Reformation Pastors

Richard Baxter and the Ideal of the Reformed Pastor

STUDIES IN CHRISTIAN HISTORY AND THOUGHT

A full listing of titles in this series
appears at the end of this book

STUDIES IN CHRISTIAN HISTORY AND THOUGHT

Reformation Pastors

Richard Baxter and the Ideal of the Reformed Pastor

J. William Black

Foreword by John Morrill

Wipf & Stock
PUBLISHERS
Eugene, Oregon

Wipf and Stock Publishers
199 W 8th Ave, Suite 3
Eugene, OR 97401

Reformation Pastors
Richard Baxter and the Ideal of the Reformed Pastor
By Black, J. William
Copyright©2004 Paternoster
ISBN: 1-59752-768-8
Publication date 6/10/2006
Previously published by Paternoster, 2004

This Edition Published by Wipf and Stock Publishers
by arrangement with Paternoster

Paternoster
9 Holdom Avenue
Bletchley
Milton Keyes, MK1 1QR
PATERNOSTER Great Britain

STUDIES IN CHRISTIAN HISTORY AND THOUGHT

Series Preface

This series complements the specialist series of *Studies in Evangelical History and Thought* and *Studies in Baptist History and Thought* for which Paternoster is becoming increasingly well known by offering works that cover the wider field of Christian history and thought. It encompasses accounts of Christian witness at various periods, studies of individual Christians and movements, and works which concern the relations of church and society through history, and the history of Christian thought.

The series includes monographs, revised dissertations and theses, and collections of papers by individuals and groups. As well as 'free standing' volumes, works on particular running themes are being commissioned; authors will be engaged for these from around the world and from a variety of Christian traditions.

A high academic standard combined with lively writing will commend the volumes in this series both to scholars and to a wider readership.

Series Editors

Alan P.F. Sell, Visiting Professor at Acadia University Divinity College, Nova Scotia, Canada

David Bebbington, Professor of History, University of Stirling, Stirling, Scotland, UK

Clyde Binfield, Professor Associate in History, University of Sheffield, UK

Gerald Bray, Anglican Professor of Divinity, Beeson Divinity School, Samford University, Birmingham, Alabama, USA

Grayson Carter, Associate Professor of Church History, Fuller Theological Seminary SW, Phoenix, Arizona, USA

For Stephanie,
Linnea and Caroline

Psalm 34:3

Contents

FOREWORD

Richard Baxter holds a special place in the affections of all those who love the seventeenth century and all those who seek to find within the seventeenth century truths that can speak to us today.

Why this is so is fairly easy to explain. He was a passionately autobiographical author, laying himself and his soul bare for the edification of others. Thus we know more about him and about his life than we do about almost any other godly man in the seventeenth century. Others wrote journals of the soul, but their over-scrupulosity and preoccupation with reifying every temptation makes them if not repellent, then out of focus. Baxter is better at telling about the light and shade of his life. Similarly Baxter is a man who not only saw ministry as service rather than power (all ministers claim to recognize this) but who actually lived out his life as one of pure service. The tirelessness of his ministry – a pulpit ministry, an epistolary ministry, a pamphlet ministry – a ministry of words, damaged his health but never his sense of vocation. And it allowed him to negotiate between being a spokesman for the visible and invisible churches of Christ.

What makes Baxter so remarkable, of course, is that he achieved this towering reputation as a preacher and evangelist with so little education. He achieved a moral authority and leadership amongst the 'orthodox' puritans of the 1650s and 1660s without spending a day at a university, while those content to give him first place had spent seven, fourteen, or even more years in deep study. His learning was osmotic and one consequence of his humbler background is that he wore it lightly. He has occasionally been accused by some scholars – including by me, and I stand by it! – of suffering an inferiority complex when he had the chance to lead the godly in refashioning the Church at the time of the restoration of the monarchy in 1660-62 and that at the Savoy Conference he overplayed a tricky hand. But faced by anything less than a lordly prelate or a cavalier with a superiority complex, he was as meek as a lamb. His patience and self-effacement in building up the Association movement in the 1650s or in working out a strategy of partial conformity after 1662 are exemplary.

The result is that Richard Baxter has been much studied – at least twenty serious biographies, for example, in the course of the twentieth century. And yet there is room for far more study, and in this book, William Black offers something startling, convincing and of great interest whether we approach Baxter from the point of view of the historian trying to make sense of the particularity of the past or from the point of view of the theologian examining how men and women in the past who have a strong sense of God's presence in their lives try to bring to others that burning sense of His immanence and imminence.

So this is a study of Richard Baxter as gentle catechist. At its core is an analysis of one of Richard Baxter's most revered tracts – the *Gildas Salvianus*, or apologia for his pastoral ministry – of 1656. Black's research seeks to locate the tract within a tradition of writing on protestant pastoral ministry stretching back to 1550; it seeks to correlate Baxter's theory with his practice in Kidderminster; and it examines the influence of the work on succeeding generations of 'post-puritans' (my term).

Amongst its major claims is the insistent linking of Baxter's theory and practice to those of Martin Bucer. I myself wish that Black had suggested a *consonance* between their ideas rather than claimed a central significance for the connection. But this is his book and he has lived with the issues more than I have. It is usually better to overstate a case than to understate it, after all! Beyond that, I think Black offers us a wonderfully rich and convincing account of how and why Baxter placed so much emphasis on a particular style of family catechising; there is a superb chapter on the origins of the Worcestershire Association and the claim that it needs to be seen less as a triumph of ecumenism than as a determined attempt to shore up the pastoral effectiveness of ministers who could expect no support from the state or from the civil magistrate; and there is a telling chapter suggesting that Samuel Clarke and his silent amanuenses portrayed pre-war puritans like Samuel Fairclough as enthusiastic catechisers, not because they were, but because, by the Restoration, Baxter had made it essential for any godly minister to be seen to have been an enthusiast for it.

Throughout, Black offers careful readings of Baxter himself, very thoughtfully contextualised, with equally thoughtful and wide-ranging reference to the secondary literature. Here he is equally at home in, and able to engage with the distinctive hermeneutics of, the literatures of secular historians and denominationally-driven evangelical theologians. The Baxter who emerges from this study is a better listener, and a man both more generous-spirited and more compassionate than he often comes across as being. Black's book is a distinguished one, shedding new light not only on a neglected aspect of a giant amongst the godly protestants of the English Reformation but on the perennial dilemmas that face any pastor confronting the confusion and helpless frailty of the bulk of humanity.

John Morrill
Professor of British and Irish History, University of Cambridge
Permanent Deacon in the Roman Catholic Diocese of East Anglia,
Parish of St Etheldreda Newmarket, Suffolk, UK

PREFACE

Pastoral ministry is not by nature a profession. But its very ambiguity as a role within the church leads many to attempt entrance requirements that increase respectability, job descriptions that make it seem like a career, and promotions to bigger and more prominent congregations that give the appearance of upward mobility. There has always been tremendous pressure to make the pastor a religious professional. And yet violence is done when it is edged in that direction, whether by the sheep or the shepherds themselves, their neighbours in the surrounding community, or even by historians attempting to make sense of its practitioners and what they do. It is an old problem.

Over its long history, as Christianity has moved in and out of favour in the eyes of its host cultures, those outside the circle of the local gathering of believers have often either ignored the spiritual aspects of Christian leadership, or assumed that the worst examples among them are the norm. Pastors are often viewed with a nervous condescension, marginalized as irrelevant or safely caricatured as hypocritically scrupulous or hopelessly out of step with the dance of society. And yet from within, there is mystery at work. Men and women are co-opted into a mission much bigger than themselves. The apostle Paul observed that Jesus Christ himself 'gave some to be apostles, some to be prophets, some to be evangelists, some to be pastors and teachers' (Ephesians 4:11) who together oversee the telling and application of the Christian good news, which is 'the power of God for the salvation of everyone who believes' (Romans 1:16). For those on the inside, becoming a pastor is not a career choice, it is a commission.

Richard Baxter (1615-1691) was primarily a pastor. Yet a survey of the vast literature that has accumulated about this complex figure, who seems to have been in the middle of and to have had something to say about everything that happened during England's revolutionary seventeenth century, shows a curious inability to put the pieces together into a meaningful whole. Baxter has been explored as a theologian, a best-selling author of practical divinity, a self-taught scholar, a man of letters, an army chaplain, a preacher, a polemicist, a pastoral genius, a historian, a catechist, a poet, an autobiographer, a hagiographer, a promoter of Christian unity, a wrecker of Christian unity, a casuist, a lover, an economist, a hypochondriac, a Nonconformist hero, a Nonconformist villain, and a cranky old man. But rather than view his two decades of pastoral involvement with St Mary's parish in Kidderminster as simply one line among many in Baxter's long *curriculum vitae*, I would suggest that it is his identity as a pastor that defines and makes sense of everything else about him.

Richard Baxter's remarkable tenure in Kidderminster transformed the parish. And by publicizing his successes and publishing his thoughts on ministry in the form of an exhortation to his fellow ministers, his *Gildas Salvianus, the Reformed Pastor* (1656), Baxter changed the way English Protestants understood and practised pastoral ministry. Three hundred and fifty years later, the aftershocks of his pastorate continue to reverberate in surprising and unexpected places, not only throughout the English- speaking church, but throughout the world wherever English-speaking missionaries succeeded in establishing new communities of Christians. This present work is not a biographical study to revise previous attempts to tell Baxter's life story. Rather, this is an effort to understand pastoral ministry as Baxter understood it. This study places Baxter's pastorate in general, and his *Reformed Pastor* in particular, in their historical contexts. As we look more closely at the pastoral motives and strategies adopted by Baxter's predecessors in the aftermath of England's tumultuous Reformations, Baxter's own motives and the reasons behind his own strategy in Kidderminster will become increasingly clear. Baxter's own ministry was in fact his response to the long, often rancourous conversation among England's Protestants since the Reformation on how best to shepherd England's Protestant flock. Making sense of Baxter's ministry means picking up on the conversation as he heard it. And understanding Baxter the pastor takes us a long way towards better understanding Richard Baxter the man and the times in which he lived.

One might think that academic research is a solitary adventure. I've learned otherwise. During the course of this study, I have accumulated, one by one, debts of gratitude to what has become a small army of individuals for specific acts of kindness, counsel and generosity, without whom this book could never have been written.

I am grateful first to the late Dr Nigel Kerr who taught me Church History at Gordon-Conwell Theological Seminary, and who nurtured in me an appreciation for those sixteenth- and seventeenth-century Christians in England and later in America known today as 'puritans'. And I have Dr Garth Rosell, also of Gordon-Conwell, to thank for suggesting that I think about devoting my doctoral thesis to a study of Richard Baxter's pastoral ministry.

I am indebted to the input and encouragement I have received from many of my colleagues. I have been helped in particular by the kindness, advice and critique of Dr Geoffrey Nuttall, Professor John Morrill, Professor Neil Keeble and Mr Don Gilbert. Paul Lim, John Brouwer, John Coffey, Michael and Auriel Schluter, Sue Mutimer, Pam Bush, Courtney Stevens, Nancy Lee, Ranald and Susan Macauley, Mark Ashton, Mark and Barbara Phippen, Michael Lawrence, Vern and Jane Farewell, and Father John and Denise Jillions have all provided the context of encouragement and support that have sustained me during this long labour. I am grateful most of all to Professor Eamon Duffy, who was my supervisor during my years in Cambridge. To recast the puritan metaphor of high praise, he has been both a *Barnabas* and a timely *Boanerges* as well. He graciously endured my progress, and by example, counsel and critique tutored me in the historian's craft and joy. Though whatever faults remain in this study are mine alone, informed readers will recognize everywhere the silent impact of those who have served as my mentors.

The luxury of being able to devote one's complete attention to research is an expensive gift. And many individuals have given sacrificially to make the research behind the book possible. I am grateful to my wife's parents, Jim and Nancy Larsen, and also to my father and step-mother, Joe and Kaye Black for their substantial support. And I am grateful for the astonishing generosity of the members, leadership and staff of First Presbyterian Church in Reading, Pennsylvania, without whom this project would have been impossible. The members of Kempsville Presbyterian Church of Virginia Beach, Virginia, were also munificent in their support of my family. I am also grateful to the trustees of the Archbishop Cranmer fund for awarding me a studentship in 1997-98 and again in 1998-99, as well as to the Master of Fitzwilliam College and the trustees of the Fitzwilliam Trust Research Fund who have helped to cover travel expenses incurred in my many trips to libraries and public records offices in London, Oxford and Worcester.

No reliable history can be written without access to the evidence contained in the primary sources, and I am thankful for the permission given me by staff from the following libraries and records offices to consult their collections: the Cambridge University Library, the British Library in London, Dr Williams's Library in London, Guildhall Library in London, the Bodleian Library in Oxford, Sidney Sussex College Muniments Room in Cambridge, Westminster Theological College Library in Cambridge, the Wren Library in Trinity College in Cambridge, St John's College Library in Cambridge, Fitzwilliam College Library in Cambridge, the Public Records Office in Kew, London, the Worcester Diocesan Records Office and the Hereford and Worcestershire Records Office in Worcester. In particular, I am grateful for the cheerful and consistently helpful assistance given me by the staff of the Cambridge University Library Rare Books Room who somehow managed to keep me plentifully supplied with piles of old books. I am also indebted to the Librarian and Trustees of Dr Williams's Library in London for access to Baxter's correspondence and treatises, and for their permission to quote from them. And I must give special thanks to the Warden and Librarian of Tyndale House in Cambridge for welcoming my wife Stephanie and me into the community of scholars there and for providing us with a desk from which to base our researches.

An earlier version of chapter three was published as 'Richard Baxter's Bucerian Reformation', in *Westminster Theological Journal* (2001). An earlier version of chapter five was published as 'From Martin Bucer to Richard Baxter: "Discipline" and Reformation in Sixteenth and Seventeenth Century England', in *Church History* (2001). I am grateful to the respective editors for their kind permission to make use of the material in these articles here.

I am also indebted to a number of friends and colleagues here in Addis Ababa who, when I became too enmeshed in the material to be any good at proofing, helped me during the final stages by reading portions of this manuscript with an eye towards correcting mistakes. Michael Madany, Vicki van Gorkom, RoxAnn Cox, Ruth Cremer, Ginny Holt, Nicola Ayers, Aimee MacFarland, Art Volkman, Christine Davidson and Lila Balisky undertook this tedious task, for which I am very grateful. Whatever mistakes remain are, of course, entirely mine.

Finally, during the course of working on this book, I have often marveled at the intense love Richard Baxter had for the men and women and children of St Mary's parish in Kidderminster where he served as pastor. Though there are many facets which combine to make a pastor effective in a particular congregation, the fact that he or she often meets the individuals under their care when they are most vulnerable—at times of spiritual or relational crisis, illness or bereavement—often serves to forge relationships of mutual loyalty, trust and compassion. Having served as a pastor, though more than three centuries after my subject, I have experienced a similar dynamic at work. Life lived on the edge of eternity focuses the mind, tries the motives, and makes fellowship a precious thing. For that reason, I again wish to acknowledge my debt of gratitude to the congregation of First Presbyterian Church in Reading, Pennsylvania. They were our home before we came to Cambridge. They endured my efforts to serve as a pastor in their midst. They encouraged my love of study, and when the time was right, released me and with their blessing sent me to undertake the labour of this book. Thus in acknowledgement of those brief, intense and good years we spent in their midst, and in gratitude for their ongoing encouragement and support, I dedicate this book to the members and friends of First Presbyterian Church in Reading, Pennsylvania.

J. William Black
17 Yekatit 1996 (Ethiopian Calendar)
Ash Wednesday 2004
Addis Ababa, Ethiopia

Abbreviations

AEH	*Anglican and Episcopal History*
BHST	*Baptist Historical Society Transactions*
BJRL	*Bulletin of the John Rylands Library*
BL	British Library, London
BNS	*Baxter Notes and Studies*
BQ	*Baptist Quarterly*
BT	Baxter Treatises
BxL	Baxter Letters
Calendar	N.H. Keeble and G.F. Nuttall, *Calendar of the Correspondence of Richard Baxter* (Oxford: Clarendon Press, 1991).
CHR	*Catholic Historical Review*
CHST	*Congregational Historical Society Transactions*
CL	*Christianity and Literature*
CQ	*The Congregational Quarterly*
CR	A.G. Matthews, *Calamy Revised: Being a Revision of Edmund Calamy's Account of the Ministers and Others Ejected and Silenced, 1660-2.* Oxford: Clarendon Press, 1934.
CUL	Cambridge University Library
DNB	*Dictionary of National Biography,* Sir L. Stephen and Sir S. Lee, eds. (London: Oxford University Press, 1908-09).
DWL	Doctor Williams's Library, London
EHR	*English Historical Review*
EQ	*Evangelical Quarterly*
ER	*The Epworth Review*
ET	*The Expository Times*
fol(s).	folio(s)
Foster	Joseph Foster, *Alumni Oxonienses: The Members of the University of Oxford, 1500-1714* (Oxford: Oxford University Press, 1891-1892).

FQ	*Friends Quarterly*
HLQ	*Huntington Library Quarterly*
JBS	*Journal of British Studies*
JEH	*Journal of Ecclesiastical History*
JMH	*Journal of Modern History*
JMHRS	*Journal of the Merioneth Historical and Record Society*
JPHSE	*Journal of the Presbyterian Historical Society of England*
JTS	*Journal of Theological Studies*
JURCHS	*Journal of the United Reformed Church History Society*
LGL	London Guildhall Library
LTQ	*Lexington Theological Quarterly*
MC	*Modern Churchman*
MQR	*Mennonite Quarterly Review*
n.d.	no date of publication
n.p.	no place of publication
NPNF	*Nicene and Post Nicene Fathers*
P&P	*Past & Present*
PR	Parish Records
PRO	London Public Records Office, Kew
PROB	Probate
ODNB	*Oxford Dictionary of National Biography, in Association with the British Academy,* Brian Harrison and Colin Matthew, eds. (Oxford: Oxford University Press, forthcoming 2004).
PS	*Prose Studies*
QH	*Quaker History*
Rel. Bax..	Matthew Sylvester, ed., Reliquiae Baxterianae, Or, Mr. Richard Baxters Narrative of The most Memorable Passages of his Life and Times (London, 1696).
RTR	*Reformed Theological Review*
SC	*Seventeenth Century*
sig(s)	signature(s)
SCJ	*Sixteenth Century Journal*
SMRT	*Studies in Medieval and Reformation Thought*
SR	*Sewanee Review*
TCHS	*Transactions of the Congregational Historical Society*
TSAS	*Transcripts of the Shropshire Archeological Society*
TWAS	*Transactions of the Worcestershire Archeological*

	Society
unp.	unpaginated
v	*verso*
Venn	John Venn and J.A. Venn, *Alumni Cantabrigienses* (Cambridge: Cambridge University Press, 1924).
Wing	D.G. Wing, *Short Title Catalogue of Books Printed in England, Scotland, Ireland, Wales and British America, and of English Books Printed in Other Countries, 1641-1700*, 2nd edition (New York, 1982-1998).
WR	A.G. Matthews, *Walker Revised: being a revision of John Walker's Sufferings of the clergy during the Grand Rebellion, 1642-1660* (Oxford: Clarendon Press, 1988, reissue of 1948 edition).
WTJ	*Westminster Theological Journal*
§(§)	section(s)

Quotations throughout this study retain their original spellings, capitalisations and punctuations. Abbreviations and contractions in handwritten manuscripts unfamiliar in modern usage have been silently expanded. Because the spelling in many of the primary sources can seem random, those who may be tempted to despair at having to read sixteenth- and seventeenth-century English can take comfort in the fact that most spellings (unless it is a typesetting error) make sense phonetically. I also find that by reading passages out loud I can usually get the sense of what is being said. Dates follow the modern format, with the New Year beginning on January 1. If the old format for date is used in titles, the modern date is inserted in brackets in the form of 1613[4]. For all primary sources in both footnotes and bibliographies, the city of publication is London unless otherwise indicated. In the footnotes, all twentieth- and twenty-first century sources list the author, title and date of publication in the first instance. Full publisher information for all twentieth- and twenty-first century printed sources can be found in the bibliography.

CHAPTER 1

Baxter and the Experts

Introduction

This study examines Richard Baxter's practise of pastoral ministry in its broader historical context. Called in 1641 by leading Kidderminster laymen impressed by his preaching skills to supplement perceived insufficiencies in the ministry of their vicar, within two years Baxter was forced by the outbreak of local unrest preceding the civil wars to flee to the relative safety of Coventry. In 1647 Baxter returned to Kidderminster after recovering from the illness that ended his career as an army chaplain. His subsequent ministry succeeded in redefining English pastoral practise until the Restoration brought his experiment in pastor-led, parish-based reformation to a frustrating end. The tracts and treatises he published on ministry during those brief years are significant, not only for the full picture they provide of Baxter's own ministry, but also for their influence on his colleagues and on the character and emphases of later Dissent. But because he also viewed himself as the heir and defender of England's 'godly, learned and faithful' ministry in their long battle for reformation against Roman Catholics, prelatists, separatists and hard-hearted parishioners, these published works and private correspondence also provide an intriguing and heretofore unused perspective from which to view the development of England's Protestant ministry. The picture that emerges of what conventionally has been understood as 'puritan' ministry is, however, unexpected, as is Baxter's relationship to it. And even if prevailing perceptions are overturned, placing Baxter's ministry in its historical context helps us not only to understand, finally, Richard Baxter as pastor, but also how the diverging strategies of pastoral ministry that defined England's Protestants and their restless quest for reformation were ultimately, if unsuccessfully, resolved in Baxter's Kidderminster ministry. At the Restoration in 1660, Baxter was forced to concede his position as minister in Kidderminster to the sequestered vicar. The re-establishment of episcopacy and the rush to redress the perceived suffering of those clergy who had remained loyal to crown and prayer book drew the curtain not only on Baxter's pastoral ministry in Kidderminster but on the hopes of many that reformation might finally and fully come to the Church of England.

Baxter Studies is a crowded field. A whole spectrum of publications continues to pour out, from popular sketches and web page introductions to the more subtle investigations of academic historians and theologians.[1] One set of admirers has

---

[1] See, for example 'The Richard Baxter Homepage', 'The Baxter Institute' and 'The Richard Baxter Society', some of the many links accessible online by entering Richard Baxter in a search engine. Even Baxter's parish church, St Mary's and All Saints Church in

founded an Institute of Pastoral Ministry in his name.[2] Another circle, based appropriately in Kidderminster, founded a small journal in conjunction with the tercentenary of Baxter's death in 1991.[3] Even in the broader areas of seventeenth-century history, historical theology and literary studies, Baxter is a ubiquitous feature of footnotes and indices, and his posthumously published *Reliquiae Baxterianae* (1696) is regularly plundered for his take on the decisive decades of Civil War, Interregnum and Restoration England.[4]

In Protestant circles, despite long-standing concerns from certain quarters over his views on justification and redemption,[5] Baxter has been considered by many to be the apogee of puritan ministry and practical divinity.[6] And long after the pastoral labours of nearly all his contemporaries and predecessors have been forgotten, and their numerous treatises and sermons on ministry relegated to the obscurity of the rare book rooms, Baxter's *Gildas Salvianus* and the ministry from which it came continued to draw the attention of churchmen and academics from the eighteenth- to the mid-twentieth century, and remains required reading in many conservative Protestant seminaries.[7] With the resurgence of academic

---

Kidderminster, has a web page with pictures and brief history of the church and an overview of Baxter's life {http://www.stmarys-kidderminster.org.uk}. Given his astonishing output with pen and parchment, the mind staggers to think what the man would have done with a laptop and email.

[2] See the Richard Baxter Institute for Ministry and its journal *Ministry Today*.

[3] See *Baxter Notes and Studies: The Journal of the Richard Baxter Society*.

[4] Christopher Durston's 'Puritan Rule and the Failure of Cultural Revolution, 1645-1660', C. Durston and J. Eales, eds., *The Culture of English Puritanism, 1560-1700* (Basingstoke: MacMillan,1996), 219, 231-32; Keith Wrightson, *Earthly Necessities: Economic Lives in Early Modern Britain*, 1470-1750 (London: Penguin, 2002), 280-281.

[5] For the most recent studies of those aspects of Baxter's theology which have been most controversial, as well as the most recent overviews of the secondary literature generated in the process, see Tim Cooper, *Fear and Polemic in Seventeenth-Century England: Richard Baxter and Antinomianism* (Aldershot: Ashgate, 2001); Paul C.H. Lim, 'In Pursuit of Unity, Purity and Liberty: Richard Baxter's Puritan Ecclesiology in Context' (University of Cambridge PhD thesis, 2001); Hans Boersma, *A Hot Pepper Corn: Richard Baxter's Doctrine of Justification in Its Seventeenth-Century Context of Controversy* (Zoetermeer, Netherlands: Boekencentrum, 1995), 1-24; see also J.I. Packer, 'The Redemption and Restoration of Man in the Thought of Richard Baxter' (Oxford University DPhil thesis, 1954), soon to be published by Paternoster; Gavin McGrath, 'Puritans and the Human Will: Voluntarism within Mid-Seventeenth Century English Puritanism As Seen in the Works of Richard Baxter and John Owen' (University of Durham PhD thesis, 1989).

[6] For a recent example, see Timothy Cooke's articles, '"Uncommon Earnestness and Earthly Toils": Moderate Puritan Richard Baxter's Devotional Writings', in *AEH*, 63 (1994), 51-72, and 'Richard Baxter and the Dictates of the Praying Classes', *WTJ*, 58 (1996), 223-235.

[7] See the list of the editions of Baxter's *Gildas Salvianus* in the bibliography. See also, for example, J.C. Ryle, *Baxter and His Times* (1853), and *The Priest, the Puritan and the Preacher* (1857); J. Stoughton, 'Richard Baxter; or Earnest Decision', in *Lights of the*

interest in puritanism during the first half of the twentieth century came renewed interest in Baxter, spurred in no small way by the meticulous researches of Dr Geoffrey Nuttall.[8] Yet despite the ongoing publication of studies which touch on Baxter's pastoral efforts, and the unrelenting proliferation of popular works, only one sustained examination of Baxter's pastoral ministry has appeared in the past thirty years: C.D. Gilbert's unpublished 1996 master's thesis, 'Richard Baxter's

---

World (1853); Joseph Napier, *Richard Baxter and His Times. A Lecture* (1855); J. Tulloch, 'Baxter', in *English Puritanism and its Leaders* (1861); W.C. Magee, 'Richard Baxter, his Life and Times', in *Lectures Delivered Before the Dublin Young Men's Christian Association* (1862); A.B. Grosart, 'Richard Baxter: Seraphic Fervour', in *Representative Nonconformists* (1879); G.D. Boyle, *Richard Baxter* (1883); J. Stalker, 'Richard Baxter', in *The Evangelical Succession* (1883); W.G. Blaikie, *Richard Baxter* (1885); J.H. Davies, *The Life of Richard Baxter, of Kidderminster, Preacher and Prisoner* (1887); John Brown, 'Richard Baxter, the Kidderminster Pastor', in *Puritan Preaching in England* (1900); George Eayrs, *Richard Baxter and the Revival of Preaching and Pastoral Service* (London: n.p., 1912); William Harris, *Richard Baxter: The Making of a Non-conformist* (1912); F.J. Powicke, *A Life of the Reverend Richard Baxter 1615-1691* (London: Jonathan Cape, 1924); A.S. Langley, 'Richard Baxter-The Director of Souls: The Man and his Pastoral Method', *BQ*, 3 (1926-27), 71-80; W.H. Haddon, 'Baxter's Work', *BQ*, 3 (1926-27), 205-210; W.H. Haddon, 'Richard Baxter-The Man', *BQ*, 3 (1926-27), 150-155; T.H. Martin, 'Richard Baxter and "The Reformed Pastor"', *BQ*, 9 (1938-39), 350-360; C.F. Kemp, *A Pastoral Triumph: The Story of Richard Baxter and his Ministry at Kidderminster* (New York: MacMillan, 1948).

[8] Nuttall's studies on Baxter include 'Richard Baxter and the Puritan Movement', in *Heroes of the Faith*, F. Ballam, ed. (London: Livingstone Press, 1949); 'Richard Baxter's Correspondence: a preliminary survey', in *JEH*, 1 (1950), 85-95; 'The Worcestershire Association: Its Membership', in *JEH*, 1 (1950), 197-206; 'A Transcript of Richard Baxter's Library Catalogue: A Bibliographical Note', in *JEH*, 2 (1951), 207-221; *Richard Baxter and Philip Doddridge: A Study in a Tradition* (1951); 'Advice to a Young Minister', in *CQ*, vol. 30:3 (1952), 231-235; 'The Death of Lady Rous, 1656-Richard Baxter's Account', in *TWAS*, 28 (1952), 4-13; 'Richard Baxter's *Apology* (1654): Its Occasion and Composition', in *JEH*, 4 (1953), 69-76; 'The Correspondence of John Lewis, Glasgrug, with Richard Baxter and with Dr. John Ellis, Dolgelley', in *JMHRS*, vol. 2:2 (1954), 120-134; *The Manuscript of the Reliquiae Baxterianae* (1954); '[Review of] H. Martin, *Puritanism and Richard Baxter'*, in *JEH*, 6 (1955), 240-41; 'The MS of *Reliquiae Baxterianae* (1696)', in *JEH*, 6 (1955), 73-79; *Richard Baxter* (1965); 'The Personality of Richard Baxter', in G.F. Nuttall, *The Puritan Spirit: Essays and Addresses* (1967); 'Richard Baxter and *The Grotian Religion'*, in *Reform and Reformation: England and the Continent, c. 1500-1750*, D. Baker, ed. (Oxford: Basil Blackwell, 1979); (with N.H. Keeble) *Calendar of the Correspondence of Richard Baxter* (1991). For bibliographies of Dr. Nuttall's publications, see Tai Liu, 'Bibliography [until 1977]', in *Reformation, Conformity and Dissent: Essays in Honour of Geoffrey Nuttall,* R.B. Knox, ed. (London: Epworth Press, 1977); for publications from 1977-1996, see Tai Liu, 'Geoffrey Nuttall: A Bibliography 1977-1996', in *JURCHS*, 5 (1996), 534-543. See also Clyde Binfield, 'Profile: Geoffrey Nuttall: The Formation of an Independent Historian', in *ER*, 25 (1998), 79-106.

Ministry in Kidderminster, 1641-1661'. Moreover, there have been no attempts to understand Baxter and his ministry within the broader context of sixteenth- and seventeenth-century pastoral practise. It is a neglect with far-reaching implications, both with respect to ongoing efforts to understand Baxter in his seventeenth-century context, as well as with regard to Baxter's role within the broader puritan and later Nonconformist community.

The purpose of this study, therefore, is to examine Richard Baxter's understanding of pastoral ministry from the perspective of his own stated concern for 'reformation' and in the broader context of Edwardian, Elizabethan and early Stuart pastoral ideals. I will investigate Baxter's major treatise on pastoral ministry, *Gildas Salvianus* (1656), and explore the background of each aspect of his pastoral strategy. I will argue that far from being novel, Baxter's practise of pastoral ministry reflects aspects of his puritan predecessors' practise, if not their rhetoric. But I will also contend that the primary contours of Baxter's ministry are derived, not from ideals for pastors assumed after the Elizabethan Settlement, but from the earlier Edwardian reformation emphases of the exiled Strasbourg reformer Martin Bucer. An examination of sixteenth- and seventeenth-century treatises and sermons on pastoral ministry, as well as a survey of contemporary understandings of 'reformation' will provide the evidence to support the argument for Bucer's influence on Baxter's pastoral strategy. Further comparisons between *Gildas Salvianus* and Bucer's writings on ministry and reformation will demonstrate the correspondence of their pastoral motives and practise. Individual studies of the primary elements of Baxter's pastoral strategy will reveal the areas of continuity with previous pastoral practise, as well as those aspects influenced by his reading of Bucer or which resulted from his own improvisations as he attempted to apply his strategies in the local context of Kidderminster. Finally, I will discuss the subsequent impact of Baxter's efforts both on the lives of individual pastors and on the subsequent perception of 'puritan' ministry, and conclude by exploring his relationship with Thomas Doolittle as an indication of how vision for ministry was passed from one generation to the next.

After an introduction and survey of the present state of research (chapter 1), the first section will investigate *Gildas Salvianus* in its context by surveying the motives, rhetoric and practise of puritan pastoral ministry. Chapter 2 will survey extant treatises and sermons on pastoral ministry from the Edwardian reformation to the British civil wars, establishing the literary context for Baxter's *Gildas Salvianus* and highlighting the difference between published rhetoric and parish practise. Chapter 3 will examine the way English Protestants used the word 'reformation' and the resulting impact on their pastoral priorities. Most significantly, this chapter will highlight Richard Baxter's recovery of a Bucerian understanding of reformation which had been overshadowed by a dominant Genevan perspective for nearly a century. The first section culminates with chapter 4's analysis of Baxter's *Gildas Salvianus*. This chapter argues that with the publication of *Gildas Salvianus*, Baxter overturns the conventional discussion of pastoral ministry by reconfiguring efforts for reformation along pastoral and evangelistic lines. This chapter demonstrates the similarities between Baxter's pastoral strategy and practise and that of Martin Bucer and suggests that Baxter's pastoral strategy was influenced by his reading of Bucer's works on ministry and reformation.

The second section will examine the core elements of Richard Baxter's ministry in Kidderminster as outlined in *Gildas Salvianus*. Although the decision not to adopt a chronological study of Baxter's pastorate, but to investigate each aspect separately, necessitates asking different sets of questions of the same historical territory as the context for each element is analyzed, I felt the resulting clarity of perspective well worth the risk of seeming repetitious. Chapter 5 takes up the contentious issue of church discipline, with an overview of prior constraints and practises, an explanation of Baxter's own practise and how it developed, and an analysis of the evidence suggesting Bucer's influence on Baxter's approach. Chapter 6 traces Richard Baxter's experiences in the Civil Wars, and identifies those influences that led to the founding of the Worcestershire Association. Chapter 7 follows the development of Baxter's dual emphases on public preaching and personal instruction and details the evangelistic core of his pastoral strategy.

The third and final section considers the immediate impact of Baxter's pastoral ministry and raises questions concerning Baxter's subsequent influence. Chapter 8 asks whether Baxter's Bucerian emphases might not be better explained by the survival of an intermediate Bucerian tradition in English Protestant ministry. It also argues that although Baxter's strategy was in part a reaction against the bankruptcy of the long-standing 'puritan' pastoral ideal, later admirers and historians overlooked its failure and mistakenly assumed continuity with Baxter's practise. Chapter 9 assesses Baxter's long-term relationship with Thomas Doolittle as an example of ministerial formation and a further means to assist Baxter's strategy to effect pastor-led, parish-centered reformation. The study concludes in chapter 10 by summarizing Baxter's role in the development of seventeenth-century pastoral ministry.

The Current State of Research on Baxter as Pastor

Richard Baxter understood himself to be, primarily, a pastor, but recent academic studies of Baxter have mostly focused on other aspects of his life and thought.[9]

---

[9] An exception to the rule is Professor Keeble's article 'Richard Baxter's Preaching Ministry: its History and Texts', in *JEH*, 35 (1984), 539-559; see also his *Richard Baxter: Puritan Man of Letters* (Oxford: Clarendon, 1982), 69-93. For more general treatments of early modern pastoral ministry, see David Cornick, 'The Reformation crisis in pastoral care' and 'Pastoral Care in England: Perkins, Baxter and Burnet', G.R. Evans, ed., *The History of Pastoral Care* (London: Cassell, 2000), 223-251; Ralph Houlbrooke, 'The family and pastoral care', G.R. Evans, ed., *The History of Pastoral Care*, 262-293; Philip Sheldrake, 'George Herbert and *The Country Parson*', G.R. Evans, ed., *The History of Pastoral Care*, 294-312; Tom Webster, *Godly Clergy in early Stuart England: the Caroline Puritan Movement 1620-1643* (Cambridge: Cambridge University Press, 1997);

Hence, although many non-academic works have undertaken to examine Baxter's pastoral technique and have uncritically passed on his own accounts of his success, we know surprisingly little about *why* Richard Baxter did what he did at Kidderminster, or even how his understanding of ministry related to that of his contemporaries and predecessors. Was he a pastoral genius or was he merely typical, or something in between? Most have simply assumed that Baxter was, in J.I. Packer's words, 'the most outstanding pastor...that Puritanism produced.'[10]

Prior to 1900, most studies of Baxter and his ministry were published for the purpose of edification.[11] His pastoral exertions and his fervour were considered exemplary, and the purpose of such 'history' was often not to provide a critical evaluation, but rather to instruct or inspire the present from the past.[12] These popular treatments have portrayed Baxter as a model for young pastors, divorcing him and his writings altogether from their historical context. In his funeral sermon for Baxter in 1691, for example, William Bates spoke of *Gildas Salvianus* as 'the accomplished model of an evangelical minister.... a copy taken from life'.[13] Cotton Mather, writing to ministerial candidates, counselled more generally that 'when your heart and your pen want the holy fire to be quickened within you, a

---

Patrick Collinson's 'Shepherds, Sheepdogs and Hirelings: The Pastoral Ministry in Post-Reformation England', W.J. Sheils and D. Wood, eds., *The Ministry: Clerical and Lay* (Oxford: Blackwell, 1989); Ian Green, '"Reformed Pastors" and *Bons Cures*: The Changing Role of the Parish in Early Modern Europe', W.J. Sheils and D. Wood, eds, *The Ministry*; see also Eamon Duffy, 'The Godly and the Multitude in Stuart England', *SC*, 1 (1986), 31-55, and 'The Long Reformation: Catholicism, Protestantism and the multitude', in *England's Long Reformation, 1500-1800*, N. Tyack, ed. (London: UCL Press, 1998); and Patrick Collinson, *Elizabethan Puritan Movement* (Oxford: Clarendon, 1990, 1967).

[10] J.I. Packer, 'Introduction', in Richard Baxter, *The Reformed Pastor*, William Brown, ed. (Edinburgh: Banner of Truth Trust, 1974, reprinted from the fifth edition, 1862), 9.

[11] See, for example, the works listed in footnote 7.

[12] Taking their cue from the rationalist historians with Enlightenment presuppositions, many of the Victorian era Church historians saw their work as providing moral or spiritual illustration. See R.J. Evans, *In Defence of History* (London: Granta, 1997), 15-16. Evans's description of 'the history of history', while helpful for secular models of historiography, is not as useful when attempting to describe Christian historiography because of the alternative teleologies a Christian perspective introduces. The absence in Evans's work of any discussion of a Christian philosophy of history is a major weakness in an otherwise excellent study. For an articulate example of this alternative teleology, see Stratford Caldecott, 'Conclusion: Eternity in Time', S. Caldecott and J. Morrill, eds., *Eternity in Time: Christopher Dawson and the Catholic Idea of History* (Edinburgh: T and T Clark, 1997); see also Robert Frykenberg, *History and Belief: The Foundations of Historical Understanding* (Grand Rapids, MI and Cambridge: Eerdmans, 1996); Michael Bauman and Martin I. Klauber, eds. *Historians of the Christian Tradition: Their Methodology and Influence on Western Thought* (Nashville, TN: Broadman and Holman, 1995).

[13] William Bates (1625-1699), *A Funeral Sermon for the Reverend, Holy and Excellent Divine, Mr. Richard Baxter* (1692), 89, 93.

[book by] Baxter will bring you a coal from the altar for it'.[14] Indeed, successive generations of evangelical ministers, from Samuel Wesley (1662-1735), Philip Doddridge (1702-1751),[15] John Wesley (1703-1791),[16] Francis Asbury (1745-1816), Thomas Chalmers (1780-1847), to Charles Spurgeon (1834-1892)[17] also found Baxter's example compelling and sought to apply his model. Describing *Gildas Salvianus* to his readers in 1830, William Orme observed that 'scarcely any of his books [have] been more extensively read, or more generally useful than this.'[18] Even James Stewart states that *Gildas Salvianus* is, 'after three hundred years still so sure a guide'.[19]

The uncritical use of *Gildas Salvianus* as a paradigm for pastoral ministry has continued even to the last decades of the twentieth century, with the publication of two more abridged editions: James Houston's *'The Reformed Pastor': A Pattern for Personal Growth and Ministry* (1986) and W. Stuart Owen's *The Ministry We Need: An abridged and rewritten version of 'the reformed pastor'* (1997),[20] as well as Paul Miller's article 'Spirituality, Integrity and Competence: Essentials of Ministry in Richard Baxter's *Reformed Pastor*' (1997), and Anglican bishop Wallace Benn's pamphlet *The Baxter Model: Guidelines for Pastoring Today* (1993).[21] Of recent treatments of Baxter's *Gildas Salvianus*, both popular and

---

[14] Mather continues, 'Yea, to fetch a metaphor from another element, he may be called...an ocean of divinity. To say of that very great man, that if he had not meddled in too many things, he would have been esteamed one of the learned men of the age, it is to speak a thing which I do not well understand: for his meddling with so many things, and writing more learnedly upon the most of them (except his expositions) than the most of them who have written upon perhaps but one or two of the things, to me renders him one of the most leaerned of the age.' Cotton Mather, *Student and Preacher; or Directions for a Candidate of the Ministry* (1789), 187-88.

[15] See Nuttall, *Richard Baxter and Philip Doddridge*.

[16] Eayrs, *Richard Baxter*, 4-6.

[17] See C.H. Spurgeon, *Autobiography, Volume I: The Early Years 1834-1859* (Edinburgh: Banner of Truth Trust, 1962, revised edition of 4 volume autobiography first published in 1897-1900), 417.

[18] William Orme, *The Life and Times of Richard Baxter: with a Critical Examination of his Writings*, II (1830), 180.

[19] Quoted in Wilkinson, 'Richard Baxter's "The Reformed Pastor"', 17.

[20] Richard Baxter, *'The Reformed Pastor': A Pattern for Personal Growth and Ministry*, James Houston, ed. (Portland, OR: Multnomah Press, 1986); W. Stuart Owen, ed. *The Ministry We Need: an abridged and rewritten version of 'the reformed pastor' by Richard Baxter...together with the Life of Richard Baxter 1615-1691* (London: Grace Publications, 1997).

[21] Paul Miller, 'Spirituality, Integrity and Competence: Essentials of Ministry in Richard Baxter's *Reformed Pastor*', in *EQ*, 69 (1997), 333-342; Wallace Benn, *The Baxter Method: Guidelines for Pastoring Today* (Lowestoft: n.p. 1993). See A.S. Langley, 'Richard Baxter—The Director of Souls', 71-80, and T.H. Martin, 'Richard Baxter and "The Reformed Pastor"', 250-261, for earlier attempts to point contemporary pastors to Baxter's example.

academic, only David Sceats, in his 'Gildas Salvianas [sic] Redevivus-The Reformed Pastor, Richard Baxter' (1993), has attempted a more critical examination of the pastoral method promoted there.[22] However, Sceat's decision to view *Gildas Salvianus* through the lens of late twentieth-century pastoral practise further muddles any sense of appropriate context and distances him from both an effective appreciation and a meaningful critique of Baxter as a pastor.

Academic studies of Baxter from the turn of the twentieth century to the Second World War benefited from the gradual loosening of ties between church history and denominational apologetics. The study of puritanism, however, was slow to gain acceptance as a valid academic pursuit. Scholars such as S.R. Gardiner,[23] C.H. Firth,[24] and A.G. Matthews[25] did much to create a respected context in which to pursue further investigations of seventeenth-century puritanism in general.[26] New researches focusing on Baxter began to upgrade the insights of earlier studies into the academic mainstream.[27] Hindsight suggests that F.J. Powicke's two-volume biography of Baxter, and the multitude of his shorter studies, provided the bridge for Baxter studies into the academy.[28]

---

[22] David Sceats, 'Gildas Salvianas [sic] Redevivus-The Reformed Pastor, Richard Baxter', in *Anvil*, 10 (1993), 135-145.

[23] See, for example, Gardiner's *History of the Great Civil War, 1642-1649*, 4 vols. (London, 1893); Gardiner, ed. *Constitutional Documents of the Puritan Revolution, 1625-1660* (Oxford: Clarendon Press, 1906, 1979 printing).

[24] See, for example, *Oliver Cromwell and the Rule of the Puritans in England* (London: Oxford University Press, 1953; London, 1900); *Last Days of the Protectorate 1656-1658*, 2 vols (London: Longmans, Green, 1909); (edited with R.S. Rait) *Acts and Ordinances of the Interregnum 1642-1660*, 3 vols (London: Stationary Office, 1911); *Cromwell's Army: a history of the English soldier during the Civil Wars, the Commonwealth and the Protectorate*, 3rd edition (London: Greenhill, 1992; London: Methuen, 1921).

[25] See Matthews's *The Works of Richard Baxter: An Annotated List* (No Place: Oxted, 1932); *Calamy Revised: Being a Revision of Edmund Calamy's Account of the Ministers and Others Ejected and Silenced, 1660-2* (Oxford: Clarendon, 1988; Oxford: Clarendon, 1934); *Walker Revised: Being a Revision of John Walker's Sufferings of the Clergy during the Grand Rebellion, 1642-60* (Oxford: Clarendon, 1988; Oxford: Clarendon, 1948).

[26] See William Lamont's discussion tracing the delineation of issues within the study of puritanism in *Puritanism and historical controversy* (London: UCL Press, 1996), 1-11, 55-193. See also Raphael Samuel, 'The Discovery of Puritanism, 1820-1914: A Preliminary Sketch', J. Garnett and C. Matthew, eds., *Revival and Religion Since 1700, Essays for John Walsh* (London: Hambledon, 1993), 201-47.

[27] See, for example, Brown, 'Richard Baxter, the Kidderminster Pastor', in *Puritan Preaching in England* (1900); Eayrs, *Richard Baxter*; Ladell, *Richard Baxter*. See also Max Weber's 1930 English translation, *The Protestant Ethic and the Spirit of Capitalism* (London: Routledge, 2001; 1930) and R.H. Tawney, *Religion and the Rise of Capitalism* (London: John Murray, 1926), both of which, significantly, make use of Baxter's *A Christian Directory* (1673) in their arguments.

[28] See F.J. Powicke, *A Life of the Reverend Richard Baxter (1615-1691)* (London: Jonathan Cape, 1924); *The Reverend Richard Baxter under the Cross, 1662-1691* (London:

For our purposes, the early work of Dr Nuttall marks a threshold in studies of Baxter's Kidderminster ministry from earlier incidental and predominantly descriptive studies to more historically nuanced analyses. Building on Powicke's pattern of brief but carefully researched investigations of well-defined questions, Nuttall's work coincided with the broader studies of a new generation of historians and theologians attracted by Baxter's own theological perspicuity and by the significant role he played in each of the major crises which defined seventeenth-century Britain.[29]

Even so, many of the studies which have focused on Baxter's Kidderminster ministry have treated him in what Collinson, Lamont and Morrill have termed a 'vertical way' and with a particular future development in mind, seeing Baxter more as one of the founders of Nonconformity and viewing him through the lens of what is attractive to a contemporary perspective rather than understanding him 'horizontally' in the context of his own times.[30] Alexander Gordon finds in Baxter the 'germs of enlightened conviction' that would eventually 'fructify' into those

---

Jonathan Cape, 1927); *A Puritan Idyll or the Rev. Richard Baxter's Love Story* (Manchester: Manchester University Press, 1918); 'Richard Baxter's Relation to the Baptists', in *BHST*, 6 (1918-19), 193-215; 'Story and Significance of the Rev. Richard Baxter's *Saints' Everlasting Rest'*, in *BJRL*, 5 (1919-20), 445-79; 'Eleven letters of John Second Earl of Lauderdale (and First Duke), 1616-1682, to the Rev. Richard Baxter (1615-1691)', in *BJRL*, 7 (1922-3), 73-105; 'Dr. Du Moulin's *Vindication*', in *CHST*, 9 (1924-6), 219-37; 'Richard Baxter and The Countess of Balcarres (1621?-1706?)', in *BJRL*, 9 (1925), 585-99; 'Richard Baxter and *The Saints Everlasting Rest'*, in *CQ*, 3 (1925), 280-90; 'Richard Baxter and William Penn', in *FQE*, 59 (1925), 151-60; 'Another Lauderdale Letter', in *BJRL*, 10 (1926), 524-31; 'An Episode in the Ministry of the Rev. Henry Newcome, and his Connection with the Rev. Richard Baxter', in BJRL, 13 (1929), 63-88; 'The Reverend Richard Baxter and his Lancashire Friend Mr. Henry Ashurst', in *BJRL*, 13 (1929), 309-325; 'Some Unpublished Correspondence of the Reverend Richard Baxter and the Reverend John Eliot...1656-1682', in *BJRL*, 15 (1931), 138-76, 442-66; *Some Unpublished Correspondence of the Reverend Richard Baxter and the Reverend John Eliot...1656-1682* (Manchester: Manchester University Press, 1931).

[29] See Packer, 'The Redemption and Restoration'; Irvonwy Morgan, *The Nonconformity of Richard Baxter* (London: Epworth Press, 1946); Hugh Martin, *Puritanism and Richard Baxter* (London: SCM Press, 1954). Of these, only Packer's contribution furthers the trend established by Nuttall.

[30] See Morrill, 'Introduction', in *Eternity in Time*, 4-7; Morrill, 'The Historian and the "Historical Filter"', in P. Geach, *et al., The Past and the Present: Problems of Understanding* (Oxford: Grandpont House, 1993), 95-97; Morrill's contribution to *The History Debate*, Juliet Gardiner, ed. (London: Collins and Brown, 1990), 91-95; Patrick Collinson, 'The vertical and the horizontal in religious history: internal and external integration of the subject', Alan Ford, James McGuire and Kenneth Milne, eds., *As by Law Established: The Church of Ireland since the Reformation* (Dublin: Lilleput Press, 1995); William Lamont, *Richard Baxter and the Millennium: Protestant Imperialism and the English Revolution* (London: Croom Helm, 1979), 22-24.

optimum characteristics of his own 'Liberal Nonconformity'.[31] N.H. Mair claims that 'Baxter's late puritanism with its emphasis upon practicality, catholicity, and simplicity was a forecast of the Latitudinarian ideas of the following decades, ideas which helped pave the way for the onset of the rationalistic era.'[32]

Further hindering a definitive appraisal of Baxter's pastoral ministry has been the tendency to pass on autobiographical descriptions without any additional interpretation or explanation. Hugh Martin's *Puritanism and Richard Baxter* (1954) uncritically accepts Baxter's account without commenting on how Baxter's ideas on preaching and ministry may have developed. Martin even provides an overview of Baxter's *Gildas Salvianus*, though again he is satisfied with merely enumerating Baxter's main ideas, stopping short of placing them in any kind of wider historical context.[33] Such treatment contributes to the false impression that twentieth-century historians have understood Baxter's pastoral identity and practise. Mostly, however, like Martin, they have simply passed on Baxter's autobiographical reminiscences as being sufficient.[34]

G.F. Nuttall, N.H. Keeble, C.D. Gilbert and J.I. Packer have produced the most substantial recent treatments of Baxter's pastoral ministry.[35] In his painstakingly researched biography of Baxter, Nuttall traces the circumstances which in 1641 led Baxter to accept the lectureship in Kidderminster. After describing Baxter's return to Kidderminster following a five-year absence brought on by the eruption of civil war, Nuttall provides a topical consideration of Baxter's ministry (preaching, catechising, services, worship, sacraments, discipline, association,

---

[31]Gordon, 'Baxter as a founder of Liberal Nonconformity', in *Heads of English Unitarian History* (1895), 101. See also E.A. George's chapter, 'Richard Baxter 1615-1691', in *Seventeenth Century Men of Latitude: Forerunners of the New Theology* (London: T. Fisher Unwin, 1909); J. H. Davies, *The Life of Richard Baxter, of Kidderminster, Preacher and Prisoner* (London: n.p. 1887), 35; Ladell, *Richard Baxter*; Grosart, 'Richard Baxter', 113-14.

[32] N.H. Mair, 'Christian Sanctification and Individual Pastoral Care in Richard Baxter' (Union Theological Seminary, New York, ThD thesis, 1966), 95. In contrast, W.R. Shealy totally modernizes Baxter's ministry by concluding that 'Universality, Institutionality, Particularity: these constitute the triplex framework of Richard Baxter's pastoral perspective.' Shealy's analysis of Baxter's ministry may satisfy certain mid-twentieth century questions, but it does not shed much helpful light on seventeenth-century pastoral ministry as Baxter and his colleagues understood it. W.R. Shealy, 'The Power of the Present: The Pastoral Perspective of Richard Baxter, Puritan Divine, 1615-1691' (Drew University PhD thesis, 1966), 52.

[33] Martin, *Puritanism and Richard Baxter*, 138, 143, 150-57.

[34] More recently, historians like Keith Wrightson have adopted a more critical stance to Baxter's perspective rather than uncritically passing on his description. See *English Society 1580-1680* (London: Hutchinson, 1982), 216-17.

[35]Nuttall, *Richard Baxter*, 24-63; Keeble, *Richard Baxter*, 69-93, and 'Richard Baxter's Preaching Ministry', 539-559; C.D. Gilbert, 'Richard Baxter's Ministry in Kidderminster, 1641-1661' (University of Birmingham MPhil thesis, 1996), and 'The Worcestershire Association of Ministers', in *BNS*, 4:2 (1996), 3-15.

assistants) and of certain immediate factors which contributed to it (his chronic poor health, concern over separatists). However, the restrictive format has forced Nuttall's study, compressed into 131 pages of text, to present each facet of Baxter's ministry in its most developed form. The resulting composite does not make much of Baxter's ongoing development or of the broader context from which such an understanding of ministry arose.

In his *Richard Baxter: Puritan Man of Letters* (1982), Keeble places his overview of Baxter's pastoral ministry in the broader context of his theological concerns over antinomianism and his efforts to execute a 'scheme for a comprehensive body of practical divinity'.[36] Keeble's main interest is 'the course of Richard Baxter's literary career'. Although not primarily concerned with Baxter as a pastor, Keeble does acknowledge 'the indebtedness of Baxter's practical writings to his pastoral experience'.[37]

In his later article, 'Richard Baxter's Preaching Ministry', Keeble comes nearest to Baxter's own position when he states that 'Baxter's multifarious activities, the involvement in so many schemes, projects and negotiations and the composition of so many books, were but a means to a pastoral end. His engagement with any issue or cause was never that merely of the writer, scholar or politician.'[38] But though Keeble notes that 'The distinctive mark of that ministry' was 'its prosecution of a sustained program of personal instruction', he forgoes any further examination on Baxter's overall pastoral agenda and focuses instead on a description of Baxter's preaching ministry and the identification of those texts from his published corpus which originated as sermons.[39]

C.D. Gilbert, in his 1996 unpublished M.Phil. thesis, 'Richard Baxter's Ministry in Kidderminster, 1641-1661', has provided the most comprehensive treatment of Baxter's pastoral ministry to date. Gilbert's work benefits from his experience as a local historian, and his sensitivity to local context enriches the value of his observations.[40] This is seen most clearly in his opening chapter on Kidderminster in 1641, the year Baxter began his lectureship under George Dance at St Mary's. Gilbert provides a helpful perspective on the dynamics at work within the parish resulting from the activities of an influential circle of puritan townsmen who were responsible for forcing Dance to agree to provide for a preacher to supplement his prayerbook ministry.[41] Gilbert also describes Baxter's insight into the challenge presented by the proliferation of Baptists, Quakers and

---

[36] Keeble, *Richard Baxter*, 69-74.

[37] Ibid., 80.

[38] Keeble, 'Richard Baxter's Preaching Ministry', 540.

[39] Ibid., 540-42. Other works by Keeble on Baxter include 'C.S. Lewis, Richard Baxter and "Mere Christianity"', in *CL*, 30:3 (1981), 27-44; *'Loving and Free Converse': Richard Baxter in His Letters* (London: Dr Williams's Trust, 1991).

[40] See, for example, C.D. Gilbert, *A History of King Charles I Grammar School Kidderminster* (Kidderminster: Tomkinson, 1980), as well as his many brief studies since 1991 in *BNS*.

[41] C.D. Gilbert, 'Richard Baxter's Ministry', 13-14.

various other 'sectaries', as well as his ongoing conflict with 'Anglican survivalism' and the particular difficulties posed by the opposition of Sir Ralph Clare within his own parish.[42] Beginning with Baxter's leadership in the development of the Worcestershire Association, Gilbert outlines his efforts to effect 'godly reformation'. With chapters on discipline, the role of the magistracy, preaching and catechising, Gilbert provides a well-rounded description of Baxter's pastoral efforts. But though Gilbert's work contributes much valuable local detail to the previous depictions of Baxter's pastoral ministry, he does not take us beyond the general outline of what was already known, nor does he attempt to locate Baxter in the broader flow of sixteenth- and seventeenth-century English history.

J.I. Packer has consistently sought to bridge the gap between academic scholarship and a broader non-specialist audience with respect to puritans in general and Baxter in particular.[43] His 1954 University of Oxford D. Phil. thesis, 'The Redemption and Restoration of Man in the Thought of Richard Baxter', supervised by Nuttall, proved a turning point in the study of Baxter's theology.[44] More recently, Packer has argued against the more constricting definitions of those who would understand 'puritan' as a label 'fastened on to advocates of more external reform for the Church of England'. Instead, 'Puritan ecclesiastical agitation was one aspect only of a many-sided religious movement that had evangelism and nurture at its heart'. Thus puritanism was primarily a 'pastoral movement, in which conformists and nonconformists, Anglicans, Presbyterians, Independents, Baptists, and Erastians' all shared similar pastoral goals.[45] For Packer, Baxter is the most articulate practitioner of pastoral puritanism at its best.[46] And yet, while Packer successfully avoids the tendency among Baxter's admirers to pass on uncritically an ahistorical account of his ministry as an example for contemporary practise, his concern to make Baxter accessible to a

---

[42] C.D. Gilbert, 'Richard Baxter's Ministry', see chapters 2 and 3.

[43] See, for example, Packer, *A Grief Sanctified: Love, loss and hope in the Life of Richard Baxter* (Leicester: Crossway, 1997); 'Richard Baxter on Heaven, Hope and Holiness', in *Alive to God: Studies in Spirituality presented to James M. Houston*, J.I. Packer and L. Wilkinson, eds. (Downers Grove, IL: InterVarsity Press, 1992), 161-175; *A Quest for Godliness: The Puritan Vision of the Christian Life* (Wheaton, IL: Crossway, 1991), also published in the United Kingdom as *Among God's Giants* (Eastbourne: Kingsway, 1991); 'Richard Baxter', in *Theology*, 55 (1953), 174-78; (with T. Beougher), 'Go Fetch Baxter', in *Christianity Today,* 35 (16/12/1991), 26-28.

[44] See Alister McGrath, *To Know and Serve God: A Biography of James I. Packer* (London: Hodder and Stoughton, 1997), 46-49. For a select bibliography of Packer's writings, see 293-308.

[45] Packer, 'The Practical Writings of the English Puritans', in *A Quest for Godliness*, 51.

[46] See Packer, 'Introduction', in Baxter, *The Reformed Pastor*, 9-19; see also Packer, *A Man for All Ministries* (1991); 'Introducing "A Christian Directory"', in Richard Baxter, *A Christian Directory* (Morgan, PA: Soli Deo Gloria, 1990, reprt of 1846 edn, 1673 first edition), unp.

non-academic audience limits the scope of his historical investigations to ground previously covered.

This study will address a series of questions not tackled in the existing literature. Was Baxter a pastoral virtuoso, or was he merely reflecting a broader consensus of under-reported pastoral practise, noteworthy perhaps as a popularizer, but not much more? Is Baxter's ministry simply a case of early Stuart practical godliness writ large, or are there elements of discontinuity between Baxter's Kidderminster and the efforts of those earlier pastors presented by Samuel Clarke in his successive galleries of 'godly' exemplars? To what extent does Baxter's understanding of 'reformation' square with that of his 'puritan' predecessors and the subsequently attempted Westminster Assembly reforms, and does their preferred rhetoric influence their ensuing pastoral strategies? Can Baxter's efforts as a pastor be best explained in terms of his immediate context, or are there further, more remote elements at work which affect his response to the situation he finds upon his return to St Mary's parish in 1647?

Richard Baxter's recognized success as a pastor and his corresponding popularity as an author propelled him into positions of leadership within Cromwell's fragmenting Settlement, where he increasingly acted in the capacity of spokesman for the 'Able, Faithful, Godly Ministry of this Nation'.[47] His role as commentator on the tumultuous events in England from the events leading to the Civil Wars to the Glorious Revolution have long made Baxter a familiar source for historians beyond the confines of what used to be called 'church history'. Yet by grappling with his identity as a pastor, we come closest to making sense of the complex facets of his own history, and why he did and wrote the things he did. Rescued from the distorting patina of hagiography and the curious neglect of the academy, Baxter's pastoral ministry becomes a lens that clarifies both the puritanism from which he emerged, and the nonconformity he subsequently embodied.

---

[47] [Richard Baxter], *The Humble Petition of Many Thousands...of the County of Worcester... In behalf of the Able, Faithful, Godly Ministry of this Nation* (1652).

PART ONE

The Reformed Pastor

CHAPTER 2

Rhetoric and Reality:
Pastoral Emphases and Practise in Edwardian, Elizabethan and Early Stuart England

Richard Baxter's *Gildas Salvianus* was the latest in a long series of published exhortations to England's Protestant pastors. The previous century of Protestantism in England had witnessed a burgeoning collection of treatises and sermons excoriating pastoral inadequacies and applying biblical standards to contemporary circumstances in the nation's parishes. Whether engaged in a polemical defence of 'godlie ministery', or concerned to expound the archetype of the 'Faithful Shepheard', these authors, often parish ministers themselves, succeeded in creating a literary reality that appears to have had little in common with the day to day experience of parish ministry. The need to stigmatize Roman Catholic ministry led Protestant pastors to displace completely the sacramental model and its communal associations with a preaching-centred model and its emphasis on individual response and faith.[1] By changing the way pastors conceived of and practiced their ministry, these Protestants introduced fundamental changes in the way Christianity was understood and lived by ordinary people. Though they met with surprising success in some areas, their attempts to reorient the lives of their parishioners around Protestant verities also succeeded in arousing significant resistance on the part of many who were not convinced of the need to change.[2] An account of this struggle between the rhetoric of an ideal Protestant pastoral ministry and the reality experienced in the parishes survives in the remarkably one-sided and idealized accounts of pastoral ministry preserved in these exhortatory treatises and sermons. This chapter undertakes to survey every extant English Protestant treatise on pastoral ministry as well as every published sermon identifiably addressing pastoral practise, with the aim both of describing the ideals that informed Protestant

---

[1] While acknowledging that the 'overwhelming impression left by the sources for late medieval religion in England is that of a Christianity resolutely and enthusiastically orientated towards the public and the corporate, and of a continuing sense of the value of cooperation and mutuality in seeking salvation', Eamon Duffy also draws attention to 'signs of a privatizing tendency' in the practise of late medieval piety. See Duffy, *The Stripping of the Altars: Traditional Religion in England 1400-1580* (New Haven and London: Yale University Press, 1992), 131.

[2] Christopher Haigh, *English Reformations: Religion, Politics, and Society under the Tudors* (Oxford: Clarendon, 1993), 278-84, 289-95.

pastors and glimpsing the reality they attempted to alter. And although the published rhetoric of England's Protestants reveals a monolithic commitment to the ideal of a pulpit-centred pastoral ministry, there are also hints that in their actual practise of parish ministry, even the most zealous Protestants found their ideal wanting, and sought further means to supplement their effectiveness as pastors.

There have been surprisingly few attempts to analyze Elizabethan and early Stuart treatises on pastoral ministry. Earlier efforts, though sympathetic to pastoral concerns, too often limited the scope of their investigations to that portion of evidence that enabled them to view puritan pastors as part of a wider tradition of pastoral care. John T. McNeill's definition of pastoral care in *A History of the Cure of Souls* (1952), for example, is so broad as to be unintelligible to those in a sixteenth- or seventeenth-century context.[3] Moreover, McNeill is selective in the evidence he considers, choosing to ignore those details that run counter to his homogenizing theme.[4] Another attempt to develop a history of pastoral care by William Clebsch and Charles Jaekle, while more refined, runs into similar difficulty by imposing a modern definition of pastoral care on previous historical ages and denominational traditions.[5] While they find ample examples to illustrate their definitions, their efforts end up telling the reader more about what *they* believe a pastor should do and be rather than providing a reliable guide through the particulars of the sources. Winthrop Hudson attempts to delineate the characteristics of puritan ministry, though his work suffers from the same tendency to project back into the sources modern definitions of 'Anglican' or 'Puritan' which in turn oversimplifies many of the pastoral realities that were faced by ministers.[6] Horton Davies also discusses puritan pastors and pastoral issues in his surveys of worship and theology in England,[7] and while helpful as a general guide through the period, his particular

---

[3] McNeill defines the cure of souls as 'the sustaining and curative treatment of persons in those matters beyond the requirements of animal life.' McNeill, *A History of the Cure of Souls* (New York: Harper, 1951), vii.

[4] His generalist approach leads him to make statements like 'Despite all the competent Anglican writing on the cure of souls, Anglicanism lacked a general treatise on the work of the pastor.' McNeill, *History*, 236.

[5] 'The ministry of the cure of souls, or pastoral care, consists of helping acts, done by representative Christian persons, directed toward the healing, sustaining, guiding and reconciling of troubled persons whose troubles arise in the context of ultimate meanings and concerns.' William A. Clebsch and Charles R. Jaekle, *Pastoral Care in Historical Perspective* (New York: Harper and Row, 1967), 4.

[6] Winthrop S. Hudson, 'The Ministry in the Puritan Age', H.R. Neibuhr and D.D. Williams, eds., *The Ministry in Historical Perspective* (New York: Harper, 1956).

[7] See Horton Davies, *The Worship of the English Puritans* (London: Dacre Press, 1948); *Worship and Theology in England: From Cranmer to Hooker, 1534-1603* (Princeton: Princeton University Press, 1970); *Worship and Theology in England: From Andrews to Baxter and Fox, 1603-1690* (Princeton: Princeton University Press, 1975).

focus does not allow for the detailed treatment of puritans as pastors or of the exhortatory literature they produced.

More recent attempts to explore the puritan tradition of pastoral ministry have proven more profitable and stimulating. Patrick Collinson's study of Elizabethan pastoral ministry highlights some of the internal tensions within the puritan pastoral perspective and traces puritan pastoral efforts and rhetoric from their high ideals to their ultimate frustration.[8] Likewise, Ian Green has provided helpful perspective on pastoral developments in England by setting them in a wider continental framework.[9] In his useful article, Neal Enssle has discussed in detail the ideals which motivated and governed puritan pastoral efforts.[10] The collection of essays found in *A History of Pastoral Care* (2000) has sought to update the earlier overviews of ministry by McNeill, Clebsch and Jaekle, and Neibuhr and Williams. In particular, David Cornick gives a helpful overview of the pastoral emphases of the continental reformers in his 'The Reformation Crisis in Pastoral Care'.[11] In the same volume, Cornick has another essay focusing more closely on early modern pastoral care in England, comparing the ministries of William Perkins, Richard Baxter and Gilbert Burnet. In this study, Cornick defines pastors such as Perkins and Baxter not simply as preachers, but as clinicians of the soul and surgeons of the conscience.[12] This line of inquiry leads Cornick to summarize Baxter's ministry in terms of 'casuistry and pastoral guidance', his primary source being Baxter's massive *A Christian Directory* (1673), the seventeenth-century pastoral equivalent of the *Physicians Desk Reference*. Cornick thereby highlights an important aspect of the English pastoral tradition, but in such a brief overview, he can provide only an introduction to the use of casuistry by early modern pastors, while other aspects of their ministries remain unplumbed.[13] But perhaps the best introduction to the context and issues which shaped pastoral ministry in post-Reformation England remains Patrick Collinson's *Elizabethan Puritan Movement* (1967). This has

---

[8] Collinson, 'Shepherds', 185-220.

[9] Ian Green, '"Reformed Pastors"', 249-286.

[10] Neal Enssle, 'Patterns of Godly Life: The Ideal Parish Minister in Sixteenth- and Seventeenth-Century English Thought', in *SCJ*, 28 (1997), 3-28. For an example of a more localized study, see J. Freeman, 'The Parish Ministry in the Diocese of Durham, c. 1570-1640' (University of Durham PhD thesis, 1979).

[11] David Cornick, 'The Reformation Crisis', G.R. Evans, ed., *A History of Pastoral Care*, 223-251. For his comments on Bucer and Calvin, see 237-247.

[12] Cornick, 'Pastoral Care in England', 315.

[13] The cursory nature of such an overview means that the complex issue of church discipline, which vexed and convulsed the Church of England from the Reformation to the Restoration, is summarized in less than three pages. See Cornick, 'Pastoral Care in England' 323-325. See also Ralph Houlbrooke's 'The family and pastoral care', G.R. Evans, ed., *A History of Pastoral Care*, 262-293. Houlebrooke helpfully explores the impact of Protestantism on English family life as reflected in the range of pastoral activities undertaken by sixteenth- and seventeenth-century Protestant pastors.

been recently supplemented by Tom Webster's *Godly Clergy in Early Stuart England* (1997). Their labours have provided me with a starting point and form the basis for the further exploration entailed in this chapter.

Priests Good and Bad

Though the differences between the late medieval Roman Catholic understanding of pastoral ministry and the Protestant ideals that began to take root in England are considerable, there are several continuities worth noting. One must be mindful that the blanket condemnation of Roman Catholic ministry by zealous Protestants was made by those who had much to gain from portraying Roman Catholic ministry in its worst possible light whilst trumpeting the alternative at its most virtuous.[14] Recent studies have asserted the vigour of the pre-Reformation church in England, and that far from being a timely corrective to a corrupt and waning form of Christian ministry, Protestant ideas competed with a system of beliefs and practises in many places entrenched and popular, which did not lie down and die in the face of a much-heralded biblical alternative.[15] Moreover, the virulent attacks by Protestants against Roman Catholic forms of ministry in the literature on ministry from Elizabeth to the Civil War betray not Protestant but Catholic strength, as well as a corresponding Protestant fear that a resurgent Counter-Reformation Catholicism might actually prevail. But we begin to tread beyond our scope.

Awareness of the negative effects a scandalous priest would have in his parish was not a Protestant innovation, nor was awareness of the positive benefits engendered by more and effective preaching.[16] Gregory the Great's *Liber*

---

[14] Ian Green is certainly correct to warn that 'If one is tempted to draw a sharp contrast between a late medieval priest with little but the sacraments to perform and a 'reformed pastor' or *bon curè* with a much wider range of tasks, one could be guilty of taking a blinkered view of the former's work and an unduly optimistic view of the latter's readiness to perform the tasks set him.' '"Reformed Pastors"', 262-263.

[15] See, for example, Haigh's discussion of Richard Whitford in his *English Reformations*, 25-28. Eamon Duffy has provided perhaps the best example of the response of an English parish through the trauma of England's reformations in his *The Voices of Morebath: Reformation and Rebellion in an English Village* (New Haven and London: Yale University Press, 2001). However, for a critique of this revisionist view, see Eric J. Carlson, 'Cassandra Banished? New Research on Religion in *Tudor and Early Stuart England'*, E.J. Carlson, ed., *Religion and the English People 1500-1640: New Voices New Perspectives* (Kirksville, MO: Thomas Jefferson University Press, 1998), 3-22. And for a discussion of the difficulty all sides have in making sense of the conflicting evidences, see Alec Ryrie, 'Counting Sheep, Counting Shepherds: The Problem of Allegiance in the English Reformation', Peter Marshall and Alec Ryrie, eds., *The Beginnings of English Protestantism* (Cambridge: Cambridge University Press, 2002), 84-110.

[16] Peter Marshall states that 'The notion that preaching was almost totally neglected by

Regulae Pastoralis is an early but influential treatment of the pastoral role of bishops for the Western Church. Concerned to show 'the manner of man the pastor ought to be' as well as 'after what manner he should teach', Gregory (540-604) provided a model instructive both to later Catholics and Protestants.[17] The evangelical nature of the pastor's responsibility demands that his life be consistent with his words: 'For...whoever enters on the priesthood undertakes the office of a herald, so as to walk, himself crying aloud before the coming of the judge who follows terribly.'[18]

Various attempts were later made in England to raise clergy standards by publishing rules and ideals, most notably by John Pecham, Archbishop of Canterbury from 1279-1292.[19] Medieval Roman Catholic handbooks on pastoral ministry, such as those written in the mid-Fifteenth Century by John Myrc, Augustinian canon of Lilleshall in Shropshire, contain frank descriptions of the shortcomings of parish ministers as well as practical suggestions to promote a more effective ministry:

> For little of worth is the preaching,
> If thou be of evil living.[20]

---

priests in the late Middle Ages is almost certainly a false one.' *The Catholic Priesthood and the English Reformation* (Oxford: Clarendon, 1994), 88.

[17] Gregory the Great, *The Book of Pastoral Rule* (James Barmby, translator), in *NPNF* 2:12, *Leo the Great, Gregory the Great* (1895, repr. Peabody, MA: Hendrickson, 1995), Part III, Prologue, 24a. Prior to Gregory, both Chrysostom ('De Sacerdotio', c. AD 382) and Gregory Nazianzen (*tou autou apolghtikoß*, c. AD 362), addressed issues of the pastor's character and duty. Gregory is aware of Gregory Nazianzen's work as he writes, but does not seem aware of Chrysostom's. See Thomas Oden, *Care of Souls in the Classic Tradition* (Philadelphia: Fortress Press, 1984), 43-73. For an overview of the pastoral concerns of early monasticism, see Benedicta Ward, 'Pastoral Care and the Monks: "Whose feet do you wash"', G.R. Evans, ed., *A History of Pastoral Care*, 77-89.

[18] Gregory the Great, *The Book of Pastoral Rule*, p. 12a. 'For he who is required by the necessity of his position to speak the highest things is compelled by the same necessity to exhibit the highest things. For that voice more readily penetrates the hearer's heart, which the speaker's life commends, since what he commands by speaking he helps the doing of by shewing.' *The Book of Pastoral Rule*, 10a-b.

[19] See also Norman Tanner's overview of the pastoral reforms attempted by the Fourth Lateran Council in 'Pastoral care: the Fourth Lateran Council of 1215', G.R. Evans, ed., *A History of Pastoral Care*, 112-125. In the same volume, see also Thomas O'Loughlin, 'Penitentials and Pastoral Care', 93-111.

[20] See John Myrc, 'Instructions for Parish Priests', in *Early English Text Society*, Original Series, 31 (1868), 1-3 (modernized). See R.M. Ball, 'The Education of the English Parish Clergy in the Later Middle Ages with Particular Reference to the Manuels of Instruction' (University of Cambridge PhD thesis, 1976), 22-78, 221-304. See also Roland Bainton, 'The Ministry in the Middle Ages', R. Neibuhr and D. Williams, eds., *The Ministry in Historical Perspectives* (New York: Harper, 1956), 82-109; and David B. Foss, 'John Mirk's Instructions for Parish Priests', W.J. Sheils and D.

As Patrick Collinson observes, 'Long before the Reformation, it was a commonplace that there were two kinds of priests, good and bad.'[21]

But along with the continuity of reaction against clerical vice, pre- and post-Reformation clergy continued to share many of the same roles in the life of individuals and in the community in which they lived. The early Protestant preacher and printer Robert Crowley, in his attack on Roman Catholic ministry, also uncovers an aspect of lay expectation of the pastoral ministry that remained immune to reform: 'What call they serving of a cure? For sooth, to say mass, matins and evensong on the holy day, to make holy water and holy bread, to conjure the fount and volow [baptize] the child, to shrive, housel, and annoint the sick, to say dirige and mass, and bury the dead.'[22] Though a Protestant pastor might criticize the theological presuppositions informing Roman Catholic pastoral duties, the Protestant faced similar expectations from the members of his parish to oversee and appropriately mark the significant rites of passage of the members of his parish: birth, marriage and death.

Nevertheless, the theological break with the Roman Church was complete, and the subsequent transformation of pastoral ministry attempted at the parish level by committed Protestants was comprehensive in scope, at least in terms of ideals. In terms of many of their duties, Roman Catholic priests and Protestant pastors might appear to be similar: both preached (or were supposed to), both led services of public prayer and worship, both celebrated sacraments, both visited the sick, both officiated the rites of passage, both took leadership roles in the community and in the resolution of personal and local conflicts.[23] But

---

Wood, eds, *The Ministry*, 131-140; Leonard E. Boyle, 'Robert Grosseteste and the Pastoral Care', L.E. Boyle, ed., *Pastoral Care, Clerical Education and Canon Law 1200-1400* (London: Variorum Reprints, 1981), 3-51.

[21] Collinson, 'Shepherds', 185. For an anthology of medieval texts on pastoral ministry, see John Shinners and William J. Dohar, *Pastors and the Cure of Souls in Medieval England* (Notre Dame, IN: Notre Dame University Press, 1998). For other studies of medieval pastoral ministry, see N.J.G. Pounds, *A History of the English Parish: The Culture of Religion from Augustine to Victoria* (Cambridge: Cambridge University Press, 2000), 155-177; William J. Dohar, *The Black Death and Pastoral Leadership: The Diocese of Hereford in the Fourteenth Century* (Philadelphia: University of Pennsylvania Press, 1995).

[22] Robert Crowley, *The Confutation of xiii articles whereunto n. Shaxton subscribed* (1548), sig Giv. See Peter Marshall's discussion in *The Catholic Priesthood*, 175-77.

[23] Ivonwy Morgan notes the similarities between early Protestant and Roman Catholic complaints against bad pastors, as well as their similar suggestions to bring about pastoral reform in *The Godly Preachers of the Elizabethan Church* (London: Epworth Press, 1965), 1-10. Diarmaid MacCulloch notes that while the 'creation of a reformed ministry was one of the great success stories of the Elizabethan Church', the lack of accompanying structural reform meant that Protestant ministers shouldered alone the burden of parish pastoral care that before had come from a 'variety of sources: monks,

however similar the practise, both understood their Bibles, their roles, the means and the ends towards which they laboured, very differently. The impetus for this transformation of the Roman Catholic practise of pastoral ministry did not come from within Roman Catholicism itself. The Roman Church had demonstrated impressive flexibility in absorbing previous movements of reform throughout the medieval period, and even again with Trent and the Counter-Reformation. Widespread public discontent with Catholic pastoral practise was not the reason behind the change. Rather, Protestants understood the change in pastoral emphasis to have occurred because of a change in theological emphases, derived ultimately from a change in the source of authority from scripture and tradition to scripture alone.[24] Thus changes in emphasis between Roman Catholic and Protestant pastoral ministry are due not to differences in *degree*, but to differences in *kind*. Though they may seem to be using similar words and sharing similar concerns over pastoral shortcomings, late medieval Roman Catholic priests and post-Reformation Protestant pastors are in fact speaking from very different perspectives and working towards different ends.[25]

For both sorts of pastors, Protestant and Catholic, it was a difference with eternal consequences. For Protestants, this realization produced both urgency that their evangelical obligations be fulfilled, and fear that their light might be quenched by a Catholic revival (whose own leaders were ironically motivated by a similar zeal). But as the sixteenth-century progressed and fault lines appeared in the attempted Elizabethan Protestant consensus, concerns to facilitate effective pastoral ministry were increasingly diverted into the polemic for further reformation. The frustration of these hopes, first by Elizabeth and then by James I, as well as the development of an alternative Protestant sacramentalist understanding of ministry, which became dominant during Charles I's reign, continued to inform the rhetoric about ministry, if not the practise, of those Protestants unhappy with the conformist *status quo*. In the following survey, effort has been made to limit its scope to those sermons and treatises that aim specifically to exhort pastors, as opposed to those which merely address pastors and their duties as one of a number of points being made. The former were published primarily for pastors, the latter as instruction for godly laypeople.

In 1551, the otherwise anonymous Peter Pykeryng published *A Myroure or*

---

friars and nuns, the diocesan and parish system, chantry foundations great and small.' MacCulloch, *The Later Reformation in England, 1547-1603* (London: MacMillan, 1990), 101-102.

[24] See Alister McGrath's chapter 'The Return to Scripture', in *Reformation Thought: An Introduction,* 3rd edition (Oxford, Blackwell, 1999), 135-158.

[25] For the most thorough recent study of the Edwardian Reformation and how the growing divergence between England's Protestants and Catholics was managed by those in power, see Diarmaid MacCulloch's *Tudor Church Militant: Edward VI and the Protestant Reformation* (London: Allen Lane, Penguin Press, 1999).

glasse for all spiritual Ministers to behold them selues in; wherein they may learne theyr office and duitie towardis the flocke comitted to their Charg.[26] Pykeryng's compilation of texts from 'holy scripture and catholyke doctours' betrays a different concern than what one finds in Myrc or other standard late medieval handbooks on pastoral duty. Pykerying is careful to stay close to biblical texts when describing pastoral duties. The 'spirituall pastoure', writes Pykeryng, 'is a preachar...that is lawfully called by the autoritie and comaundement of God, unto the cure of soulls of the congregation, which is committed unto him: to teache the Gospel and minister the Sacraments unto them.'[27] The pastor's characteristics are 'First, that he be of a Catholik fayeth. Secondarly that he be of good conuersation in liueynge. Thyrdly, that he be boeth able to exhorte with holesome doctrine, and also to reproue them that gayne saye it.'[28] Pykeryng's pastor 'is to rule and gouerne faithfully, the church that is committed unto hys charge: with the ministrying of the worde and Sacramentis, and to holde oute and expell false doctryne and offencion.' Pykeryng concludes his exhortation with the Pauline admonition that a century hence Richard Baxter himself would take as the text of the sermon that became *Gildas Salvianus*: 'Take hede unto your selves, and to al the flocke emonge whom the holy goste hath set you to be ouersears to lead the congregation of god, whych he hath purchaised in his bloude.'[29] With this introduction, Pykeryng begins his list of quotations, first from scripture, and then from early church authorities such as Augustine, Ambrose, Cyprian, Jerome and Gregory.

Though obviously not intended as a polemical piece, Pykeryng provides an early foreshadowing of what became the stock Protestant concerns of later sermons and treatises: that pastors effectively preach and rightly teach the Bible, and live a life that honours God by avoiding scandal and setting an example for the church. As we shall see, these were perennial concerns among committed Protestants that were neither quickly nor easily resolved. But Pykeryng's pastors did not have long to reflect on Protestant pastoral tactics. The unprecedented religious upheavals of the coming decade would make such concerns seem a luxury in light of more profound choices that would confront the English clergy.

Elizabethan Pastors and their Ministry

For two decades in the aftermath of Elizabeth's re-establishment of Protestant

---

[26] The remainder of Pykeryng's title continues: *Gathered out of holy scripture and catholic doctors, by Peter Pykeryng, seruant to the ryght worshipful syr Anthonie Neueil Knyght, and one of the Kingis maiesties councel established in the north, and sent to syr. Hon Codkyll vycar of South.* There is no mention of Pykeryng in either Venn or Foster.

[27] Pykeryng, *A Myroure*, sig A.iii.

[28] Pykeryng, *A Myroure*, sig A.iii[v].

[29] Pykeryng, *A Myroure*, sig Aiiii. Pykeryng here quotes Acts 20:28 and echoes 1 Peter 5:2-3.

doctrine following Mary's restoration of Catholicism, there were no handbooks or treatises on pastoral ministry published in England.[30] Once Protestantism was re-established, there seems to have been an awareness that the primary work of the first generation of Elizabethan Protestants in the English parishes was evangelism, without which there could be no pastoral care.[31] In a letter of 8 August 1580 to the Earl of Leicester, William Chaderton, Bishop of Chester could optimistically claim that 'Lancashire is in some places well reclaimed, for even in the field where 14 or 15 usually resorted to church, I have at my sermons had above 2000 attentive hearers. Many gentlemen [however] remain obstinate.... We therefore intend to proceed against them speedily, and hope in time to reclaim all or most part, especially if we might expel the vagrant priests, and place learned, zealous, and grave [preachers], at least in the chief towns, wherein we purpose to do our uttermost'.[32] Increasingly a priority was also defending the new church from the flood of doctrinal polemic from the English Catholic community in exile and from the missionary initiatives by increasing numbers of seminary priests. This response produced a counter-flood of Protestant treatises against various aspects of Roman Catholic teaching and tradition perceived as vulnerable to criticism from a biblically-informed perspective. But alongside the Catholic challenge there was a growing awareness among the more committed Protestants that Elizabeth's Settlement was not a provisional step on the road to the complete reformation that lay at the heart of their agenda for the English church, rather it was intended as the final word. Protestant energies were therefore diverted towards overcoming the block to further reform, which led them to focus increasingly on changing the government and ceremonies of the church.[33] But Elizabeth's adamant opposition to further reform made the advent of a continental or Scottish kind of discipline increasingly remote. However, with the qualified success of

---

[30] If there are tracts, treatises or sermons on the pastor's duty published during these decades, they have presently escaped my attention.

[31] Consider, for example, Edmund Grindal's recruitment, whilst Archbishop of York, of Edmund Bunney and some forty other Protestant preachers from the universities to labor throughout the north in an effort to promote the work of conversion. See Ronald A. Marchant, *The Puritans and the Church Courts in the Diocese of York 1560-1642* (London: Longmans, 1960), 16-17; Claire Cross, 'A Metamorphosis of Ministry: Former Yorkshire Monks and Friars in the Sixteenth-Century Protestant Church', *JURCHS*, 4:5 (1989), 289-304. See also George Carleton's account of the regular evangelistic preaching ministry of Bernard Gilpin in *The Life of Bernard Gilpin* (1629), 17-27. And see Claire Cross's, 'Priests into Ministers: The Establishment of Protestant Practise in the City of York 1530-1630', in *Reformation Principal and Practice*, P.N. Brooks, ed. (London: Scholar Press, 1980), 225.

[32] *Calendar of State Papers Domestic Series, Elizabeth and James, 1580-1625, Addenda*, 12, XXVII, M.A.E. Green, ed. (1872), 11-12.

[33] Patrick Collinson traces the rise of English Presbyterianism in *The Elizabethan Puritan Movement*, 101-145.

Protestant attempts to convert the parishes through the uneven provision of godly preaching came a growing awareness of the need to address the quickly growing *pastoral* needs at the parish level by exhorting parish clergy to their God-given duty.

As Protestant ideas advanced, however, resistance at the local parish level also became more defined and hindrances to the Protestant perspective were revealed in increasingly sharp relief. Specifically, the vast majority of clergy inherited by Elizabeth may have found themselves in a doctrinally reformed Church of England, but they had little if any inclination to modify the way their ministry was understood and practiced. It was in this new context that Protestants began to formulate their own description of the parish minister. The old Roman Catholic complaints against non-preaching and scandalous clergy-Collinson's 'bad priests' – were co-opted by Protestants and skillfully used as a means to root out the strongholds of local Catholic practise. And the 'good priests' intended for substitution were of course not simply better practitioners of Roman Catholicism – they were a different species altogether.

In an ordination sermon preached in Manchester and published in 1582, a young Simon Harward (1556?-1614) advanced the old complaints as a means to promote the new way: 'We of the ministery are admonished of our dutie, that we ought to be labourers, not loyterers, not to live idely and securely, but to be painfull workemen in the Harvest of the Lord.'[34] However, in a remarkable passage, Harward presents in stark terms the fundamental differences, as he viewed them, between Roman Catholic and Protestant ministries. 'To be a labourer in the Lordes Harvest,' writes Harward,

> is not to chaunt and bleat in Quiers, or it is not to iangle the Bels, and to looke to the Vestery, as was in time past the office of the Poster: it is not, to reade and singe lessons, and to hallow bread, and all greene fruite, as was the charge of the Reader: it is not, to Charme or to Coniure, as was the office of the Exorcist: it is not, to carye Candlesticks and light Tapers, as the Acolites... it is not, to serue at the Altar, & to read the Gospel, for the quick and the dead,

---

[34] Simon Harward, *Two Godlie and learned Sermons, preached at Manchester in Lancashire, before a great Audience, both of Honor and Worship. The first containeth a reproofe of the subtill practices of dissembling Neuters, and politique Worldlings. The other a Charge and Instruction , for all unlearned, negligent, and dissolute Ministers.* (1582), sigs Ciiii v, Dii. Harward describes himself on the title page as a 'preacher of the woord of God, and Maister of Arte, late of Newe Colledge in Oxford'. Harward matriculated at Christ's College, Cambridge in 1572, BA in 1575, BA at Oxford in 1577, and MA in 1578. He was chaplain of New College, Oxford in 1577, and was presented to the rectory of Warrington, Lancashire, in 1579. Resigning for unspecified reasons in 1581, Harward was 'preacher' at Crowhurst, Barnstead and Tandridge in Surrey, and Odiham in Hampshire. He was instituted vicar of Banstead on 1 December 1604. See *DNB*.

as was wickedly placed for the office of Deacons: it is not, to mumble vp Masses, and to offer vp sacrifice, for the quick and the dead, as the shaueling Priests: it is not, to sit Imperiously, with the Maiesty of a Triple Crowne, and to dispose kingdoms, nor to beare a Crosier Staffe, and blesse, and challenge power to give the holy Ghost, & remit sinnes at their own pleasure, as the Pope and his Bishops: it is not, to weare a Cardinals Hat, nor to lyue vnto them selues, and their own bellies, as the swinish Cloister men, Abbots & Priors, Munkes & Friers: it is not, to serue mens humors, as elbow Chaplaines...[35]

Instead, true ministry is

to feede the flocke of Christe, with the heavenly food of his blessed worde, as did the Apostles, Prophets and Euangelists, in the primitiue church, & is now required of Pastors & such Elders, or Bishops, which are appointed as watchmen over certain flocks & congregations, to rule and gouerne the same, by the preaching of the Gospell, by the administring of the Sacraments, & by the exercising of Ecclesiasticall discipline & of the Doctours, whose charge is especially to expand the right sence & vnderstanding of the Scriptures, & to instruct those which are Catechumenoi in ye points & principles of christian religion.[36]

With scripture and Geneva providing the inspiration, young zealous Protestants like Harward continued to press for a reconstruction of the pastor's duty along Genevan lines even in the face of stiffening resistance to the suggestions of structural change.[37] But if importance is heightened by

---

[35] Harward, *Two Godlie and learned Sermons*, sig Fvii^v-Fviii.

[36] Harward, *Two Godlie and learned Sermons*, sig Fviii. It is a definition that could have been lifted straight from Calvin. See John Calvin, *Institutes of the Christian Religion* (trans. F.L. Battles; Philadelphia: Westminster Press, 1960), Book iv, chapters 4-7, 1056-1060.

[37] By 'Genevan' I mean the influence John Calvin had on the way pastoral ministry was understood and promoted in the English Church, especially by the 'hotter sort' of Protestants such as Harward. Drawing inspiration from their experience of Calvin's Geneva during their exile under Mary, many of the returning Protestants under Elizabeth's more favorable reign sought to influence the course of reformation using a blueprint based not only on Calvin's writings but on what they themselves had seen and heard. Here we see an early example of that influence on issues pertaining directly to pastoral ministry. See Andrew Pettegree, 'The Clergy and the Reformation: From "devilish priesthood" to New Professional Elite', A. Pettegree, ed., *The Reformation of the Parishes: The Ministry and the Reformation in Town and Country* (Manchester: Manchester University Press, 1993), 8-9. For discussion of an earlier example of

emphasis, then the priority work of a pastor for Harward is that of preaching. Indeed, the primary qualifications for a pastor are that he knows 'how to doo his Embassage, how to feed [the flock] with discretion, first with Milke, and then with strong meate, how to labour in the Lords haruest, how to builde, how to leade the people of God, how to watch ouer them, how to lighten their hearts, and to season them with the knowledge of Gods holy worde.'[38] Harward concludes with the exhortation that his hearers pray to God 'that he will roote out all rauening Wolues, all Hierlings, Timeseruers, and dombe Dogges, which hinder the course of the Gospel, that he wyl giue his word free passage'.[39] Harward thus abridges the complex world of the Elizabethan church into those ministers who further God's purposes through faithful preaching of his word, and those ministers who by their negligent lives and non-preaching ministries hinder God's intentions for the English church. It is a dialectic that would serve puritan rhetoric long and well.

It was inevitable that the discussion of pastoral duties would be swept up into larger issues of controversy. Harward's assertion of a Calvinist understanding of pastoral ministry was an echo from the provinces of a much more contentious issue vexing an increasingly divided English Protestantism. Frustrated by finding Elizabeth and many bishops against the further reformation of the church, English presbyterians mounted a determined, learned, and ultimately futile attack on the unreformed aspects of the English church. Men such as Thomas Cartwright (1535-1603), Walter Travers (1548?-1635) and William Fulke (1538-1589) viewed the duties of the local parish minister in light of the larger issue of establishing a Reformed discipline. But they were forced from their influential positions at Cambridge by an ecclesiastical and political hierarchy made uneasy by the egalitarian nature of the reforms being promoted.[40]

William Fulke's *A Brief and Plain Declaration, concerning the desire of all those faithful Ministers, that have and do seeke for the Discipline and reformation of the Church of England* (1584) sets forth the presbyterian ideal of pastoral ministry, the practical outcome of what the hoped-for changes in the Church of England's structure would accomplish. Fulke himself studied at St John's College and Clifford's Inn, and was a friend of Thomas Cartwright. Having taken a major role in the Vestiarian Controversy at Cambridge, he was

---

Calvin's influence on the Reformation in Scotland, see Euan Cameron, 'Frankfort and Geneva: The European Context of John Knox's Reformation', R.A. Mason, ed., *John Knox and the British Reformations* (Aldershot: Ashgate, 1998), 51-73. See also Diarmaid MacCulloch, 'The change of religion', 101. I will discuss Calvin's influence on English understandings of Reformation in the next chapter.

[38] Harward, *Two Godlie and learned Sermons*, sig Cvi[v]-Cvii.

[39] Ibid., sig Ivii.

[40] Collinson, *The Elizabethan Puritan Movement*, 108. Collinson observes, however, that the English Presbyterians wrangled endlessly among themselves over how ecclesiastical power might be distributed. See 107, for example.

deprived of his fellowship and expelled as an extremist. Later readmitted, Fulke became Master of Pembroke Hall in 1578 and vice-chancellor in 1580.[41] He wrote *A Brief and plain declaration* in 1572 at the height of the controversy over presbyterianism, but held it back from publishing because, some have speculated, of certain differences with Travers and others on the locus of authority in the reformed congregation.[42]

In Fulke's view, England was prevented from experiencing the full fruit of the Reformation because of a preponderance of unlearned and ungodly ministers, and that 'if euer we minde suche a reformation... wee must vtterlye remooue al the vnlearned pastors, as men by no means to be tollerated to have any charge ouer the lords flok'. Such 'blinde watchmen', 'ignoraunt dumbe Dogges', 'idle greedie Curres' and 'vnlearned Sheepheardes' 'by the testimonie of God his spirite, are denied to be meet Pastours of the people of God.' Instead, the primary pastoral task is to teach people the Bible, or, in biblical terms, to feed the flock of God. For Fulke, teaching the Bible 'is the chiefe & principall office that is in the church. By that we be taught to know God, & how to serue him, & what benefits to look for at his hand, without which knowledge, ther can be no felecity but only destruction loked for'.[43]

Fulke allows that the 'second part' of a pastor's duty 'consisteth in right administration of the Sacramentes of God'. But 'the office of preaching bee more excellent...as S. Paul speaketh comparatiuely. *Christ sent me not to baptize but to preach.* 1.Cor.1.17.' Though Fulke goes on to delineate a third category of the pastor's duties, that of leading public prayer, his comments are brief and almost an afterthought. Indeed so keen is Fulke to underline the centrality of preaching and to deprecate any other inherited pastoral function that smacks even remotely of Roman Catholic tradition, that great swaths of what previously passed as pastoral ministry are dismissed out right as dangerous, such as confirmation, churching of women and certain funeral traditions.[44] Though Fulke avoids the trap of defining ministry solely in terms of what occurs in the pulpit, his preaching-centred rhetoric is strained by his expanded definition of 'preaching': 'while we intreat of preaching to be the duty of a pastor, we do not only meane publike preaching, when the congregation is assembled, but also priuate exhortation, reprehension, consolation of every particuler person within his charge'. It is the pastor's duty not only to 'teache al his flocke openly: but also he must instruct every familie priuatelie'.[45] The designs of Elizabethan presbyterians like Fulke on the structure of the English church may have been frustrated at every turn, but as we shall see, their insistence on a preaching-centred parish ministry, however

---

[41] See *DNB*.

[42] See Collinson, *The Elizabethan Puritan Movement*, 108.

[43] William Fulke, *A Brief and plaine declaration* (1584), 35, 45, 15.

[44] Ibid., 58-59, 62-63, 64, 73-75.

[45] Ibid., 51, 52.

broadly defined, was to have a long, if turbulent, future.

As Archbishop Whitgift (1583-1604) successfully enforced the royal stance against presbyterian reform, arguments previously utilized by Protestants against the shortcomings of Roman Catholic ministry were increasingly applied by presbyterian puritans against the Protestant prelacy of the Church of England. A zealous young Dudley Fenner, who had personally tasted the Archbishop's sourness towards what was taken as presbyterian subversiveness during a disastrous audience in January 1584, was one of many impatient ministers who lashed out unhelpfully against what they perceived as episcopal obstruction to further reform.[46]

Others may have had similar misgivings, but were able to express their concerns more tactfully and sidestep the rancor that had previously elicited responses in kind and served only to burn bridges. Laurence Chaderton (1536?-1640), whose long ministry in Cambridge, as first Master of Emmanuel College and as lecturer at St Clements Church, influenced generations of students who would go on to serve as ministers, held unswervingly to the principle of a pulpit-led reformation, even if it seemed an accompanying reformed polity and discipline was not to be. And though he published no treatise or sermon on pastoral ministry, according to Peter Lake, Chaderton understood that

> The minister, through his skill as a scholar, preacher and practical divine, was the mediator between the pages of scripture and the spiritual predicament of his flock; he was the channel through which the word was to be brought to the people. It was through his constant vigilance in that role that the cause of further reformation was to be advanced.[47]

Chaderton's contemporary, Robert Some (1542-1609), Master of Peterhouse in Cambridge and eventually vice-chancellor of the university, reasserted the, by now, traditional complaints but in terms that would not be perceived as overly threatening.[48] Some had a much better fix on the concerns of the authorities than the more zealous presbyterians, and was thus able to address (rather than arouse) those concerns while advancing a godly agenda:

---

[46] Dudley Fenner, *A Defence of the godlie ministers against the slaunders of D. Bridges* (1587), sig B3. See also Collinson's relation of the Archbishop's wrath against Fenner and the rest of his uninvited delegation of Kentish ministers in *The Elizabethan Puritan Movement*, 254.

[47] Peter Lake, *Moderate Puritans and the Elizabethan Church* (Cambridge: Cambridge University Press, 1982), 33; see also 127-28 and 130-31 for further examples of the 'moderate' puritan take on the task of the minister.

[48] Robert Some, *A Godly Treatise containing and deciding certaine questions, moued of late in London and other places, touching the Ministerie, Sacraments and Church* (1588), 6.

Where sounde teachers are placed, these commodities are apparant.
First, Almightie God is notablie serued. Secondly, the prince is
dutifullie obeyed. Thirdly, the enemie to religion is either wonne or
descried. Where the people are not taught, these absurdities doe
followe: First they cannot serue God, for they doe not knowe God...
Secondlie, the prince is not so dutifullie obeyed: the rebellion in the
North is a proofe of that. Lastly, the enemie to religion cannot be
wonne: for faith commeth by hearing.[49]

But Some's capitulation to the authorities' concerns was too much for the
more radical anti-episcopal element within the puritan spectrum. John Penry
(1559-1593), who was later executed for his role in the scurrilous Martin
Marprelate libels, took Some and other moderates to task for what were
considered self-serving inconsistencies.[50] Why were the bishops so resistant to
rooting out ignorant, non-preaching ministers? Did not their lack of zeal call
into question the validity of their own ministry? Penry's contention was that
there is no such thing as a ministry separated from a preaching ministry.
Therefore, 'Euery vnpreaching minister sinneth in executing the works of a
pastoral function, as the sacraments, &c therefore he hath no ministery...
because his calling is not the calling of the [New Testament] ministery.'[51] It
was therefore a sin to receive communion from such a non-minister, or for true
ministers to maintain communion with them. For Penry, who took the
complaint rhetoric to its logical ends, the refusal to rid the church of ignorant
ministers was to participate in perpetuating the soul-killing darkness
enshrouding too many parishes. Anything less than total reformation was a
damnable sell-out.

But total reformation was an idea that understandably did not sit well with the
Queen, and especially those who perhaps had the most to lose, such as John
Whitgift and his fellow bishops. Men of presbyterian or separatist persuasion
were not tolerated, and those who took leadership or published anti-episcopal
polemic found themselves marginalized, dismissed from their livings, exiled,
imprisoned, or even like Penry, executed for treason. The remaining fifteen
years of Elizabeth's reign saw few treatments of the pastor's duty, the
exceptions being John Holme's *The Burthen of the Ministerie* (1592) and
George Phillips's *The Good Sheapeheardes dutie* (1597).[52] Both are relatively

---

[49] Ibid., 7-8.

[50] John Penry, *A defence of that which hath bin written in the questions of the ignorant
ministerie* (1588). Collinson does not consider Penry to have been Martin Marprelate
himself, though he was certainly one of those involved in the conspiracy. See *The
Elizabethan Puritan Movement*, 391-96. For Penry, see *DNB*.

[51] Penry, *A defence*, 36.

[52] George Phillips, *The good Sheapeheardes dutie* (1597), sig C2ᵛ. John Holme, *The
Burthen of the Ministerie. Gathered out of the sixt chapter of the Epistle of S. Paul to*

brief sermons and both titles promise more than their contents deliver. And given the intensity of the discussion in the previous decade, both seem calculated to say as little substantively as possible.

But the near absence of a published literature on pastoral ministry in these years does not imply an absence of concern. A different kind of English Protestant pastoral concern was being forged. Protestant preaching was having its effect, as was the continual call for a learned ministry, as seen in the remarkable increase of university graduates entering the ministry.[53] Having abandoned of necessity the more radical reforming urge that had prompted presbyterians to overplay their hand, a new generation of university-trained pastors was being appointed to increasing numbers of parishes, replacing non-preaching ministries with preaching ones, thereby giving rise to different kinds of pastoral issues. And if later accounts of the lives of those whom biographers like Samuel Clarke considered exemplary are accurate, the preparation of successive generations of godly pastors appears to have occurred more by example and apprenticeship, especially in places like Cambridge or in the households of particular puritan pastors, rather than through published treatises and sermons. It seems that while the presbyterians were burning themselves out, other godly Protestants who shared many of the same concerns found conscience-saving ways to pursue more quietly their calling as pastors within the system instead of becoming reformers of the system.[54] The proliferation of these godly pastors as Elizabeth's long reign approached its end produced a growing need to get beyond the dogmatic debates of church structure and to address anew the practical issues involved in effective pastoral ministry from a

---

the Galathians, the first verse (1592), sig F-Fv. George Phillips matriculated at Trinity College, Cambridge, in 1579. He received the BA in 1583/4 and proceeded to MA in 1587. See *DNB*. John Holme, 'a North Country man', matriculated as a sizar at Christ's College, Cambridge, in 1584. He received the BA in 1587/8 and proceeded to MA in 1591. See Venn.

[53] See Rosemary O'Day, *Education and Society 1500-1800* (London: Longman, 1982), 135-150; R. O'Day, 'The Reformation of the Ministry, 1558-1642', R. O'Day and F. Heal, eds., *Continuity and Change: Personnel and Administration of the Church of England 1500-1642* (Leicester: Leicester University Press, 1976), 56, 63-71.

[54] 'Wherein then lay their puritanism?' asks Patrick Collinson. 'These pastorally-minded puritans cared deeply about the failings of the established Church as they knew them at the parochial level: the lack of preachers, the shortcomings of the poorer clergy and the carelessness of the wealthy and the nonresident, the powerlessness of the pastor with no weapon of discipline in his hand. And although the label "nonconformist" does not begin to describe what was distinctive about these men, nonconformists they were, and they could be stung into defiance by too peremptory a demand to conform. Presbyterians in an active, militant sense most of them were not, but they had little sense of loyalty to their ordinaries or to the Church conceived in an Anglican, hierarchical way; and by contrast a strong sense of belonging to their fellow preachers, gathered in conference.' *Elizabethan Puritan Movement*, 128-129.

godly perspective.

Richard Greenham was one who strove to pursue parish ministry rather than become embroiled in the debates over further reformation. Greenham's ministry generated a tremendous amount of attention, especially among the rising generation of Protestant ministers studying just five miles away in Cambridge.[55] It is striking that Greenham's reputation among the generation of 'godly' ministers that succeeded him derived not from his pulpit prowess but from his pastoral skill. His *Workes* were posthumously published in 1599, and while rich in pastoral insights and advice, they include no treatise where he focuses extended attention on pastors and the nature of their duties.[56] During his lifetime, Greenham published precious little, and contributed nothing to the published discussion on pastoral ministry.[57] However, the posthumously published folio volume of his *Workes* went through four revised editions. The significant amount of new material brought to the editor's attention, often in the form of letters and notes taken down from sermons and discourses, speaks of the esteem in which he was held, especially among his younger colleagues, many of whom had made the five mile hike from Cambridge to Dry Drayton to see first-hand what 'godly' ministry was about.[58] That so many young men resorted to Dry Drayton to hear Greenham preach, observe his ministry and sit around the family table with him discussing the practical issues of parish ministry provides our first hint that the realities of pastoral ministry were not as straight forward as the pulpit prescriptions of the published rhetoric would care to admit.[59]

---

[55] See the discussion of Greenham's 'household seminary' in chapter 9.

[56] See, however, chapter 48 of his *Works*, 'Of the Ministerie', in *The Workes of the Reverend and Faithful Servant of Iesus Christ M. Richard Greenham, Minister and Preacher of the Word of God* (3rd edition, 1601). See also Greenham's 'The Fourth Sermon' expounding Hebrews 13:17 in Greenham, *Workes* (4th edition, 1605), 777-785.

[57] See Greenham's *A godly Exhortatation [sic], and fruitfull admonition to virtuous parents and modest Matrons* (1584), clearly not a reputation-making publishing event. A letter of his to Richard Cox, Bishop of Ely was also published, probably without his permission, in the Nonconformist anthology *A parte of a register* (1593), 86-93. See Eric. J. Carlson's discussion of Greenham's publications in his excellent study of Greenham's ministry and influence in '"Practical Divinity": Richard Greenham's Ministry in Elizabethan England', E.J. Carlson, ed., *Religion and the English People, 1500-1640* (Kirksville, MO: Thomas Jefferson University Press, 1998), 147-193, here 149, note 8.

[58] Carlson, '"Practical Divinity"', 180-81.

[59] Greenham defined pastoral ministry as 'none other thing, but to preach the word of God sincerely, and purely with a care of the glory of God, and a desire of the salvation of our breathern: & secondly a reverent administration of the sacraments, according to the order and institution of our Saviour Jesus Christ'. *Works* (4th edition, 1605), 781-82. However, Parker and Carlson state that 'the lived reality of his ministry was much more complex, since "preaching" subsumed a variety of teaching functions, including catechizing and confirming'. See K.L. Parker and E.J. Carlson, *'Practical Divinity': The*

Called to Preach

In response to the crackdown against presbyterian reform, godly pastors began to limit the scope of their pastoral concern to the horizons of their local parishes and fellow ministers. Nevertheless, they continued to face local opposition as they sought to impose their biblically-informed perspective on life and ministry through the medium of the Protestant pulpit. Their pastoral zeal was often labeled as 'puritane' zeal and understood as presbyterian agitation for structural reform by those whose position in English social and religious hierarchy, from James I on down, made them naturally suspicious of anyone who promoted change in any form.[60] And puritanism became increasingly caricatured as an hyper-scrupulous, hypocritical censoriousness by the majority of people who had no interest in acquiescing to any religious demands upon their lives beyond a tolerable minimum.[61] Writing to justify the centrality of preaching in Protestant ministry, Samuel Hieron recognized the problem of official and popular prejudice against committed Protestants: 'The common saying is, that there are none usually so bad as these Puritanes (for in their ignorance not knowing truly what a Puritane is, and in their malice seeking to disgrace honest men, they terme euery man that makes conscience of hearing the word, for the building of himself *in holy faith*)'. These 'Puritanes' were therefore unjustly tarred as 'nothing but a pack of hypocrites, men that are not to be trusted for al their faire shewes, holy horses, and the like names of disgrace, which hell can inuent'. Most troubling for Hieron was that 'out of this puddle of reproachfull speeches against the louers of preaching, they gather up filth to cast in the face of preaching itself.'[62]

The son of the vicar of Epping in Essex, educated at Eton and King's College, Cambridge, Hieron (1576?-1617) had taken orders only four years before when he wrote in 1604 *The Preachers Plea...making known the worth and necessary vse of Preaching.*[63] Presented to the living of Modbury in Devon, his preaching ability made him immediately popular, but his own strict conformity to the Church of England made him useful to the Bishops. He was given numerous opportunities to preach at gatherings of clergy, several of his sermons to fellow

---

Works and Life of Revd. Richard Greenham (Aldershot: Ashgate, 1998), 59-116, here 59; see also J.H. Primus, *Richard Greenham: Portrait of an Elizabethan Pastor* (Macon, GA: Mercer University Press, 1998) for another perspective on Greenham.

[60] James VI, *BASILIKON DWRWN. Or His Maiesties Instrvctions to His Dearest Sonne, Henry the Prince.* (Edinburgh, 1603) sigs B3-b3; pp. 38-44.

[61] See, for example, Giles Widdowes (Rector of St Martins Church, Oxford), *The Schysmatical Puritan* (1630); see also John Taylor (poet), *A Swarme of Sectaries, and Schismatiques* (1641).

[62] Samuel Hieron, *The Preachers Plea: Or A Treatise in forme of a plain Dialogue, making known the worth and necessary vse of Preaching* (1604), 64.

[63] See *DNB*.

pastors being published posthumously.[64] It is a measure of Hieron's confidence in the efficacy of godly preaching that he collapses the sum of Protestant pastoral ministry into 'two things principally required in a Minister: the one, that he be able to exhort with wholesome doctrine: the other, that he have skill to improue them that say against it.' But Hieron has biblical reasons for doing this. Answering the question why God requires every minister to be able to preach, Hieron declares that, based on Romans 10:14-15, 'the hearing of a Preacher which is sent, is the ordinary means ordained of God to beget faith. From thence ariseth another point: that the whole ministery must be the meanes and instrument to beget faith, must be a man sent [to preach]'.[65] It is the same argument used by the presbyterians of the previous generation, yet stripped of its subversive edge. Hieron applies parochially what had previously been applied nationally, and finds a more receptive audience. Though the popular stigma against 'Puritanes' remained, the survival of puritan pastoral emphases through the debacle of the presbyterian failure and official disfavour occurred as a result of calculated decisions like Hieron's not to pursue the implications of his rhetoric too far beyond the bounds of the local parish, at least in print.

Experience as a pastor would later temper Hieron's diagnosis and treatment from the stark black-and-white problems and solutions of *The Preachers Plea* to the later more qualified sermons to fellow clergy.[66] Clerical incompetence and apathy over matters of eternal life and death, however, continued to stagger Hieron as unconscionable: In the hands of an incompetent '*Miller* we loose but our meale, of the *Farrier* but our horse, of the *Taylour* but our garment, of the *Lawyer* but our money, of the *Physitian* but our bodyes: but in the hands of an vnfaithfull minister a man looseth his soule and his everlasting portion in heaven.' But if the bane of God's church was an idle, distracted and greedy ministry, Hieron was convinced that God's blessing would be poured out on local parishes and on the church as a whole if pastors would busy themselves with the biblical mandate for their calling. From his matured perspective, the essence of that calling was threefold: preaching the word, administering the sacraments and what Hieron refers to as '*private inspection,* by reprooueing Sinners by admonishing, exhorting, by comforting the afflicted & those which are cast downe, & all to this end, that the elect whome sinne hath loosened, & disjoynted from *Christ* their head, may be restored to their place again'.[67]

---

[64] See Hieron's *The Spirituall Fishing. A Sermon Preached in Cambridge* (1618), and *Aarons Bells A-sounding. In a sermon, tending chiefly to admonish the ministerie, of their charge, & duty* (1623).

[65] Hieron, *The Preachers Plea*, 139, 126-127. For a variant reading, see Samuel Hieron, *All Sermons of Samuel Hieron* (1614), 510.

[66] See, for example, Hieron, *Aarons Bells A-sounding* (1623), 12.

[67] Hieron, *Aarons Bells A-sounding*, 4, 8. See also Bryan Crockett's exploration on the discussion by Hieron and others on the difficulties of reproducing a preached sermon's impact in print in his 'The Act of Preaching and the Art of Prophesying', in *SR*, 105 (1997), 48-49.

This shift in strategy away from national ecclesiastical reformation to ministerial and parish reformation was already taking place prior to Elizabeth's death and is seen in the posthumous publication of William Perkins's *Of the Calling of the Ministerie: two Treatises, describing the Duties and Dignities of that Calling* in 1605. Perkins (1558-1602), was a fellow at Christ's College, Cambridge, until 1595, when he moved across the street to become lecturer at St Andrew the Great until his death seven years later. Perkins's preaching and pastoral skills exercised considerable influence on the rising generation of young men preparing for parish ministry.[68] Though Perkins may have been sympathetic to the presbyterian cause, he publicly skirted the issue and declared the primary need for reformation was in the lives of the pastors themselves.[69] For if any minister desires any 'fruite' from his labour, 'let them first sanctifie themselues, & clense their heartes by repentance, afore they presume, to stand vp to rebuke sinne in others, else let them not thinke, that their golden words shall doe so much good, as their leaden liues shall doe hurt.'

If hypocrisy deforms the pastoral fruit, worldly distractions also compromise ministers and keep them from ever achieving the goal of Biblical ministry: 'to saue soules'. Perkins acknowledges that such a goal may not be popular in a given parish, where the people may have certain other expectations of what their pastor should be and do. But a pastor should not imagine that by fulfilling popular expectations he has then had an effective ministry, especially if it has meant neglecting preaching:

> They therefore are greatly deceiued, who thinke a Minister to discharge sufficiently his duitie, though hee preach not, if hee keepe good Hospitalitie, and make peace amongst his Neighbors, and performe other workes of charitie and good life: for if a Minister... preach not...he hath no conscience, nor can haue any comfort, for that is the principall dutie of a Minister (though all the other bee required to make him compleate): the wante of them may condemne him before men, but it is the pollution of his lippes, which presently checkes him before God.[70]

Perkins gives here a rare glimpse into the other aspects of a pastor's ministry

---

[68] See, for example, Samuel Clarke's record of Richard Blackerby's conversion and subsequent call to pastoral ministry under Perkins's influence, in *The Lives of Sundry Eminent Persons in this Later Age* (1683), 58. For further biographical detail on Perkins, see Ian Breward, 'Introduction', *The Work of William Perkins* (Abingdon (Berks): Sutton Courtenay Press, 1970) and J.I. Packer's lecture, *An Anglican to Remember, William Perkins: Puritan Popularizer* (London: St Antholin's Lectureship Charity, 1996).

[69] William Perkins, *Of the Calling of the Ministerie* (1605), 51.

[70] Ibid., 56, 8, 24.

and the other roles that he played in the lives of his parishioners.[71] He also gives the reason for his almost exclusive focus on preaching in a work that is advertised as describing the pastoral ministry. For Perkins, tension exists in pastor and parish because pastoral ministry is an uneasy combination of call from above and expectations from below. Perkins was clearly aware of the different communal and priestly roles pastors were expected to play, especially in the religious marking of the various rites of passage of the members of the community.[72] But puritans like Perkins and Hieron wrestled with what they considered to be a divine imperative about a pastor's ministry that superseded social, political and local realities and expectations. Recognition of that imperative shifted the pastor's primary duty from being a priestly intermediary between God and humanity to that of a herald and a guide, announcing God's agenda and leading people towards the promised land of salvation. Tension between these two roles both in the minister and in the parish member creates much of the spiritual discord which then gets translated into the wider ecclesiastical conflicts that dominated local and national affairs throughout the sixteenth and seventeenth centuries. While recognizing the tension, Perkins insists on the precedence of preaching over all other duties, not because he and his fellow puritans were keen on excluding or ignoring other aspects of ministry, but to insure that the one means that God had provided his church to ignite faith would be rightly applied.[73] Parish ministry was, after all, not the

---

[71] Aside from the expected pastoral duties, some ministers also served their communities 'by exercising justice in the commonwealth and the practicing of Physick and Chirugerie'. See John Favour, *Antiquities triumphing over Novelties* (1619), epistle. Also Collinson, 'Shepherds', 190.

[72] Collinson states that 'These occasions, invested as they were with the inevitability of life and death and the capacity to make and break, resolve and dissolve the bonds of human society, brought the parish clergy into the most meaningful and certainly the most earthbound of their involvements with their flocks. These offices, as well as the sacramental office of ministering communion, interlocked with what John Bossy has identified as the primary social task entrusted to the parish priest or his equivalent throughout the rural parishes of Europe between the fourteenth and seventeenth centuries, that of a settler of conflicts, the principal instrument of what Bossy has elsewhere called the social miracle.' Collinson, 'Shepherds', 190. See also John Bossy, *Christianity in the West 1400-1700* (Oxford: Oxford University Press, 1985), chapter 4.

[73] See Bremer, *Shaping New Englands: Puritan Clergymen in Seventeenth-Century England and New England* (London: Prentice Hall International, 1995), 25-28. When seeking to make a different point about the interplay between preaching, faith, and other aspects of the minister's duty, other puritans were quite willing to allow the usefulness of other pastoral means besides preaching as an aid to faith. Richard Greenham, for example, counsels fellow pastors that 'The meanes to increase our faith, is the word preached, praier, the Sacraments, and the discipline of the church. The word crucifieth thee anew in thine heart. Prayer giueth thee a feeling of faith. The Sacraments confirm both thy faith, and feeling; and discipline continueth vu in obedience both of the word and prayer, and the sacraments, and consequently is a meanes to continue in vs all these

parish's idea, but God's.

In 1607, Richard Bernard (1568-1641) published what amounted to a 355 page encyclopædia of puritan pastoral practise, *The Faithful Shepheard*. Though Collinson compares Bernard's treatise unfavorably with medieval Catholic manuals such as *Oculus Sacerdotis*, *Pupilla Oculi*, the *Memoriale Presbiterorum*, and Myrc's *Instructions*, because of his lack of a comprehensive treatment of all the various duties a minister might be expected to perform, Bernard's concern, like each Protestant author already considered, was to make sure that Protestant pastors were clear on the fundamental task to which God had called them.[74] But within the bounds of that concern, however restrictive it might appear from a modern (or sacramentalist) perspective, Bernard provides a practical compendium of advice for those who wanted to shepherd their flock in the puritan way, in effect a casuistry of a godly preaching ministry. Educated in Perkins's shadow at Christ's College, Cambridge, Bernard was himself the pastor of Worksop, Nottinghamshire, from 1601 until 1613, when he became the minister in Batcombe in Somersetshire, where he served until his death.[75]

Not surprisingly, the foundational task facing Bernard's faithful shepherd is that of preaching.[76] Other aspects of his ministry would be empty of spiritual value unless they were built upon the cornerstone of a regular ministry of the word. Bernard is well aware that his particular emphasis upon preaching would appear foolish to those outside godly circles, but he argues that his emphasis is Pauline, and that God himself has chosen what 'carnall judgement' views as a foolish message (the cross) brought by foolish means (preaching) to effect his plan of salvation.[77] But foolish as it may appear, it is the one and only means God appoints to elicit saving faith from his people.[78]

But having established the pre-eminence of preaching, Bernard makes a remarkable qualification: 'Experience shewes how that little profit comes by preaching when Catechising is neglected. Many there are who teach twise or three times in a weeke: and yet see lesse fruit of many yeeres labour by not Catechising, than some reape in one yeere, who performe both together.'[79]

---

comfort which by the other means are found in Christ.' *The Workes,* third edition (1601), chapter 48 (Of the Ministerie), §15, 396.

[74] Collinson, 'Shepherds', 193-194, 196.

[75] Bernard received the BA in 1594/5, and the MA in 1598. See *DNB*. Though he was active early in his career in separatist circles, he later broke with them and pursued his pastorally puritan goals within the Church of England. See also William Haller, *The Rise of Puritanism; or The Way to the New Jerusalem as set forth in pulpit and press from Thomas Cartwright to John Lilburne and John Milton, 1570-1643* (New York: Columbia University Press, 1938), 137-139.

[76] Richard Bernard, *The Faithful Shepheard* (1607), sig A3.

[77] Bernard takes his imagery from 1 Corinthians 1:18-31. Bernard, *The Faithful Shepheard*, 1.

[78] Ibid., 2.

[79] Ibid., 9. Bernard makes a similar point in a later published sermon addressing

Though hitherto the published literature has seemed to indicate a one-dimensional focus on preaching, Bernard implies that puritan pastoral practise has been somewhat more pragmatic in its local strategy all along. Indeed beginning with Bernard, the hegemony of preaching in puritan pastoral works is increasingly modified by an emphasis on the complementary roles of preacher and catechist.[80] Bernard deals similarly with other pastoral responsibilities such as public prayers ('Halfe houre Praiers are too tedious'), how to read the Scriptures, how to choose sermon text, begin a sermon, make appropriate application, as well as what gestures to avoid whilst preaching ('smiting on the Pulpit, ...stamping downe very unaduisedley,... spitting, rubbing the brows,... nodding of the head,... fidling with the fingers upon the breast, buttons, stroaking of the beard and such like toies.').[81] Bernard's goal in giving all this practical instruction is the formation of an exemplary ambassador whose charge it is to represent the agenda of the king. Such an ambassador must be worthy of his embassage, as well as equipped to discharge his duty.

Ian Green has confirmed what appears to be a massive attempt on the part of English Protestants to supplement their preaching with catechizing. Surveying some 680 catechisms in *The Christian's ABC: Catechisms and Catechizing in England c. 1530-1740* (1996), Green finds the most popular Elizabethan and early Stuart catechists concerned not so much with imprinting controversial doctrinal distinctives on impressionable minds as with insuring that catechumens were presented with the fundamentals of the evangelical gospel.[82] Moreover the sheer numbers of catechisms produced and the range of audiences envisioned by them (from children and servants to adults) indicates that though catechizing lacked 'the rhetorical and polemical glamour of the sermon' and though 'as a tool for changing beliefs it has been considered [by modern historians] too mechanical to be effectual', parish ministers found them an indispensable help in accomplishing their pastoral goals.[83] The proliferation of catechizing thus provides a second hint that actual Protestant pastoral practise went far beyond the impression given by the rhetoric of their pastoral manuals.

Despite the efforts of authors like Richard Bernard, however, many pastors continued to be discouraged at what appeared to be a lack of progress in their attempts to promote the spiritual reformation of the parish church. William Harrison voiced his frustration in a sermon published in 1614: '*Again wee*

---

catechism: *Two Twinnes: or Two part of one portion of Scripture. I. Is of Catechising. II. O the Ministers maintenance* (1613), 1-10.

[80] Bernard, *The Faithful Shepheard*, 9-10.

[81] Ibid., 14-19, 72-73, 89.

[82] Ian Green, *The Christian's ABC: Catechisms and Catechizing in England c. 1530-1740* (Oxford: Clarendon, 1996), 31-36.

[83] Felicity Heal, '[Review of] *The Christian's ABC: Catechisms and Catechizing in England c. 1530-1740.* By Ian Green', in *JMH*, 71:1 (1999), 185.

cannot but acknowledge that the Lord hath sent many skilfull and painefull Husbandmen to sowe his fielde with us: who according to their office and dutie, sow it in due season, after a good maner, and with the best seede. And yet it yeeldeth litle fruite. People heare much, learn litle, and practise lesse.'[84] Rather than question the received puritan pastoral tradition, Harrison instead chooses to find fault with the congregations who regularly sit under godly preaching. The apparent barrenness *'cannot be imputed to the want of good preaching, but rather to the want of good hearing: the fault is rather in the ground, then in the sower, or in the seede. The seede is good, and great store is sowne, but the ground is barren.'* Or, more to the point, *'the doctrine is sound, and the maner of teaching profitable, but the people heare amisse, and so for want of good-hearing loose the fruite of many good sermons'.*[85]

In contrast, when given the opportunity to address the gathered clergy of Bath and Wells at the triennial episcopal visitation in July of 1612, Samuel Crooke uses deferential boldness to raise more familiar puritan pastoral complaints with his 'Reverend Fathers, and Brethren, Fellow-labourers in the worke of the Gospell', placing fault for the failings of the ministry squarely in their laps.[86] Crooke (1575-1649) came to the pulpit in Bath with impeccable puritan credentials. A student at Pembroke Hall, Cambridge, he was elected fellow, but his election was then refused by the Master. Crooke then became one of the first fellows at Emmanuel College. After preaching in and around Cambridge in 1601, he was presented to the rectory at Wrington, Somerset. At Wrington, 'where the people had never before...a preaching minister, he was the first that by preaching...brought religion into notice and credit.'[87] After a long ministry, Crooke would be chosen in 1642 to represent Somerset at the Westminster Assembly.

Crooke likens the pastor's work to that of a gardener and spends many pages developing a horticultural metaphor. But like Richard Bernard, Crooke gives a backhanded acknowledgment that the puritan emphasis on a preaching ministry has met with increasing success, admonishing his colleagues that their ministry consists in more than just preaching: 'Oh then, God forbid the *minister* should thinke all his worke done, when hee hath ended his exhortation!... Neither let the *hearer* imagine, that when the sound is out of his eare, hee hath *done* with

---

[84] William Harrison, *The Difference of Hearers. Or, an exposition of the Parable of the Sower* (1614), sigs A4v-A5. Of William Harrison, little is known. William Hunt makes the following observation in passing: 'William Harrison, a serious Protestant but hardly a puritan in any useful sense of the word...' in *The Puritan Moment: The Coming of Revolution in an English County* [Essex] (Cambridge, MA: Harvard University Press, 1983), 95.

[85] Harrison, *The Difference of Hearers*, sig A5.

[86] Samuel Crooke, *Three Sermons, viz. The Waking Sleeper, The Ministeriall Husbandrie, The Discourse of the Heart* (1615), here *The Ministeriall Husbandry and Building*, sig A2.

[87] *DNB*, V, 205-206.

God, or God with him.'[88] But with his scope limited by the parameters of a sermon, Crooke does not go into the same practical detail as Bernard, choosing instead the broad brush of critique over and against ideal.

Another visitation sermon, Jerome Phillips's *The Fisher-man*, was published in 1623. 'Preached at a Synode held at Southwell in Nottinghamshire', Phillips's sermon gives an indication of how effective complaints against non-preaching ministers had been: 'Many to auoide the imputation of dumbe dogs in the Church, breake silence, and become Preachers, sometimes (through ignorance) of vnsound doctrine, many times of vnsauory, that worketh nothing either to the information of the iudgement, or to the reformation of the affections of the hearer'.[89] According to Phillips, it was these unlearned, unskilled pretenders that were giving genuinely 'painful' pastors a bad reputation. Phillips simply assumes that an effective parish ministry is a preaching ministry. Only by preaching is the Law of God effectively applied, and only by preaching can God's grace through Christ be made known. 'A skillful Pastor must sometimes be a *Boanerges*, that is, the sonne of thunder, to thunder out the curses of the Law against obstinate sinners. Again he must sometimes be a *Barnabas*, that is, the sonne of consolation to comfort with the sweet promises of the Gospell those that feele the weight and burden of their sinnes.'[90] That such a message would be preached in a context of episcopal oversight demonstrates how mainstream so-called puritan perspectives on pastoral ministry at least had become.[91]

Robert Mandevill's posthumously published *Timothies Taske* (1619) was, in most respects, a conventional restatement of previous pastoral emphases. Ministers should live lives that demonstrate the truth of the gospel, and they should give themselves to the task of communicating the gospel through every means at hand. Mandevill also continues to defend the primacy and necessity of preaching. Above all, he is convinced of the exalted calling of pastors in God's church. However despised by fallen humanity, the pastor was both prophet and priest to the Lord's people, commissioned with God's message of judgement and salvation.[92]

Mandevill's appropriation of the language of Old Testament priesthood to describe the pastor's mediatorial role as God's messenger was an ironic foreshadowing of a new crisis already in the making at the hands of a growing number of sacramentalist clergymen who were increasingly influential at

---

[88] Crooke, *Three Sermons*, 86.

[89] Jerome Phillips, *The Fisher-man. A Sermon Preached at a Synode held at Southwell in Nottinghamshire* (1623), 13.

[90] Ibid., 13-14, 16.

[91] See Kenneth Fincham, *Prelate as Pastor: The Episcopate of James I* (Oxford: Clarendon, 1990), 112-146, 250-276.

[92] Mandevill, *Timothies Taske: A Christian Seacard* (Oxford, 1619), 28, 32, 37.

court.[93] Despite puritan protestations to the contrary, at the time of Mandevill's premature death in 1618, efforts to promote local reform through the provision of a learned preaching ministry were increasingly, if unevenly, successful. Preaching and catechising were having a profound effect in parishes where a pulpit-centred ministry was able to take root. Even so, such pastors were never more than a minority among their colleagues, and as a rival reinterpretation of Protestant pastoral duty gained influential supporters among the bishops and at court, such pastors once again found themselves with more than scandalous and non-preaching colleagues to worry about. Within ten years, the relatively benign ecclesiastical oversight and Calvinist consensus under James which had provided the context for the extraordinary flowering of puritan pastoral skill and influence would be undone.[94] In its place would arise a Protestant sacramentalist understanding of the minister's duties that stressed conformity and order in worship, while de-emphasizing preaching and Calvinist doctrine.[95] Mandevill would have viewed the change in emphasis as an abdication of the pastor's high call, in exchange for a slippery slope that would lead back to the seat of Antichrist himself, the Church of Rome.[96] It was a recipe for conflict, a conflict that is reflected in the subsequent literature on the duties of the godly pastor.

---

[93] Richard Hooker (1554-1600) and Bishops Lancelot Andrewes (1555-1626), Richard Neile (1562-1640) and William Laud (1573-1645) led a reappraisal of the Church of England's polity, theology and pastoral practise, with their views gaining the authority of enforcement with the accession of Charles I in 1626 and the death of Archbishop George Abbot (1562-1633) and the translation of William Laud in 1633 as his replacement. Though the debates as to the nature of what became known as Laudianism are beyond the scope of this paper, the core reforms/innovations sought by Neile and Laud include 1) an accommodation of the theological views of Jacobus Arminius (1559-1609), who sought to temper what he perceived as the rigidity of Calvinist predestinarianism; 2) a renewed emphasis of the efficacy of the sacraments in the process of salvation; 3) a renewed emphasis upon liturgy and ceremony in church services, and a corresponding de-emphasis upon the role of preaching; and 4) a re-establishment of royal and ecclesiastical authority using arguments of divine right. See Nicolas Tyacke, *Anti-Calvinists: The Rise of English Arminianism c. 1590-1640* (Oxford: Clarendon, 1987).

[94] This generalization, however, has been questioned. See, for example, Kenneth Fincham & Peter Lake's 'The Ecclesiastical Policies of James I and Charles I', Kenneth Fincham's 'Episcopal Government, 1603-1640' and Peter Lake's 'The Laudian Style', all in *The Early Stuart Church, 1603-1642*, K. Fincham, ed. (Basingstoke: MacMillan, 1993).

[95] See, for example, John Fielding, 'Arminians in the Localities: Peterborough Diocese, 1603-1642', K. Fincham, ed., *The Early Stuart Church, 1603-1642* (Basingstoke: MacMillan, 1993), 94-95.

[96] The final half of Mandevill's treatise/sermon is devoted to a diatribe against the Roman Catholic understanding of pastoral ministry. See *Timothies Taske*, 38ff.

Against the Tide

On the 3rd of December 1626, nearly twenty months after Charles I succeeded to the throne, John Cosin preached 'A Sermon at the Consecration of Dr. Francis White, Bishop of Carlisle'.[97] Cosin (1594-1672), who would become bishop of Durham after the Restoration, had long been associated with Bishop Richard Neile's Durham House circle in London. Having studied at Caius College, Cambridge, taken orders and become prebendary of Durham in 1625 under Neile's patronage, Cosin chose the opportunity afforded him as preacher for the consecration of one of Charles's first new bishops to make a very different and public point about how ministry in the Church of England should be conceived. 'I would not be mistaken, I come not here to preach down preaching. But this I wonder at, that preaching now-a-days should be counted our only office, as if we had nothing else to do, and an office independent too, as if we were all bishops when we preach.'[98] Cosin acknowledges that 'Christ was sent to Preach the Gospel to the poor; and of the same errand are His Apostles and bishops sent'. But for Cosin, preaching is an *episcopal* office: 'The priests' office not so large, who preach too, but yet under the bishop's license only; they then to be the great pastors of the diocese, and we but as servants and substitutes under them, to preach by their commission and not by our own.' Reverting to a terminology of priesthood that made puritans queasy, Cosin also called for a reversion to priestly function as the primary role of the parish minister: 'For by virtue of our orders we are only put to offer up the prayers and sacrifices of the Church, to administer the Sacraments, to bind and to loose, and not to preach unless we be thereunto appointed'.[99] Cosin's rationale is that bishops are the true pastors and that the responsibility for preaching lies with them. Moreover, if priests were busy fulfilling the duties given them by the bishop, they would have little time for preaching, unless specifically asked to do so by the Bishop. Citing the example of Chrysostom

---

[97] Francis White (c.1564-1638) was educated in Cambridge and ordained in 1588. He published several anti-Catholic treatises and was employed by James I in several disputes with the Jesuit John Fisher. He was made dean of Carlisle in 1622, and after being made bishop of Carlisle in 1626, he was translated first to Norwich (1629) and then to Ely (1631). A friend of Laud, his later publications were devoted to disputing puritan views of the Sabbath.

[98] John Cosin, 'A Sermon at the Consecration of Dr. Francis White, Bishop of Carlisle', in *The Works of the Right Reverend Father in God, John Cosin, Lord Bishop of Durham*, I (1843), 96.

[99] Puritans had been so successful with their pulpit-centred rhetoric that earlier critics such as Richard Hooker reacted against what appeared to be a single-minded focus on preaching to the exclusion of worship. See Richard Hooker, *On the Laws of Ecclesiastical Polity*, V, J. Booty, ed. (London: Belknap Press, 1982), chapters lvii, lx. See also Peter Lake's discussion of Hooker's position in *Anglicans and Puritans? Presbyterianism and English Conformist Thought from Whitgift to Hooker* (London: Unwin and Allen, 1988), 162-63, 176-77.

and other early church fathers, Cosin observes that 'they thought priests had a deal to do besides [preaching], to say their hours, to sing their service, to visit the sick, to reconcile penitents, and not to preach so much, though they neglected not this neither, but then it was when the bishop set them awork when he was otherwise employed, and could not so often attend it, for there must be preaching however.'[100] One needs only to compare Simon Harward's scathing caricature of Roman Catholic ministry from 1582 with Cosin's intentional subversion of the 'godly' pastoral ideal to imagine the acute horror felt by England's evangelical Protestants in the face of this nascent reversion to sacramentalist priorities. Even so, Cosin's choice of the pulpit as the medium through which his countervision of pastoral ministry is broadcast is itself a tacit recognition of the significance attained by preaching through nearly seventy years of sustained Protestant emphasis. The power of the pulpit itself was not in dispute; ironically it was magnified by this attempt to redefine ministry and assert episcopal control over the pulpit.

Astute observers recognized early on the dangers posed by this revival of 'prelacy'. David Calderwood (1575-1650) had long been an opponent of James's attempts to impose episcopacy in Scotland. Educated at the College of Edinburgh and ordained in 1604 as minister of Crailing in Roxburghshire, Calderwood set out his concerns over the new direction in the 1628 treatise, *The Pastor and the Prelate, or reformation and conformitie shortly compared.* For Calderwood, the contraposition and its implications could not be clearer: 'The Pastor thinketh it the principal part of his ministry to labour in the word and doctrine, because woe is unto him if he preach not the gospel.... The Prelate thinketh of preaching as accessory, and would have it worn out of use by a long dead liturgy.'[101] The order envisioned by Cosin would, for Calderwood, hamstring effective pastoral ministry by substituting lesser ends for the overriding evangelical goals of what he considered to be biblical ministry.[102]

But if Calderwood's polemic polarized the pastoral issues at stake, in other contexts, the distinctions between puritan and Laudian pastoral emphases could be uncomfortably blurred. Barnaby Potter (1577-1642) was one of the few Calvinists to be appointed by Charles to the episcopal bench between 1625 and 1641.[103] Preaching the sermon at his consecration (and displaying no little theological dexterity) was his nephew, Christopher Potter (1591-1646), who having abandoned earlier puritan leanings, had more recently attached himself to the rising star of William Laud, succeeded his uncle as provost of Queen's

---

[100] Cosin, 'A Sermon', 95-96.

[101] David Calderwood, *The Pastor and the Prelate* (Edinburgh, 1843 repr of 1628 edition), 4. For David Calderwood, see *DNB*.

[102] Calderwood, *The Pastor and the Prelate*, 26.

[103] See Fincham and Lake, 'The Ecclesiastical Policies of James I and Charles I', in *The Early Stuart Church, 1603-1642* (Basingstoke: MacMillan, 1993), 37.

College, Oxford, and become chaplain in ordinary to Charles I.[104] Having spent 49 pages discussing the first half of his text (from John 21:17), 'And Jesus said unto him', from which he expounds the authority of Peter's commission, Potter turns his attention to the commission itself: 'Feed my sheep.'[105] Potter displays awareness of evangelical concerns over preaching, but he transposes to the office of bishop those attributes of spiritual oversight that any 'puritan' commentator would have applied to parish ministry: 'What are the duties of a good and wise Pastor[?]... One word in my Text implies all, *Feed*.' Indeed, says Potter, in a restatement of the quintessential Protestant pastoral concern, 'The prime care and vertue of a good Bishop is faithfully and fruitfully to dispense the word of Life, the doctrine of salvation to his people, and to live himselfe the life which he commends.' While Potter is convinced that episcopal authority must be reasserted for the health of the church, he remains suspicious that corresponding episcopal grandeur has tempted bishops to absent themselves from their primary pastoral duty: 'By *wholsome doctrine*... I mean the plaine preaching of that *truth* which is *according to godlinesse*... this [that is, preaching] is the ground, all other discourses (though profitable) are but the descants.'[106] Although he pointedly appropriates puritan pastoral rhetoric and applies it to his episcopal audience,[107] Potter's sermon defies easy caricature. But this attempt to implement godly concerns within the nascent Laudian order was probably satisfying to no one, except perhaps his uncle.

With the top-down imposition of a Laudian agenda gathering momentum, climaxing with Laud's elevation to Canterbury in 1633, published treatments of 'godly' pastoral duties all but disappear. A few bold pastors managed to address the issue of ministry, but they did so usually in the context of sermons whose main thrust was not aimed at pastors or the ministry. In his sermon series *The True Convert* (1632), for example, Nehemiah Rogers, the pastor of Messing in Essex, addresses pastors during the course of his exposition of the parable of the good shepherd.[108] In an observation about Christ's own ministry obviously not conceived in a vacuum, Rogers declares that '*Christ was no dumbe Priest....* Yea it was his custome euery Sabboth to goe into the Synagogue and preach, as witnesseth Saint *Luke* 4.16. So then, though hee was dumbe as a *Sheepe* before the *Shearer*, yet neuer dumbe as a *Shepheard* amongst his *Sheepe*.'[109] But Rogers's most striking description of pastoral

---

[104] In his early years, Potter had been a protégé of the puritan provost and opponent of Laud, Henry Airay. Potter also held a lecture at Abington, 'where he was much resorted to for his edifying way of preaching.' See *DNB*, XVI, 212-214.

[105] Christopher Potter, *A Sermon preached at the Consecration of the Right Reverend Father in God Barnaby Potter D.D. and L. Bishop of Carlisle* (1629), 1-49.

[106] Potter, *A Sermon*, 52, 55-56, 56-58.

[107] Ibid., 75-76.

[108] Nehemiah Rogers, *The True Convert: or an exposition upon three Parables. The lost sheep. The lost groat. The lost sonne.* (1632), 119-142.

[109] Ibid., 124.

ministry is autobiographical. Taking a moment to address his own parish in the prefatory 'Letter to the Reader', Rogers reveals his primary motivation for publishing these sermons, and uncovers something of his pastoral methodology as well: 'I desire to feede you, both by the Eye and Eare; by one, or both, I would get into your hearts.' Resorting to metaphor, Rogers explains his strategy: 'You are nailes of the Sanctuary, it is not one blow that fastens you: your need calls for the same hand againe; the same heart; the same hammer: I have trauelled in birth againe and againe, that Christ may be formed, and confirmed in you...(now eleuen years and vpwards) wherein you haue not beene blest with the former and latter raine; Preaching, Catechising'. Moreover, he has faithfully led them to celebrate the Lord's Supper, 'joyntly renewing our Couenant with God, and (in him) with another, ouer the bleeding wounds of our Crucified Sauiour.' Over all is his passion for their conversion: 'Many a night and day haue I wrastled with God (as *Iacob* in *Bethel*) by Prayer to gaine a blessing for you; and in you, and your saluation to my owne soule; with what... fruits many eyes who behold your order, both in the Celebration of Gods worship, as likewise in Conuersation and holy life, can witnesse'. Though probably not untroubled, the bond between such a pastor and his parish is strong: 'you are as deare to mee as a Flock can be vnto a Shepherd; my labours; my life; my refusall of better and greater meanes (if greater meanes be better) for your sakes, I trust will say much.'[110]

Though Roger's stylized description of his ministry cannot be forced to bear too much interpretive weight, he does provide valuable insight into both the dynamics of the bond between pastor and parish as well as an overview of the threefold emphases of his ministry—preaching, catechizing and sacraments. Unconcerned to be prescriptive about what pastoral ministry *ought* to be, Rogers gives us a glimpse as to the major elements of his ministry as actually practiced.

Much more common, however, are those published sermons which use the worst of puritan excesses to discredit all who do not comfortably fit in the new order. The tendency of some pastors to use preaching as an opportunity to rail against sin was a frequent target of conformist criticism. George Wall, in a sermon preached before Archbishop Laud himself during the 1635 metropolitical visitation in Worcester, digresses from expounding the 'dignity of the Ministerial office' to complain about 'those hot-spirited and indiscreet Teachers, who speake stones, and have words as sharpe as arrows... who are no sooner clasped in their Pulpits, but as if they were on Mount *Sinai* giving the law, breath nothing but Thunder and Lightning, Hell and Damnation to their afflicted Brethren.'[111] Such preachers actually hinder the work of the gospel, for 'Little doe such rigid Orators consider, how that ten *Barnabasses* (sons of

---

[110] Ibid., 'To the Reader', unp.

[111] George Wall, *A Sermon at the Lord Archbishop of Canterbury his Visitation Metropolitical, held at All-Saints in Worcester* (1635), 12.

Consolation) cannot often put to silence the voice of despaire; which one *Boanerges* (sonne of Thunder) hath Coniured up.'[112]

In 1632, three years after becoming the rector of Bemerton, near Salisbury, George Herbert (1593-1633) produced an explication of thirty seven characteristics of a pastor and his ministry. Unpublished for nearly two decades following his early death, Herbert's *A Priest to the Temple, or The Country Parson* (1652) expands upon each of these characteristics through the lenses of English Protestant pastoral tradition and of his own experience. Herbert's treatment of pastoral ministry is altogether different from the literature surveyed thus far, although Christopher Hodgkin's claim that *The Country Parson* is 'the first attempt by a Protestant English churchman of any party at a practical, and especially a thorough, pastoral manual' must be qualified in light of the evidence reviewed in this chapter.[113] Even so, the difference between Herbert's *Parson* and the previous works published for pastors is significant. Part of the difference is explained by his deliberate decision not to involve himself in the ecclesiastical controversies gripping the wider church under Charles. Unlike the other sermons and treatises we have viewed, Herbert is not attempting to persuade or exhort or score polemical points. Herbert is not intending to address anyone else but himself. Thus while *A Priest to the Temple* certainly reflects aspects of the contemporary genres of character studies or conduct books,[114] Herbert intends his work as a private meditation to aid him in his pastoral duties, 'Being desirous...to please Him... I have resolved to set down the Form and Character of a True Pastor, that I may have a Mark to aim at: which also I will set as high as I can, since he shoots higher that threatens the Moon, than he that aims at a Tree.'[115]

As one would expect, Herbert covers staple aspects of Protestant and puritan concern, with chapters on preaching, catechising, the sacraments, diligence

---

[112] Ibid., 12. Michael Wigmore issues a similar critique in his visitation sermon, *The Meteors. A Sermon preached at a visitation by Michael Wigmore, Rector of Thorseway in Lincolnshire, and sometimes Fellow of Oriel college in Oxford.* (1633), 10-11.

[113] Christopher Hodgkins, *Authority, Church, and Society in George Herbert: Return to the Middle Way* (1993), 105.

[114] *Contra* Collinson, see 'Shepherds', 197. See also John N. Wall, 'Introduction', J.N. Wall, ed., *George Herbert: The Country Parson, The Temple* (New York: Paulist Press, 1981), 25-35.

[115] George Herbert, *A Priest to the Temple* (1652), sigs A3-A3^v. However, when Barnabas Oley republished *A Priest to the Temple* in 1671, he clearly had in mind Herbert as an example and guide for young ministers: And there will not be so much need to beseech them, to buy Fathers, Councils, and other good classic books; to mortify the flesh, with study, fasting, and prayer, and to do every thing becoming a curate of souls: using this book, as a looking-glass, to inform them what is decent.' *A Priest to the Temple* (1671), sigs v-vi. See also John Spurr, *The Restoration Church of England, 1646-1689* (New Haven and London: Yale University Press, 1991), 169-70.

against false teaching and dangerous living, and the pastor's own godliness.[116] But Herbert also considers more private concerns such as the pastor's prayer life, his state in marriage or singleness, his home life and his Sunday routine. Herbert treats character attributes such as the pastor's charity, his generosity, his condescension and his courtesy. Professional pastoral duties that either go unmentioned or are merely touched on in other works are explored more carefully by Herbert, such as visiting families, comforting the sick or bereaved, confronting the obstinate, and taking stock of the strengths and weaknesses of the people of his parish. Herbert's chapter, 'The Parson in Mirth', explores the appropriate place for a sense of humor, 'knowing that nature will not bear everlasting droopings, and that pleasantness of disposition is a great key to do good; not only because all men shun the company of perpetual severity, but also for that when they are in company, instructions seasoned with pleasantness, both enter sooner, and root deeper.'[117] Herbert's concern is so practical as to include even a chapter on coping with church wardens![118]

Herbert's 'Mark to aim at' was the most comprehensive published analysis of the pastor's duty that Protestant England had seen. The discontinuity of Herbert's meditation on ministry with the previous thrust of Protestant literature on pastoral ministry raises a warning flag to those who would impute ministerial poverty to those early Protestants and later puritans whose diagnoses of the ailments facing the English church led to a single-minded concern for preaching as the corrective for those ills. Previous sermons or treatises on ministry were intended not so much for inclusive instruction on all possible pastoral duties as for particular exhortation on points considered at risk. In contrast, Herbert covers more pastoral territory because he simply *assumes* the Protestant perspective and has deliberately chosen not to argue or debate Protestant priorities. Thus he is free to transcend what had become the standard issues of discussion in print and focus instead on how he actually spent his time in ministry. Herbert provides the clearest indication yet that Protestant pastoral practise extended well beyond the embattled pulpit-centred ideal for Protestant ministry. Yet to insinuate that Herbert was the only one among his colleagues attempting this full-orbed vision of a pastor's life is to disregard the differences in purpose behind the previous Protestant discussions of pastoral ministry and Herbert's treatise. Even so, while Herbert's actual ministry may not have been unique, he was certainly the only one who stepped out of the bounds of the contemporary discussion to write about it.

A Priest to the Temple allows us to say that there was much more to sixteenth- and seventeenth-century Protestant and puritan pastoral ministry than

---

[116] For a discussion of Herbert's catechizing ministry, see Stanley Fish, *George Herbert and the Living Temple* (Berkeley: University of California Press, 1978), 12-14.

[117] Herbert, *A Priest to the Temple*, 95-96.

[118] See Herbert's table of contents, *A Priest to the Temple*, sigs A8-A8ᵛ. Herbert's chapter on Church Wardens (XXIX) may be found on 99-101.

meets the press. But it also suggests that it is doubtful that conscientious Protestant pastors were ever solely dependent upon the small library of more narrowly focused sermons and treatises inspected here for their training as pastors. Evidence considered in chapter 9, already hinted at in our discussion of Richard Greenham's ministry earlier, indicates an intentional, if informal, effort on the part of established pastors to model effective ministry and pass on their skills to the rising generation of young men who sensed God's call to parish ministry.[119] Herbert's work is significant, not because it is a singularity of well-rounded pastoral ministry in a sea of puritan pulpitolatry, but because of the glimpse, unobstructed by the demands of polemic, which Herbert gives into the parish realities faced by every man who undertook a pastoral charge in the seventeenth century. Of course Herbert, too, gives us an ideal pastor, but it is an ideal constructed from the very real issues facing every minister in a local parish. Though Herbert may have been a Calvinist, he had little sympathy with nonconformity. And though he may have agreed with Laudian positions on certain issues, he was not a Durham House man. Herbert was much more an Elizabethan Settlement Protestant than he was of either the puritan or Laudian parties.[120] And with respect to pastoral concerns, he betrays only what would have been universally recognized as *Protestant* concerns. In 1632 at least, in the few remaining months before the gathering Laudian storm would dash the remnants of the balance struck by Elizabeth and maintained by James I, it was still possible for a pastor to stand in the middle.

With puritan pastors constrained by the Laudian hierarchy to conform and puritan ideas censored from publication, published exhortations for a godly ministry all but disappear in the latter half of the 1630s. Published visitation sermons during these years were increasingly utilized as a platform to promote a Laudian emphasis, or, more often than not, as an opportunity for a pastor to display his learnedness.[121] One later example, Richard Bayly's *The Shepheards*

---

[119] See, for example, Clarke's comments on Richard Greenham's efforts to help young men prepare for ministry in *A General martyrologie...whereunto is added the lives of Thirty Two English Divines, Famous in their generation for Learning and Piety, and most of them Sufferers in the Cause of Christ* (1677), 14. For a discussion of some of the difficulties in making use of Clarke's material, see chapter 8 below.

[120] See Christopher Hodgkin's chapter, 'Herbert's Protestant Priesthood', for example, in *Authority, Church, and Society in George Herbert* (Columbia, MO: University of Missouri Press, 1993), 103-105. See also Daniel Doerksen, *Conforming to the Word: Herbert, Donne, and the English Church before Laud* (Lewisburg, PA: Bucknell University Press, 1997), 13-24.

[121] See, for example, Thomas Twittee, *Ad Clerum proforma concio habita Marii 13 1624* (1624); Bishop Richard Parr, *Concio ad clerum habita Oxoniae Jul.12.1625* (1625); Robert Bedingford, *Cura pastoralis, concio ad clerum* (1629); Richard Gardiner, *Concio ad clerum habita in templo beatae Oxon* (1631); and Richard James, *Concio habita ad clerum Oxoniensem de ecclesia* (1633). An exploration of Laudian sermons *ad clerum* is beyond the scope of this present research.

Starre, or the Ministers Guide (1640), is an extensively developed metaphor on ministers and their likeness to the stars of the night sky, ranging over classical Greek and Latin writers, Greek and Latin Fathers and the most current astrological learning available to inform the comparison. Bayly is forced to stretch somewhat to pull this otherwise standard exhortation from his cosmic metaphor.[122]

Laud may have succeeded in silencing nonconforming perspectives on ministerial duty, but the repression of godly ministers combined with what appeared to them as license granted for clerical laxity galled painful pastors who saw their hopes of reformation erode before their eyes. Oliver Bowles (c. 1577-1646), 'Pastor of Sutton in Bedfordshire', was one who placed the blame for the deplorable state of the clergy at the beginning of the Long Parliament's reforms squarely on the Laudian policy of enforcing conformity at the expense of preaching.[123] Bowles would later revisit the theme of a godly parish ministry in his posthumously published *De pastore evangelico tractatus* (1649), a tedious restatement of the pre-Laudian Protestant understanding of pastoral ministry. The minister's dignity comes not as a priest handling sacraments, but as God's messenger announcing the way of life. The minister's authority comes not from one's position in an episcopal hierarchy, but from the spiritual weapons provided by God's word rightly used in preaching. God has sent the priceless treasure of his gospel into the world so that sinners might be saved, and ministers are the stewards, their ministry in effect serving as the keys of life and death.[124] The pastor's primary task is, not surprisingly, preaching,[125] for the pastor is *'Os dei ad populum'*.[126] While the sacraments are important, they are

---

[122] 'The Starres of Heaven are ever restlesse in their motion, and yet never wearyed. These starres in Christs hand must imitate the diligence of their pattern by the practise of unwearyed patience in the motion of their restlesse function. The office of a Minister did never consist in idlenesse.' *The Shepheards Starre*, 30. Bayly, who was Laud's half-brother, was Prebendary of St Paul's, dean of Salisbury, President of St Johns, Oxford, and Rector of Bradfield during his full career. See *WR*, 67.

[123] Oliver Bowles, *Zeal for Gods House Quickned: Or, A Sermon Preached before the Assembly of Lords, Commons, and Divines at their solemn Fast July 7.1643. In the Abbey Church at Westminster. Expressing the Eminencie of Zeale requisite in Church Reformers* (1643), 16. See also 40-47. Oliver Bowles was born at Sawtry, Hunts, in c. 1577. He matriculated Sizar at Queens' College, Cambridge, c. 1593, took his BA in 1596/7 and his MA in 1600. He was a fellow of Queens' from 1599-1607. Ordained a deacon and a priest in Colchester on April 5, 1601, Bowles became rector of Abbots Ripton, Hunts, from 1605-1607. He became rector of Sutton, Bedfordshire, 1607-1635. See Venn.

[124] Bowles, *De pastore evangelico tractatus*, sig A3.

[125] Bowles explains that there are many aspects of the pastor's duty which will not be discussed in this work. *De pastore evangelico tractatus*, sig B4.

[126] Ibid., sig B4; see also *Liber I, capit xxii*. Bowles also devotes considerable attention to helping the pastor discern the spiritual state of the individuals under his care so that

clearly secondary to the work of proclaiming God's truth. Even catechising is understood as a *'minus principalis'*.[127]

Conclusion

In the nearly one hundred years from Peter Pykeryng's *Myroure or glasse for all spiritual ministers* to Oliver Bowles's *De pastore evangelico Tractatus*, English society, politics, and religion had been utterly, and sometimes catastrophically transformed. The year that Charles I was executed for treason found Oliver Bowles making essentially the same points about pastoral ministry that Protestant writers and preachers had been making since the reign of Edward VI. With reformation as the goal and preaching as the primary means, English Protestant pastors remained remarkably consistent, at least in their published attempts to complete what the first reformers had begun. But it was a rhetoric that never quite matched the reality that existed in thousands of parishes, providing more a starting point for Protestant ministers rather than a general road map. And if Herbert's *A Priest to the Temple* serves to illustrate the disparity between rhetorical and real pastoral ministry among Protestants, it also serves to demonstrate just how Protestant the underlying assumptions about Christian ministry had become. The debate, at least, if not the reality, had moved from arguing a Protestant pastoral and preaching agenda to assuming it. But if Protestant and puritan rhetoric had long worn thin, circumstances were now conspiring to make a reappraisal of Protestant pastoral ministry urgently necessary. Nevertheless, it would take a new generation of Protestant pastors, freed from the restraints of a sacramentalist episcopate and fresh from the traumas of civil war to revise the pastoral inheritance and make what would be one final push for the reformation of the English Church. But before we consider Richard Baxter's contribution to the discussion on pastoral ministry, it will repay our trouble to examine more closely the primary motive behind the unprecedented pastoral efforts of England's Edwardian, Elizabethan and early Stuart Protestants—the perceived need for further reformation.

---

his preaching might find its mark. And he concludes by discussing several cases of conscience facing pastors, including whether or not it was permissible for a pastor to leave his present parish and move to another, and whether or not is was permissible for a pastor to flee in times of persecution. Sig B4; *Liber II, capit v.*

[127] Ibid., sig B4; *Liber II, capit v.*

CHAPTER 3

Richard Baxter's 'Reformation' and its Precedents

At the heart of Richard Baxter's agenda for pastoral ministry lay his understanding of "reformation".[1] But as one who viewed himself firmly within the tradition of England's "godly, learned and faithful" Protestant pastors, Baxter's rhetoric, at least, was hardly unique. For more than a hundred years, the prospect of further "reformation" informed the strategies and inflamed the rhetoric of committed Protestant ministers preaching in pulpits from Great St Mary's in Cambridge to St Margaret's in Westminster, and from the pulpits of hundreds if not thousands of more ordinary parish churches throughout the kingdom. Even so, only recently have historians' own utilization of "reformation" begun to reflect the range and complexities of use discernible in sixteenth- and seventeenth-century sources. Not surprisingly, "reformation" has become a term that is increasingly problematical for historians attempting to describe England's transformation from a kingdom of Roman Catholics to one of Protestants. With perspective enhanced by more diverse sources of evidence, the argument viewing England's reformation as a convoluted process that extended far beyond the successive Tudor settlements of religion in the middle years of the sixteenth-century has found persuasive proponents.[2]

While the present-day controversy continues over a reformational time frame,

---

[1] An earlier version of this chapter appeared as an article in *Westminster Theological Journal*. See J. William Black, 'Richard Baxter's Bucerian "Reformation"', *WTJ*, 63:2 (2001), 327-349. I am grateful to the editor for permission to make use of it here.

[2] See Haigh, 'The Recent Historiography of the English Reformation', M. Todd, ed., *Reformation to Revolution*, 14-32; Patrick Collinson, 'Comment on Eamon Duffy's Neale Lecture and the Colloquium', N. Tyacke, ed., *England's Long Reformation*, 71-72, 78-84; A.G. Dickens, 'The Early Expansion of Protestantism in England 1520-1558', M. Todd, ed., *Reformation to Revolution*, 157-78; Dickens, *The English Reformation* (London: Batsford, 1989); D.J. Peet, 'The Mid-Sixteenth century Parish Clergy, with particular consideration of the dioceses of Norwich and York' (University of Cambridge PhD thesis, 1980), 84-156; and Haigh's revisionist *English Reformations*. For an earlier reading of reformation not so much as from Roman Catholicism as to the fragmentation following the civil wars, see William Haller's chapter, 'Reformation without Tarrying', in *The Rise of Puritanism*, 173-225.

as well as the vantage from which to judge its relative success or failure,[3] it is helpful to recall that for several generations, many of England's early Protestants were themselves under no illusions as to the incompleteness of England's reformation.[4] It was their fundamental unhappiness with Elizabeth's religion "established by law" and attempts to revise it that polarized the English church, particularly over the issues of ceremonies and government, and established a pattern of confrontation that would dominate the Church of England through James II. While a spectrum of clergy and laity took as the goal of their exertions the task of completing the "reformation", *how* reformation was understood changed as the more zealous of England's Protestants were forced by a succession of frustrations to reevaluate both their means and ends. Moreover, "reformation" itself covered a range of meaning, used often to denote the overall process of religious change from Roman Catholicism to Protestantism, but just as often when speaking of smaller changes, be it community behavior, or with respect to particular tell-tale ceremonies or structures within the Church.

An attempt to chart Tudor and early Stuart concepts of reformation would be to rewrite the story of English Protestantism, which is obviously beyond the scope of this study.[5] Instead, this chapter will employ a series of examples to suggest more modestly that, when used to describe the overall process, the meaning of "reformation" constantly shifted, depending at any given time on the particular deficiencies perceived and the goals envisioned by their correction.[6] But more importantly, for our purposes, we will see how the long-

---

[3] See Nicolas Tyacke's overview in his 'Introduction: re-thinking the "English Reformation"', N. Tyacke, ed., *England's Long Reformation*, 1-32; also Jeremy Gregory, 'The making of a Protestant nation: "success" and "failure" England's Long Reformation', N. Tyacke, ed., *England's Long Reformation*, 307-33.

[4] See Collinson's chapter '"But Halfly Reformed"', in *Elizabethan Puritan Movement*, 29-44.

[5] Collinson has provided the best overview of the contention between the puritan and conservative wings of the Church of England in the sixteenthth century in *Elizabethan Puritan Movement*. Tom Webster has provided a similar survey for the early seventeenth century in his *Godly Clergy*.

[6] This survey assumes that descriptive concepts such as 'reformation' carry meaning identifiable from their contexts. Contemporary usage demonstrates a general consensus as to what reformation signified in a given context, and it also demonstrates that meaning developed, though not necessarily progressed (in a Whiggish sense) as circumstances changed. Charting this horizontal development of meaning provides a helpful contrast to what Robert Ashton describes as 'the vertical fragmentation of historical studies' by demonstrating the interconnectedness of ideas from one person to another and providing a framework in which to discuss the relative influence of one person's ideas or meaning on another's. See Robert Ashton, *Reformation and Revolution 1558-1660* (London: Granada, 1984), xv. See also Herbert Butterfield, *The Whig Interpretation of History* (London: G. Bell and Sons, 1931; repr. New York: Norton, 1965); and Evans, *In Defence of History*.

buried understanding of reformation advocated by the exiled Strasbourg reformer Martin Bucer during his time in England was resurrected nearly a century later by Richard Baxter and to astonishing effect. Under Baxter's influence during the "godly" Indian Summer of post-Civil War England, English pastoral practise was reconfigured under an overtly Bucerian perspective on reformation. The killing frost of the Restoration, however, put an end both to Baxter's Kidderminster and Worcestershire Association experiments and, ultimately, to the English puritan hope of finishing the reformation.

Setting the Record Straight

Richard Baxter's take on England's "Long Reformation" was that of a pastoral disaster. Baxter was persuaded that the breach between England's Protestants over the speed and extent of reformation in England was ultimately to blame for those events that led to civil war. Bypassing political explanations, Baxter drew a straight line from the "sad division" between English Protestants during the Marian exile in Frankfort to "those daies of blood that we have seen" and the resulting "great mutations in Church and State".[7] In an early example of what D.R. Woolf has called an ideological use of history "to explain the disasters of the present in such a way as to cast blame on their opponents," Baxter uses the conflict between the "Prelates" and the "Puritans" as a prism through which to reinterpret England's reformation history.[8] This use of history, while becoming standard practise after the civil wars, hardly ever accomplished its author's intent. As Thomas Fuller noted, "Such as wrote *in* or *since* our *Civil Wars*, are seldome apprehended *truely* and *candidly*, save of such of their owne *perswasion*, whilest others *doe not* (or what is worse *will not*) understand them aright."[9]

But Baxter was also participating in a long line of Christian historiography, articulated most famously by Augustine's *The City of God*, which viewed history as reproducing the conflict between godly Abel and corrupt Cain.[10] Early Protestant historians found the Old Testament stories of Israel's repeated declensions into idolatry and episodes of reformation particularly instructive for their own struggles with the perceived corruptions of Roman Catholicism.

---

[7] Baxter, *Gildas Salvianus,* 150, 161.

[8] D.R. Woolf, *The Idea of History in Early Stuart England* (Toronto: University of Toronto Press, 1990), 247.

[9] Thomas Fuller, *The Appeal of Iniured Innocence: unto The Religious Learned and Ingenuous Reader* (1659), 1. See Woolf, *The Idea of History,* 247-50.

[10] See Samuel Clarke's utilization of a Cain *versus* Abel framework in *A Generall Martyrologie* (1651), 1. Given Baxter's friendship with Clarke, it is likely that Baxter was familiar with this particular work and that it was influential in the development of Baxter's own reading of history.

Philip Melanchthon used this Old Testament pattern as a means to understand the present in his edition of John Carion's *Chronicles*, which also influenced William Harrison's 'Great English Chronology'.[11] Finding this dualism a convenient interpretative tool, Harrison understood reformation in the Old Testament sense of a complete purging from the corrupting practises and idolatries of the surrounding nations, effected only by the obedience of both individuals and community to patterns of true worship and right living laid out in Scripture.[12] Heated by such biblical reflections, Harrison and many of his godly colleagues, as we shall see, became increasingly ambivalent as to which side of the historical division Elizabeth's Church might fall.[13]

For Baxter, writing in his 1656 *Gildas Salvianus; The Reformed Pastor*, England's reformation was marred from its earliest days by Protestant confusion over the continuing role of ecclesiastical government and ceremonies inherited from the Roman Catholic past. It did not bode well that "so many godly learned men that had forsaken all for the Reformed profession" "should...fall in pieces among themselves, and that about a Liturgy and Ceremonies, so far as to make a division."[14] After Mary's death, the "party that was for Prelacy and Ceremonies, prevailed for the countenance of the state, and quickly got the staff into their hands, and many of their Brethren under their feet." Those not "of their mind and way" and "who desired the Discipline and order of other reformed Churches" were harassed, others were deprived or imprisoned, and all were tarred with "the nick-name of Puritans, as knowing how much names of reproach and scorn could do with the vulgar for the furthering of their cause."[15]

But the great tragedy of this fraternal persecution for Baxter was that those who scrupled the unreformed ceremonies and government of the Church were "made uncapable of being Preachers of the Gospel in *England*, till they would change their mind." Such, for Baxter, was akin to spiritual treason, for the Church was thereby deprived of many of its most effective pastors, "and that at a time of such necessity" "when Popish Priests were newly cast out, and multitudes of Congregations had no Preachers at all." Baxter views the hostility between the "Prelatical" party and the "Puritans" as continuing without relief

---

[11] See Philip Melanchthon, *The thre bokes of Cronicles whych John Carion...gathered*, translated by Walter Lynn (London, 1550); William Harrison, 'The Great English Chronology', cited by G.J.R. Parry, *A Protestant Vision: William Harrison and the Reformation of Elizabethan England* (Cambridge: Cambridge University Press, 1987), 3-137.

[12] Ibid., 16.

[13] Ibid., 30-31, 55-56.

[14] Baxter, *Gildas Salvianus*, 149. See Collinson's discussion of Baxter's probable source, 'The Authorship of *A Brieff Discours off the Troubles Begonne at Franckford*', in *Godly People: Essays on English Protestantism and Puritanism* (London: Hambledon Press, 1983), 191-212.

[15] Baxter, *Gildas Salvianus*, 150-51.

through the reigns of Elizabeth I and James I, reaching a climax in the "new impositions" under Charles I at the instigation of Archbishop Laud. At this point, even "conformable Puritans began to bear the great reproach (there being few of the Non-conformists left)." The resulting provocations to puritan consciences became intolerable: "Altars must be bowed to," "All must publish a Book for dancing and sports on the Lords day" thereby licensing the profaning of the Sabbath, "Lectures were put down, and afternoon Sermons, and expounding the Catechism or Scripture." Those whose consciences forbade conformity were hauled before church courts "to be presented together with Adultery and such like sins." Such was the violence against the godly "that many thousand families left the Land...most in the remote *American* parts." Baxter concedes that it would hardly be worth complaining had the authorities taken steps to provide "competent men for their places." "But alas the Churches were pestered with such wretches as are our shame and trouble to this day." And those who did preach, spent more time preaching against the puritans than against sin or for salvation. The atmosphere became so poisoned that Baxter reports, "it was become commonly in *England* a greater reproach to be a man truly living in the fear of God, then to live in open prophaness, and to rail at godliness." Preachers with an eye towards preferment "were well ware that the rising way was to preach against the precise Puritans, and not to live precisely themselves." All of which leads Baxter to the decidedly Deuteronomic conclusion concerning the civil wars: "And thus both Ministry and people grew to that sad pass, that it was no wonder if God would bear no longer with the Land."[16]

Up to this point, however, Baxter was attempting to set the record straight by historicizing the standard godly line that reformation could not proceed until the hindrances of an unreformed diocesan prelacy were removed.[17] But unlike

---

[16] Ibid., 151-52, 156-57, 157-58. See a similar line taken in Stephen Marshall's Parliamentary Fast Day warnings to the same end in his *Reformation and Desolation: or A Sermon tending to the Discovery of the Symptomes of a People to whom God will by no meanes be reconciled* (1642). See also R. Paul House, 'Old Testament Historians', M. Bauman and M.I. Klauber, eds., *Historians of the Christian Tradition: Their Methodology and Influence on Western Thought*, 16-27.

[17] 'Setting the record straight is an important part of Baxter's business, but only as a means, not an end. He has...a case to argue.' Keeble, 'The Autobiographer as Apologist: *Reliquiae Baxterianae* (1696)', in *PS*, 9:2 (1986), 114. Joan Webber has noted that 'what frightens Baxter perhaps most of all is the prospect that slander may be taken for history.' Webber, *The Eloquent 'I': Style and Self in Seventeenth-Century Prose* (Madison, WI: University of Wisconsin Press, 1968), 140. For other studies of Baxter's use of autobiography, see Margaret Bottrall's chapter 'Richard Baxter', in her *Every Man a Phoenix: Studies in seventeenth century autobiography* (London: John Murray, 1958), 111-40; K.J. Weintraub's *The Value of the Individual: Self and Circumstance in Autobiography* (Chicago: University of Chicago Press, 1978), 242-51; Donald Stauffer, *English Biography Before 1700* (Cambridge, MA: Harvard University Press, 1930),

the sixteenth-century Presbyterians and their Long Parliament progeny, Baxter was not against bishops *per se*, for "it was not all the Prelates of the Church that thus miscarried: we have yet surviving our *Usher*, our *Hall*, our *Morton*, learned, godly and peaceable men." Baxter even suggests that if more of the bishops had "been such," the incurable divisions which provoked the civil wars would never have occurred, and the subsequent "great mutations in Church and state" avoided altogether.[18] Nevertheless, Baxter has a point to make with his history, and as Keeble observes of his later *Reliquiae*, he marshals his evidence "in the service of an interpretation of events. Baxter discerns in the complexities of history a simple and fundamental opposition" between those who live for God and those who do not.[19] Even more intriguing is that Baxter assumes a continuity of reformational intent amongst committed Protestants from Cranmer to himself, a kind of godly solidarity against worldly opposition, with his own experience presented as wholly typical.[20] The cause is that of the gospel, and those who seek its advance will of necessity view reformation as preliminary means to that end. Conversely, those unconcerned with the advance of the gospel will betray their true orientation as its enemies by resisting attempts to reform. "Just such a holy war," adds Keeble, "is discernible in every historical event. Indeed in the fallen world, it is this conflict which constitutes history."[21] But as we shall see, Baxter's updated Bible dualism oversimplified the puritan predicament. By viewing England's "Long Reformation" as a conflict between "Prelatical" Cain and "Godly" Abel, Baxter was able to gloss the fundamental differences which existed in how even the "Puritans" themselves understood and attempted reformation. What Baxter neglects to point out is that for most of England's Protestant history, reformation was viewed from a Genevan perspective. Baxter's own vision, however, predates the zeal of the returning Marian exiles and finds its closest

---

192-94, as well as a discussion of Baxter's biographical style in his *A Breviate of the Life of Margaret Baxter* (1681), 167-69.

[18] Baxter, *Gildas Salvianus*, 161.

[19] Keeble, 'The Autobiographer', 114; Cooper, *Fear and Polemic*, 198-201.

[20] This tendency is more pronounced in Baxter's later polemical histories such as *A Treatise of Episcopacy* (1680), *Church History of the Government of Bishops* (1680), *An Apology for the Nonconformist Ministry* (1681), *The Nonconformists Plea for Peace* (1679), *The Second Part of the Nonconformists Plea for Peace* (1680), *A Third Defence of the Cause of Peace* (1681), *The True History of Councils Enlarged* (1682), *Cain and Abel Malignity* (1689), *The English Nonconformity* (1690), and *Reliquiae Baxterianae* (1696). Even so, all of the elements of Baxter's concern with what Keeble calls 'the grand strife' and 'personal apologetic' are present in this relatively early accounting of England's Protestant history. See Keeble, *Richard Baxter*, 117, 149. 'His story matters only so far as it illustrates a larger story: personal experience exemplifies general experience.' Keeble, 'The Autobiographer', 112. I am grateful to Professor Keeble for his interaction with me on this subject.

[21] Keeble, 'The Autobiographer', 114.

affinities with Reformation Strasbourg.

Martin Bucer's English Reformation

The most sophisticated of the proposals to finish the reformation in England was also one of the first-that of the exiled Strasbourg reformer Martin Bucer (1491-1551).[22] Bucer's name had been connected with the cause of reformation in England from its earliest days, and a 1535 translation of his *Das einigerlei Bild* (1530) was the first book that openly promoted the case for iconoclasm in English.[23] Forced by Charles V's Interim to leave Strasbourg in 1549, Bucer had come to England at the invitation of Archbishop Cranmer and was installed as Regius Professor of Divinity at Cambridge in 1550.[24] Bucer's passionate concern to reform pastoral ministry and institute an effective church discipline permeate the lectures he gave on Ephesians, as well as the sermons he preached at Great St Mary's. His critique informed Cranmer's final revision of the Book

---

[22] See Constantin Hopf, *Martin Bucer and the English Reformation* (Oxford: Basil Blackwell, 1946); Mark E. Vander Schaaf, 'Archbishop Parker's Efforts Toward a Bucerian Discipline in the Church of England', in *SCJ*, 8:1 (1977), 85-103; Collinson, 'The Reformer and the Archbishop: Martin Bucer and an English Bucerian', in *Godly People*, 19-44; Collinson, *Archbishop Grindal 1519-1583: The Struggle for a Reformed Church* (London: Cape, 1979); Richard L. Harrison, 'Martin Bucer on the Nature and Purpose of Ministry: The View from Exile', in *LTQ*, 16:2 (1981), 53-67; H.C. Porter, *Reformation and Reaction in Tudor Cambridge* (Cambridge: Cambridge University Press, 1958); D.F. Wright, 'Martin Bucer and England-and Scotland', C. Krieger and M. Lienhard, eds., *Martin Bucer and Sixteenth Century Europe*, ii (Leiden: Brill, 1993), 523-32; Basil Hall, 'Martin Bucer in England', D.F. Wright, ed., *Martin Bucer: Reforming Church and Community* (Cambridge: Cambridge University Press, 1994), 144-60; Rosemary O'Day, *The English Clergy*, 27.

[23] Martin Bucer, *A treatise declaryng and shewing...that pyctures and other ymages...ar in no wise to be suffred in...churches* [1535]. A Latin translation appeared in England before it was translated into English. See John Foxe, *Acts and Monuments*, iv, ed. J. Pratt (1853-8, 1877), 669. See Margaret Aston, *Faith and Fire: Popular and Unpopular Religion 1350-1600* (London: Hambledon, 1993), 277, 296; Aston, *England's Iconoclasts*, i (Oxford: Clarendon, 1988), 240. For Bucer's further interaction with English reformers during the Henrician reformation, see Diarmaid McCulloch, *Thomas Cranmer: A Life* (New Haven and London: Yale University Press, 1996), 174-84.

[24] Bucer was the most prominent of a number of European reformers invited to England by Cranmer to further the work of reforming the English Church. Others include Peter Martyr Vermigli, John a Lasco, Ochino and Bucer's colleague in Strasbourg, Paul Fagius. See Basil Hall, 'Cranmer, the Eucharist and the Foreign Divines in the Reign of Edward VI', P. Ayris and D. Selwyn, eds., *Thomas Cranmer: Churchman and Scholar* (Woodbridge, Suffolk: The Boydell Press, 1993), 236; MacCulloch, *Thomas Cranmer*, 2, 469-71, 481-82; Horton Davies, *Worship and Theology in England*, I, 106-07.

of Common Prayer.[25] Moreover, his own experience as a reforming pastor made him sensitive to the practical issues involved in shepherding a newly Protestant parish on the narrow road between Roman Catholic relapse and Anabaptist excess. His published counsel to reformation pastors, *Von der Waren Seelsorge* (Strasbourg, 1538), was later translated into Latin and included as *De Vera Animarum Cura* in his posthumously published collection *Scripta Anglicana fere Omnia* (Basle, 1577).

For Bucer, the pastor was the key figure if any programme for reformation was to be successful. Bucer's pastoral agenda for reformation was dominated by the goal of facilitating the conversion of the unbelieving majority in his parish. His most significant contribution to the cause of reform in his adopted home came in *De Regno Christi* (1551), his hastily written and subsequently neglected blueprint for the furthering of reformation in England, published as a belated New Year's gift to Edward VI.[26] Bucer observed that while England's reformation had been advanced by royal edict and legislated settlement, most people had been minimally exposed to Protestant doctrine and untouched by Protestant discipline, much less converted to evangelical faith.[27] Writing to John Calvin in 1550, Bucer presented a downbeat assessment of the overall status of the English reformation. With bishops unable "to come to agreement as to Christian doctrine, much less as to discipline," Bucer reported that the primary hindrance to reformation was the deplorable state of the parish clergy. And with most parishes either "sold to the nobility" or held in absentia by pluralists who appointed poor, ignorant "substitute" who were "in heart mere papists," he complained that it was not surprising "how little can be effected for the restoration of the Kingdom of Christ by mere ordinances, and the removal of instruments of superstition."[28] Directly addressing this deficiency, Bucer argued in *De Regno Christi* that a reformed ministry was central to the advance of a reformation "by devout persuasion."[29] Such ministry involved effective

---

[25] See Bucer, *Censura De Caeremoniis Ecclesiae Anglicanae* (1551); and E.C. Whitaker's English translation in *Martin Bucer and the Book of Common Prayer* (Great Wakering: Mayher-McGrimmon, 1974). See Bucer's appendix on the desperate need for well-trained pastors, 148-72.

[26] The immediate impact of *De Regno Christi* was negligible due to Bucer's death on 28 February 1551, and the death of Edward VI in 1553. It was printed in Basle only in 1557, though it was later included in *Scripta Anglicana* (1577). See Wilhelm Pauck, 'Editor's Introduction', in *Melanchthon and Bucer*, Library of Christian Classics, XIX (London: SCM Press, 1969), 170.

[27] Bucer, *De Regno Christi*, 268.

[28] 'Cambridge letter of Bucer to Calvin, 1550', H.C. Porter, ed., *Puritanism in Tudor England* (London: MacMillan, 1970), 60-61.

[29] Bucer, *De Regno Christi*, 268, 271. See N. Scott Amos, '"It is Fallow Ground Here": Martin Bucer as Critic of the English Reformation', *WTJ*, 61 (1999), 48-49. Amos assumes that Bucer's prescription for reformation is a programme for more and better

evangelical preaching, the right administration of the sacraments, the exercise of church discipline, and the practise of catechizing for confirmation.[30]

Though he had been in England only a short while, Bucer found disturbing parallels between the incomplete course of reformation in England and that of his German homeland. For despite efforts to insure "right preaching" so that "the religion of Christ be rightly established," neither in Germany or England had the Church "become entirely subject to Christ's gospel and Kingdom, [or] allowed the Christian religion and the discipline of the churches to be restored throughout."[31] Instead, the supporters of reformation "seem to have learned only these things of the gospel of Christ: first to reject the tyranny of the Roman Antichrist and the false bishops. Next to throw off the yoke of any kind of discipline." In a withering critique of German reformation intended to prick English consciences as well, Bucer continues,

> Thus it was not displeasing to them to hear that we are justified by faith in Christ and not by good works, in which they had no interest. They never seriously considered what was explained to them about the nature and power of true faith in Christ, and how necessary it is to be prolific in good works. A number of them accept some preaching of the gospel only in order that they might confiscate the rich properties of the Church. And so it has happened that in a great many places this entire doctrine of the Kingdom of Christ has been faithfully announced to the people, but I for one cannot say in what churches it has yet been firmly accepted and Christian discipline publicly constituted.[32]

By discipline, Bucer meant an integrated system of pastoral oversight, whose end was a process by which professing Christians whose lives were a scandal to the gospel were either restored to the church through repentance or excluded from the church through their continued impenitence.[33] The key to discipline

---

preaching. Bucer, as we shall see, certainly wanted more and better preaching, but viewed reformation as the result of a far more extensive pastoral strategy.

[30] Bucer, *De Regno Christi*, 225-47. Part of Bucer's programme also involved a reformed understanding of penance. See his chapter (IX) on 'The Ministry of the Discipline of Penance', 247.

[31] Ibid., 211.

[32] Ibid., 212-13. Scott Amos rightly questions why, apart from a few references in Haigh's *English Reformations* (see 193, for example), Bucer's critique of England's reformation was not cited as evidence for the prosecution in works such as J.J. Scarisbrick's *The Reformation and the English People* (Oxford: Basil Blackwell, 1984), and Duffy's *The Stripping of the Altars*. Amos, "'It is Fallow Ground Here'", 51.

[33] For Bucer's practise of church discipline, see A.N. Burnett, "Church Discipline and Moral Reformation in the thought of Martin Bucer", in *SCJ*, 22 (1991), 439-56; A.N. Burnett, *The Yoke of Christ: Martin Bucer and Church Discipline* (Kirksville, MO:

was Bucer's insistence that, prerequisite to receiving the privileges of adult membership, every person baptized as an infant must make a profession of faith and of obedience to Christ and the church.[34] This exigency transformed the minister's role from that of simply a herald of good news to that of a shepherd called to careful oversight of each member of his flock through "teaching and admonishing them not only publicly but also at home and privately."[35]

Bucer's reconfiguration of pastoral ministry replaced the inherited sacramental paradigm for parish ministry with one that was primarily evangelistic. While Bucer was in full agreement with using legislative means to rid the land of "Antichristian'" abuses, retool the universities to become Protestant seminaries, and even reform such social concerns as marketing, civil law, and the role of the magistrate in a Christian community, he recognized that these would ultimately be superficial changes apart from widespread individual spiritual transformation.[36] Reformation itself would be facilitated by reformed pastors and would occur as a result of the accumulated conversions within a given parish, as people were then enabled by God's Spirit to keep God's law.[37]

Reformation by Reaction

Bucer died in Cambridge on 28 February 1551, and Protestant hopes in any case were dashed with the death of Edward VI in 1553 and the subsequent failure of attempts to secure a Protestant succession. However, Mary's early death in 1558, and the accession of Anne Boleyn's daughter Elizabeth to the throne resurrected Protestant hopes for a completed English reformation. But as

---

Sixteenth Century Journal Publishers, 1994); Henry G. Krahn, 'Martin Bucer's Strategy against Sectarian Dissent in Strasbourg', in *MQR*, 50:3 (1976), 163-180; Kenneth R. Davis, 'No Discipline, No Church: An Anabaptist Contribution to the Reformed Tradition', in *SCJ*, 13 (1982), 42-58.

[34] Bucer, *De Regno Christi*, 211-12.

[35] Ibid, 235. See also Bucer, *Concerning the True Care of Souls and Genuine Pastoral Ministry and how the latter is to be ordered and carried out in the church of Christ* (privately translated by Peter Beale) (Strasbourg, 1538), 40-41. See also *De Vera Animarum Cura*, in *Scripta Anglicana*, 293. I am grateful to Dr. Janet Tollington, librarian of Westminster College, Cambridge, for her assistance in locating Beale's translation. Children and "ignorant Christians" were to be carefully catechized, with an eye towards rehabilitating confirmation as an essential element of discipline. See *De Regno Christi*, 222.

[36] Bucer, *De Regno Christi*, 273-77, 279-315, 333-84.

[37] '[There are] so many who by all possible means which they dare employ either oppose, postpone, or delay this reformation.... That is why it is fitting for Your Majesty to be quite seriously concerned about the restoration of [the clergy's] duty and ministry and to act with a more burning energy toward this very goal, the more the renewal of this office contributes toward the salvation of all and the more its neglect endangers and its dissipation damages everyone's salvation.' Bucer, *De Regno Christi*, 266.

Baxter's narrative points out, the Protestant leadership who had escaped Mary's persecution by fleeing to continental centers of reformation returned to England already nursing disagreements over what course Elizabeth's reformation should take. Elizabeth's compromise settlement and the subsequent dissatisfaction of many who had been influenced by the examples of reformation in cities like Geneva and Zurich served to consign Bucer and his programme to the sidelines of debate. Though a Latin edition of *De Regno Christi* was published in Basle in 1557, there is little evidence of its widespread circulation in the English Protestant community. Moreover, Conrad Hubert's edition of Bucer's later works, *Scripta Anglicana*, did not appear until 1577. By then, Bucer had been further relegated as merely one of many continental authorities cited by the various parties in their attempts to win polemical points.[38]

In the meantime, the issue confronting England's Protestants had shifted from one of defining and applying reformation to reacting to Elizabeth's definition and whether or not it was sufficient. Anthony Gilby was a veteran of the "sad division" of 1557 in Frankfort, which found him moving with John Knox and William Whittingham to Geneva after the row in the exiled English congregation over whether the 1552 Book of Common Prayer should to be replaced by a reformed order of worship.[39] When he returned to England, Gilby had been astonished that Elizabeth's 1559 Settlement had retained certain "relics of popery," ceremonies and clerical dress which were used by Roman Catholics but which were viewed as matters indifferent with respect to Scripture.[40] Attempts by the bishops to suppress all nonconformity were met by outraged and increasingly radicalized responses among the more earnest Protestants like Gilby:

> [our enemies and persecutyrs] can not thinke the worde of God
> safelye ynough preachid, & horably inough handlyd, without cap,

---

[38] The one exception is Thomas Sampson's attempt in 1573 to undo damage done to the cause of further reformation by the publishing of *An admonition to Parliament* (1572) by reminding Lord Burleigh that a programme for the reform of church and state had been underway in King Edward's time, a programme which Bucer had addressed in his *De Regno Christi*. Sampson, who had been a fellow at Pembroke Hall when Bucer was in Cambridge, made a digest of Bucer's book for Burleigh and urged him to consider its potential for the present situation. For Sampson's letter to Burleigh, see John Strype, *Annals of the Reformation* (1824), II, i, 392-95. See Collinson, 'The Reformer and the Archbishop', 30-31.

[39] Gilby was born in Lincolnshire and attended Christ's College, Cambridge, where he achieved BA in 1531/2 and MA in 1535. After Mary's accession, he fled in 1554 from his living in Leicestershire to Frankfort in 1554. Upon his return to England under Elizabeth he was presented by Henry, Earl of Huntingdon to Ashby de la Zouch. Gilby died in 1585. See *DNB*; Collinson, *Elizabethan Puritan Movement*, 33, 72; Collinson, 'The Authorship of *A Brieff Discours'*, 191-212.

[40] Collinson, *Elizabethan Puritan Movement*, 35.

cope, surplis. But that the sacraments the maryinge, the buryinge, the chirchin of wemen, & other church service, as they call it, mus nedes be decored with crossinge, with capping, with surplessing, with knelinge, with preti wafer cakes, and other knackes of poperi.[41]

Discomfort over the unreformed "popish" taint contaminating English worship provoked a further conviction that the entire fabric of the Church's government and ministry was similarly untouched by reform. Archbishop Parker's crackdown on nonconformity in 1565 pushed Gilby to view the bishops not as friends in the battle for the further reformation of the church but as reformation's chief impediment. Bitterly addressing the bishops, some of whom had shared the hardships of the Marian exile, Gilby vented:

> O beware you, that wilbe Lordes over the flockes, that you be not sore punyshed for your pryd, towardes your brethren, and your cowardlines in gods cause, that for Princes pleasures and pompse liuinges, do turne poperi into policie, and to become our persecutors under the cloke of policie. It were better to lose your liuings, then to displease god on persecutinge of youre brethren, & hinder the course of the worde.[42]

Gilby's perspective on both the problems facing England's reformation and the solutions required take us into a different world from that addressed by Martin Bucer only 15 years earlier. For Gilby, reformation became primarily a crusade to free the English Church of all continuity with its Roman Catholic past and to settle the Church's worship, government and ministry on Scriptural foundations. For *"if this Poperie continewe, [the bishops] wilbe younge Popes doubtlesse, and poperie it self will growe up again."* *"Therefore, let all good men labour all that they can, to plucke up these wicked weedes of Poperie, the remmenauntes of superstition and Idolatrie."*[43] For Gilby, resisting "popery" was a matter of conscience. In the words of his "Souldier of Barwick": "my harte ariseth in my body, when I see thee and they fellows cloathed like [the Pope's] Chaplaines, that burned the blessed Bible, and our faythfull fathers, and deare Brethren in our eyes."[44] Gilby's programme for reformation was correspondingly simple: "This is the summe of the request...of the Godly Ministers of London...that after so long preaching of Christ in London (almost

---

[41] Anthony Gilby, *To my louynge brethren that is troublyd abowt the popishe apparrell, two short and comfortable Epistles* (1566), sig A2v.

[42] Ibid., sig B3.

[43] Gilby, *A Pleasaunt Dialogue...between a Souldier of Barwick, and an English Chaplain* (1573), sigs A6-A6v.

[44] Ibid., sig C5.

these thirtie yeares) they may put in practise, the doctrine of Christ, and minister his holy sacraments in that simplicitie, that Christ and his Apostles hath left them, without the ceremonies and garments abused by the papistes."[45] With Anthony Gilby, reformation has shifted from Bucer's emphasis on evangelism and its implications for church forms and structures to a primary emphasis on the purity of the forms and structures themselves.

Completely overwhelmed by the increasingly bitter rhetoric was the reality that there were a number of bishops in Elizabeth's Protestant church who were concerned to promote a lively Protestant faith within their dioceses, albeit within the parameters set by Elizabeth.[46] Bishops Richard Cox of Ely (1559-1581), John Jewel of Salisbury (1560-1571), Edwin Sandys of Worcester (1560-1570), James Pilkington of Durham (1561-1576) and Edmund Grindal of London (1560-1570) each sought to advance Protestant faith and uproot Roman Catholic superstition in their local contexts. Motivated by a vision of a national church 'devoid of the old religion's rites and symbols and led by theologically grounded bishops and pastors under the Crown's authority', they were nevertheless pressured by Elizabeth's government to compromise their national goals and focus instead on the more pressing issue of suppressing the significant minority of insistent Catholics and enforcing conformity, both by Catholics and the more radical Protestants.[47] This, of course, made conflict inevitable with those like Gilby for whom any delay in the complete reformation of the Church was unconscionable.

It was a short step from viewing an unreformed episcopal government as part of the problem to demanding that the government and ministry of the church as well as its worship undergo reformation. That step was taken in 1570 by Thomas Cartwright in his series of Cambridge lectures on the Acts of the Apostles and again but with popular force with the publication of the anonymous *Admonition to Parliament* in 1572.[48] Later acknowledged as the work of John Field and Thomas Wilcox, the *Admonition* exhorted Parliament not only to reject "all popish remnants both in ceremonies and regiment," but also to establish "those things only which the Lord himself in his Word commandeth because it is not enough to take pains in taking away evil but also

---

[45] Ibid, sig C1.

[46] See, for example, S.A. Wenig, *Straightening the Altars: The Ecclesiastical Vision and Pastoral Achievements of the Progressive Bishops under Elizabeth I, 1559-1579* (New York: Peter Lang, 2000).

[47] Donald McKim, '[Review of] Straightening the Altars', *CH*, 71:3 (2002), 658-659.

[48] For Cartwright see Collinson, *Elizabethan Puritan Movement*, 112-13, 122-25. For the *Admonition*, see W.H. Frere and C.E. Douglas, eds., *Puritan Manifestoes* (London: Church Historical Society, 1907, repr. London: SPCK, 1954), 5-55; Collinson, 'John Field and Elizabethan Puritanism', in *Godly People*, 339-41; *Elizabethan Puritan Movement*, 118-21; D.J. McGinn, *The Admonition Controversy* (New Brunswick, NJ: Rutgers University Press, 1949).

to be occupied in placing good in the stead thereof."[49] The reforming "good" in mind was of course a Presbyterian polity or "discipline," with Calvin's Geneva as the model. Like Bucer, the Presbyterians had a programme for the further reformation of the Church, though the focus was almost entirely on supplanting episcopacy with presbytery and, Patrick Collinson adds, "pragmatism with dogma."[50] Furthermore, they "found it hard, if not impossible, to think of reformation in any other terms than as a public act to be imposed on the Commonwealth by law and discipline."[51] Reformation, therefore, involved exchanging an unscriptural government, discipline and ceremonies for a system more in line with the teaching of Scripture. As such it involved the legislated resettlement of the Church,[52] as well as, in the meantime, an underground movement to establish a system of pastoral conferences that would provide the framework upon which a Presbyterian discipline could be erected when the time was right.[53]

The harsh crackdown on the Presbyterians led by Archbishop Whitgift effectively crushed the movement, and the cause of further reformation was thereafter unhelpfully connected, in royal and episcopal eyes, with subversive Presbyterian agitation. Unsurprisingly, all overt references to the further reformation of the church disappear from the title pages of treatises and sermons from the last half of Elizabeth's reign into that of James I. Because tampering with the 1559 Settlement was forbidden by Elizabeth and again by James after the 1604 Hampton Court Conference, reforming zeal either spun out in a harried separatism or was redirected towards issues that all parties could agree on, such as the need to amend the clergy or to promote individual godliness.[54]

F.J. Bremer states that '[t]he leadership of the Puritan effort to reform England rested primarily on the shoulders of the clergy.'[55] Ministers increasingly urged their fellows to be faithful in their God-appointed task. Following Elizabeth's death, there was a marked upsurge in published sermons and treatises exhorting clergy to bring their lives and ministries into conformity with the reformed ideal of the preaching pastor. In one of these treatises, the

---

[49] McGinn, *The Admonition Controversy*, 373. For John Field and Thomas Wilcox, see Collinson, 'John Field', 335-370; *Elizabethan Puritan Movement*, 85-86, 116-21.

[50] Collinson, *Elizabethan Puritan Movement*, 105. For the Presbyterians' reforming objectives, see 105-07.

[51] Ibid, 131-32.

[52] For the efforts of Elizabethan parliaments to further the cause of Presbyterian reformation, see Collinson, *Elizabethan Puritan Movement*, 269-88, 303-16; J.E. Neale, *Elizabeth I & her Parliaments, 1559-1581* (London: Cape, 1953) and Neale, *Elizabeth I & her Parliaments, 1584-1601* (London: Cape, 1957).

[53] See Collinson's section 'Presbytery in Episcopacy', *Elizabethan Puritan Movement*, 333-84.

[54] Ibid., 432-47.

[55] Bremer, *Shaping New Englands*, 14.

posthumously published *Of the Calling of the Ministrie* (1605), William Perkins lamented that "In many places of our land, there is by Gods blessing much teaching, yet there is little reformation, in the liues of the most: but contrariwise, some fall to Atheisme; some to Papisme: some into soule sinnes, not to be named among Christians." The cause of this declension was not, for Perkins, to be found in the gospel, "nor in our doctrine, nor in the teaching of it" but rather because too many ministers live unreformed, scandalous lives "in the face of their people."[56] For Perkins, the need for reformation was just as urgent as it was for Bucer, Gilby, and Presbyterians like Field. But reflecting the late Elizabethan context in which he wrote, the scope of Perkins' reformation is more confined. He allows that the Elizabethan Church of England could be called "reformed," and suggests that the glory of such a church is "to haue their doctrine powerfull, & effectuall for the winning of soules." It was therefore incumbent to insure "that their ministers be godly men, *as good Schollers*, & their *liues inoffensiue* as wel as their *doctrine sound*;" otherwise, "they will find in woefull experience, that they pull downe as much with one hand, as they build vp with the other."[57]

Concern for reformation was not the monopoly of an obstreperous minority on the verges of church affairs. As visitation records demonstrate, the ecclesiastical hierarchy was also concerned with many of the same issues that vexed the more zealous "godly" clergy.[58] Church courts were utilized not only

---

[56] William Perkins, *Of the Calling of the Ministerie* (1605), 51-52.

[57] Ibid., 52-53. Further examples of Perkin's concern could be multiplied from the published writings of "godly" ministers such as Richard Bernard (1568-1641), Samuel Hieron (1576?-1617), Robert Mandevill (1578-1618) and Samuel Crooke (1575-1649). For Bernard, the vicar of Worksop, Nottinghamshire from 1601-1613, and afterwards the rector of Batcombe, Somersetshire, see *The Faithful Shepheard* (1607) and *Two Twinnes* (1613). For Hieron, vicar of Madbury, Devonshire, see *The Preachers Plea* (1604), *Aarons Bells A-sounding* (1623) and *The Spirituall Fishing* (1618). For Mandevill, vicar of Holme, Cumberland, see *Timothies Taske* (1619). For Crooke, the rector of Wrington, Somerset, see *Three Sermons..viz. The Ministeriall Husbandry* (1615).

[58] See, for example, Bishop John Williams's articles for Lincoln Diocese in 1635, in particular his concern with Sabbath breakers, 5.(30.), 5.(31.) and 5.(32.), in Kenneth Fincham, ed., *Visitation Articles and Injunctions of the Early Stuart Church*, II (Woodbridge, Suffolk: The Boydell Press, 1998), 101-102. See also Archdeacon Theophilus Aylmer's 1625 visitation articles for London Archdeaconry, particularly his concern that ministers not lead scandalous lives and also for the disciplining of 'common swearers, drunkards, blasphemers, simoniacall persons, or usurers...witches, coniurers, southsayers, charmers, fornicators, adulterers, incestuous persons, brawlers, common slanderers of their neighbours, raylers, scolds, filthy and lascivious talkers, sowers of discord betwixt neighbours....' Canons 71-75 (6), 109 (20), 14, 17. Fincham states that 'The fact that many sets [of visitation articles from 1603-42] underwent constant revisions suggests that they were valued as a means to exercise ecclesiastical

to enforce conformity but to uphold standards of public morality. Efforts were made to improve the quality and effectiveness of the clergy.[59] Puritan clergy found the church courts better than nothing as a means of troubling the unrepentant; but they also sought to gain the cooperation of like-minded local magistrates who were in a position to use their authority as a partner in effecting local reformation.[60]

Nevertheless, consistent royal and ecclesiastical policy against the more radical aspects of church reformation forced many concerned clergymen to find a less offensive outlet for their reforming zeal. This redirection of "godly" zeal for reformation is perhaps most transparent in the series of four sermons published by Richard Sibbes in 1629 as part of *The Saints Cordials*, and separately in 1637 under the title *Josiahs Reformation*.[61] Had such a work appeared in Bucer's day, the connections with England's reformation would have been obvious, as Bucer along with Cranmer and others had likened boy-King Edward VI to the Old Testament reforming king Josiah. But even under the watchful eyes of the Bishop of London and soon-to-be Archbishop of Canterbury William Laud, no such connotations were intended or taken. Instead, Sibbes presents a guide for a wholly internalized and subjective reformation of the individual heart. When Sibbes calls his hearers to "remove the impediments that hinder" reformation, his concern is not with "popish relics" or hypocritical ministers, but rather "a hard and stony heart, which is opposite to tenderness." When Sibbes finally addresses the nature of Josiah's reformation, he chooses his words carefully: "Let us have such a resolution and purpose of reformation as Josiah had; for his prayers were joined with a purpose of reformation, which he...performed in so strict a manner, that there was never such a reformation among all the Kings of Judah as he made."[62] Sibbes's conformable conclusions take us far from the clamoring visions of

justice and to recommend good practise and pastoral aspirations.' xxviii. See also Kenneth Fincham, *Prelate as Pastor*, 129.

[59] Keith Wrightson, *English Society*, 208.

[60] See Sir Nathaniel Barnardiston's partnership with Samuel Fairclough in Kedington, Suffolk, in Samuel Clarke, *The Lives of Sundry Eminent Persons*, 161-163B, 169. For a full discussion of the Fairclough account, see chapter 8. See also John White's cooperative relationship with magistrates in Dorchester in David Underdown's *Fire from Heaven: The Life of an English Town in the Seventeenth Century* (London: Harper-Collins, 1992), 128-30; Wrightson, *English Society,* 208.

[61] Richard Sibbes, *The Works of Richard Sibbes*, A. Grosart, ed. (1862-64, repr. Edinburgh: The Banner of Truth Trust, 1983), vi, 28. For Sibbes, master of St Catherine's College in Cambridge and preacher at Gray's Inn in London, see M.E. Dever, *Richard Sibbes: Puritanism and Calvinism in Late Elizabethan and Early Stuart England* (Macon, GA: Mercer University Press, 2000), and 'Richard Sibbes and the "Truly Evangelical Church of England"' (University of Cambridge PhD thesis, 1991).

[62] Sibbes, "The Art of Mourning", in *Josiahs Reformation, The Works of Richard Sibbes*, vi, 67, 75.

reformation from the preceding century: "Reformation makes all outward things fall into a good rule, but they are to be called only by the authority of the prince, and when a fit time and occasion requires." And if his readers missed his meaning the first time, he adds even more submissively, "But this must be done by the consent of authority, otherwise it would be an impeachment to government."[63]

The political realities that forced Sibbes to redefine the locus of reformation inwardly are more widely reflected in the proliferation of published works of "practical godliness". The intense, predominantly Calvinist spirituality which formed the basis and informed the exhortations of this literature grew out of the preaching ministries of the increasing circle of university educated clergy, R.T. Kendall's "'affectionate practical" school of "experimental predestinarians".[64] This "carefully nurtured godly clerical society, rooted in spiritual needs" and "the ability of this community to organise, communicate and foster a sense of embattled minority with a mission to change the spiritual state of the country" reveal Sibbes and his "godly" colleagues to be participants in what Thomas Webster describes as an "early Stuart Puritan movement." Though surprisingly Webster does not acknowledge early Stuart continuity with Elizabethan puritan concerns for reformation *per se*, he nonetheless observes that "the means of this movement were different those [sic] of their forebears, concentrating of the particular, both individual and parochial, on producing better ministers through colleges, seminaries and pastoral care, rather than delivering petitions and admonitions to monarch and Parliament."[65] Thus, the motivating vision of a reformed English Church is the same, even if both means and goals have shifted yet again.

Godly discontent simmered under the Laudian reversion to a sacramentalist perspective on worship and ministry, distaste for Calvinism and intolerance of nonconformity.[66] But an unforeseen conjunction of royal arrogance and political ineptness combined with spectacular ecclesiastical overreaching in Scotland, disastrous military responses, the collapse of royal authority in Scotland and Ireland, and the congealing of fears of a vast popish conspiracy undermining English Protestantism to create the conditions which made

---

[63] Sibbes, "The Saints Refreshing", in *Josiahs Reformation, The Works of Richard Sibbes*, vi, 90.

[64] See R.T. Kendall, *Calvin and English Calvinism to 1649* (Oxford: Oxford University Press, 1979), 6-9; Packer, *A Quest for Godliness*, 49-77; Charles Hambrick-Stowe, *The Practice of Piety: Puritan Devotional Disciplines in Seventeenth-Century New England* (Chapel Hill, NC: University of North Carolina Press, 1982).

[65] Webster, *Godly Clergy*, 338.

[66] See Nicolas Tyacke, *The Fortunes of English Puritanism 1603-1640* (London: Dr Williams's Trust, 1990); Tyacke, "Puritanism, Arminianism and Counter-Revolution", M. Todd, ed., *Reformation to Revolution*, 53-70; Tyacke, *Anti-Calvinists: The Rise of English Arminianism c. 1590-1640* (Oxford: Clarendon, 1987).

reformation, civil war and indeed revolution possible.[67] If James had been perceived as guiding the Church in the right direction (even if far too slowly for his more 'Puritan' subjects), Charles increasingly alarmed them "by frogmarching it away from reformation."[68] John Morrill speaks of a "'coiled spring" of "godly" zeal in 1640, wound tight by Laudian innovation and provocation, and a "willingness to contemplate fundamental change in the English Church which had not been seen since the 1580s and perhaps not even then."[69] Willingness became opportunity as the Long Parliament capitalized on Charles I's political weakness and began to dismantle the edifice of Laudian episcopacy.[70] Finishing Elizabeth's halfway reformation, or even leveling the English Church to its foundations and building anew along biblical lines, seemed suddenly within reach.

The pent-up desire for reformation was reflected, and to a certain degree promoted by the rhetoric in which the members of the Long Parliament were immersed as they gathered for monthly Fast Day sermons in St Margaret's Church.[71] Edmund Calamy (1600-1666), minister of St Mary Aldermanbury,

---

[67] John Morrill, *The Nature of the English Revolution* (London: Longman, 1993), 5-25; Morrill, "The Coming of War", M. Todd, ed., *Reformation to Revolution*, 143-54.

[68] Morrill, *The Nature*, 270.

[69] Ibid, 270.

[70] John Graham wryly observes that "Back in the 1640s…the unity which all reformers valued was to be more precisely described in terms of a common enemy than it was in terms of a common aspiration." J.K. Graham, "Searches for the New Jerusalem: The History and Mystery of Reformation in Mid-Seventeenth Century England" in *Religion, Resistance, and Civil War*, G.J. Schochet, ed. (Washington, DC: The Folger Institute, 1990), 37.

[71] See Stephen Baskerville, *Not Peace But a Sword: The political theology of the English Revolution* (London: Routledge, 1993). Baskerville's attempt to isolate a puritan "political theology" of revolution wholly misses the point of the many "preachers" he cites as evidence. No mainstream puritans had as the goal of their preaching the kind of "revolution" which Baskerville describes. The term "revolutionary Puritan" (1, 209-11) unhelpfully conflates the godly preachers of the 1630s and 40s with the radical sectarians of the middle to late 1640s whose control of the army and of the rump transformed the intended reformation into a more inclusive political and institutional revolution. The failure to distinguish between the competing factions among the godly wrongly tars puritanism with a political radicalism its leaders would have repudiated. Baskerville confuses the puritans' passionate desire for reformation, pursued through political and religious means, with the intentional attempt to overturn the foundations of English society-monarchy, law and church-the thought of which was abhorrent to puritans, both episcopal and Presbyterian alike. Moreover, Baskerville presents a range of "Puritan preachers" like Perkins, Sibbes, Calamy, Marshall and Owen without regard to their own contexts as though they shared the same perspective and could therefore speak with the same voice. This failure to appreciate the spectrum of "puritan" positions and agendas, even among the "preachers" who regularly addressed the Long Parliament in the 1640s, casts doubt on the validity of his conclusions. And though he states that he

London, saw direct historical continuity with Elizabethan Presbyterian efforts to complete the reformation in his own pulpit manifesto for reformation preached to the gathered members of the House of Commons on 22 December 1641.[72] Calamy preached the imperative of reformation in stark Old Testament terms: "Nationall turning from evill, will divert Nationall judgements, and procure Nationall blessings."[73] Reflecting continuity with the diverted reformational concerns of Perkins and Sibbes, Calamy also acknowledges that this reformation "must be Personall", but he picks up the earlier Presbyterian demand by also insisting that reformation "must be Nationall".[74] Personal reformation will occur when the "wicked" majority acknowledge their sins and change their behavior in repentance. This personal "humiliation" provided the necessary foundation on which the institutional reformation of Church and society could take place, for *"Humiliation without Reformation, is a foundation without a building: Reformation without Humiliation, proves often a building, without a foundation."* Significantly, this metaphor bridges the gap for Calamy between Elizabethan and early Stuart concepts of reformation, for "Both of them together, comprehend the Essentialls of this great duty, which is the very quintessence of Practicall Divinity."[75]

For Calamy, the means to procure this reformation is the thoroughly conventional call for Parliament to send "a faithfull and painfull Ministery thorowout the Kingdome." Possessed by a conviction in the efficacy of godly preaching to promote "Personall Reformation", Calamy observes that "those

---

has "no intention of arguing what William Ames called 'that Machiavellian blasphemy, that religion is nothing but a politic engine'" (7), Baskerville's approach leads him to see the efforts of the puritan preachers as but revolutionary politics hypocritically dressed in religious jargon. By minimizing religion and maximizing politics, Baskerville misreads the puritan *raison d'être*.

[72] Calamy received the BA in 1620 and MA in 1623 from Pembroke Hall, Cambridge. He served as chaplain to Nicolas Felton, Bishop of Ely and became vicar of St Mary's in Swaffam Prior, Cambridgeshire in 1626. He resigned the next year to become a lecturer at Bury St Edmunds, Suffolk, where he remained for ten years. From 1637-39, he served as rector at Rochford, Essex. In October 1639 he was elected to the perpetual curacy of St Mary Aldermanbury in London and became one of the leading figures in the attack on Episcopacy. See E.C. Vernon's 'The Sion College Conclave and London Presbyterianism during the English Revolution' (University of Cambridge PhD thesis, 1999), especially his first chapter, '"Calamy, and the *Junto* that meet at his house": Puritan Networks, the London Clergy and the Outbreak of the English Civil War', 26-71; W.S. Barker, *Puritan Profiles* (Fearne, Scotland: Mentor, 1996), 207-18; *DNB*; Samuel Palmer, *The Nonconformist's Memorial* (1802), I, 76-80; Matthews, *CR*, 97; Richard L. Greaves, *Saints and Rebels: Seven Nonconformists in Stuart England* (Macon, GA: Mercer University Press, 1985), 10.

[73] Edmund Calamy, *Englands Looking-Glasse, Presented in a Sermon Preached before... Commons... December 22, 1641* (1642), 22-23.

[74] Ibid, 39, 44-45.

[75] Ibid, 26.

places...where the least Preachers hath beene, are the greatest enemies to Reformation."[76]   But when Calamy turns to specifics for institutional reformation, his concerns are consistent with those of the earliest puritan agitators, and his focus is squarely on the national church: "Many pollutions have crept into our Doctrine, much defilement into our Worship, many illegall innovations have been obtruded upon us." Moreover, not only are many of the clergy woefully insufficient, but the entire episcopal structure has been tried and found wanting: "the very posts and pillars of this House, many of them are rotten; the stones are loose and uncemented; the House exceedingly divided and distracted with diversity of opinions; the very foundation is ready to shake, and the House to fall down about our ears." The solution was not to waste time remodeling a structurally flawed house, but to rebuild it "according to the pattern in the Mount." For Calamy, it would not be enough "to bring us back...to our *first Reformation* in King *Edwards* dayes". Instead, the time had come "to *reform the Reformation it self.*"[77]

Calamy's reformation was interrupted by the onset of civil war and by the army-led revolution which oversaw the regicide and emptied parliament's already diluted national Presbyterian Church of any pretense to authority.[78] While parliament had overseen the dismantling of most of the offending structures and ceremonies of the Laudian Church, the failure to replace

---

[76] Ibid, 56-57.

[77] Ibid, 46. Calamy pursues a similar theme in another Fast Day sermon preached two months later, *Gods True Mercy to England... In a Sermon Preached before... Commons Feb.23.1641[2]* (1642), 50.

[78] Of 40 English counties (plus London), only 16 plans for the implementation of parliament's Presbyterian settlement were produced. In the end, only London, Lancashire and Essex established functional classical systems and provincial synods, while of the rest, only Suffolk, Middlesex, Shropshire, Somerset, Cheshire and Surrey (and later, Derbyshire and Nottinghamshire) made any attempt to erect a Presbyterian system of the parliamentary model. Counties where plans were produced but were either never approved by Parliament or implemented include Westmorland, Durham, Northumberland, Hampshire, Wiltshire and Yorkshire. See Vernon, 'The Sion College Conclave'; Morrill, *The Nature of the English Revolution*, 156-57; see Bolam and Goring's description of the reactions against Parliamentary Presbyterianism in "Presbyterians in the Parish Church: English Presbyterian Beginnings", in *The English Presbyterians*, C.G. Bolam, J. Goring, H.L. Short and R. Thomas, contributors (London: Allen and Unwin, 1968), 41-45. See also Morrill, "The Impact of Puritanism", John Morrill, ed., *The Impact of the English Civil War* (London: Collins and Brown, 1991), 63; Christopher Hill, *The Century of Revolution, 1603-1714* (London: Thomas Nelson, 1961), 129; Anthony Fletcher, "Oliver Cromwell and the godly nation", J. Morrill, ed., *Oliver Cromwell and the English Revolution* (London: Longman, 1990), 216-28. See also Ann Hughes, *Godly Reformation and its Opponents in Warwickshire, 1640-1662* (Stratford-upon-Avon: The Dugdale Society, 1993), 1-8; W.A. Shaw, *A History of the English Church During the Civil War and Under the Commonwealth 1640-1660,* II (London: Longmans and Company, 1900), 1-174.

episcopacy with an enforceable alternative government brought to a frustrating end the long campaign to oversee a national reformation along Presbyterian lines.[79] Without Presbyterian structures, a Presbyterian-based agenda for national reformation could not be sustained. The resulting vacuum of ecclesiastical authority made the job of godly parish ministers outside the few existing classes very difficult, especially in the face of the rising influence of those with a separatist or sectarian agenda. The fundamental issue of the lack of effective parish discipline remained unaddressed in most parts of the country. This put ministers under great pressure from within their parishes by those who were scandalized by the prospects of sharing communion with unrepentant sinners and grossly ignorant parishioners. Many pastors improvised means to prohibit the scandalous and ignorant from participating in the sacraments, whether by some sort of examination or by suspending communion altogether.[80] Some pastors attempted to appropriate the Separatists' use of adult membership covenants as a means to differentiate between the godly and profane within the parish. But for the vast majority of parish clergy who were appalled by its implications, the luxury of separation was not an option.[81]

Baxter's Kidderminster Reformation

In 1647 Richard Baxter returned to Kidderminster after a five year absence, becoming *de facto* pastor over St Mary's parish just when it was becoming obvious that the long-hoped for Westminster reforms were fatally stuck in the birth. And yet for Baxter, reformation remained a very live issue. As glimpses of his pastoral practise emerge in his earliest writings, *Aphorisms of Justification* (1649), *The Saints Everlasting Rest* (1650), and most profoundly in *Christian Concord* (1653), it becomes increasingly obvious that Baxter was marching to the beat of a different drum. Gone is the emphasis on a legislated religious settlement. Gone is the insistence on discipline through hierarchical church courts. Gone is the insistence on viewing reformation as contingent upon more "godly" preaching. Instead, Baxter's agenda for reformation was

---

[79] See Derek Hirst, "The Failure of National Reformation in the 1650s", G. Schochet, ed., *Religion, Resistance, and Civil War*, 51-61.

[80] Ibid, 54.

[81] See Ralph Josselin, *The Diary of Ralph Josselin*, A. MacFarlane, ed. (Oxford: Clarendon, 1991), 4/25/1647 (92), 6/20/1647 and 6/21/1647 (97), and 2/23/1651 (235-36). Though Josselin does not mention a covenant *per se*, he did organize a meeting where he "invited divers" to "tast their spirits in reference to discipline". See 6/20/1647 (97). See also Alan MacFarlane, *The Family Life of Ralph Josselin: A Seventeenth Century Clergyman* (Cambridge: Cambridge University Press, 1970), 24. On church covenants among separatists, see Nuttall, *Visible Saints: The Congregational Way 1640-1660* (Oxford: Basil Blackwell, 1957), 43-69 (on separation), 75-81 (on covenants), 131-139 (on distinguishing between the prophane and the godly).

local, pastoral and practical. The thrust was overtly evangelistic.[82] The means were a complex of pastoral tasks designed specifically to give pastors the opportunity to confront each parishioner personally with the claims of the gospel. The goal was a converted parish, which thereby enabled it to become a "godly" or reformed parish.

The fullest exposition of Baxter's pastor-led reformation is found in his *Gildas Salvianus* (1656). Arguing that the nation's religious declivities were a direct result of the "pravity of their Guides," Baxter posited that reformation would be effectively furthered, not by legislative fiat, but *"by endeavouring the Reforming of the Leaders of the Church."*[83] With the long-lived Elizabethan impulse to finish the halfly-done reformation itself at a dead end and but halfly-done, Baxter sought to redirect godly zeal for reformation in a pastoral direction: *"Will you shew your faces in a Christian Congregation, as Ministers of the Gospel, and there pray for a Reformation, and...the Conversion and Salvation of your hearers, and the prosperity of the Church: and when you have done, refuse to use the means by which it must be done?"*[84] And though the vision for reformation which Baxter articulates is different in emphasis and means from the failed Parliamentary efforts of the 1640s, he cannily maintains the blessing of "antiquity," the "consent of Reformed Divines," and the appearance of continuity between Kidderminster and the Westminster Assembly itself.[85] Baxter bolstered his case with a rare citation of the 1644 *Directory for the Publique Worship of God*:

> It is the duty of the Minister not only to teach the people committed to his charge in publike, but *Privately* and *Particularly* to admonish, exhort, reprove and comfort them upon all seasonable occasions, so far as his time, strength, and personal safety will permit. He is to admonish them in time of health to prepare for death: And for that purpose, they are often to confer with their Minister about the estate of their souls, *&c. Read this over again and consider it.*[86]

Baxter's attraction to such a statement is significant. The fact that such a pastoral direction was published by the Westminster Assembly indicates the

---

[82] R.S. Paul describes Baxter's controlling pastoral agenda as "the missionary imperative". R.S. Paul, 'Ecclesiology in Richard Baxter's Autobiography', in *From Faith to Faith: Essays in Honor of Donald G. Miller on his Seventieth Birthday*, D.Y. Hadidian, ed. (Pittsburgh, PA: The Pickwick Press, 1979), 383.

[83] Baxter, *Gildas Salvianus*, sig A5.

[84] Ibid., sigs (a7)v-(a8).

[85] Ibid., sig (a7).

[86] Ibid., sig (a7)-(a7)v. See *A Directory for the Publique Worship of God Through out the Three Kingdoms of England, Scotland, and Ireland* (1644) (1980), 26.

survival of a Bucerian pastoral emphasis underneath the rhetoric of the pulpit-centered ideal. However, the fact that such a passage was buried in the direction "Concerning Visitation of the Sicke" demonstrates just how marginal such a pastoral vision had become to the main thrust of puritan reformation. Baxter's reference to this paragraph points us not so much to the source of his pastoral strategy as to his efforts to legitimize his own approach and to move his readers beyond the ineffective reformational rhetoric of the Long Parliament to consideration of a practical strategy that appeared to be producing real results, in Kidderminster at least.

But Baxter's programme for reformation was not simply puritan pastoral business-as-usual, shorn of its Presbyterian pretensions and transposed for play not in the halls of power but in the nation's parishes. Rather, his agenda was of an altogether different order. Baxter appears to have left the puritans' Genevan ideal at its Westminster Assembly dead-end and returned to England's reformation foundations to rebuild a pastoral ministry according to Bucer's pattern found in *De Regno Christi* and *De Vera Animarum Cura*. For all his efforts to maintain continuity between Kidderminster and the puritan past represented by the Assembly, Baxter's starting point was not with the overall Settlement, or with altering doctrine and ceremonies. He began instead with individual pastors, seeking to insure either their conversion or their repentance and thus their reformation into an instrument that God could then use to transform a growing circle of individuals within the parish.[87] Baxter's 'Reformed Pastor' was thus the key to reformed parishioners, reformed parishes, and ultimately a reformed nation. To put it another way, Baxter argues that it will take a *reformation* pastor and strategy to bring about the hoped for personal, parochial and national reformation.

"To be a Bishop or Pastor," summarized Baxter, "is...to be the guide of sinners to salvation."[88] By deliberately equating parish pastors with bishops (and having the freedom for the only time in the Church of England's history to do so), Baxter gave the impression of agreement with the Assembly on the equality of ministers.[89] But by refusing to freight this equality with the disputed system of Presbyterian courts, Baxter opened the door for effective local parish discipline while allowing for a range of views on the most effective theory of church government. Thus freed from the paralyzing debates which doomed the hoped-for Westminster reformation, Baxter was able to devise an evangelistic emphasis which enabled him to remake the English Protestant pastoral inheritance of preaching, sacraments, catechizing, visitation and association

---

[87] Baxter, *Gildas Salvianus*, sig A5.

[88] Ibid., 248.

[89] See *Jus divinum ministerii evangelici* (1654), which Baxter cites with approval in *Gildas Salvianus*, sig (d2)v. See also Baxter's later defense of this view in his *Whether Parish Congregations Be True Christian Churches, and the Capable Consenting Incumbents, be truly their Pastors, or Bishops over their Flocks* (1684).

into a process that actively promoted conversion and parish reformation.[90]

When set side-by-side, Baxter's understanding of reformation bears an uncanny correspondence to that advanced by Bucer a hundred years earlier. Moreover, the pastoral strategies which each designed to further their vision of parochial reformation are almost identical. Even so, the case for Baxter's use of Bucer in devising an alternative strategy for reformation rests solely on these remarkable similarities in their programmes, as nowhere in his published works or his private correspondence during the 1640s and 50s does Baxter mention Bucer in a ministerial context.

Despite the dramatic shift in reformational emphases contained in his work, nowhere does Baxter herald his alternative strategy for reformation as such. In a 1656 letter to Thomas Wadsworth, Baxter allowed himself the boast that 'I see hope of successe that convinceth me, we never hitt the way of pulling downe the Kingdome of the Devill till now.'[91] Baxter assumes his perspective on reformation rather than expounds upon it. As a result, there was little in Baxter's *Reformed Pastor* that his contemporaries would have perceived as

---

[90] Baxter's understanding of conversion has not been adequately explored. His own experience did not fit neatly into existing 'puritan' categories, for he 'could not distinctly trace the workings of the Spirit' on his heart. Nor did he know the 'Time' of his conversion, 'whether sincere Conversion began now, or before, or after, I was never able to this day to know.' *Rel. Bax.*, I, 3, 22. Thus while convinced of its necessity, Baxter remained flexible in how he gauged spiritual response. His own lack of a convincing conversion experience may have contributed to the development of his soteriology, and how the gospel was to be communicated evangelistically, as well as the kind of response that was appropriate to the gospel's offer of forgiveness and new life. As Charles Cohen observes, '[p]uritan religious experience centered around conversion'. Thus to take up this issue here leads us in directions that go far beyond the more modest scope of this study. See Cohen, 'Two Biblical Models of Conversion: An Example of Puritan Hermeneutics', in *CH*, 58:2 (1989), 182. For a further introduction to the small library that has accumulated around the issue of the puritan understanding of conversion, see Norman Pettit, *The Heart Prepared: Grace and Conversion in Puritan Spiritual Life* (New Haven and London: Yale University Press, 1966); David D. Hall, *The Faithful Shepherd: A History of the New England Ministry in the Seventeenth Century* (Chapel Hill, NC: University of North Carolina Press, 1972), 61-66; Patricia Caldwell, *The Puritan conversion narrative: The beginnings of American expression* (Cambridge: Cambridge University Press,1983); Mary Cochran Grimes, 'Saving Grace among Puritans and Quakers: a study of seventeenth- and eighteenth-century conversion experiences', in *QH*, 72 (1983), 3-26. Paul Lim gives the best recent introduction to Baxter's understanding of conversion. See Lim, 'In pursuit of unity, purity and liberty', 24-38. A good place to find out what Baxter himself says on the matter is his *A Treatise on Conversion* (1657) *Directions and Persuasions to a Sound Conversion* (1658). Both are expanded sermon series preached in the midst of his Kidderminster ministry.

[91] DWL, MS 59, BxL ii, 249. See also *Calendar*, no. 290. See also William Lamont, "[Review of] Calendar of the Correspondence of Richard Baxter", in *JURCHS*, 5:1 (1992), 56-58.

novel or controversial, which is why they, and subsequent generations of admirers and historians, simply assumed that he was another, if more successful, *puritan* pastor of the Genevan sort. Even so, conscientious pastors had understood for years, tacitly if not rhetorically, that painful preaching was itself insufficient as an instrument of both conversion and reform.[92] Pastors had long been seeking to supplement their pulpit work with catechizing the young, and some even used catechizing as a means to instruct the more ignorant adults of their parishes.[93] Pastors had also since the 1560s been vexed over the lack of church discipline,[94] and some sought to examine those parishioners who wished to participate in communion. And due to the prevalence of "gross ignorance" and "scandalous livers", some pastors felt it necessary to suspend communion altogether.[95] Moreover, there were many clergy who understood the evangelistic imperative inherent in their call.[96] Nevertheless, the primary model informing Elizabethan and early Stuart pastoral efforts was the reactionary model of the returning Marian exiles which repeatedly expressed itself in opposition to the perceived insufficiencies of the Church of England's discipline and ceremonies, and was betrayed as such again in the 1640s as soon as the Long Parliament lifted the lid of official repression.[97] This "puritan" reformation was informed by the example of Calvin and Beza's Geneva and sought primarily to break away from all things Roman Catholic, establish godly preachers in the nation's pulpits, and enforce a more biblical government and discipline through a nationally legislated settlement. The reformation sought by preachers from Anthony Gilby to Edmund Calamy all but ignored the day to day labors of the faithful parish shepherd, at least in their published rhetoric.[98]

---

[92] See William Harrison's *The Difference of Hearers* (1614), sig A4v-A5; see also George Carlton's description of Bernard Gilpin's ministry in *The Life of Bernard Gilpin* (1629), 19-27.

[93] See Ian Green, *The Christian's ABC*.

[94] There was also concern among Roman Catholic clergy over clerical and lay discipline prior to the beginnings of the English reformation. See Peter Heath, *The English Parish Clergy Prior to the Reformation* (London: Routledge, 1969), 105-34.

[95] See Webster, *Godly Clergy*, 119-21; Stephen Mayor, *The Lord's Supper in Early English Dissent* (London: Epworth Press, 1972). Early in his ministry, Baxter himself scrupled serving communion to an unworthy congregation, see *Aphorisms of Justification* (1649), 251.

[96] See Simon Harward, *Two Godlie and learned Sermons* (1582), CVI-CVI(b).

[97] Jacqueline Eales makes a similar argument in "A Road to Revolution: The Continuity of Puritanism, 1559-1642" in *The Culture of English Puritanism, 1560-1700*, C. Durston and J. Eales, eds. (Basingstoke: MacMillan, 1996), 184-92. Though it was a road that ultimately (and for most puritans, regrettably) led to "revolution", it was a road originally intended by those pushing events in Parliament in the early 1640s to lead to reformation.

[98] Of all the sixteenth- and seventeenth-century treatises and sermons on pastoral ministry, only George Herbert's *A Priest to the Temple* (1652) gives sustained attention

In contrast, the reformation sought by Martin Bucer, and by Richard Baxter after him, saw those day-to-day pastoral duties as the most important part.

It may be that Baxter's silence about Bucer's influence was part of an intentional effort to maintain the semblance of continuity between his puritan predecessors and the his own reconfiguration of Puritan ministry that his return to Bucerian priorities necessitated. His disastrous 1649 foray into theological polemic, *Aphorisms of Justification*, had already made him suspect in the eyes of many English Calvinists.[99] But as we have seen, there survived enough of a Bucerian echo in English pastoral practise, if not rhetoric, to insure that even Calvinists committed to Presbyterian reform who were unhappy with Baxter's theology could still be challenged by his perspective on ministry. Moreover, as we have seen, Baxter's own historiography glossed over the failure of puritan reformation and presented a united 'Puritan' continuum from Cranmer (and therefore Bucer) to himself, as if the eighty-year diversion of Geneva-induced Presbyterian agitation had not existed.[100] Baxter's choice to focus on the antagonism between the 'godly' and the prelates enabled him to avoid mention of the differences between Edwardian and Elizabethan reformational priorities. Ironically, it is possible that Baxter himself may have been unaware of the differences in the way 'reformation' was understood in his own efforts to recount its English history.

Conclusion

In this chapter I have sought to provide a context for Richard Baxter's pastoral ministry within the broader attributes of English Protestant pastoral practise, and I have drawn attention to features of Martin Bucer's understanding of reformation that seem to anticipate Baxter's pastoral breakthrough in the 1650s. I have also observed that, during the intervening century, the understanding of reformation was profoundly affected by the experiences of the returning Marian exiles, and their subsequent reaction to the perceived insufficiencies of

---

to those aspects of pastoral ministry which occupied most of a parish minister's time and attention. See my section on George Herbert in chapter 2 of this work. See also Philip Sheldrake, 'George Herbert and *The Country Parson*'.

[99] See, for example, Christopher Cartwright's animadversions against Baxter's *Aphorisms of Justification* preserved in Baxter's *A Treatise of Justifying Righteousness* (1676). Baxter's account of their exchange is found on sigs A2-A5. See also John Troughton's later critique of Baxter's "Arminianism" in his *Lutherus Redivivus: or The Protestant Doctrine of Justification by Faith onely, Vindicated* (1677), sigs A2v-A3, 6-7. See Tim Cooper's analysis of Baxter's *Aphorisms* in *Fear and Polemic*, 87-121.

[100] In fact, his only comment during his Kidderminster years on the impact of the Assembly's failed reformation is found in a personal aside buried in his "Explication" in *Christian Concord*: "We in this county did seek for authority from the Parliament some years ago for the establishing of the Presbyterian Government; and all our endeavours were frustrate." Baxter, *Christian Concord* (1653), "Explication", 31.

Elizabeth's 1559 Settlement. This reaction to Elizabeth's "halfway reformation" took the discussion about reformation in a direction that was different in both emphasis and means from that which Bucer had previously urged. Influenced in particular by Calvin's reformation of Geneva, this Elizabethan revision of reformation priorities sought through legislated means to rid the church of the remnants of Roman Catholicism and to replace medieval ecclesiastical structures and discipline with those perceived as more biblical. Moreover, the need to evangelize unreformed parishes was addressed by the demand for more and better preachers, the success of whose labors would lead to conversion to Protestantism and usher in the advance of godliness and true piety. However, the uneven results of Protestant preaching and the ultimate frustration of attempts to enforce the Long Parliament's legislated reformation may have made Bucer's alternative vision of a pastor-led reformation both attractive and feasible to Richard Baxter in the aftermath of England's Civil Wars. Even if the absence of direct evidence restrains us from claiming that Baxter's strategy for pastoral ministry was influenced directly by his reading of Martin Bucer, the consonance between their reformational goals and the pastoral means they used to achieve them is remarkable.[101] The fruit of his own attempts to reconfigure his pastoral ministry along what are strikingly Bucerian lines, Richard Baxter's exhortation to his fellow ministers in his *Gildas Salvianus* succeeded in reconnecting England's 'Puritan' pastors with their Edwardian heritage.

---

[101] 'Consonance' is a helpful word in this context, and I am grateful for the suggestions of John Morrill to this end. See 'Foreword', xiv.

CHAPTER 4

Baxter's *Gildas Salvianus* (1656) and the Reformation of Parish Ministers

Richard Baxter's *Gildas Salvianus; The Reformed Pastor*, published late in the summer of 1656, was not a conventional book on pastoral ministry. Part scathing indictment of pastoral failures and confession of pastoral sins, part exhortation to pastoral duty and explication of pastoral strategy, part sermon, part treatise, and part breathless face-to-face imploration, *Gildas Salvianus* introduced a conception of parish ministry, progressively tested by Baxter in Kidderminster and tried in surrounding Worcestershire parishes, the effect of which challenged British clergy not simply to try harder, but to reconfigure their practise of pastoral ministry. Hailed as a pastoral genius by his colleagues, Baxter nevertheless offered a strategy bearing a remarkable resemblance to that which the Strasbourg reformer Martin Bucer recommended to the leaders of the Edwardian reformation more than a century before. The purposes of this chapter, therefore, are to understand *Gildas Salvianus* within the wider context of Baxter's ministry in Kidderminster and explore his conviction that his experience could furnish the model for the wider reformation of the English Church. Moreover, this chapter will examine evidence that suggests that Baxter's own pastoral practise may have been decisively influenced by Martin Bucer's writings on ministry and reformation.

Gildas Salvianus did not appear in a vacuum. For all the talk of reformation emanating from the Long Parliament and Westminster Assembly in the 1640s, reforming zeal that might have been channeled into rethinking local pastoral practise was quickly siphoned off into the unworking of Laudian sacramental emphases and the episcopal structures which had been used to enforce them. There was also endless wrangling over what ecclesiastical arrangement should take over from the dismantled episcopal Church of England. Moreover, with the constraining lid of Laudian uniformity removed, all manner of church-related concerns clamored for redress, from the need for relief from the non-preaching ministries of inadequate or scandalous ministers, to keeping the unworthy from church communion, and inhibiting the proliferation the sects. While the Long Parliament's efforts to reform the English Church attempted traditional top-down means to enact and enforce a uniform religious settlement, Baxter seems to have recognized early on the implications of their failure to produce a workable national plan. His response was to focus on *parish* reformation rather than on a monolithic national reformation.[1] In the absence of an authoritative national settlement, it was the one time in early modern England when a local and decentralized pastoral agenda for parish reformation such as Baxter's was actually feasible.

But *Gildas Salvianus* was also much more than an attempt on Baxter's part to add his bit to the national debate. It was the culmination of a sequence of pastoral initiatives, beginning as early as his return to Kidderminster in 1647, each of which will be explored more fully in chapters 5, 6 and 7.[2] Having touched on the desperate need for a workable system of church discipline in his *Aphorisms of Justification* (1649), and having already introduced the wider reading public to his concerns for godly ministry, and specifically the need for house to house pastoral oversight, through the dedicatory epistle of his very popular *The Saints Everlasting Rest* (1650), Baxter again attempted to influence the disordered state of the Cromwellian Church by publishing the founding articles of the Worcestershire Association along with his apology for them in *Christian Concord* (1653).[3] By doing so, Baxter used his own example and that of his colleagues to raise again the issue of church discipline. Moreover, Baxter proposed the establishment of voluntary ministerial associations as the means to bypass the stalemate over church government which had remained unresolved following the army's takeover in 1647. With each of these initiatives, Baxter sought to fill the vacuum of spiritual authority left by a banished episcopacy and the failed Presbyterian alternative.

As his own pastoral initiatives took hold in Kidderminster and began to produce results, Baxter found it increasingly difficult to resist taking every opportunity to advance both his diagnoses of the failings of parish ministry, and his prescriptions for its reformation. For reasons that we shall explore later, he never once doubted that his own experience in Kidderminster had significance for conscientious ministerial colleagues struggling in parishes across England. His experience within the Worcestershire Association and the encouraging

---

[1] Baxter, *Christian Concord* (1653), 'Explication', 31. See also *Rel. Bax.*, II, §28, 148.

[2] In 1658, Baxter published *Confirmation and Restauration, The necessary means of Reformation and Reconciliation*, which returns to the vexing issues surrounding parish discipline and seeks to reclaim confirmation as a means to enable parishioners to become full participants in church communion. As such, Baxter's ideas do not represent a new development, but a further refining of the processes he had already initiated to help the 'grossly ignorant' understand and practice their faith. Although covering much of the same descriptive ground as *Gildas Salvianus* and in some sense its sequel, *Confirmation and Restauration* failed to achieve the impact generated by *Gildas Salvianus*, perhaps on account of being simply lost in the torrent of works pouring from Baxter's pen.

[3] For an overview of the Church during Cromwell's Protectorate, see J.M. Murphy, 'Oliver Cromwell's Church: State and Clergy During the Protectorate' (University of Wisconsin PhD thesis, 1997).

feedback he received there served only to strengthen this conviction.

These pastoral concerns spilled over into each of his seven works published in 1655. In the two assize sermons which he preached in Worcester and published as *True Christianity*, Baxter uncovered the hypocrisy of those who claim to be devoted to God and yet 'despise his Ministers, reject his Word, abhor Reformation, scorn at Church-Government', with the uncolored warning, 'Your salvation will be such as your Christianity is.'[4] In a sermon preached in London in 1654 and published as *Making Light of Christ and Salvation*, Baxter took the lack of concern with parish reformation and purity as a symptom of the absence of a true work of Christ. His published discourse, *A Sermon of Judgement*, preached in London at St Paul's in December 1654, is prefaced by an impassioned plea to the Lord Mayor Christopher Pack to throw the support of the magistrate behind the beleaguered attempts by preachers to initiate effective church discipline.[5] In the tract *The Quakers Catechism*, Baxter begins by flaying 'the Separatists and Anabaptists in England' for their monstrous sin of separating from their parish churches, claiming that the proliferation of sects like the Quakers are evidence of God's judgment against separation.[6] In *Richard Baxter's Confession of his Faith*, written to draw a line under the six years of controversy generated by his *Aphorisms of Justification*, he provides a succinct analysis of the failings of England's ministers and offers his own example as a means to reformation.[7] Even in his groundbreaking apologetic treatise *The Unreasonableness of Infidelity*, Baxter inevitably digresses to give what he takes to be the Biblical basis informing submission to pastoral ministry.[8]

Seen in this light, *Gildas Salvianus* is the zenith of a ten-year effort to effect the conversion and reformation of his parish transposed to a national congregation of fellow pastors. It is hindsight, however, that views *Gildas Salvianus* as the apex of Baxter's ministry. As we shall see, the decision to publish was not so much part of a greater strategy to call the English clergy to account as the *ad hoc* opportunity to publish a fast day sermon, which then grew in Baxter's mind as he reworked it for publication into something more significant.

At some point during the autumn or early winter of 1654, in the midst of his prodigious schedule, Baxter decided to make what was to be the most significant improvisation of his pastoral strategy—a commitment to meet with

---

[4] Baxter, *True Christianity* (1655), 54-55, 153.

[5] Baxter, *Making Light of Christ and Salvation* (1655), 28; *A Sermon of Judgement* (1655), sigs A7-A10v. Christopher Pack was himself a Presbyterian lay elder.

[6] Baxter, *The Quakers Catechism* (1655), sigs A4v-Dv.

[7] Baxter, *Richard Baxter's Confession of his Faith* (1655), sigs (b)-(b3)v.

[8] Baxter, *The Unreasonableness of Infidelity* (1655), 'The Second Part', 150-152. See also his pamphlet, *Humble Advice...Offered to Many honourable members of Parliament* (1655).

and catechize every family in his parish. It was a decision he long resisted.[9] But once the decision was taken, the process of organizing the parish for what became a massive administrative undertaking proceeded apace.

Baxter states that first he 'breifly explained to the reasons of our undertakinge in the open Congregation, & reade them over the Agreement, Exhortation & Catechism [*The Agreement of Divers Ministers* (1656)]'. Then he preached for several Sundays 'from Heb. 5.11.12.' on the necessity and benefits of personal oversight and instruction. After procuring catechisms for each household, Baxter sent his assistant Richard Sargent and one of the deacons to deliver the copies of *The Agreement* personally to every family in the parish, using the opportunity for more direct conversation this afforded to persuade further those who were reluctant to participate.[10] After giving families six weeks to learn the catechism, 'the Clark goeth a week before to every family to tell them when to come'.[11] At the appointed hour, a family would come to Baxter's house (later, after he was trained, Baxter's assistant Richard Sargent would visit the homes of parishioners who lived outside Kidderminster), at which time 'they recited the Catechism to us'. 'After that I first helpt them to understand it, and next enquired modestly into the State of their Souls, and lastly, endeavoured to set all home to the convincing, awakening, and resolving of their Hearts'. Each family was given an hour's time, and the effort cost Baxter 'the Labour of a Sermon'.[12]

Baxter would later write in his *Reliquiae Baxterianae*, 'Of all the Works that I ever attempted, this yielded me most Comfort in the Practice of it.'[13] And though one hesitates to accept uncritically Baxter's estimation of the success that met his efforts, the fact that his Worcestershire Association colleagues were willing to commit themselves to the same rigorous practise within months of his own initial efforts indicates a consensus that Baxter's report of impressive initial results warranted a wider trial of his method. By late winter of 1655, personal oversight and instruction were at the top of the Worcestershire Association's agenda: 'I propounded the Business to the Ministers, and they all (upon Debate) consented that I should turn our brief Confession into a Catechism, and draw up a Form of Agreement for the Practicing of that Duty'. Accordingly, Baxter 'drew up the Catechism in Two

---

[9] *Gildas Salvianus*, sig (a6)v. See chapter 7 for a full account of Baxter's concerns.

[10] Baxter's letter to Thomas Wadsworth, the rector of Newington Butts, Surrey, in late January 1656, DWL MS 59, BxL ii: 249; also *Calendar*, nos. 290, 202.

[11] *Gildas Salvianus*, sig (a7).

[12] *Rel. Bax.*, II, §41, 179-180. Baxter gives differing estimates of the numbers of families he and Sargent were able to see in a given week. In his letter to Wadsworth (*Calendar*, no. 290) he states that he himself met with six families each week. In *Gildas Salvianus*, he states that the total is 'about 15 or 16 families a week' (sigs (a6)v-(a7). In *Rel. Bax.*, Baxter states that he and Sargent 'took fourteen Families every Week' (II, §41, 179).

[13] *Rel. Bax.*, II, §41, 179; *Gildas Salvianus*, Sigs (b2)- (b2)v.

leaves in 8*vo.* comprehending as much as is *necessary to be believed, consented to* and *practised*; in as narrow a room and just a Method as I thought agreeable to the Peoples Understandings'.[14] When he presented both the catechism and the agreement to the association in May, 58 ministers subscribed.[15]

Baxter records that his colleagues 'judged it unmeet to enter upon the work, without a solemn humbling of their souls before the Lord, for their long neglect of so great and necessary a duty'. Organizing a day of fasting, humiliation and prayer to be held on 4 December 1655 in Worcester, the Association asked Baxter if he would preach, and thereby lead them in the inauguration of the work. *'In answer to their desires I prepared the following Discourse; which...proved longer then could be delivered in one or two Sermons.'* But on the appointed day, Baxter was incapacitated *'by the increase of my ordinary pain and weakness'*, and was unable to make the journey to Worcester. *'To recompence which unwilling omission, I easily yielded to the requests of divers of the Brethren, forthwith to publish the things which I had prepared, that they might* see *that which they could not* hear.'[16] By Christmas 1655, Baxter had finished 480 pages of expanded sermon, and by 15 April 1656, added a further 76 pages of prefatory letters.[17] By August, he was receiving the first letters written by ministers who had just read the newly published work and were writing to express their gratitude.[18]

Gildas Salvianus: **The Prefatory Letters**

Baxter undertakes in his prefatory letter 'To my Reverend and Dearly beloved Brethren, the faithful Ministers of Christ, in *Brittain* and *Ireland*', to urge the implementation of the three main elements of the pastoral strategy he had put into practise in Kidderminster. The 'first and main matter' of Baxter's appeal is for 'the generality of Ministers in these three Nations, to set themselves presently to the Work of Catechizing, and Personal Instructing all...who will be persuaded to submit thereunto'.[19] For more than fifteen months, Baxter's energies had been poured into establishing the programme of personal catechizing, and promoting it amongst his colleagues in the Association. Though he had found it to be the single most effective aspect of his ministry, Baxter was quick to acknowledge that catechizing would not be sufficient of

---

[14] *Rel. Bax.*, II, §40, 179.

[15] [Baxter], *The Agreement of Divers Ministers of Christ In the County of Worcester...For Catechizing or Personal Instructing* (1656), 4-15. The 'Exhortation to all our Parishioners' (17-33) is dated 'May 4th 1655'.

[16] *Gildas Salvianus*, sig A2v.

[17] The date on Baxter's final page of text is 'Decemb. 25. 1655'. *Gildas Salvianus*, 480.

[18] See letters from Stephen Streete, rector of Buxted, Sussex, and Samuel Corbyn, Conduct of Trinity College, Cambridge: *Calendar*, nos. 320 and 321.

[19] *Gildas Salvianus*, sig (a4).

itself to bring about the desired reformation of a parish. Baxter's second request, therefore, urged the nation's ministers 'unanimously [to] set themselves to the practice of those parts of Christian Discipline, which are unquestionably necessary, and part of their work.'[20]   The lack of effective church discipline in the nation's parishes had, from Baxter's perspective, been responsible for providing separatists with a pretext for dividing parishes to form their own congregations of the visibly godly. This breakdown had opened the floodgates allowing for all manner of heterodox sects to proliferate, further threatening to upend the ministry of godly pastors in parish churches.

Baxter's third request is that 'all the faithful Ministers of Christ would without any more delay Unite and Associate for the furtherance of each other in the work of the Lord, and the maintaining of Unity and Concord in his Churches.'[21] Baxter saw that a local context of ministerial cooperation and encouragement was an essential prerequisite if the reformation of ministry was to take hold and produce the intended local reformation.[22]

Though Baxter's main thrust was to outline his pastoral strategy, the sheer force of his rhetoric reveals that his fundamental concern was to argue that the reformation of the English Church could begin only with the reformation of her ministers: 'Too many that have set their hand to this sacred work, do so obstinately proceed in Self-seeking, Negligence, Pride, Division, and other sins, that it is become our necessary duty to admonish them.'[23] As self-appointed 'monitor' of the clergy, Baxter found correspondence with the similarly direct indictment of pastoral sins from the early Christian writers Salvian and Gildas, from whom he drew inspiration: 'The Title of the Book it self is Apologetical', for by using their names 'I offer you an excuse for plain dealing.'[24]

---

[20] Ibid., sig (b2)v. See chapter 5 below for a full description of Baxter's practise of 'Christian Discipline'.

[21] Ibid., sig (c)v. See chapter 6 below for a discussion of the origins of Baxter's Worcestershire Association.

[22] Each of these three aspects of Baxter's pastoral strategy will be examined more closely in subsequent chapters.

[23] *Gildas Salvianus*, sigs A5, A4v. This of course, places Baxter firmly in the long line of both Protestant and Catholic clergy concerned to improve the quality of England's shepherds traced in chapter 2.

[24] Ibid., sig (a3v). See C.D. Gilbert, '"Repent O England": Richard Baxter as Gildas Salvianus', in *BNS*, 5:1 (1996), 3-10. For Salvian (c.400-c.470), born near Cologne and later presbyter of Marseilles, see *The Writings of Salvian, the Presbyter*, J.F. O'Sullivan, tr. (New York: Cima Publishing Company, 1947); Salvian, *A Treatise of God's Government and of the justice of his present dispensations in this world*, 1700; G.W. Olsen, 'Reform after the Pattern of the Primitive Church in the Thought of Salvian of Marseilles', *CHR*, 68 (1982), 1-12. Of the British monk and historian Gildas (6th century), Baxter writes in his *Christian Directory*: 'Gildas...is called Sapiens, and our eldest writer; and yet he calleth the multitude of the lewd British clergy whom he reprehendeth in his "Acris Correptio," traitors and no priests; and concludeth seriously,

Most telling for our purposes are the reasons Baxter gives for his exposé of ministerial sins, for they go far to explain his own rationale for drafting such a sermon, as well as his decision to go further and prepare it for a wider audience through publication. His first reason was his fear of a Catholic conspiracy to use the divisions and scandals of Protestant ministry as a pretext for undermining Protestantism in England.[25] In this light, Baxter viewed the Quakers as Catholic plants whose purpose was to sow confusion and undermine the authority of Protestant pastoral leadership. The best way to neutralize their effect was through a public confession of ministerial sins and subsequent repentance. *'What is it but our sins that is the strength of all these enemies?...* *The tongues of Quakers, and Papists...are all at work to proclaim our sins, because we will not confess them ourselves'.*[26]

The second reason pushing Baxter to publish his call to repentance was his fear that the recent parliamentary attempts to 'overthrow' (disestablish) the ministry were but the first pangs of God's judgment against the sins of the ministry. *'Hath it not been put to the Vote in...Parliament...whether the whole frame of the stablished Ministry, and its legal maintenance should be taken down? and were we not put to plead our Title to that maintenance, as if we had been falling into the hands of Turks'?*[27] The very fact that there were *'swarms of Railers at the Ministry'* should force ministers to remove everything in their lives or performance of duty which might cause scandal in the eyes of God and humanity. Leveling a sobering challenge to his colleagues, Baxter admonishes, *'I think it is no time now to stand upon our credit, so far as to neglect our duty, and befriend our sins, and so provoke the Lord against us. It rather beseems us...to confess our transgressions, and to resolve upon a speedy and through reformation, before wrath break out upon us, which will leave us no remedy'.*[28]

However distressing such shortcomings might be, chief in Baxter's mind was the unpardonable setback such lack of ministerial repentance caused to the Church's evangelistic task. For the 'welfare of the Church and the saving of mens souls' was contingent upon the 'faithful endeavours' of devoted ministers, and for individual ministers to be negligent themselves, 'or silently to

---

that he that calleth them priests, is not...any excellent christian. Yet those few that were pious he excepteth and commendeth.' (From the 1846 edition of *A Christian Directory* [1673], rpr. Morgan, PA: Soli Deo Gloria, 1996), 634b. For Gildas, see his history *De Excidio et Conquestu Britanniae*; Michael Winterbottom, ed., *Gildas: The Ruin of Britain and Other Works* (London: Philmore, 1978); T.D. O'Sullivan, *The De Excidio of Gildas: Its Authenticity and Date* (Leiden: Brill, 1978); Michael Lapidge and David Dumville, *Gildas: New Approaches* (Woodbridge, Suffolk: The Boydell Press, 1984).

[25] *Gildas Salvianus*, sig A3v.

[26] Ibid., sig A3v.

[27] Ibid., sig A3v, (c7)-(c7)v. For the Barebone's Parliament debates on the maintenance of tithes in the summer of 1653 see Austin Woolrych, *Commonwealth to Protectorate* (Oxford: Clarendon, 1982), 235-250; Hill, *The Century of Revolution*, 135, 164.

[28] *Gildas Salvianus*, sig A4.

connive at, and comply with the negligent', the evangelistic purpose to which God had called them would be frustrated.[29] Though all the previous reasons cited certainly formed part of the pretext behind *Gildas Salvianus*, by raising the issue of parochial evangelism Baxter introduces the key for understanding both his primary purpose in writing as well as the passion with which it is written. Curiously, Baxter never directly explains this purpose, apparently considering it obvious to the reader, just as he leaves the nature of conversion unexplained here as well. However underdefined by Baxter though, as we shall see evangelism is by far the most significant purpose informing his pastoral vision. Moreover, it is this aim which sets him as a pastor and *Gildas Salvianus* as a treatise on pastoral ministry apart from almost anything else the English Church had seen since the fervent Protestants of the Edwardian reformation. Baxter was utterly persuaded that the pastor's primary task was evangelistic in nature, and that failure at this point meant the shipwreck of God's purposes for the Church and eternal disaster for untold thousands of souls. It was one thing to foil Catholic conspiracies or frustrate the sectaries' designs to demolish effective parish ministry, but in bringing *Gildas Salvianus* to press, Baxter's ultimate passion was to facilitate the salvation of men and women, and pastors were God's chosen means to be their 'Guides' into the promised land.[30] Compelled by the logic of both the need of the people and the nature of his pastoral call, Baxter devised a strategy that could advance his mission within the particular constraints of 1650s Kidderminster. This inescapable logic provides the clearest explanation of the motives and energy behind Baxter's pastoral efforts, and thus behind his motivation to write these letters and sermons and put them into print. The 480 pages of text which follow are simply Baxter's attempt to explain the implications thereof.

Gildas Salvianus: The Book

The opening pages of *Gildas Salvianus* betray its origin as a sermon. And the book's slapdash organization has long been recognized as its primary weakness as a literary effort. In 1766, Samuel Palmer complained that Baxter's style 'is remarkably diffuse: the method is surprisingly perplexed; the same thoughts... being often repeated'. As a result, according to Palmer, the book was rendered 'much more tedious and disagreeable, and consequently much less useful, than otherwise it might have been.'[31] But Palmer's abridgment proved just as unsatisfactory to later readers. Correcting Baxter's style neutered Baxter's impact. William Brown complained, 'we would...greatly prefer the work in its original form, with all its faults, to the abridgment of it by Palmer: if the latter

---

[29] Ibid., sig A5.
[30] Ibid., sigs A5v, (d)v.
[31] Samuel Palmer, 'The Preface', in Baxter, *The Reformed Pastor; A Discourse on the Pastoral Office*, abridged by Samuel Palmer (1766), ix.

was freed from many of its defects, it also lost much of its excellence.'[32] Because the text reads much more like an impassioned conversation, written in the heat of a particular moment, than a properly disciplined treatise, its impact is more immediate than cumulative. And as a sermon whose original intention was more to provoke repentance than to discourse learnedly on pastoral ministry, this was surely as Baxter intended.[33] Nevertheless, the impulse by later admirers to edit Baxter and thereby make him more accessible to contemporary readers (and applicable to contemporary agendas) has served rather to distance him and his work from their original contexts.[34]

Gildas Salvianus takes as its starting point the biblical text, Acts 20:28: 'Take heed therefore to yourselves, and to all the flock over which the Holy Ghost hath made you Overseers, to feed the Church of God, which he hath purchased with his own blood.'[35] Baxter' outline is clear enough, endeavoring first to define what the Apostle Paul means when he uses the term 'Overseer', which he considers synonymous with 'Pastor' and 'Bishop'. He then sets out to explain 'what it is to Take heed to ourselves, and wherein it must be done', as well as giving 'some brief Reasons' in support. Next, 'I shall show you, What it is to Take heed to all the Flock in our Pastoral Work, and wherein it must be done.' In conclusion, Baxter proposes to 'make some Application of all'.[36]

With his opening definitions of 'overseer' and 'church', Baxter entered into the heart of contentious debate on church government which he traced to divisions amongst the exiled Protestant community during the Mary's reign.[37] While an overview of the debate is beyond the scope of this chapter, Baxter was characteristically unhappy with aspects of each of the major ecclesiological positions, be it Laudian prelacy, Presbyterianism, Independency or separatism. His own pastoral experience had demonstrated to him the need for local parish pastors to be given the same authority for discipline as had previously been the prerogative of the episcopate alone. In effect, he was arguing that local parish pastors corresponded to the 'bishops' or 'overseers' mentioned in the New Testament. In Baxter's view, the inherited system of bishops, each of whom

---

[32] William Brown, 'Preface', in Baxter, *The Reformed Pastor*, W. Brown, ed. (1829), 63. His own abridgment of *Gildas Salvianus* reached five editions and is still in print. The fifth edition was published in 1862.

[33] Baxter, *Gildas Salvianus*, 92.

[34] For an example of this tendency, see in the Bibliography the many English editions of *Gildas Salvianus* which have appeared since Baxter's death.

[35] Baxter's version slightly varies from the 1611 Authorized Version (Baxter: 'overwhich'; AV: 'over the which'), as well as with the 1602 Geneva Bible (Baxter: 'overwhich'; GB: 'whereof'). The difference may be explained by the fact that Baxter may have refined his own translation, or that he preferred to rephrase either 'over the which' or 'whereof' with the stronger 'overwhich', adding further weight to his view of the pastor's position of authority over the parish.

[36] Baxter, *Gildas Salvianus*, 12.

[37] Ibid., 150, 161.

had oversight of hundreds of parishes, made church discipline as he understood it unpracticeable. Baxter was aware of similar views in Archbishop James Ussher's proposals for a modified episcopacy.[38] However, rather than citing Ussher, he preferred to base his argument on his interpretation of the text. By equating the Ephesian elders, who are the objects of the apostle's exhortation in the text, with both pastors and bishops, the biblical foundation for his own revision of the parish minister's task was laid. The power of the keys (discipline and excommunication) and of ordination previously reserved for diocesan prelates were, according to Baxter's exegesis, the province of every parish minister. Moreover, Baxter claimed that the pastoral oversight envisaged by Paul was not titular or administrative, but functional and personal. This reading lead Baxter to argue that local parishes or churches 'should be no greater then the Pastors can personally over-see, so that they may *Take heed to all the Flock'*. The church is thus defined as existing primarily locally: 'that particular society of Christians of which these Bishops or Elders have charge, associated for personal Communion in Gods publike worship, and for other mutual assistances in the way to Salvation.'[39]

Unlike the separatists who preferred to redraw the spiritual map by segregating the serious Christians from the unholy mix of the parish, Baxter chose to work with the parish system as it was. The resulting dilemma of how a mixed field like an English parish could be a true church drove him to find a way to preserve the inclusiveness of the national church and its parochial structure while maintaining the integrity of its gospel and ordinances. Baxter's goal of national reformation was essentially the same as that of previous generations of 'godly' clergy. However, his primary means were not reformed structures or ceremonies, but rather the personal reformation of individual pastors, the reconfiguration of parish ministry along evangelistic lines, and the resulting conversion of parishioners that inevitably followed.[40] Having laid the

---

[38] See Baxter's own discussion of the issues of church government, and the explanation of his own preference for 'primitive episcopacy' in the third of his *Five Disputations of Church-government and Worship* (1659). See also James Ussher, *The Reduction of Episcopacie unto the Form of Synodical Government received in the Antient Church* (1656). For a discussion of Ussher's views, see R.B. Knox, *James Ussher: Archbishop of Armaugh* (Cardiff: University of Wales Press, 1967), 128, 140-145; Michael Mendle, 'Untimely Compromises: Moderate Proposals for Church Government in 1641', in *Conference on Puritanism*, S. Bercovitch, *et al* (London: n.p., 1975), 1-27; D.S. Hopkirk, 'The Reduction: Archbishop Ussher's Historic Effort in Accommodation', in *RTR*, 11 (1952), 61-71. For further discussion of Baxter's views, see N.H. Keeble, *Richard Baxter*, 27, 190; Nuttall, *Richard Baxter,* 80-81, 86-87; Irvonwy Morgan, *The Nonconformity of Richard Baxter,* 117-143; A.H. Wood, *Church Unity Without Uniformity: a study of seventeenth century English church movements and of Richard Baxter's proposals for a comprehensive church* (London: Epworth Press, 1963).

[39] Baxter, *Gildas Salvianus*, 9, 10, 13.

[40] Ibid., 387, 413-414.

biblical foundations, his goal in the remainder of this treatise is to provoke ministerial reformation and to advocate the most effective means reformed pastors can then use to spur reformation in their parishes.

The Pastor's Task

'The Pleasing of God, and the Salvation of our People' were, for Baxter, the two great ends of the pastor's call. But in practise these ends were too often frustrated by hypocrisy, complacency and the absence of a relationship with and commitment to God. Fundamentally, Baxter felt that any clergyman 'that is not himself taken up with the predominant love of God, and is not himself devoted to him... [or is] not addicted to the pleasing of God, and maketh him not the Center of all his actions... that man that is not a sincere Christian himself, is utterly unfit to be a Pastor of a Church'. Moreover, pastors who themselves had no experiential knowledge of the salvation they proclaimed, and whose examples contradicted rather than confirmed their teaching were not only themselves in danger of condemnation, but were a curse to those under their care. In light of their calling and privileges, pastoral apathy was incomprehensible. Not only did pastors 'have a Heaven to win or lose', but 'the souls of your hearers, and the success of all your labours' hang in the balance. Indeed, such heavenly-mindedness was a pastoral imperative, for 'no man is fit to be a Pastor...that doth not set his heart on the life to come.... For he will never set his heart on the work of mens salvation, that doth not heartily believe and value that salvation.'[41]

After exhorting his fellow pastors to examine their fitness for their calling, his next concern is to establish the scope of the pastor's charge. For Baxter, it is not enough for a pastor to preach regularly to the gathered parish, or to be merely available to everyone within a certain geographical boundary. His text mandates care over *all* the flock, which he takes as meaning particular care over every member: *'We should know every person that belongeth to our charge.* For how can we take heed to them, if we do not know them?' But he qualifies the extent of the pastor's charge, as he did in *Christian Concord* (1653), to include only those who consent to his oversight and own the responsibilities and rights of church membership.[42] And though he acknowledges that such oversight would be difficult in large parishes, especially without the help of an assistant, the implications of the text are, for him, inescapable.

Upon clarifying the issue of parochial oversight, Baxter summarizes a pastor's duties. Though thirty pages later he protests that 'I intend no such thing

---

[41] Ibid., 57, 55, 25, 38, 56.

[42] Ibid., 60, 61. This key aspect of Baxter's understanding of church membership and discipline is touched on only in passing here, though he picks up and more thoroughly develops the theme again on 95-115, 155-56, 213-221.

as a Directory for the whole Ministerial Work', his methodical list furnishes the
most developed exposition yet of his understanding not just of a pastor's duties
but of his sense of pastoral priorities as well.[43] Rather than provide a list of
duties, however, he begins first by describing the kinds of people each parish
will contain and the relative priority of their pastoral needs.[44]

Corresponding to the primary evangelistic thrust of a pastor's call, Baxter
finds that the primary pastoral need confronting parish clergy 'lyeth *in bringing
unsound Professors of the faith to sincerity*'.[45] As Eamon Duffy observes, 'the
parish was indeed mission territory'.[46] 'The work of conversion', urged Baxter,
'is the great thing that we must first drive at, and labour with all our might to
effect.' Moreover, he confesses that this 'lamentable necessity of the
unconverted' has forced him 'frequently to neglect that which should tend to
the further increase of knowledge in the godly'. But 'who is able to talk of
Controversies or nice unnecessary points...how excellent so ever, while he
seeth a company of ignorant, carnal, miserable sinners before his face, that
must be chang'd or damn'd?'[47] As we shall further explore in section II, the
driving purpose behind each aspect of Baxter's reconfiguration of pastoral
ministry is to facilitate the conversion of the unconverted majority within the
parish.

Only when the pastor is satisfied that he has done what he can for the
conversion of the unconverted under his care can he turn his attention to the
needs of those who are truly Christian. These he divides into six categories.
Some are 'young and weak' and 'of small proficiency or strength'. Some
'labour under some particular distemper, that keeps under their graces, and
maketh them temptations and troubles to others... [and are] addicted to
Pride...worldliness... frowardness... disturbing passions....' Others are
'Declining Christians, that are either fallen into some scandalous sin, or else
abate their zeal and diligence and shew us that they have lost their former
Love'. Some have 'fallen under some great Temptation'. Still others have
become depressed and have need for their pastor to 'settle the Peace' of their
souls. The rest of the pastor's work must be directed to 'those that are yet
strong: For they also have need of our assistance'.[48]

Baxter presents a catalogue of means to enable pastors to address their
parishioners in their varied circumstances. First is the 'publike preaching of the

---

[43] Ibid., 92. Baxter's overview begins on page 68 and continues through 116.

[44] Baxter provides a similar list of twelve categories in describing the makeup of his own
parish, though for a different purpose, in *Confirmation and Restauration* (1658), 157-
165. See Eamon Duffy's 'The Godly and the Multitude in Stuart England', in *SC*, 1
(1986), 38-40.

[45] Baxter, *Gildas Salvianus*, 68.

[46] Duffy, 'The Long Reformation', N. Tyacke, ed., *England's Long Reformation*, 49.

[47] Baxter, *Gildas Salvianus*, 68, 70.

[48] Ibid., 71-77.

word', which, for Baxter, is 'the most excellent, because it tendeth to work on many'.[49] Secondly, the pastor must 'administer the holy mysteries...Baptism and the Lords Supper'.[50] Thirdly, pastors must lead public worship.[51] Fourthly, pastors must take 'special care and oversight of each member of the Flock'.[52] Fifthly, pastors are to counter the spread of false teaching and hinder the success of false teachers. Sixthly, pastors are to encourage those who are strong and growing in their faith, that they may provide helpful examples to the rest of the flock. Seventhly, pastors should give deliberate care to the sick and dying, 'helping them to prepare either for a fruitful life or a happy death.'[53] Eighthly, pastors should resolve cases of troubled consciences. Ninthly, pastors should admonish the impenitent.[54] Lastly, pastors should oversee the formal use of church discipline.[55]

Catechizing and Personal Instructing

After breaking the flow of his discussion to return to his original purpose for the sermon, which was 'to humble our souls before the Lord',[56] Baxter

---

[49] Ibid., 78.

[50] Ibid., 80.

[51] 'Me thinks, the solemn Praises of God should take up much more of the Lords day then in most places they do.' Ibid., 80-81.

[52] Ibid., 81-86. Keeble calls this aspect of Baxter's practise 'the distinctive mark of the Kidderminster ministry'. See *Richard Baxter*, 82-85.

[53] Baxter, *Gildas Salvianus*, 87, 88-94. Baxter here goes into surprising detail, giving explicit directions of how to approach and counsel those in extremity.

[54] Ibid., 94.

[55] Ibid., 95-115. Baxter concludes his overview with the observation that 'from what hath been said, we may see that the Pastoral office is another kind of thing then those men have taken it to be, who think that it consisteth in preaching and administering the Sacraments only', 115.

[56] For Baxter, the three great sins afflicting the nation's godly clergy were pride, the *'undervaluing the Unity and Peace of the whole Church'*, and most of all, a corporate unwillingness to 'seriously, unreservedly and industriously, lay out ourselves in the work of the Lord' (Ibid., 168, 183, 208). This third sin was evidenced by laziness in studies and preparation (208-09), dull and 'drowsie' preaching (211), the neglect of 'acknowledged duties', particularly the 'business of discipline' (213, 217), and *'the Prevalency of worldly fleshely interests too much against the Interest and work of Christ'* (234). The result of these pastoral sins could be seen in the fragmentation of the godly into competing sects as well as the increase in 'common prophaness' (244). Earlier, in a remarkable digression, Baxter retells the history of the English reformation and casts the resulting divisions among English Protestants as an example of the ongoing opposition to God's purposes for his Church. Though the sins of England's committed Protestant pastors have contributed to the continuous frustration of further reformation in England, Baxter makes it clear that the real culpability lay with those of the 'Prelatical Party' who have consistently set themselves against God's word and

relaunches without pause into the task of persuading his ministerial audience of the usefulness, indeed the necessity of parish-wide catechizing, focusing first on its benefits. For Baxter, no other pastoral practise had so facilitated the conversion of the 'unsound Professors' among his parish. Its effectiveness in evangelism derived from the opportunity to apply the truths of the gospel to each person's particular situation.[57] But there were undeniable pastoral benefits as well: the individual concerns of those already converted could be personally addressed, parishioners could be better equipped to listen to sermons with understanding, preaching would be more effective as the pastor better understood the particular issues with which his parishioners struggled, and pastors could better satisfy themselves concerning the status of those who partook in communion.[58]

Baxter was fully persuaded that his pastoral programme, with parish-wide catechizing at the head, constituted the necessary means to effect the long-sought reformation of the English Church. Moreover, he argued that government-imposed changes in Church structures and ceremonies alone made for a hollow reformation. The true reformation long-sought by faithful ministers would come about person by person, parish by parish, through diligent application of pastoral means for the conversion and edifying of each person under each pastor's care.[59]

Though he carefully catalogued the difficulties that he faced in implementing his scheme for catechizing, he could also point to signal successes which had made it more than worth the trouble: 'I have found by experience, that an ignorant sot that hath been an unprofitable hearer so long, hath got more knowledge and remorse of conscience in half an hours close discourse, then they did from ten years publike preaching'. 'For my part I apprehend this as one of the best and greatest works that ever I put mine hand to in my life.'[60]

Baxter concludes his discourse by providing 'Directions for the right managing of this Work'. With his own practise providing the model, Baxter recommends first preaching a series of 'effectual convincing Sermons' on the value and necessity of catechizing. Next, catechisms should be personally delivered by the minister to every family, giving him further opportunity to persuade them to participate. Moreover, the minister should use these visits to compile a list of all those able to participate.[61]

God's faithful ministers, to the bane of the English Church (117-136, 137). See my discussion in the previous chapter for Baxter's perspective on England's reformation and his use of history to further his argument.

[57] Ibid., 313.

[58] Ibid., 315-319.

[59] Ibid., 345.

[60] Ibid., 357, 386.

[61] Ibid., 417, 420. Baxter goes so far as to suggest ways that the catechisms might be paid for: either by the minister himself, or by 'the best affected of his people of the richer sort', or through a collection taken at a 'day of Humiliation in preparation to the

Baxter then scripts an entire catechetical session and provides a sample introductory speech for the minister to give when the family first arrives and are nervously awaiting the session to begin. He suggests taking family members aside privately one by one, for 'I find by experience, people will better take plain close dealing about their sin and misery and duty when you have them alone then they will before others'. To avoid scandal, however, he recommends meeting women 'only in the presence of some others'.[62]

He suggests that the pastor begin each session with the catechism, and 'if they are able to recite but a little or none of it, try whether they can rehearse the Creed, and the Decalogue.' The pastor should then 'choose out some of the weightiest points, and try by further Questions how they understand them'. Once engaged in this conversation, however, Baxter counsels pastoral restraint and compassion, for some of the most soundly converted people he knows experienced great difficulty in their attempt to learn the words of the catechism in spite of their godly habits and good company. This 'teacheth me what to expect from poor ignorant people that never had such company and converse for one year or week: and not to reject them so hastily as some hot and too high professors would have us do'.[63] The pastor should seek to determine the person's spiritual status, and 'when you have...discerned an apparent probability that the person is yet in an unconverted state, your next business is...to bring his heart to the sense of his condition'. The session should be brought to a conclusion by pressing the person to make 'closure with Christ', and exhorting him to amend his previously sinful life. Baxter suggests that a record be kept 'in a book' of 'who come and who do not, and who are so grossly ignorant as to be utterly uncapable of the Lords Supper... and who not: and as you perceive the necessities of each, so deal with them for the future.' Lastly, he urges the pastor to 'extend your charity to those of the poorest sort, before they part from you: Give them somewhat towards their relief, and for the time that is thus taken from their labours'.[64]

'I have done my Advice, and leave you to the Practice.' Having methodically taken his readers through an impassioned consideration of the components of an effective pastoral ministry, Baxter argued: 'I doubt not, but God will use it...to the awakening of many of his servants to their duty'.[65] But as we shall see, Richard Baxter was concerned about much more than challenging pastors with their God-given obligations.

---

work' (421).

[62] Ibid., 425-26, 426.

[63] Ibid., 427, 432. See also 449-451 for further instructions on how to deal with other kinds of people (the 'dull', 'timorous', 'youthful', 'aged', 'inferiours', 'superiours', 'rich', 'poor', etc.).

[64] Ibid., 440, 442, 447, 448, 452.

[65] Ibid., 480.

Reforming the Church by Reforming Pastors

Permeating the entire work is a passionate concern for reformation. Baxter's use of the word is, however, elastic. From the beginning, he uses reformation to refer to the renovation of individual ministers, and the entire thrust of his argument concerns the transformation of ministry.[66] But throughout, Baxter is unequivocal in his conviction that these are means to a greater goal, for the 'Reforming of the Leaders of the Church' will 'more effectually further a Reformation'.[67] But as we have seen, reformation was not primarily a matter of altering church government and ceremonies; rather, its derivation was in the spiritual reorientation of individuals. Using imagery similar to New Testament metaphors depicting regeneration, he describes reformation first as the sloughing off of an obstructed disposition: a work that 'must dispell our common prevailing ignorance', 'that must bow the stubborn hearts of men', and 'that must answer their vain objections, and take off their prejudices'.[68] But reformation also compelled individuals to transcend the petty, often political differences that had too often frustrated the advance of the gospel throughout Britain and Ireland. Rather than being caught up in the cynical political maneuvers that viewed reformation as a humanly devised programme promoting religious change, the success of which was dependent upon whether the proponents were in or out of political favour, Baxter urged his readers to understand that *this* programme 'hath its rise neither from them nor us, but from the Lord, and is generally approved by his Church.'[69] With eyes opened to what he maintained was the Lord's agenda for individuals and the church, differences that were thereby revealed as petty could be laid aside. Reformation itself begat further workers for reformation, for reformed individuals 'must reconcile their hearts to faithful Ministers; and help on the success of our publike preaching', the result of which 'must make true godliness a commoner thing'.[70]

While acknowledging that it was God himself who gave or withheld the blessing of reformation upon his church, Baxter also noted that God's grace ordinary 'worketh by means'.[71] With this caveat, he could recommend his own Kidderminster experience as a means to reformation that had been attended by God's blessing. The 'awakening of many of [God's] servants to their duty' and the further 'promoting of the work of a Right Reformation' could only bring 'his much greater blessing' upon their pastoral efforts, which Baxter defined as

---

[66] In light of their sins, Baxter calls upon his colleagues to make a 'speedy and thorough reformation, before wrath break out upon us, which will leave us no remedy.' Ibid., sig A4.

[67] Ibid., sig A5.

[68] Ibid., sig (a6)v.

[69] Ibid., sig (a6).

[70] Ibid., sig (a6)v.

[71] Ibid., 480, sig (a6)v.

'the saving of many a soul'. This 'much greater blessing' was the crucial, unifying emphasis behind his own concern for reformation and informing his own pastoral efforts. The work of evangelism was the church's reason for existence. It was therefore reasonable for him to expect God to enable his church to do what he created it to do. Moreover, his own experience demonstrated that focusing all of his pastoral energy into parish evangelism was also the means of yet further reformation, as an increasing circle of parishioners experienced salvation and began to view their world from the same God-centred perspective. The derivative effects seemed well worth the effort, too, as the pastor seeking reformation would experience the peace that God gives to those who do his will, and witness 'the exciting of his servants through the nation to second' them in their efforts, ultimately leading to the true 'unity of [the] Churches'. For Richard Baxter, writing these final words of his treatise on 'Decemb.25.1655', it was an intoxicating vision.[72] And from those heady days at what hindsight would view as the peak of his Kidderminster ministry, he might be pardoned if to him they were hopes that seemingly lay within reach.

Baxter's Bucerian Pastor

We have already drawn attention to the similarities between Baxter's understanding of reformation and that of Martin Bucer. But more specifically, Baxter's description of the pastoral needs found in a given parish and the pastoral means to address them also bears remarkable resemblance to a similar presentation of pastoral ministry made by Martin Bucer (1491-1551) in his *Von der Waren Seelsorge* (Strasbourg, 1538), later translated into Latin and included as *De Vera Animarum Cura* in the posthumously published *Scripta Anglicana fere Omnia* (Basle, 1577).[73] For Bucer, the cure of souls involved five primary tasks. First, the pastor is 'to lead to Christ our Lord and into his communion those who are still estranged from him, whether through carnal excess or false worship.' Secondly, the pastor is to seek the restoration of those who through temptations had been drawn away from the faith. Thirdly, the pastor is 'to assist in the true reformation of those' in the church whose lives are entangled in sin and worldliness. Fourthly, the pastor is to 're-establish in true Christian strength and health those who, while persevering in the fellowship of Christ and not doing particularly or grossly wrong, have become somewhat feeble and sick in the Christian life'. And fifthly, the pastor is to give aid to those who remain strong in the faith, to further their progress and keep

---

[72] Ibid., 480.

[73] For Bucer, see Wright, 'Martin Bucer and England', 523-532; Basil Hall, 'Martin Bucer in England', 144-160; Basil Hall, 'Cranmer, the Eucharist and the Foreign Divines', 236; Rosemary O'Day, *The English Clergy,* 27.

them from falling away.[74]

Bucer further identifies the various kinds of people within a given parish. Within the church, first of all, are 'lost sheep'. These Bucer defines as 'those whom God has elected to his Kingdom but do not yet recognize Christ...and are strangers to his church, whether they were baptized...or not.' Secondly, 'stray sheep' are those who at one time were part of Christ's flock apparently as true believers but who have moved away from their first love, 'but not yet to the extent that they have completely fallen away from Christ and been lost'. Thirdly, Bucer describes the 'injured and broken sheep', those Christians within the church who are 'hurt and injured in their inner being'. Fourthly, the 'weak sheep', while remaining faithful participants in the life of the church, are 'weak in faith and love and all the strengths of the Christian life'. Lastly, the 'sleek and strong sheep are the real Christians, who are growing well and are stable in the Christian life.'[75]

As we have seen in the previous chapter, Bucer, like Baxter, was persuaded that the 'Kingdom of Christ must be renewed not only by edicts but also by devout persuasion.'[76] And like Baxter, Bucer viewed godly ministry as central to the advance of reformation. Such ministry involved the effective evangelical preaching, the right administration of the sacraments, the exercise of church discipline, and the practise of catechizing for confirmation.[77] Most strikingly, Bucer, like Baxter, exhorted pastors to go house by house in their efforts to draw their parishioners to Christ:

> The pastors and teachers of the churches who want to fulfill their office and keep themselves clean of the blood of those of their flocks who are perishing should not only publicly administer Christian doctrine, but also announce, teach, and entreat repentance towards God and faith in our Lord Jesus Christ, and whatever contributes toward piety, among all who do not reject this doctrine, *even at home and with each one privately*.[78] (emphasis mine)

Collinson observes that Bucer's pastoral programme was never a practical option for the English Church in his day, frustrated by universities as yet unmobilized for the task of clerical reformation, deficiency in the number and

---

[74] Bucer, *Concerning the True Care of Souls*, 40. See also *De Vera Animarum Cura*, in *Scripta Anglicana*, 293.

[75] Bucer, *Concerning the True Care of Souls*, 41. *De Vera Animarum* in *Scripta Anglicana*, 294-295.

[76] Bucer, *De Regno Christi*, 268.

[77] Bucer, *De Regno Christi*, 225-247. Part of Bucer's programme involves a reformed understanding of penance. See his chapter (IX) on 'The Ministry of the Discipline of Penance', 247ff. For Bucer's understanding and practise of church discipline, see A.N. Burnett, 'Church Discipline', 439-456; A.N. Burnett, *The Yoke of Christ*.

[78] Bucer, *De Regno Christi*, 235.

quality of clerical recruits and the poverty of most clerical livings.[79] A century later, however, the presence of an educated, motivated and godly core amongst English clergy put implementation of many of Bucer's prescriptions for ministry within reach. Though we have seen hints that, despite their pulpit-centered rhetoric, 'puritan' ministers utilized many of the same pastoral tools advocated by Bucer such as catechizing, visitation and discipline, there is no evidence until Baxter of a corresponding survival of Bucer's pastoral *strategy*.[80]

However, when Baxter's practise is placed side by side with Bucer's ideal, the correspondence is startling. Baxter, like Bucer, recognized that reformation was a pastoral task and not a governmental responsibility.[81] Baxter, like Bucer, saw the conversion of the unconverted majority within his parish as his primary goal.[82] Baxter, like Bucer, urged pastors to supplement their preaching by meeting with every individual under his pastoral care and instructing them in the gospel.[83] Baxter, like Bucer, viewed an adequate confession of faith and profession of Christian obedience as prerequisite to participation in church privileges.[84] Baxter, like Bucer, saw confirmation as a tremendous opportunity both to evangelize and to reestablish the concept of both privileges and responsibilities in adult church membership.[85] Baxter, like Bucer, saw the preservation of the integrity of church membership and participation in the sacraments through the pastor-led exercise of church discipline as indispensable to the integrity of Christian witness, especially in the face of pressure from separatists.[86] The only major pastoral priority that Baxter does not bring forward from Bucer is Bucer's use of a Protestant form of penance.[87]

---

[79] Collinson, 'The Reformer and the Archbishop', 37.

[80] This distinction between pastoral tools and pastoral strategy will be more fully developed in chapter 8.

[81] Bucer, *De Regno Christi*, 268; Baxter, *Gildas Salvianus*, sig (a8).

[82] Bucer, *De Regno Christi*, 235; Bucer, *Concerning the True Care of Souls*, 74-75; Baxter, *Gildas Salvianus*, sig A5-A5v.

[83] Bucer, *De Regno Christi*, 222, 235; Baxter, *The Saints Everlasting Rest* (1650), sig A4; Baxter, *Gildas Salvianus*, sig (a4); Baxter, *The Agreement of Divers Ministers of Christ in the County of Worcester* (1656), 11, 17-19.

[84] Bucer, *De Regno Christi*, 229-230; Baxter, *Christian Concord* (1653), sig B2-B3v, C2.

[85] Bucer, *Censura De Caeremoniis Eccleisiae Anglicanae in Martin Bucer and the Book of Common Prayer*, 100-104; Baxter, *Confirmation and Restauration*, 10-11, 172-181, 194-205.

[86] Bucer, *De Regno Christi*, 238-241; Bucer, *Concerning the True Care of Souls*, 40; Baxter, *Gildas Salvianus*, sig (b2)v.

[87] See Bucer, *Concerning the True Care of Souls*, 55-74. Amy Burnett observes that Bucer's emphasis on penance and church discipline, while mainly 'theoretical and theological' in the 1520s, became increasingly practical in the early 1530s. 'During these years Bucer directed his energies towards two tasks: promoting concord between Lutherans and Zwinglians and establishing an institutional structure for the evangelical

Though Baxter does not cite Bucer in *Gildas Salvianus,* twenty-five years later in a letter to six moderate bishops of the Restoration Church of England prefacing *An Apology for the Nonconformists Ministry* (1681), Baxter gives an unprecedented commendation of Bucer's pastoral strategy:

> O that all our Clergy would read and weigh what Bucer saith copiously and vehemently for Parish-Discipline, and pure Communion, *de Regno Dei, de Animarum Cura, in censura Liturg.* specially *de Confirmatione* and what he saith of Pastoral Government, Ordination and Order, and of imposing such Ceremonies as ours (It was written in *England*, and for *England*):[88]

Although Baxter is primarily concerned to persuade these moderate bishops that his ensuing arguments against the Church of England's arbitrary impositions which prevented ejected clergy like himself from conforming with a clear conscience are both biblically correct and consistent with pre-Laudian policy, he allows what may be an astonishing glimpse into the reformation pedigree of his own positions, not only of comprehension within the Church of England but of discipline, confirmation and the role and authority of the local pastor-all major planks of his own pastoral strategy. Based on the similarity of their pastoral programmes, and on this late but unprecedented (for Baxter) commendation of Bucer's pastoral strategy, it may be that Baxter's *Reformed Pastor* is actually the revival of the Bucerian pastor. But given that Baxter's impassioned referral occurs thirty years after the instigation of his own Kidderminster reforms, the argument that Baxter was directly influenced by Bucer's writings on pastoral ministry runs into difficulty.[89] The major obstacle remains the fact that Baxter nowhere mentions Bucer when writing about pastoral ministry during his Kidderminster years. Even when engaged in defensive polemic, when it might seem in his interest to demonstrate continuity with someone of Bucer's standing, no reference is forthcoming. This objection can be countered somewhat by the observation that Baxter rarely if ever cites *anyone* when laying out the various aspects of his pastoral programme.[90] Even

---

church in Strasbourg. Both activities forced Bucer to think through the implications of his ideas on penance and church discipline.' Burnett, *The Yoke of Christ,* 55.

[88] Baxter, *An Apology for the Nonconformists Ministry,* sig A3. Each of Bucer's works cited by Baxter are found in *Scripta Anglicana: De Regno Christi:* 1-170; *De Vera Animarum cura:* 265-355; *Censure:* 456-503. As Bucer did not publish any work under the title *de Confirmatione,* Baxter may be referring to what Bucer has to say specifically about confirmation in the works that he lists.

[89] Baxter cites Bucer's authority, always in a crowd with others, on three additional issues in *An Apology the Nonconformists Ministry:* see 117, 131 and 215.

[90] Exceptions include Baxter's citations of Thomas Ball and 'his late Book for the Ministry' (*Pastorum Propugnaculum,* 1656), as well as William Lyford (*William Lyford his Legacy, or a Help for young People to Prepare them for the Sacrament,* 1656),

so, the absence of a direct reference to so likely a source, or at any rate so potent a potential ally, remains curious.

Baxter does, however, cite Bucer in discussions of several unrelated theological issues in works published while he was still in Kidderminster. In 1658, for example, Baxter cites Bucer in his *Certain Disputations of Right to Sacraments* as one of thirty-two divines in support of a particular argument.[91] The earliest is an explicit reference to Bucer's position on episcopacy in his 'Explication' in *Christian Concord* (1653).[92] Thus Baxter was aware of Bucer's *Scripta Anglicana* and citing it the same year he was overseeing the Worcestershire Association implementation of what is arguably a Bucerian programme of parish discipline. And even if direct evidence of Bucer's influence on Baxter is not forthcoming from his early works and extant letters, the extraordinary correspondence between their understandings of reformation and strategies for pastoral ministry suggests that Baxter may have been familiar with Bucer's *Scripta Anglicana* works on reformation and ministry and that his reading of them greatly influenced the direction his ministry subsequently took.

As we shall see in subsequent chapters where we examine more closely the particulars of Baxter's ministry, there were some precedents to various aspects of Baxter's pastoral practise in the ministries of his contemporaries and predecessors. But nowhere prior to Baxter does one find direct evidence of English clergy advocating pastor-led parochial reformation.[93] Nor does one find evidence of pastoral strategies deliberately reorganized to maximize parish

---

Zachary Crofton (*Catechising Gods Ordinance*, 1656), the London minister's *Jus divinum ministerii evangelici* (1654) and Henry Hammond (*Of the Power of the Keyes*, 1647). See *Gildas Salvianus* (1656), sigs (b6)-(b7), (d2)v. All of these publications, however, postdate the implementation of Baxter's own strategy in Kidderminster. With each of these citations, Baxter demonstrates his familiarity with contemporary discussion, while at the same time shedding no light on the sources for his own thinking.

[91] Baxter's citation, however, is suspicious: '30. [of 32] *Bucer*, and *Martorate* citing him, on Joh. 15.2. Quomodo ergo...'. *Certain Disputations of Right to Sacraments*, 470. It is possible that Baxter had not in fact read Bucer himself, but had only come across this quote in another source. In material dating from shortly after the restoration of Charles II in 1660, Baxter again cites Bucer when arguing for moderation with respect to the reimposition of episcopacy. See *Rel. Bax.*, II, §7, 250.

[92] Baxter, 'Explication', in *Christian Concord*, 76-77. While it is possible that Baxter made a derivative use of Bucer based on his readings of other authors who cited Bucer in similar contexts, there is no reason to believe that Baxter's own scholarship here is not genuine. Baxter certainly owned a copy of 'Buceri Opera': G.F. Nuttall, 'A Transcript of Richard Baxter's Library Catalogue: A Bibliographical Note', in *JEH*, 2 (1951), 210. See Baxter's recommendation of Bucer's writings in *A Christian Directory*, 734, Questions CLXXIV, XXX, 12. While it is possible that Baxter made a derivative use of Bucer based on his readings of other authors who cited Bucer in similar contexts, there is no reason to believe that Baxter here is misleading his readers.

[93] Samuel Clarke provides intriguing exceptions in *The Lives of Sundry Eminent Persons* (1683) that will be considered in chapter 8.

evangelism. Nor does one find a sophisticated awareness of the spiritual condition and pastoral needs of different members of the congregation. Nor does one find anyone advocating systematic pastoral visitation and instruction as the chief means to promote conversion and thus reformation. But each of these emphases are found in Bucer's *Scripta Anglicana*, which we know Baxter possessed at the end of his life, and which evidence suggests he read and cited at least as early as 1653. The lack of *direct* evidence, however, prevents me from positing Bucer's immediate influence on the development of Baxter's understanding of reformation, or on Baxter's pastoral practise in general or on the emphases communicated in his *Gildas Salvianus* in particular. My subsequent investigations into the particulars of Baxter's pastoral strategy uncover various additional precedents for the associational, disciplinary and catechetical aspects of his ministry. But whether these represent echoes of Bucerian emphases which survived in Elizabethan and early Stuart pastoral practise (if not rhetoric) and which were picked up as part of a 'godly' inheritance of pastoral practise and refined by Baxter for his own purposes in Kidderminster, or whether there are other non-Bucerian sources which better explain Baxter's strategy-these are questions which must remain in tension for the time being. It is enough at this stage to acknowledge the remarkable correspondence that exists between Richard Baxter's strategy for parish reformation and his subsequent pastoral practise with that of Martin Bucer. That correspondence alone would seem to argue that there is more going on between Baxter and Bucer than mere coincidence.

A *Puritan* Pastor?

Gildas Salvianus has been described as the *'locus classicus* of puritan thinking about ministry'.[94] That Baxter's pastoral labours were respected and admired by many of his contemporaries is beyond question. What is less clear is whether Baxter can be seen as the epitome of a 'puritan' understanding of pastoral ministry, when in fact much of what he emphasizes in terms of strategy deliberately challenges the conventional wisdom of a pulpit-centered ministry.[95]

---

[94] David Sceats, 'Gildas Salvianas [sic] Redevivus-The Reformed Pastor, Richard Baxter', 135.

[95] See my survey of pastoral treatises in chapter 2. Much of the confusion comes from the imprecise use of 'Puritan' and 'Puritanism' by 19th and 20th century admirers of the many sixteenth- and seventeenth-century English conformists and nonconformists whose theological and pastoral priorities resonated most nearly with their own. Such contemporary admirers tend to be either unaware or skeptical of recent academic attempts to sort out the historical context and significance of that spectrum of English (and American) clergy and laity who have been labeled Puritans, by both their enemies and their later admirers. That a quartet such as Baxter, Owen, Sibbes and Perkins could all be neatly classified as being Puritans necessitates an oversimplistic telescoping of sixteenth- and seventeenth-century English history. This ahistorical usage is further

While claiming to be within the tradition of England's godly, faithful and learned ministry, his quiet revival of a Bucerian pastoral agenda combined with his curious use of corroborating sources in *Gildas Salvianus* together tell a different story. There is not a single mention of any of the treatises, tracts or sermons on pastoral ministry produced by Baxter's ministerial predecessors. The vast majority of sources are early Church Fathers, with Gregory the Great and Augustine emerging as favorites.[96] Of British authors, Baxter cites Ussher and Ames three times, Whateley twice, and Bolton, Thorndike, Dod, Gillespie, Hooker and Rainolds each once, and each of these are cited on matters of peripheral controversy rather than as sources of pastoral inspiration.[97] But none of the authors of major Elizabethan and early Stuart treatises on pastoral ministry, such as William Perkins, Richard Greenham, Richard Bernard, Oliver Bowles or George Herbert, receives a mention. The omission of the first four is perhaps explained by Baxter's concern to take his audience beyond the pulpit-centred assumptions about ministry that characterize their efforts. More surprising, perhaps, is the absence of any mention of George Herbert (whose poetry Baxter admired), as his own treatise on ministry had been posthumously published only four years prior to *Gildas Salvianus*. A closer comparison of

---

demonstrated by the 18th- and 19th-century practise of collecting and publishing the 'Works' of these various authors by the likes of such as William Orme and Alexander Grosart (often with each piece edited in a way that removes it from its original context), and is further perpetuated by their subsequent reprinting in the 20th century by publishers such as Banner of Truth Trust and Soli Deo Gloria. See, as an example, Robert P. Martin's *A Guide to the Puritans* (Edinburgh: The Banner of Truth Trust, 1997). In his concordance of Puritan works that have been reprinted in the 20th century, Martin does not cite a single date, either of the publication of the reprinted edition, or of when the original first edition came forth!

[96] While fascinating, Baxter's use of the early church Fathers takes us beyond the scope of this paper. Gregory the Great (usually *de cura pastorali,* but also *Moralia in Job*) is cited 16 times, while Augustine is quoted (various works) 15 times. Baxter quotes both Salvian and Seneca 9 times, with Jerome, Bernard and Vincentius Lerinensis cited 5 times each. Luther is cited 3 times, as is Grotius, while Calvin is quoted twice. These figures are for the treatise proper and do not include the prefatory letter.

[97] Baxter cites Archbishop James Ussher (1581-1656), *Veterum episotlarum hibernicarum sylloge* (1632), 49, 50 (*Gildas Salvianus*, 148), and *A briefe declaration of the universalitie of the church of Christ* (1624), 44-45 (*Gildas Salvianus*, 462); William Ames (1576-1633) *Medulla Theologiae* (third edition, 1629), cap. 37 (*Gildas Salvianus*, 302, 303, 415); William Whately (1583-1639), *The New Birth* (1618) and *The Redemption of Time* (1606) (Gildas Salvianus, 85, 394; Robert Bolton (1572-1631), *Instructions for a Right Comforting Afflicted Consciences* (1631) (*Gildas Salvianus*, 77); Herbert Thorndike (1598-1672), no text cited; John Dod, *A Treatise or Exposition upon the Ten Commandments* (1603) (*Gildas Salvianus*, 85); George Gillespie (1613-1648), *Aarons Rod Blossoming* (1646) (*Gildas Salvianus*, 302); Thomas Hooker (1586?-1647), *The Soules Preparation for Christ* (1632) (*Gildas Salvianus*, 322); and John Rainolds (1549-1607), no text cited (*Gildas Salvianus*, 412).

Herbert's method and strategy with that of Baxter's does, however, provide a clue that may explain Herbert's exclusion.

As we have seen in chapter 2, at its publication in 1652, Herbert's *A Priest to the Temple* was the most comprehensive analysis of the pastor's duty that Protestant England had seen. Though Herbert's portrayal of the realities of day-to-day pastoral life compares favorably with Baxter's, a close comparison reveals that these two treatises are being realistic about two very different pastoral agendas. As Herbert demonstrates, the toolbox which Protestant pastors made use of to facilitate their ministries remained essentially unchanged from Elizabethan times-pastors preached, catechized, ministered sacraments, visited, resolved conflicts and sought to discipline the obstinate. The difference between Herbert and Baxter was not that they made use of different tools, but that they used the tools they had to different ends. Herbert assumes that the primary pastoral concern is that the sheep be fed, while Baxter's concern is that the sheep be first converted.[98] Though Herbert recognized that catechizing, for example, also had use as a means for conversion, the pastoral strategies which result from these differing foundational assumptions take Herbert's Country Parson and Baxter's Reformed Pastor in fundamentally different directions.[99] It is perhaps this fundamental difference in purpose which made works like Herbert's *A Priest to the Temple*, and indeed the other English treatises on ministry, essentially useless for Baxter's purposes.

Conclusion

Richard Baxter was the most influential pastor in sixteenth- and seventeenth-century England. And though he does not acknowledge it, his *Gildas Salvianus* reintroduced a Bucerian model of pastoral ministry into an England whose ecclesiastical agenda since Grindal had largely been set along Genevan lines. Just as concerned as his godly predecessors and contemporaries were for the reformation of England's Church and society, Baxter shared Bucer's conviction that true reformation would result, not when church structures or ceremonies

---

[98] Baxter's own undramatic process of becoming a Christian coloured his view of the nature of conversion. Allowing that it was possible to become a Christian without the spiritual crisis found in many published accounts of conversion, Baxter was also concerned to guard against false 'antinomian' assurances of salvation when not accompanied by a demonstrable change of life. For Baxter, conversion involved turning away from a godless way of life and turning to Christ and living in a manner consistent with his government. See *A Call to the Unconverted to Turn and Live* (1658); *Rel. Bax.*, I, i, §§213, 6 (3); see also Nuttall, *Richard Baxter*, 6-7; Lim, 'In pursuit of unity, purity and liberty', 24-38. For a wider discussion of the early modern notion of conversion see Duffy's 'The Long Reformation', N. Tyacke, ed., *England's Long Reformation*, 34-53.

[99] F.E. Hutchinson, *Works of George Herbert* (Oxford: Clarendon, 1941, repr. 1978), 257; Eamon Duffy, 'The Long Reformation', N. Tyacke, ed., *England's Long Reformation*, 44. See discussion in chapter 8.

were changed, but through the cumulative effect of the conversion of the multitude of 'unsound Professors' who made up the majority of any given parish. 'The whole design and business of this discourse', wrote Baxter in his preface to the appendix of the second edition, is 'the Propagation of the Gospel and the saving of mens souls'.[100] Baxter, like Bucer, perceived pastors to be the linchpin in local efforts to facilitate conversion, and thus, by extension, in the efforts to achieve the overall reformation of church and society. Having experienced what he took to be the first fruits of just such a reformation in Kidderminster, Baxter was confident that the conversion of England's parishes and the resulting reformation lay at hand, if only the nation's pastors could be stirred up to do their gospel duty. From Baxter's perspective, pastoral negligence had long been the bane of the English Church. Thus in an attempt to wake his pastoral colleagues up to their evangelical duty, Baxter expanded what had been intended as a fast-day sermon and brought forth what became the most influential treatise on pastoral ministry Protestant England had heretofore seen.

Baxter's example was widely hailed, less widely followed, and finally, perhaps more often than not, simply abandoned even before the Restoration made it redundant.[101] Even in Kidderminster, as we shall see, efforts to woo his parish to submit to his pastoral oversight and thus be eligible for communion resulted in only 600 out of 1600 who voluntarily consented to his pastoral regimen, with the other 1000 passively opting out, choosing to remain 'hearers' only 'for fear of Discipline'.[102] Baxter's hopes for the conversion of multitudes were mostly unfulfilled. His goal for the reformation of the English Church remained merely a dream. Though he would later blame Restoration churchmen as having ruined England's best and last hope for a godly reformation,[103] Baxter's own strategy had already been sinking under its own weight.

Gildas Salvianus ultimately failed to achieve its author's purposes. In his labors to facilitate the long-sought puritan reformation of the Church of England, Baxter may have made use of the Puritan components of godly ministry at hand, but combined with Bucerian priorities, the sum of their parts went beyond anything the godly had hitherto envisioned. He recognized with Bucer that the Church's primary pastoral need is to evangelize her own nominal adherents, and that the Church's unreformedness necessitates that the *cure* of souls be the pastor's primary aim before he undertakes their care. Richard Baxter's reworking of the pastor's task recovered the long-buried emphases of England's earliest Protestants and ignited the hope in Kidderminster and the

---

[100] Baxter, *Gildas Salvianus*, sig Nn2.

[101] 'When I attempted to bring them [members of the Worcestershire Association] all conjunctly to the work of Catechizing and Instructing every Family by it self, I found a ready consent in most and performance in many.' *Rel. Bax.*, I, i, §136, 85.

[102] Ibid., I, i, §137 (25), 91.

[103] Ibid., I, i, §139, 97.

surrounding parishes of Worcestershire that reformation was at hand. And through *Gildas Salvianus*, for a brief time, at least, it seemed possible that the fire might spread.

PART TWO

The Reformed Ministry

CHAPTER 5

Baxter's Discipline and the Foundations of the Reformed Parish

In the first section, I have placed Baxter's *Gildas Salvianus* within the broader context both of the rhetoric and the reality of English Protestant pastoral practise as well as the undergirding motive of reformation. In this section, I will examine more closely the main components of Baxter's own pastoral practise and investigate both the continuities and divergences with existing pastoral precedent. At the core of his efforts to bring reformation to Kidderminster lay his efforts to establish a parish-based system of church discipline that would preserve the integrity of the sacraments and thus rob separatists of one of their primary excuses for abandoning the parochial system. This chapter seeks to place Baxter's effort to develop a strategy for an effective church discipline in its historical context. In particular, I will first consider the precedents to the system that Baxter developed for St Mary's parish.[1] Special attention will be given to Martin Bucer's Reformation-era prescription for reforming the discipline of the church, and I will explore further the possibility that Baxter's strategy was actually a recovery of Bucerian emphases. Secondly, I shall also examine why church discipline was of such concern to Baxter and his ministerial colleagues, and trace the evolution of his own programme for discipline. Finally, we shall consider the impact Baxter's discipline had on his wider goal of reformation, both in his parish and beyond.

During a frank exchange of letters in 1656 with his most prominent parishioner, Sir Ralph Clare, who had scrupled to receive Communion at services divergent from the Book of Common Prayer, Richard Baxter stepped back from the discussion and bluntly addressed what he took to be the real issue at stake: the controversial core of his pastoral agenda—the establishment of a procedure for church discipline:

---

[1] An earlier version of this chapter appeared as an article in *Church History*. See J. William Black, 'From Martin Bucer to Richard Baxter: "Discipline" and Reformation in Sixteenth and Seventeenth Century England', *CH*, 70:4 (2001), 644-673. I am grateful to the editor for permission to make use of it here.

...I take it to be a heinous, scandalous sin, to live from under Discipline... And therefore I dare not admit such [to the Lord's Supper] till they repent, no more than I would do a Drunkard or Adulterer.... I dare not be an Instrument of hindering Reformation, and the Execution of just Discipline, by gratifying the Unruly that fly from it, and set themselves against it...

Besides, the Office of a Pastor is not only to Preach and Administer the Sacrament, but also to admonish, rebuke, and exercise some Discipline for the Good of the Church: And he that will not profess his consent to these, doth not by his partial submitting to the rest [i.e. attending services] shew his consent that I be his Pastor. I will be a Pastor to none that will not be under Discipline: That were to be a half Pastor, and indulge Men in an unruliness and contempt of the Ordinance of Christ.[2]

Devising and implementing a system of discipline for his parish proved Richard Baxter's most daunting task as a pastor. And it is easy to forget that Baxter was one of many hundreds of ministers attempting to cope with the undermining of parish ministry in the fragmenting aftermath of the civil wars.[3] As we shall see, it took several years of trial and error to hit upon a process that gave some hope of success. But while other pastors laboured in obscurity, Baxter's publishing successes and his leadership in developing the Worcestershire Association ensured that his own efforts as a pastor to bring reformation to his parish would increasingly attract a nationwide audience. And because so many of his colleagues took note of his efforts and claims of success, Baxter's example served, in the few years before the Restoration, to

---

[2] *Rel. Bax.*, II, §33, 160-62. Baxter's letter is dated 2 February 1656. Sir Ralph Clare (1587-1670) of Caldwall (or Caldwell) Hall, writes Baxter, was 'an old Man, of great Courtship and Civility, and very temperate as to Dyet, Apparel and Sports, and seldom would Swear any lowder than [*By his Troth*, &c.] and shewed me much Personal Reverence and Respect (beyond my desert) and we conversed together with Love and Familiarity'. And though Baxter acknowledged Sir Ralph's piety, and found him helpful as an intermediary in his discussions with Peter Heylyn and Henry Hammond, Baxter also stated that he 'did more to hinder my greater Successes, than a multitude of others could have done'. 'All the Disturbance I had in my own Parish was by Sir *Ralph Clare's* refusing to Communicate with us, unless I would give it to him kneeling on a distinct Day, and not with those that received it sitting.' *Rel. Bax.*, I. 94, §137 (27); II, 208, §66; II, §33, 157. See C.D. Gilbert and Richard Warner, *Caldwall Hall Kidderminster* (Kidderminster: Tomkinson, 1999), 1-6; see also *DNB*.

[3] John Morrill suggests that the threat posed by the radical sects was exaggerated by the fears of both parliamentarian and royalist clergy. The perception of a fragmenting religious and social order was enough to provoke a response from Baxter and others. See Morrill's essay, 'Order and Disorder in the English Revolution', in *The Nature*, 384-391.

redefine the way puritan ministry was both understood and practiced.

'Before these times of Examination...'

Scandalous discrepancy between a Christian's profession and a Christian's behavior has vexed local churches from New Testament days.[4] The operative Biblical model for establishing a procedure for discipline in local communities of Christians is found in Matthew 18:15-17.[5] A right application of this passage became of increasing concern to many continental and English Protestants attempting to reconstruct New Testament polity and community life. But in both the discussion and events as they unfolded in sixteenth- and seventeenth-century England and in later historical literature, the tendency has been to confuse the actual pastoral practise of local church discipline with the wider issue of ecclesiology.[6] While the two are certainly related, this confusion has served to obfuscate the local pastoral issues with which clergy struggled and which provided tinder for their debates on reforming church structures and polity. And though the struggles by England's more zealous protestants to complete the reformation of the Church of England's government and worship have been capably handled by recent historians, the *pastoral* concerns and practises which lay at the heart of this puritan agitation have attracted little attention. Even if the impulse to escalate the discussion into the wider issues of polity and worship is impossible to resist entirely, the focus of this study remains the pastoral issue of local church discipline.

As with his perspective on reformation and his strategy for pastoral ministry, Martin Bucer presented England's Protestant leadership with the most comprehensive prescription to date for reforming the Edwardian Church's

---

[4] The story of Ananias and Sapphira in Acts 5:1-11 and the Corinthian believer brazenly sleeping with his father's wife in 1 Corinthians 5:1-5 served as signal examples of the seriousness with which God treated the unrepentant sinner in the church. However, consideration of the disciplinary practises of the early church and later Western Catholicism takes us beyond the more modest scope of this chapter.

[5] 'Moreover if thy brother shall trespass against thee, go and tell him his fault between thee and him alone: if he shall hear thee, thou hast gained thy brother. But if he will not hear thee, then take with thee one or two more, that in the mouth of two or three witnesses every word may be established. And if he shall neglect to hear them, tell it unto the church: but if he neglect to hear the church, let him be unto thee as an heathen man and a publican.' *The Holy Bible,* Authorized Version (1611).

[6] See, for example, Irvonwy Morgan's chapter 'A Draft of Discipline', in *The Godly Preachers*, 175-217. Heinz Schilling, however, does not allow enough room for the genuine religious concern as a motivation for ecclesiastical discipline in his '"History of Crime" or "History of Sin"? -Some Reflections on the Social History of Early Modern Church Discipline,' E.I. Kouri and T. Scott, eds., *Politics and Society in Reformation Europe: Essays for Sir Geoffrey Elton on his Sixty-fifth Birthday* (London: MacMillan, 1987), 305-06.

medieval discipline.[7] As Bucer was the first Protestant in England to argue for a revision of parish discipline in light of reformation priorities, his significance to any further discussion of later Elizabethan and Stuart efforts to reform the Church's discipline cannot be overstated.[8] Fresh from what appeared to be the crushing defeat of reformation in Strasbourg, he hoped to help his adopted Church of England avoid the disaster that struck the Protestant churches of his homeland which had occurred, he was convinced, through their neglect of discipline.[9]

Bucer's understanding of church discipline, championed during his remaining months in England, evolved during his twenty-five years of ministry in Strasbourg.[10] Bucer's discipline incorporated four interrelated elements into the life of the church: public profession of faith and of obedience to the church and its pastors as a prerequisite to participation in Communion (most effectively implemented through an involved process of confirmation); catechetical instruction and private oversight of children and adults through regular meetings between pastor and his parishioners; the oversight of morality in the parish by the pastor and lay elders, combined with the exercise of mutual admonition amongst the members; and the establishment of a disciplinary process along with the use of penance to promote either a notorious sinner's repentance or their exclusion from Communion and the community through excommunication.[11]

As we have seen, Bucer felt any reformation of doctrine was contingent upon

---

[7] See MacCulloch, *Thomas Cranmer*, 364-66; Amos, '"It is Fallow Ground Here"', 41-44.

[8] 'John Foxe's *De censura sive exommunicatione ecclesiastica rectoque eius usu*, published in 1551 was the earliest tract to be written by an English Protestant on the subject of ecclesiastical discipline.' C.M.F. Davies and J.M. Facey, 'A reformation dilemma: John Foxe and the problem of discipline', in *JEH*, 39 (1988), 37-65, here 37. See also C.M.F. Davies, '"Poor Persecuted Little Flock" or "Commonwealth Christians": Edwardian Protestant Concepts of the Church', P. Lake and M. Dowling, eds., *Protestantism and the National Church in Sixteenth Century England* (London: Croom Helm, 1987), 78-102. The complete absence of Martin Bucer in Davies' discussion of discipline and the Edwardian Church here is striking. For other Edwardian treatments of discipline, see the official catechism in which discipline is described as a mark of the Church, *A short Catechism or Plain Instruction containing the sum of Christian learning* (1553), sigs Civ-G3; Thomas Lancaster, *The Right and True Understanding of the Supper of the Lord* (1550?), sig D4; John Hooper, *A Declaration of Christ and His office* (Zurich, 1547), in *Early Writings*, S. Carr, ed. (Cambridge, 1843), 90-91.

[9] Burnett, 'Church Discipline', 439.

[10] See Burnett, *The Yoke of Christ;* René Bornert, *La Réforme Protestante du Culte à Strasbourg au XVIe Siècle (1523-1598): Approche Sociologique et Interprétation Théologique,* in *SMRT,* xxviii (Leiden: Brill, 1981), 84-207.

[11] Burnett, 'Church Discipline', 439.

the transformation of both ministry and discipline at the parish level.[12] From his perspective, the traditional, sacrament-centered practise of ministry had served to inoculate parishioners against any sense of their need for Christ, and had distanced them from any awareness of the biblical means for their salvation.

> For the people have been led by [those who defend the 'papistical tyranny'] into thinking that if they have been baptized and take part in the common ceremonies, and do not interfere in the affairs of the so-called priests, then they belong to the church and congregation of Christ, even though they may never really have come to know Christ our Lord, and live in open sin, relying for their comfort in God not on Christ, but on the ceremonies of the so-called priests, their own good works, and the merits of dead saints. Indeed, they would be unable to place their trust in Christ the Lord, since in all their life and conduct they contemptuously despise him and his holy word.[13]

Bucer was therefore concerned to use church discipline as a means to pastoral, indeed evangelistic ends.

At the heart of Bucer's concern lay care for the integrity of the Lord's Supper, because of the 'grievous harm done by sharing the Lord's table with those whose sin is known and repentance unknown.' Great damage was done to the Church's witness in the world when so many 'who perhaps live for a long time at enmity with their neighbors or who have fallen into wild sexual immorality, serious blasphemy and contempt of God, and yet come to the Lord's table without any penance or sign of repentance, without even acknowledging their sins..., indeed sadly often without turning from their offenses and without being reconciled to their neighbors.' Because of this, Bucer took steps to ensure that Communion was 'not to be shared with anyone whose repentance has not yet been recognized.'[14]

In *De Regno Christi*, Bucer elaborated the necessity of making adult church privileges such as Communion contingent upon a profession of faith and of obedience to the church and pastors, especially through an enhanced process of confirmation:

> [Pastors] should require of individual Christians their personal profession of faith and Christian obedience: of adults before they are baptized; and of those who are baptized as infants, when they have been catechized and instructed in the gospel of Christ; and if

---

[12] See Bucer, *De Regno Christi*, 212-13, 266.

[13] Bucer, *Concerning the True Care of Souls,* 2; also in *De Vera Animarum Cura, Scripta Anglicana*, 260.

[14] Bucer, *Concerning the True Care of Souls*, 74; *De Vera Animarum Cura*, 323.

any do not present themselves to be catechized and taught and refuse to follow all the precepts of Christ and to make a legitimate profession of faith and of the obedience to be rendered to Christ and his church, they ought to be rejected from the company of the saints and the communion of the sacraments...[15]

Bucer recognized, however, that such discipline could not stand alone without intensive pastoral oversight. Clear teaching from the Word must be supplemented by personal involvement in the lives of each parishioner. Effective pastors who wish to 'keep themselves clean of the blood of those of their flocks who are perishing should not only publicly administer Christian doctrine, but also announce, teach, and entreat repentance towards God and faith in our Lord Jesus Christ, and whatever contributes toward piety, among all who do not reject this doctrine, even at home and with each one privately'.[16]

Even under Edward VI's Protestant regime, Bucer's finely tuned scheme for discipline was never implemented; and when Protestantism was re-established under Elizabeth, Bucer's model was apparently never considered.[17] The missionary task confronting English Protestants in the earliest days of Elizabeth's reign served for many to make any discussion of church discipline a luxury.[18] Even so, the increasing frustration expressed by the returning Marian exiles and their converts over the perceived incompatibility between a Protestant and reformed gospel and a medieval Catholic and essentially unreformed episcopal government drove many among the more zealous Protestants to press for the completion of what, hitherto had been a reformation of doctrine only. Though the Genevan redaction of reformation held discipline to be one of the marks of a true church, the version finally adopted in the Church of England's Thirty Nine Articles made no such ecclesiastical commitment.[19] As Patrick Collinson notes, 'No blemish of the Elizabethan

---

[15] Bucer, *De Regno Christi*, 228-230. See Burnett's 'Confirmation and Christian Fellowship: Martin Bucer on Commitment to the Church', in *CH*, 64:2 (1995), 202-217. Burnett also describes how Bucer's understanding of confirmation was developed in a broader context of ongoing controversy with Anabaptist separatists. See Burnett, 'Martin Bucer and the Anabaptist Context of Evangelical Confirmation', in *MQR*, 68:1 (1994), 95-122.

[16] Bucer, *De Regno Christi*, 235.

[17] See Wright, 'Martin Bucer and England-and Scotland', 525; Basil Hall, 'Martin Bucer in England', 145, 157.

[18] See Duffy, 'The Long Reformation', especially 36-42. Commenting on the challenge undertaken by England's early Protestants, Duffy states that 'Conversion, therefore, meant not merely bringing the heathen to knowledge of the gospel, but bringing the tepid to the boil by awakening preaching, creating a godly people out of a nation of conformists' (42).

[19] Article XIX mentions only two marks of a true church: faithful preaching of the Word of God and the right celebration of the Sacraments. See also James Cameron, 'Godly

Church was more prominent or more wounding to the puritan conscience than the general absence of discipline, in the reformed sense of the term.'[20] The situation was not, however, irremediable. The preface of the 1559 Prayer Book service of Commination contained a candid acknowledgement of the place of effective discipline and its absence in the church as presently constituted. Moreover, the preface appeared to stress the transitional nature of the church's present government, holding the door open to a future continuation of the reformation's progress: 'until the said discipline may be restored again, (which is much to be wished,)'.[21]

The resulting concern for discipline, however, diverged from Bucer's strategy. Rather than focus on transforming local pastoral practise, many Elizabethan Protestants sought to change those aspects of Elizabeth's reformation perceived as unfinished, namely the ceremonies and government of the established Church.[22] 'Discipline' became a code word pointing to the establishment of a system of church government that most closely reflected New Testament priorities. For most, the model in mind was Geneva.[23] As a result, Bucer's notion of a reformed parish discipline was essentially squeezed out of the discussion.

The inherited system of parish discipline within the Church of England was the provenance not of the local minister, but of the bishop, and subject to the judgment of the bishop on visitation or of the diocesan consistory court system.[24] If a potential disciplinary case succeeded in arousing the attention of

---

Nurture and Admonition in the Lord: Ecclesiastical Discipline in the Reformed Tradition', L. Grane and K. Hørby, eds., *Die danische Reformation vor ihrem internationalen Hintergrund* (Gottingen: Vandenhoeck and Ruprecht, 1990), 264-276.

[20] Collinson, *Elizabethan Puritan Movement,* 346. Stephen Brachlow states that 'In the context of puritan soteriology, a disciplined, obedient life was the primary means for gaining personal assurance of everlasting life'. Stephen Brachlow, *The Communion of Saints: Radical Puritan and Separatist Ecclesiology 1570-1625* (Oxford: Oxford University Press, 1988), 123.

[21] W. Keating, ed., 'A Commination', *Book of Common Prayer* (1559), in *Liturgical Services: Liturgies and Occasional Forms of Prayer set forth in the Reign of Queen Elizabeth* (Cambridge: Cambridge University Press, 1847), 239.

[22] Collinson's distinction between the puritan movement which pressed for ecclesiastical reform along a Genevan model and ultimately failed, and puritan religion which 'was something now widely dispersed and year by year growing roots which were not to be easily torn out' helps explain the existence of parallel conceptions of discipline amongst the godly. See Collinson, *Elizabethan Puritan Movement,* 385.

[23] See, for example, Euan Cameron, 'Frankfurt and Geneva: The European Context of John Knox's Reformation', R.A. Mason, ed., *John Knox and the British Reformations* (Aldershot: Ashgate, 1998), 51-73.

[24] See Fincham, *Prelate as Pastor,* 147-176. See Webster's description of the complexities of this system of ecclesiastical discipline in Essex in *Godly Clergy,* 180-184. For a sympathetic overview of the role of episcopal discipline, see Martin Ingram, 'Puritans and the Church Courts, 1560-1640', C. Durston & J. Eales, eds., *The Culture*

the parish church wardens, the offender would be presented before the visitation or consistory court, and a decision made as to the appropriate punishment and means of restoration.[25] Though 'reform [was] the aim of every visitation', ecclesiastical justice as such served more as a deterrent and a statement of the boundaries of tolerable behaviour than as an attempt to exercise discipline at the local parish level.[26] Such discipline, if it occurred at all, was intended to punish notorious and unrepentant offenders as examples to the rest and thereby enforce outward conformity not just to the Church but to societal norms as well.[27] But for many clergy influenced by Calvin's example, the episcopal system inherited from the medieval Roman Catholic church had usurped the prerogatives for discipline that were, by biblical right, local and congregational, and to be administered by the local pastor and elders.[28] Nevertheless, national and local efforts to modify or overturn the existing

---

of English Puritanism, 1560-1700 (Basingstoke: MacMillan, 1996), 58-91.

[25] Fincham, *Prelate as Pastor*, 129-146.

[26] Fincham, *Prelate as Pastor*, 129. See Fincham's discussion of Bishop Samuel Harsnett's use of stiff sentences against Sabbath breakers more as general deterrent than as particular justice, 174. Along a different line, Collinson highlights some of the fraternal benefits resulting from gatherings of clergy at visitations and synods. See *The Religion of Protestants: The Church in English Society 1559-1625* (Oxford: Clarendon, 1982), 122-130. Ingram states that 'In retrospect it is clear, contrary to puritan complaints, that these courts proved to be by no means ineffective agents of further reformation in England... ecclesiastical jurisdiction was not divorced from the pastoral mission of the church but part and parcel of it.' 'Puritans and the Church Courts', 69. Unfortunately, individual puritans had neither the luxury of hindsight nor the benefit of several generations with which to chart the reformation progress Ingram cites. These ministers complained precisely because the wheels of ecclesiastical justice seemed to turn so maddeningly slowly and could appear to be arbitrary and ineffective.

[27] See Collinson, *The Elizabethan Puritan Movement*, 346-355; Meic Pearse, *The Great Restoration: The Religious Radicals of the 16th and 17th Centuries* (Carlisle: Paternoster, 1998), 167-174; Collinson, 'The Cohabitation of the Faithful with the Unfaithful', O. Grell, J. Israel and N. Tyacke, eds., *From Persecution to Toleration: The Glorious Revolution and Religion in England* (Oxford: Clarendon, 1991), 52-54. On the coalescing of religious and social standards through the exercise of episcopal discipline, see Martin Ingram, 'Religion, Communities and Moral Discipline in Late Sixteenth- and Early Seventeenth-Century England: Case Studies', K. von Greyerz, ed., *Religion and Society in Early Modern Europe 1500-1800* (London: German Historical Institute, 1984), 179-181.

[28] See Collinson, *Elizabethan Puritan Movement*, 346, 101-155. The dilemma facing puritans was that the inherited and unreformed government of the Church of England as it stood was fundamentally incapable of effecting Biblical discipline. For many, like Thomas Cartwright and Walter Travers, the obvious solution was to proceed forthwith to a reformed government and discipline. Their solution called for a recasting of the entire church structure along a Genevan model, a transformation, it was argued, that would go a long way towards resolving local declensions in discipline.

episcopal structure met with repeated frustration. Under the pretext of enforcing conformity, these more fundamental disagreements with respect to local church discipline under both Elizabeth and James were pushed by the bishops to the margins, where they either simmered in a frustrated state of semi-conformity, or radicalized, leading ultimately to the rejection of the episcopal structure altogether as being beyond reform.[29]

Conformable puritans were tolerated under Archbishop Abbot, but those with a separatist agenda were not. While concerned to cope with the notoriously ungodly in their parishes, the more accommodating puritans were still hopeful that the existing parish system itself could be reformed. But even amongst these more patient puritans, there grew an increasing frustration with a structure and a hierarchy that seemed to fear more the implications of nonconformity and separatism than blatant hypocrisy and scandal at communion.[30]

The most intriguing sources for the pastoral practises of Jacobean and Caroline clergy are Samuel Clarke's collections of biographies of exemplary puritan worthies.[31] Clarke was himself a friend of Baxter's and well acquainted with Baxter's work in Kidderminster. It is, therefore, difficult to gauge the extent to which he presents pre-Baxterian examples of godly ministry that are

---

[29] The point must be made, however, that many of these early radical Protestants were actually against forming gathered churches of visible saints, agreeing instead with the notion of a state church to which everyone belonged. See Pearse, *The Great Restoration,* 161-62. By their call for true Christians to withdraw from what they considered to be corrupt and worldly local parishes and form true churches of visible saints, early separatist leaders such as Robert Browne and Robert Harrison were perceived as posing a direct threat to the existing order and ensured that official displeasure over calls for discipline would continue unabated. And by insisting that effective church discipline could only be instituted by 'gathering the worthy and refusing the unworthy' for church membership and communion, disillusioned separatists broke with those puritans who were still willing to work more or less patiently for reformation from within a Church of England which clearly still needed it. Appalled by the implications of separation, conforming and 'moderate puritans' felt it scandalously arrogant for separatists to pass judgment on the majority of parish members by presuming to establish a true church of the truly saved. See Robert Browne (1550-1633), *A treatise of reformation without tarying for anie* (1582); Robert Browne, *The Writings of Robert Harrison and Robert Browne,* A. Peel and L. Carlson, eds. (London: George Allen and Unwin, 1953), 402, 404; and see, for example, William Bradshaw's *The Unreasonableness of the Separation* (1614). See also Peter Lake's discussion of William Bradshaw's polemic against the separatists in *Moderate Puritans and the Elizabethan Church* (Cambridge: Cambridge University Press, 1982), 272-278. Lake observes that 'it is undeniable that there was a tension between Bradshaw's anti-conformist and his anti-separatist positions. It was the tension experienced, to a greater or lesser degree, by every mainstream puritan ideologue' (276).

[30] John Spurr, *English Puritanism 1603-1689* (Basingstoke: MacMillan, 1998), 30-31.

[31] For Clarke see *CR*, *DNB*, and chapter 8.

influenced by a post-Baxterian pastoral agenda.[32] Though Clarke's *Lives* prove accurate enough when checked against parallel accounts where they exist, his didactic agenda necessitates caution in their use.[33] Often it is the material he chooses *not* to include that raises questions concerning his overall reliability as a source.[34] Even so, Clarke's biographies remain valuable sources when used with caution. For many of these ministers, without his material there would be no story to tell.

In his *Collection of the Lives of Ten Eminent Divines* (1662), Clarke appears to confirm an early use by some ministers of additional means to insure the integrity of the Lord's Supper. The example of William Gouge (1578-1653) seems intended, however, to make contradictory points. On the one hand, Gouge's efforts to 'fence the table' are presented as an exception to contemporary practise. But on the other hand, Clarke also wishes to depict Gouge's efforts as part of a longstanding emphasis among puritan pastors to enforce parish discipline with respect to Communion. Clarke observes that

> Before these times of Examination of persons, before their admission to the Sacrament of the Lords Supper, [Gouge] used to go to the houses of the better sort in his Parish... that he might examine how fit they were to be admitted to that Ordinance... and then his manner was, not to admit any of the younger sort to the Sacrament, till in his judgement he found them fitted for it.[35]

Shortly before his death in 1683, Clarke published an anonymous account of Samuel Fairclough's life in his *Lives of Sundry Eminent Persons* to make similar points. Though I shall more fully analyze issues raised by this account in chapter 8, the author emphasizes the co-operative relationship that existed between Fairclough and the local magistrate, Sir Nathaniel Barnardiston, particularly in the matter of parish discipline. Their strategy 'was to hinder the *intrusion*, or *approaching* of the *visibly prophane* unto the Table of the Lord.' To facilitate this, 'it was unanimously *agreed*, that everyone who should desire to *Communicate*, should first publickly *own his Baptismal Covenant for once*,

---

[32] See Collinson, '"A Magazine of Religious Patterns": An Erasmian Topic Transposed in English Protestantism', in *Godly People*, 499-526. This concern will be explored in greater detail in chapter 8.

[33] See, for example, Jacqueline Eales's 'Samuel Clarke and the "Lives" of Godly Women in Seventeenth Century England', W.J. Sheils and D. Wood, eds., *Women in the Church, Studies in Church History*, 27 (Oxford: Basil Blackwell, 1990), 375.

[34] In the case of Margaret Baxter, it is clear that Clarke edited Richard Baxter's text out of concern for the potential for controversy. See Eales, 'Samuel Clarke', 375.

[35] Samuel Clarke, *A Collection of the Lives of Ten Eminent Divines, famous in their Generations for Learning, Prudence, Piety, and painfulness in the Work of the Ministry* (1662), 107. For Gouge (1578-1653), longtime pastor of St Anne's, Blackfriars, and member of the Westminster Assembly, see Barker, *Puritan Profiles*, 35-38.

before his admission to the Lord Supper; and that *afterwards* they should submit unto *admonition*, in case of the visible and apparent breach of that Covenant.'[36] The author comments that this 'administration of *Confirmation*...could not but make a very effectual *Reformation* in that Town'. As a result, 'prophaneness was *forced* now to hide its head; Drunkenness, Swearing, Cursing, Bastardy, and the like, as they were not *practised*, so they were scarce *known*; divers persons having *lived many years* in that Parish and in the whole time they have never heard *an Oath* sworn, or even saw *one person drunk*, as they have professed'.[37]

Laying aside for the moment questions over the reliability of these portraits, Clarke's accounts square with other sources detailing the persistence of puritan concerns over the lack of local discipline, especially with respect to the celebration of the sacraments and a desire to promote a 'reformation of manners' within the parish.[38] The Fairclough account appears to be another example of the powerful leverage for the regulation of parish life that occurred when ministers who were concerned to effect reformation were able to co-operate with magistrates who were concerned to control social disorder on the basis of a shared religious world view, though without corroborating evidence from parish and court records, it is difficult to confirm the extent of Fairclough's success beyond that of reputation. Where evidence does exist from studies of individual parishes over several generations, such as Drs Wrightson and Levine's study of Terling in Essex, it suggests that the 'confrontational reformist impulse took root most strongly in a particular segment of local society, and that it converged in this social milieu with social anxieties to produce ultimately a programme of reformation which in practise became directed primarily at the village poor.' Although Wrightson allows that 'Puritanism' itself was not a crude form of 'class ideology', but that its

---

[36] Clarke, *The Lives of Sundry Eminent Persons*, 169. Arnold Hunt claims that, for the 1630s, Fairclough's example is an 'exceptional case, made possible by the support and protection of...Barnardiston', and that, however widespread godly concern for discipline might be, Fairclough's practise of discipline appears to be a singularity. Arnold Hunt, 'The Lord's Supper in Early Modern England', in *P&P*, 161 (1998), 64-65.

[37] Clarke, *The Lives of Sundry Eminent Persons*, 169. The author's perception of the connection between the cooperation of ministry and local magistrates in setting up effective discipline and the puritan promised land of reformation is significant, whether or not things in Kedington were actually that different. For a similar, though later example of godly ministry leading to local reformation, see Clarke's account of Thomas Wilson (1601-1654?), 18-35. Clarke gives 1651 as the year of Wilson's death (18), but based on the evidence of Joseph Baker's April 24, 1664 letter to Baxter, announcing Wilson's death, Keeble and Nuttall recommend revising the date to early April 1654. See *Calendar*, 137, no. 177, note 2.

[38] The dramatic increase in the number of separatists choosing exile in the Netherlands or the American colonies in the 1630s combine with the diary entries of pastors such as Ralph Josselin cited above to support such a reading.

'reformatory ideals [fused] with expressions of social anxiety', one wonders if puritan concern for verifiable 'reformation' and magistrate concern for social control were not mutually exploited in such situations, one for the authority to impose a reforming regime, and the other for the theological justification of a particular social policy.[39] However, the fact that William Gouge focused his disciplinary efforts on 'the better sort in his Parish' raises a cautionary flag to those who might be tempted to view 'godly' concern for discipline simply as a means to control the parish poor.[40] Nevertheless, attempts by Elizabethan 'puritan' clergy and laypeople to impose a legislated reformation on the way religion was practiced witness to the long-held assumption that the optimum state for further reformation and the advance of the gospel involved this co-operation between ministry and magistrate. But under an unsympathetic Laudian regime (and indeed throughout the Elizabethan and early Stuart period), these attempts to impose local 'puritan' reformation through the exercise of parish discipline were actually illegal, and were perceived as locally divisive and potentially subversive. Though Archbishop Laud shared many of the same concerns for parish order and morality, his efforts to control preaching and impose uniformity along a more sacramentalist and 'anti-Calvinist' line enflamed desires for a reformed national church government and discipline, which were further frustrated by an episcopal discipline that, from the perspective of its 'puritan' victims, was going after entirely the wrong crowd.[41]

But 'puritan' concern for discipline was more than a reaction to the perceived shortcomings of the episcopal order. Anxiety was also fuelled by a growing sophistication in the way puritans understood the sacraments, particularly the Lord's supper.[42] Laudian concern that the Lord's Supper be rightly celebrated

---

[39] Keith Wrightson, 'Postscript: Terling Revisited', in Keith Wrightson and David Levine, *Poverty and Piety in an English Village: Terling, 1525-1700* (Oxford: Clarendon, 1995), 207, 210-211. For critiques of the 'Terling thesis', see Margaret Spufford, 'Puritanism and Social Control?', A. Fletcher and J. Stevenson, eds., *Order and Disorder in Early Modern England* (Cambridge: Cambridge University Press, 1985); Martin Ingram, 'Religion, Communities and Moral Discipline'; Marjorie K. McIntosh, 'Local Change and Community Control in England, 1465-1500', in *HLQ*, 49 (1986), 219-242. For Wrightson's discussion of these and other critiques, see 'Postscript: Terling Revisited', 198-211.

[40] See Duffy, 'The Godly and the Multitude', 31-55.

[41] See Fincham, 'Introduction', in *Visitation Articles*, xvii. See also Tyacke, 'Puritanism, Arminianism and Counter-Revolution'.

[42] See the evolution of sacramental concern from William Perkins's *A Reformed Catholic* (1611); John Preston, *The Cuppe of Blessing: Delivered in Three Sermons upon 1 Cor.10.16* (1634), and *Three Sermons upon the Sacrament of the Lords Supper* (1631); Lewes Bayly, *The Practice of Pietie: Directing a Christian how to walke that he may please God*. 30th edition (1632), 522-624; Robert Bolton, *The Saints Selfe-enriching Examination. Or, A Treatise concerning the Sacrament of the Lords Supper* (1634). See Hunt, 'The Lord's Supper in Early Modern England', 39-83; Davies,

through conformity to proper external ceremony was curiously matched by puritan clergy. Though scandalized by the reintroduction of what they felt were popish externals, these ministers were nonetheless concerned to ensure proper internal preparation, namely that participants examine their hearts so that they might partake in the sacrament in a worthy manner.[43] Under Laudian censorship, however, puritan concerns over worthy participation were allowed expression only as helps to personal piety; the actual practise of church discipline remained appallingly insufficient.[44] It would take the collapse of the Laudian regime, the shocking proliferation of separatists and sects, and the new political and religious reality wrought by the civil wars to create the conditions in which a new paradigm for local church discipline could be forged.

Efforts to reform church structures along Genevan lines were reignited with the collapse of Laud's episcopal regime, and puritan gentry seized the initiative in parliament to finish England's reformation.[45] Once again, however, concern over local church discipline became subsumed in the general rush to reform the entire structure and worship 'according to the Word of God, and the example of

---

Worship and Theology in England, II, 76-123.

[43] Davies, *Worship and Theology in England*, II, 286-325. Davies traces the puritan attempts to preserve the use of the Lord's Supper from Catholic abuse, but fails to note the increasing importance to puritans of Christ's spiritual presence in the sacrament, and the use to which this truth was put by godly pastors assisting their parishioners to prepare for communion. As a result, Davies is surprised to find Baxter's view of the Lord's Supper to be 'higher' than what was implied in the 1552 and 1559 Prayer Books (320-323). But as we shall see, such a 'high' view of the Lord's Supper goes far to explain puritan concern to receive the sacrament in a worthy manner, which brought the issue of local parish discipline as a means to facilitate worthy reception into sharp and practical focus. See also Margaret Spufford, 'The Importance of the Lord's Supper to Seventeenth-Century Dissenters', in *JURCHS*, 5:2 (1993), 62-79.

[44] Baxter writes, 'The main reason that turneth my heart against the English Prelacy [i.e. the Laudian practise of episcopacy] is because it did destroy Church Discipline, and almost destroy the Church for want of it, or by the abuse of it, and because it is (as then exercised) inconsistent with true Discipline.... And I must say, that I have seen more of the Ancient Discipline exercised of late, without a Prelate, in some Parish Church in *England*, than ever I saw or heard of exercised by the Bishops in a thousand such Churches all my dayes.' Baxter's prefatory letter to the second disputation, to the 'Christian Reader', in *Five Disputations of Church Government, and Worship* (1659), sigs P4v-Q. For the rise of 'Laudianism', see Nicolas Tyacke, *Anti-Calvinists*. In contrast, see Kevin Sharpe, 'Archbishop Laud', M. Todd, ed., *Reformation to Revolution*.

[45] Laud's demise was part of a larger collapse of royal authority throughout England, Scotland and Ireland. See John Morrill's overview of the events precipitating the Civil Wars in his 'Politics in an Age of Revolution 1630-1690', J. Morrill, ed., *The Oxford Illustrated History of Tudor and Stuart Britain* (1996), 364-366. See also Morrill, *The Nature of the English Revolution*.

the best reformed Churches'.[46] But overthrowing episcopacy and the system of church courts proved by far the easier task. As Ingram observes, 'So swiftly did [the church courts] fall...that no proper plans were made for their replacement; and in any case the courts had dominated the scene for so long and performed such complex functions that an adequate substitute was hard to find. Only when they had gone did it become apparent what an important role they had, for all their imperfections, managed to play.'[47]

Following the army's failure to enforce the Westminster Assembly's reforms, clergy beyond London and the counties of Essex and Lancashire where presbyterianism had been established were left to their own devices with respect to local discipline.[48] In the resulting confusion, clergy such as Ralph Josselin of Earls Colne, Suffolk, struggled to channel the discontent felt by the committed minority of his flock with the larger, more prophane parochial community, in ways that might neutralize the urge to separate and form a gathered congregation.[49]

Disappointment with the frustration of legislated reformation was soon displaced by horror at the rapid proliferation of separatists and sects responding to the vacuum of ecclesiastical authority and encouraged by the professed concern for (certain kinds of) 'tender consciences' on the part of Cromwell and the new regime.[50] English separatists took full advantage of the gap between the pulling down of episcopacy and the setting up of its replacement and made lack of discipline a pretext for gathering verifiable saints from the hopelessly corrupt local parishes to form true churches.[51] The possibility of Roman Catholics capitalizing on the resulting religious confusion spawned by the separatists and

---

[46] From 'The Solemn League and Covenant', September 25, 1643, in S.R. Gardiner, ed., *The Constitutional Documents of the Puritan Revolution*, 268.

[47] Ingram, 'Puritans and the Church Courts', 91.

[48] See Morrill, 'The Church in England 1642-9', 156-57. See also W.M. Lamont, 'Episcopacy and a "Godly Discipline", 1641-6', in *JEH*, 10 (1959), 88-89.

[49] '[23 February 1650/1] so now we resolved on the work, how few so ever would joyne and trust god with the same, and to give publike notice to prevent offence, and yett admit none but such as in charity wee reckon to be disciples...we mett at Priory, divers presd that persons must make out a worke of true grace on their hearts in order to fellowship and this ordinance... I...turned them to all places in the Acts and shewed that beleeving admitted into Communion, and none rejected that professed faith, and then if their lives were not scandalous that we could not turn away from them in this ordinance...' Ralph Josselin, *The Diary of Ralph Josselin*, 235-36.

[50] For a more sympathetic treatment of the emerging Cromwellian Church, see Nicolas Tyacke, 'The "Rise of Puritanism" and the Legalizing of Dissent, 1571-1719', in *From Persecution to Toleration*, 29-32. See also Claire Cross, 'The Church in England 1646-1660', G.E. Aylmer, ed., *The Interregnum: The Quest for Settlement 1646-1660* (London: MacMillan, 1974), 99-120.

[51] See Nuttall, *Visible Saints*, 43-69 (on separation), 131-139 (on distinguishing between the profane and the godly).

radical sects was taken very seriously by increasingly alarmed puritan clergy. When Richard Baxter resumed his pastoral ministry upon his return to Kidderminster in 1647, the fact that radicals cited the lack of local church discipline as their primary pretext justifying their separating agendas did not escape his attention.[52]

'[T]he work that may Reform indeed'

In his *Reliquiae Baxterianae* (1696), Richard Baxter paints the sunny picture of a Kidderminster experiencing the double blessing of an effective parish discipline and the resulting reformation.[53] What he does not mention, however, is that discipline and its beneficial effects were the result of a painstaking process that occupied his pastoral attention for more than a decade following his return to Kidderminster in 1647.[54] Though he nowhere describes the precise sequence by which he devised and implemented his programme for church discipline, his thoughts were never far from his latest pastoral initiative. Through his correspondence and published writings, it is possible to reconstruct his progress as he attempted to lead the three thousand souls of St Mary's parish into the promised land of a properly disciplined church.

Baxter was persuaded from his study of Scripture that parish ministers were endowed with episcopal authority with respect to discipline, a view which we have seen forms the biblical foundations of his arguments in *Gildas Salvianus*. While the fall of prelatical episcopacy theoretically allowed the power of the keys to revert to local pastors, the failure to enforce the Westminster Assembly's substitute Presbyterian settlement confronted clergy like Baxter with the unprecedented absence of any guiding structure for local discipline. Some pastors responded by suspending the celebration of the Lord's Supper in their parishes for fear of incurring God's judgment by offering the sacrament to people whose less-than-godly lives and inability to articulate their faith called into question their true standing before God. This led to the scandal of some parishes going for months or even years without communion being offered.[55]

---

[52] Baxter would later point out in a prefatory letter to the Lord Mayor of London, Christopher Pack, that 'the Separatists reproach them for suffering the Impenitent to continue members of their Churches, and make it the pretense of their separation from them; having little to say of any moment against the authorized way of Government, but only against our slackness in the Execution.' Richard Baxter, *A Sermon of Judgement*, sig A9.

[53] *Rel. Bax.*, I, §136, 84-85.

[54] For another recent treatment of Baxter's understanding of discipline, see Lim, 'In pursuit of unity, purity and liberty', 97-109.

[55] Baxter gives the logic behind his own reluctance to administer the Lord's Supper in Kidderminster before 1648: 'And no Minister can groundedly administer the Sacraments to any man but himself, because he can be certain of no mans justification and salvation, being not certain of the sincerity of their faith... And who then durst ever administer a

Even so, it is unlikely that he would have troubled with such a mammoth undertaking had it not been for the provocation of the separatists he encountered during and after the civil wars. Baptists, Quakers and other separatists were having increasing success in recruiting disaffected parishioners from the mixed fields of the parishes to the gathered churches of true believers. The repeated flashpoint was the perceived scandal of allowing notorious and unrepentant sinners to partake of the Lord's Supper along with the saints. There was an urgent sense on the part of clergy that something must be done. But in the absence of an enforceable common discipline, pastors were left on their own to provide for their parishes as best they could.[56] The resulting ecclesiological emergency provided the final impetus pushing Baxter into action. But as Baxter was quick to learn, the issue of discipline reached far beyond providing an adequate fence around the communion table. The nature of the sacraments, the definition of church membership, the role of confirmation, the establishment of disciplinary procedures, the nature of pastoral oversight-Baxter discovered that a review of discipline necessitated a review of each of these areas of church life and ministry, with major implications for the way Christianity was experienced at the local level.

Later, reflecting on the confusing aftermath of the Westminster Assembly, Baxter acknowledged a certain indebtedness to the 'Anabaptists' as God's warning providence to stop the 'common, *secret, unobserved transition* of all people into the name...and Priviledges of Adult Christians', by ceasing to take 'Infant-baptism, and Profession of our Parents, as sufficient Evidence...[for the] Priviledges of [adult] Christians'. Instead, such separatists were God's

---

Sacrament, being never certaine but that he shall thus abuse it: I confesse ingeniously to you, that it was the ignorance of this one point which chiefly caused mee to abstaine from administering the Lords Supper so many yeeres.' *Aphorisms of Justification*, 258-259; see also 251.

[56] Writing for the associated ministers of Cumberland and Westmorland, Richard Gilpin stated, 'When we compare the present miseries and distempers with our former confident expectations of unitie, and reformation, our hearts bleed, and melt within us... Prophanness thrives through want of Discipline'. [Richard Gilpin], *Agreement of the Associated Ministers & Churches of the Counties of Cumberland and Westmerland: With something for Explication and Exhortation Annexed* (1656), sig A2, 2. The agreement had been in effect since 1653, having been devised contemporaneously with, yet independently from Baxter's Worcestershire Association. For Richard Gilpin (1625-1700), pastor at Greystoke, Cumberland, and the grand-nephew of Bernard Gilpin, see *DNB & CR*. Such comments were echoed by an anonymous author writing on behalf of godly ministers in Norwich and Norfolk: 'We cannot in the least doubt... that many of you...have with an equall moving of Bowels with (if not exceeding any of) us, considered the sad effects, which the want of a *setled Discipline* in the Church...have produced in...this Nation.' *The Agreement of the Associated Ministers In the County of Norfolk and City and County of Norwich, Concerning Publick Catechizing* (1659), sig A2-A2v.

providential scourge to drive pastors (such as himself?) to 'require of [parishioners] a sober, serious Profession and Covenanting by themselves, in owning their Baptismal Covenant, before we number them with Adult Christians'. By forcing pastors to make fundamental changes in the way church membership was understood, Baxter perceived that the trouble caused by the separatists would 'prove a mercy to us in the End, if we have the wit and grace to learn this...and then the Reformation will do us more good, then ever the Anabaptists did us harm.'[57]

Baxter's commitment to the exercise of church discipline was already clear in 1649 with the publication of his first book, *Aphorisms of Justification*. Answering questions on how one can discern whether someone is able to receive Communion and how a parish not involved with one of the new presbyteries can hope to effect church discipline, Baxter urges implementation of disciplinary procedures, both to stop the mouths of lazy separatists who abandon the weak and lost for the sake of purity, and to maintain the integrity of the Lord's Supper.[58] His letter 'To my dearly beloved Friends...of Kederminster' prefacing his *Saints Everlasting Rest* in 1650 also reveals finely honed ideals when it comes to descriptions of the pastor's office and the processes of mutual admonition and discipline.[59] It was his attempt to implement these ideals, however, that caused Baxter trouble. His later recollections allude to a controversy during the period after his return to Kidderminster during which he met with significant resistance within the parish to his initial attempts to establish discipline, particularly as it related to the Lord's Supper: 'the state of my own Congregation, and the necessity of my Duty, constrained me to make some Attempt [to establish discipline in Kidderminster]. For I must administer the Sacraments to the Church, and the ordinary way of Examining every Man before they come, I was not able to prove necessary, and the people were averse to it: So that I was forced to think of the matter more seriously.'[60]

Other than this last hint, we know tantalizingly little about Baxter's response to this parish-wide rebuff to his initial attempts to institute discipline. We do not know what colleagues he may have consulted, for his surviving letters show him only dispensing advice or arguing his positions, not asking for input. Nor are we given any indication of anything he might have read during this time that proved influential.[61] We do have his recollection that, once he resolved on

---

[57] Baxter, *Confirmation and Restauration*, 248-249. See Lim, 'In pursuit of unity, purity and liberty', 67-77.

[58] Baxter, *Aphorisms of Justification*, 248-251.

[59] Baxter, *The Saints Everlasting Rest*, sigs A4, A5v.

[60] *Rel. Bax.*, II, §28, 148.

[61] Baxter does cite William Lyford (*William Lyford his Legacy, or a Help for Young People to Prepare them for the Sacrament*, 1656) and Thomas Ball (*Poimhnopurgoz. Pastorum Propugnaculum. Or, the Pulpits Patronage Against the Force of Un-Ordained*

a new attempt to establish a workable discipline that was 'most agreeable to the Word of God', it struck him that 'if all the Ministers did accord together in one way, the People would much more readily submit, than to the way of any Minister that was singular.'[62] This idea, as we shall see, set in motion the proceedings leading to the establishment of the Worcestershire Association. But at the heart of the Association lay Baxter's already-formulated strategy to establish a workable church discipline.

It appears that by attempting to enforce a kind of church discipline on the parishioners in Kidderminster, Baxter found himself having to choose between two unworkable options: he could either begin the process of identifying, admonishing and, if necessary, banning all the impenitent sinners within the parish, or he could continue as before and forebear the practise of parish discipline. His conscience would not allow the latter, for then he would betray his calling from God to shepherd God's flock and simply hand the church over to godlessness.[63] However, 'if we shall exercise the Discipline of Christ upon all in our ordinary Parishes what work shall we make? I will tell you what work, from so much experience'. Baxter gives a bleak answer to his own question:

> We shall have such a multitude to excommunicate, or reject that it will make the sentence grow almost contemptible by the commonness.... But all this is nothing: but that which sticks upon my heart is this: ...We shall be the cruellest enemies to the Souls of our poor peple in the world: and put them the very next step to Hell. For as soon as even we have rejected them, and cast them under publique shame, they hate us to the heart, and either will never heare us more, or hear us with so much hatred and malice or bitterness of spirit, that they are never like to profit by us...[64]

Grappling with these two options forced Baxter to step back and re-examine the ends and means of puritan ministry, and his resulting strategy for discipline was at a level of sophistication new to the English context. 'Either we must have Churches without the Discipline of Christ', writes Baxter, 'or else we must utterly undo our people, body and Soul forever, and plunge them into a

---

Usurpation, and Invasion, 1656) as authorities in support of his programme of church discipline. However, they were both published too late to be considered sources of his views. See *Gildas Salvianus*, sigs b6-b7.

[62] *Rel. Bax.*, II, §28, 148.

[63] For 'he that dare take on him to be an Overseer and Ruler of the Church, not to oversee and rule it, and dare *settle* on such a Church-state, as is uncapable of Discipline is so perfidious to Christ, and ventureth so boldly to make the Church another thing, that I am resolved not to be his follower.' Baxter, *Confirmation and Restauration*, 173-174.

[64] Ibid., 174-176.

desperate state, and make all our following labours in vaine to multitudes of them'. 'Or else', he determines, 'we must take another course, than to admit all our Parishes to Adult Church-membership, as was formerly done, without preparation, and fitness for such a state.'[65] It is likely that this alternative 'course' provided the insight that transformed Baxter's understanding of pastoral ministry and became the foundation for each of the distinctive modifications he would make in his pastoral practise.

Baxter does not divulge the source of this new 'course'. But his later emphatic commendation of Martin Bucer's strategy for 'Parish-Discipline, and pure Communion' in *An Apology for the Nonconformists Ministry* (1681)[66], suggests that the solution to Baxter's dilemma may have come from a timely reading of Bucer's *Scripta Anglicana*. We have already noted the consonance between Bucer and Baxter in their understandings of reformation and their overarching pastoral strategy. With respect to church discipline, the similarities in emphasis and detail between Bucer's conception of church discipline and that which Baxter developed are equally striking.

By finding 'another course', Baxter formulated a sustainable pastoral strategy in which church discipline could work, not by becoming the negative and censorious tool of overly-moralistic pastoral efforts, but by providing the procedural boundaries in which an effective and essentially positive pastoral ministry might take place. The way forward for Baxter was suggested by a distinction (which Bucer had also made) between infant and adult church membership which preserved both the integrity of the parish system and the validity of infant baptism.[67]

Against the arguments of the separatists, Baxter affirmed that the parishes of the Church of England were true particular churches, though he agreed with them that they were in dire need of reform. The members of the parish had been baptized and received into the church as infants, and thus every parishioner was entitled to the rights of infant church membership.[68] Provision had been made in church canons for those baptized as infants to proceed to the privileges and responsibilities of adult membership through the process of confirmation, a process that was supposedly secured by episcopal verification of the confirmands' grasp of the faith.[69] But as Baxter's own *ad hoc* experience of being 'bishopped' indicates, confirmation remained in many places a mere

---

[65] Ibid., 180.

[66] Baxter, *An Apology for the Nonconformists Ministry*, sig A2.

[67] See Baxter's discussion of the relative merits of confirmation rightly practiced versus the believer's baptism of the 'Anabaptists': *Rel. Bax.*, I, §137, 25, 92-93.

[68] Ministers should extend pastoral care to all such members, 'denying them nothing that lawfully we can yield them, in matters of Buryal, Marrying, Praying, Preaching, or the like.' Baxter, *Confirmation and Restauration*, 284.

[69] See Fincham, *Prelate as Pastor*, 123-29.

formality, despite episcopal protestations to the contrary.[70] Baxter recalled, 'And though the Canons require, that the Curate or Minister send a Certificate that children have learnt the Catechism; yet there was no such thing done... This was the old careless practise of this Excellent Duty of Confirmation... the common way, by which our Parishes come to be Churches, and our people to be Christians...'[71] Thus 'by this untried Entrance of all sorts into our Churches', men and women who were ignorant of basic Christian teaching and whose lives were a scandal to Christian profession were admitted into full adult membership and given the right to participate in the Lord's Supper, and given the assurance thereby that their eternal well-being was secure. It was this considerable block of people in any given parish that constituted the greatest hindrance to an effective church discipline, and indeed an effective ministry.[72]

But the solution would require far more than simply tightening the procedure of episcopal confirmation. In the absence of a functioning episcopate, Baxter was free to improvise a process, managed by the local pastor within the local parish, whereby the rights of adult church membership were made contingent upon a credible profession of faith and of consent to submit to pastoral oversight and discipline. Those who found themselves unfit for such a step could undergo a period of preparation to acquaint themselves with the fundamentals of Christian faith without calling their baptismal rights into question. The pastor could apply himself directly to helping them come to Christian faith and profession. Discipline would be exercised only on those who had willingly consented to place themselves under it. Thus the Lord's Supper would be reserved for those in the parish who understood and professed the faith and who had willingly agreed to place themselves under the pastor's oversight. The ignorant or otherwise ungodly members of the parish were excluded from the Lord's Supper, but given a clear procedure by which they might become full adult members.[73]

Baxter put his new 'course' into practise in Kidderminster sometime between 1650 and 1652. And because his neighbor pastors liked what they saw

---

[70] For Baxter's account of his own confirmation by Bishop Morton, see *Confirmation and Restauration*, 154-156.

[71] Ibid., 155-156.

[72] Ibid., 166. Says Baxter, '...by this hastening and admitting all the unprepared in to the Number of Adult Christians, and members of the Church, we do either put a necessity upon our selves to throw away Church-discipline, or else to be most probably the damnation of our peoples Souls, and make them desperate, and almost past all hope, or remedy.' *Confirmation and Restauration*, 172.

[73] For similarities between Baxter's 'covenant' and the covenants devised by separatist and Congregational churches during 1640-1660 as a means for protecting the purity of the Sacraments and local church fellowship, see G.F. Nuttall, *Visible Saints*, 70-81. Whether Baxter drew inspiration for his notion of 'parishioner consent' from his congregational or separating brethren or from his reading of Martin Bucer, or both, remains an open question. For a further discussion of this issue, see chapter 6.

happening in Kidderminster, when presented with Baxter's concurrent ideas for ministerial association, they made Baxter's church member covenant the heart of their 1653 Agreement and the basis of associational discipline. Like Baxter, they had discovered that 'Discipline cannot be exercised without the peoples consent...and we have at present no full discovery of their consent'.[74]

Within the context of Baxter's redefined relationship between pastor and parishioners, dealing with errant members became a relatively straight-forward application of the dominical process outlined in Matthew 18:15-17.[75] Enforcement of this discipline, at least as Baxter himself put it into practise, involved a significant logistical commitment on the part of ministers, magistrates and church members. Even before the pastor was involved, church members were required to attempt loving admonishment of their wayward fellow-member in private in the presence of a witness. If such private admonishment was unsuccessful in promoting repentance, then the case was to be brought to the attention of the church officers, who would 'hear the case, and admonish them with authority'. If repentance was still not forthcoming, then it was the minister's duty 'to rebuke such before all the Church, and to call them publickly to repentance.'[76] If, after all this there was no change, the person would be warned by the minister in private of the eternal and temporal consequences of their continued impenitent heart. At this point, Baxter would enlist the help of two councils designed specifically to help recalcitrant sinners understand the seriousness of their condition. Once a month on the day before the meeting of the Association, Baxter scheduled a 'parochial meeting', attended by three local Justices of the Peace, three or four ministers (including Baxter and his assistants), three or four deacons and 'twenty of the ancient and godly Men of the Congregation, who pretended to no Office, as Lay-Elders, but

---

[74] [Baxter], *Christian Concord*, sig B2, article XVIII. *Christian Concord* contains models of the profession of faith and of the profession of consent for pastors to use in their own parishes, see sigs C3-C3v. Baxter hints at a similar covenantal process that predicated his original coming to Kidderminster in 1641. See *The Saints Everlasting Rest*, 601. Samuel Clarke recounts a similar episode of covenant-making as part of the negotiations concerning his return to Alcester following the Civil War. Clarke, *The Lives of Sundry Eminent Persons*, 9. The significant change introduced by Baxter was in making the adult rights of church membership contingent on the profession and consent with which the covenant was comprised. See chapter 6 for a detailed discussion on the formation of the Worcestershire Association.

[75] Baxter was sensitive to charges that his covenantal basis for the exercise of church discipline promoted either separation or the formation of *ecclesiola in ecclesia*. His response was that 'we require not this Profession as a Church-making Covenant, but for Reformation of those that are Churches already; and as a means for our more facile and successful exercise of some Discipline and Government of our Congregations'. Baxter, 'An Explication of some Passages in the foregoing Propositions and Profession', appended to *Christian Concord*, 10.

[76] [Baxter], *Christian Concord*, sigs A4-B.

only met as the Trustees of the whole Church'.[77] The offender was required to be present, and his case was heard, and he was urged to repent. If he was still unwilling to repent, he was then required to attend the meeting of the Association, which would be held on the following day. There he would be further admonished, 'with all possible tenderness'. This failing to produce repentance, his case would be referred back to the local minister who, after several Sundays of further unsuccessful public admonition and prayer, would act to remove the impenitent sinner from Communion and fellowship.

There are certainly similarities between Baxter's 'course' and discipline as attempted by an increasing number of godly pastors during Civil War and Interregnum England, such as efforts to restrict the 'visibly prophane' from participating in Communion, 'owning' one's baptismal covenant and submitting to 'admonition'. But at the heart of Baxter's reconfiguration of discipline in the 1650s was the redefinition of the pastor's relationship with the parish in general, and those parishioners who wished to own the rights and privileges of full adult membership in the church in particular.[78] Summarizing the emphasis which enabled effective discipline and sustained the heart of his pastoral agenda, Baxter argued:

> Readers, because as it is not *having food*, but *eating* it that must nourish you, nor *having clothes*, but *wearing* them that must keep you warm, nor *having* a Physician, but opening your cases to him, and taking and following his advice, that must cure you; so it is not *having faithful Pastors*, but understanding their Office, and use, and applying your selves to them for necessary advice in publike and private, and submitting to their holy Ministrations, that must make you savingly partakers of the blessing of their Office and labours.[79]

For Baxter, church discipline involved more than the mutual admonition and

---

[77] Baxter's aversion to the Presbyterian understanding of eldership is here transparent. In Baxter's expansion of the duties of these 'trustees', he states that 'they were chosen once a year here unto (as *Grotius de Imperio Sum Potest*. adviseth)'. The asterisk refers to a note in the margin, '*The Principles of which Book I most liked and followed.' *Rel. Bax.*, II, §31, 150. See Hugo Grotius, *De Imperio Summarum Potestatum Circa Sacra* (Paris, 1647). See also Harm-Jan van Dam, '*De Imperio Summarum Potestatum Circa Sacra*', H.J.M Nellen and E. Rabbie, eds, *Hugo Grotius Theologian* (Leiden: Brill, 1994), 19-39.

[78] Baxter gives twelve reasons why discipline is necessary in his retrospective *Universal Concord* (1660), sigs a6-a7. See also *Rel. Bax.*, I, §137, 25, 92, for a more concise list.

[79] Richard Baxter, 'To the Reader', in Samuel Clark (the younger), *Ministers Dues and Peoples Duty* (1661), unpaginated. Baxter's letter is dated 'Nov.10.1660'. For Clark (1626-1701), ejected Rector of Grendon Underwood, Buckinghamshire, see *CR*, 119-120.

church censure implied in Matthew 18:15-17. And it went further than simply preventing the impenitent from participating in the Lord's Supper. It necessitated the redirection of the minister's time and energy into the personal oversight of each person's spiritual condition. This meant, first of all, knowing the people of his parish so that as their shepherd he might know their spiritual condition and needs. Baxter recognized that this could only occur through a process of systematic visitation.[80] But he also observed that this personal oversight served to make his preaching more effective.[81] Secondly, it meant redefining the relationship between pastor and parishioner by calling each adult parish member to demonstrate that they understood the basics of their faith and that they were willing to have Baxter as their pastor.[82] This would be expressed through the use of a written covenant professing faith and expressing consent to Baxter's pastoral oversight, along with a public profession of faith and obedience.[83] Participation in the special rights of adult members, such as the Lord's Supper, was made contingent on willingness to profess faith and obedience, though other parish rights such as burial, marriage and visitation of the sick were still available to baptized parishioners.[84] Thirdly, it involved a process by which those not yet ready to make such a profession might be taught the basics of the faith through the use of a catechism. As we have seen in *Gildas Salvianus*, Baxter later decided to go beyond the standard practise of catechizing children and servants weekly in the church by adding an element of catechesis in his regular round of visitation to all the families of his parish.[85] Fourthly, it involved a process of confirmation, by having young people who were of age make a covenant and profession of faith and obedience, by which they gained the rights of adult church members, namely participation in the Lord's Supper.[86] And fifthly, it involved establishing a disciplinary process by which those who had consented to pastoral oversight could be admonished if found in a state of unrepentant sin, with the hopes of provoking repentance, first in private by fellow members and, if unsuccessful, by successively more

---

[80] Baxter, *The Saints Everlasting Rest*, sig A4, 508-509; *Christian Concord*, sig A3v.

[81] Baxter's own practise of 'knowing' his parishioners is reflected in his sophisticated diagnosis of his parishioners' spiritual state contained in *Confirmation and Restauration*, 157-165. 'Of these twelve sorts of People, this Parish is composed, which I therefore mention, that the state of our Parishes may be truly known; while others are compared with this: For everyone hath not had the opportunity which I have had, to know all their people, or the most.' (165). See Duffy, 'The Godly and the Multitude', 37-40.

[82] Baxter, *The Unreasonableness of Infidelity*, 150-152; *Christian Concord*, sigs B2, C2.

[83] *Christian Concord*, especially sigs C2-C3v; *Certain Disputations of Right to Sacraments*, Disputation 1.

[84] Baxter, *Certain Disputations of Right to Sacraments*, Disputations 4 & 5; see also *Rel. Bax.*, I, §137, 25, 91.

[85] [Baxter], *The Agreement of Divers Ministers of Christ*; *Gildas Salvianus*; *Universal Concord*, 34-35; *Rel. Bax.*, I, §135, 83; I, §136, 85; also II, §40-42, 179-180.

[86] Baxter, *Confirmation and Restauration*; *Universal Concord*, sigs G2v-G3.

public means.[87] If the offender remained impenitent even after the pastor's rebuke and admonition before the whole church, he or she would be banned from Communion and shunned by the rest of the community.

Baxter admitted this final aspect of discipline was a last resort, when the pastor's focus was forced to shift at last from the care of the individual to the welfare and purity of the whole church.[88] What set Baxter apart from the separatists' concern for the purity of the church and the integrity of the sacraments, however, was his concern that the 'poor people' of the parishes be given the opportunity to make amends if it were a matter of ungodliness or comprehend the gospel if it were a matter of ignorance:

> Do not do as the lazy separatists, that gather a few of the best together, and take then [sic] only for their charge, leaving the rest to sink or swim... If any walk scandalously, and disorderly, deal with them for their recovery... If they prove obstinate after all, then avoid them and cast them off; But do not so cruelly as to unchurch them by hundreds & by thousands, and separate from them as so many Pagans, and that before any such means hath been used for their recovery.[89]

Instead 'we must use all the means we can to instruct the ignorant in the matters of their salvation', through public preaching and private personal instruction, laboring 'to be acquainted with the state of all our people as fully as we can' and applying the remedy thereunto.[90] Baxter had understood all along that the real need for most of the people in his parish was for their conversion. He now possessed the means to do everything humanly possible to effect it.

With the possible exception of Samuel Clarke's 1683 portrayal of Samuel Fairclough's ministry, Baxter's reconfigured programme of church discipline was a different species altogether from anything being practiced by the pastors of England at the time. But when set alongside Martin Bucer's instructions for discipline published in Latin folio of his collected English works, *Scripta Anglicana*, the likeness suggests more than coincidence. At the very least, Baxter implemented a Bucerian programme of pastoral oversight and discipline. For as he points out to the moderate bishops addressed in his *An Apology for the Nonconformists Ministry* (1681)[91], he was not the first person to

---

[87] See Baxter, *Aphorisms of Justification*, 248-251; *The Saints Everlasting Rest*, sig A5v; *Christian Concord*, sigs A3v-B; *Universal Concord*, 18-19.

[88] Baxter, *Gildas Salvianus*, 98.

[89] Baxter, *The Saints Everlasting Rest*, 509.

[90] Baxter, *Gildas Salvianus*, 81.

[91] 'To the Right Reverend Dr. *Compton*, Lord Bishop of *London*, Dr. *Barlow*, Lord Bishop of *Lincoln*, Dr. *Grosts*, Lord Bishop of *Hereford*, Dr. *Rainbow*, Lord Bishop of *Carlisle*, Dr. *Thomas*, Lord Bishop of St *Davids*, Dr. *Lloyd*, Lord Bishop of

call the English Church to reform the local parishes by reforming the ministry, or to challenge English pastors to know their flock and teach them from house to house, or to insist that participation in the Lord's Supper be restricted to those in the parish who would publicly profess their faith and their obedience to the church and pastor, or to make confirmation a process of owning one's Christian profession and taking on adult church responsibilities and rights, or to demand that all true Christians in the parish submit to discipline and pastoral oversight, or to make the establishment of discipline within the parish to be the chief means to promote the conversion of the ungodly multitude and the reformation of the community. Baxter's was a call to systematic parish discipline that England had heard before.

The results, if we can credit his own account, were startling. Writing in 1656 in the midst of his labours in Kidderminster, Baxter reflected, 'I must confess I find by some experience that this is the work that may Reform indeed; that must expell our common prevailing ignorance; that must bow the stubborn hearts of men; that must...help the success of our publike preaching; and must make true godliness a commoner thing, through the grace of God, which worketh by means.'[92] Later, summarizing the 'successes' that marked his ministry, Baxter noted that his preaching was met by 'an attentive diligent Auditory', and that so many began to be converted through his preaching and 'private conferences' that he was unable to keep count. The 'capacious' sanctuary was 'usually full, so that we were fain to build five Galleries after my coming thither'. And in what became a model description of reformation come to a town, he stated that on Sundays 'there was no disorder to be seen in the Streets, but you might hear an hundred Families singing Psalms and repeating Sermons, as you passed through the Streets'. Moreover, he claimed that 'when I came thither first, there was about one Family in a Street that worshipped God and called on his Name, and when I came away there were some Streets where there was not past one Family in the side of a Street that did not so; and that did not by professing serious Godliness give us hopes of their sincerity.'[93]

Baxter was convinced that church discipline played a decisive role in his success, the exercise of which 'was no small furtherance of the Peoples Good: For I found plainly that without it I could not have kept the Religious sort from Separations and Divisions.'[94] However, he did not deny that the institution of

---

Peterborough'. Baxter, *An Apology for the Nonconformists Ministry* (1681), sig A2. For the Restoration episcopate, see Spurr, *The Restoration Church,* 132-65.

[92] Baxter, *Gildas Salvianus,* sig (a6)v.

[93] *Rel. Bax.,* I, §136, 84-85. For the similar role played by separatists in Bucer's development of church discipline, see Henry G. Krahn, 'Martin Bucer's Strategy Against Sectarian Dissent in Strasbourg', in *MQR,* 50:3 (1976), 163-180; Kenneth R. Davis, 'No Discipline No Church: An Anabaptist Contribution to the Reformed Tradition', in *SCJ,* 13:4 (1982), 43-58.

[94] *Rel. Bax.,* I, §137, 91.

discipline 'displeased many', and that 'for fear of Discipline, all the Parish kept off [i.e. refused to participate in communion] except about Six hundred, when there were in all above Sixteen hundred at Age to be Communicants. Yet because it was their own doing [having chosen not to own their adult membership], and they knew that they might come in when they would, they were quiet in their Separation'.[95]

Having endured the scorn and abuse of separatists on the one hand, who had given up on the Church of England parish system as hopelessly corrupt and beyond remedy, and the contempt of Prelatists as being party to the general collapse of authority and the rise of the sects, Baxter looked upon his experience in Kidderminster with a sense of vindication. Those Independents and Baptists, who 'had before conceited that Parish Churches were the great Obstruction of all true Church Order and Discipline... did quite change their Minds when they saw what was done at *Kiderminster*, and began to think now, that it was much through the faultiness of the Parish Ministers, that Parishes are not in a better Case; and that it is a better Work thus to reform the Parishes, than gather Churches out of them'.[96] And against the Prelatists' revisionary charge that post-civil war Nonconformity had left nothing but scandalous disorder in its wake, Baxter countered,

> Look into this County where I live, and you shall find a faithful, humble, laborious Ministry, Associated and walking in as great unity as ever I read of since the Apostles daies.... Was there such a Ministry, or such love and concord, or such a godly people under them in the Prelates reign? There was not.... Through the great mercy of God, where we had ten drunken Readers then, we have not one now: and where we had one able godly Preacher then, we have many now: and in my own charge, where there was one that then made any shew of the fear of God, I hope there is twenty now: And the Families that were want to scorn at holiness, and live in open impiety, are now devoted to the worship and obedience of the Lord. This is our loss and misery in these times which you so lament.[97]

Baxter could demonstrate that discipline was producing results. But privately, he also wondered if most of those attempting to further reformation in the English Church had not been diverted into a huge *cul de sac*. Writing in 1655 to Thomas Wadsworth, the Rector of Newington Butts in Surrey, Baxter commented: 'It is the com*m*on err*ou*r that hath confounded us in church affairs,

---

[95] Ibid., I, §136, 85; I, §137, 25, 91.

[96] Ibid., I, §136, 85-86.

[97] Baxter, 'A Preface to those of the Nobility, Gentry, and Commons of this Land, that adhere to Prelacy', in *Five Disputations of Church Government, and Worship*, 28-29.

to lay too much upon the *forme* or *way* of Government or Order, & too little upon the prudent, resolute Industrious execution.' While Independents, Presbyterians and Anglicans debated the relative merits of their systems, want of earnest implementation at the parish level meant inevitable frustration of godly aims. 'Of the three sorts of Government now contended for, I thinke the worst well executed by good men will do much more good, than the best if formally & negligently carried on.'[98] Throughout his remaining years in Kidderminster, Baxter would continue his attempts to persuade his colleagues to go beyond mere talk and to *practice* church discipline; it did not hurt that he had also recovered for England's parishes one of the most effective means to that end.

Conclusion

Richard Baxter had long argued that 'publick Preaching is not all the ordinary Work of a faithful Minister' and that an over-emphasis on preaching had failed to accomplish the reformation it sought to induce.[99] Moreover, attempts to cure the Church's ills by fixing its government and ceremonies had been frustrated. And efforts to resolve the parochial 'holy war' between the godly and their less-than-godly neighbours by breaking away from the parish system to establish separate churches of 'visible saints' served only to alienate further the very people who needed the gospel. Something more was needed. Baxter's adaptation of a Bucerian blueprint for parish discipline not only preserved the sacraments from profanation and kept potential separatists from causing trouble, but gave him hope that the resulting conversion of nominal parish members would lead to the reformation of the entire community. It was this 'something more' that Baxter put into practise in Kidderminster.

But Kidderminster was not the Kedington of Clarke's Fairclough hagiography. And the absence of cooperation between ministry and Kidderminster's leading magistrate meant that reformation, impressive enough as it was, would never be entirely realized. Moreover, Baxter's discipline could only function in the context of the relative religious freedom of the Interregnum years or under a modified form of episcopal government. With Cromwell's death in 1658, the former could not last, and in the increasingly vindictive attitude of the Restoration Anglicans, the latter was not to be. The 'prelatical' Anglicans who came to dominate the restoration proceedings made much of their authority and of submission and conformity to their government. They had, according to Baxter, 'since the War...gone to a greater Distance, and

---

[98] The letter is dated 20 April 1655. DWL, BxL, MS 59, ii, 252. For Thomas Wadsworth (1630-76), who served at Newington Butts from 1653-1660, and then as curate of St Lawrence Pountney, London, from January of 1662 until he was ejected in August, see *CR, DNB, Calendar* I, no. 235, note, 172. See also no. 238.
[99] *Rel. Bax.*, II, §40, 179.

grown higher than before, and denied the very being of the Reformed Churches and Ministry; and avoided all ways of Agreement with them, but by an absolute Submission to their Power (as the Papists do by the Protestants)'.[100] Under legislation that restored previously sequestered Anglican ministers to their former livings, Baxter's place in Kidderminster was taken by George Dance.[101] But as Baxter noted, 'The Ruler of the Vicar, and all the Business there was, Sir *Ralph Clare*, an old Man, and an old Courtier, who carried it towards me all the time I was there with great Civility and Respect, and sent me a Purse of Money when I went away (but I refused it).' Though he respected Baxter's abilities, he found the changes which Baxter introduced in the pastor's role and the church's discipline to be incompatible with his Laudian predispositions. 'His Zeal against all that scrupled Ceremonies, or that would not preach for Prelacy, and Conformity, &c. was so much greater than his Respects to me, that he was the principal Cause of my Removal (though he has not owned it to this Day').[102]

Given the striking ability that English parishioners had demonstrated for generations of avoiding the ire of the authorities and conforming (eventually) their practise of religion to the prevailing whims of the Sovereign (through Henrician and Edwardian reforms, the Marian return of Catholicism, the half-way Elizabethan reforms, the Caroline re-emphasis of a sacramentalist orientation and de-emphasis of a Calvinist perspective),[103] Sir Ralph may, with some justification, have thought that one more redefinition of right religion would be met yet again with pliable conformity: 'I suppose he thought that when I was far enough off, he could so far rule the Town as to reduce the People to his way.' But as Baxter saw it, a fundamental change seems to have taken place in many parishioners' understanding of the role of religion: for Sir Ralph 'little knew (nor others of that Temper) how firm conscientious Men are to the Matters of their everlasting Interest, and how little Mens Authority can do against the Authority to God, with those that are unfeignedly subject to him.'[104] Religion of convention and convenience had, from Baxter's point of view, been transformed by the 'Discipline of Christ', in Kidderminster at least, to religion of the heart. In the wake of the Restoration dismantling of his Kidderminster pastoral strategy, however, hindsight would persuade Baxter that England's reformation had once again been narrowly averted by England's reluctant Protestants.

---

[100] Ibid., II, §66, 207.

[101] For Dance, see *WR*.

[102] *Rel. Bax.*, II, §152, 298.

[103] Duffy's *Voices of Morebath* gives a superb example of what this process was like in the experience of one small English parish during the Henrician, Edwardian and Elizabethan Reformations. See also Robert Whiting, *Local Responses to the English Reformation* (London: MacMillan, 1998), 135-36.

[104] *Rel. Bax.*, II, §151, 298.

CHAPTER 6

Baxter's Worcestershire Association and the Emergence of Reformed Pastors

In the previous chapter we examined Baxter's programme for parish discipline and the central role it played in his overall strategy to promote local reformation. In this chapter we will investigate the development of the Worcestershire Association and see how concerns over the absence of viable ecclesiastical structures and the perceived threat from separatists and sects led Baxter to modify an existing associational convention into a regional structure that could assist parish ministers in their efforts to maintain discipline and encourage parish reformation.

Surveying the wreckage of English Nonconformity some six years after he was forced into early retirement from his Kidderminster ministry, Richard Baxter writes:

> And I must add this to the true Information of Posterity, That God did so wonderfully bless the Labours of his *unanimous faithful Ministers*, that had it not been for the Faction of the Prelatists on one side that drew men off, and the Factions of the giddy and turbulent Sectaries on the other side (who pull'd down all Government, cried down the Ministers, and broke all into Confusion, and made the People at their wits end, not knowing what Religion to be of); together with some *laziness* and *selfishness* in many of the Ministry, I say, had it not been for these Impediments, *England* had been like in a quarter of an Age to have become a Land of Saints, and a Pattern of Holiness to all the World, and the unmatchable Paradise of the Earth. Never were such fair opportunities to sanctifie a nation, lost and trodden under foot, as have been in this Land of late! Woe be to them that were the Causes of it.[1]

---

[1] *Rel. Bax.*, I, §139, 97. A few pages earlier, Baxter prefaces some comments about the godly citizens of Kidderminster, 'though I have been now absent from them about six years....' I, §136, 86.

Baxter's exercise in hindsight is significant in that it treats his labours for Christian unity not as a singularity or as the noble but frustrated pursuit of an ecumenical ideal.[2] Instead it places his passion for church concord squarely within the context of his concern for the reformation of the English Church and its ministry. The energy with which he pursued the organizing and facilitating of the Worcestershire Association, the immediate nation-wide approbation which met his associational ideas in *Christian Concord* (1653), and his bitter dejection when the Worcestershire Association and the sixteen sister associations which sprang up in its wake were demolished with the re-imposition of episcopacy at the Restoration-none of these makes sense apart from viewing the Worcestershire Association as a means to further Baxter's *pastoral* agenda for parish reformation.[3] What follows is a re-examination of the extensive evidence relating to the Worcestershire Association from the perspective of Baxter's own stated concerns and pastoral agenda, and an account which views his efforts as part of a long-standing impulse among 'godly' pastors in the Elizabethan and early Stuart Church to associate for purposes of mutual encouragement and for the promotion of local reformation.

The Worcestershire Association, those *'unanimous faithful Ministers'*, formed and guided under Baxter's initiative in 1653, has been regarded as 'one of his greatest achievements',[4] and as an organization for which there was 'no previous precedent in England'.[5] Such acknowledgements have led succeeding generations of historians to reassemble Baxter's descriptions of its development and functions and to locate its members in their local contexts.[6] But while the particulars of the Association's genesis and Baxter's indefatigable efforts in its

---

[2] See, for example, A.M. Derham's perspective on Baxter's purpose for the Worcestershire Association in 'Richard Baxter and the Oecumenical Movement', *EQ*, 23 (1951), 96-99.

[3] N.H. Keeble states that the Worcestershire Association was Baxter's 'attempt to create by practical Christianity' 'what force and politics had failed to achieve-reformation'. Keeble, *Richard Baxter*, 155.

[4] Gilbert, 'Richard Baxter's Ministry', 60.

[5] Gordon, *Heads of English Unitarian History*, 65. Nuttall quotes Gordon with approval in *Richard Baxter*, 69. Contrast Gordon's view with that of Tom Webster in a more recent study of Caroline clerical associations in *Godly Clergy*, 75-92. There were also other associations which formed in the 1650s amongst General, Seventh Day and Particular Baptists, and later, of a sort, among Quakers. See, for example, Nuttall's 'The Baptist Western Association', 213-218; see also Nuttall's 'Association Records of the Particular Baptists', 14-25. A comparison of these associations with the voluntary association movement would be fruitful, but is beyond my present scope.

[6] See Powicke, *A Life of the Reverend Richard Baxter*, 163-176; Nuttall, *Richard Baxter*, 64-84; Nuttall, 'The Worcestershire Association: Its Membership', 197-206; Gilbert, 'Richard Baxter's Ministry', 59-74; and Gilbert's 'The Worcestershire Association of Ministers', in *BNS*, 4:2 (1996), 3-15.

promotion and maintenance have been capably demonstrated, the tendency to view the Worcestershire Association in isolation from Baxter's efforts as a pastor in Kidderminster, or as an example of a particular theological or ecclesiastical concern, or from a later perspective informed by modern ecumenism, has contributed to an unintentionally distorted picture of the purpose Baxter intended the Association to play. Baxter was not aiming at ministerial concord as an end in itself, but rather as a means to promote effective local pastoral ministry.[7] Indeed as we have seen, the evidence suggests that Baxter's mature strategy involved an intentional amalgam of awakening preaching, parish-wide catechizing, consensual pastoral oversight and discipline allowing access to the Lord's Supper, with the regularly meeting association of like-minded pastors providing the capstone of accountability and motivation that enabled the overarching strategy to work. But in order to appreciate his purpose for the Worcestershire Association, we must first step back and consider the vacuum of ecclesiastical authority and accountability that Baxter and his colleagues faced in revolutionary England and attempted to address.

Out of Egypt and into the Wilderness

Although the story behind Baxter's Association lies alongside a well-trodden path, it will repay our efforts to remind ourselves of the larger picture. The regime of doctrinal innovation, ceremonial retrogression and enforced order and uniformity within the Church of England under Archbishop William Laud during the 1630s recast the never easy balance of interests in the settlement of the Church under Elizabeth and James. This eventually provoked a reaction which, in combination with volatile fears of a connection between Charles I and papists, soon achieved a momentum and life of its own, resulting in the obliteration of the very order and society which it had originally sought to buttress.[8] The pressure of repression forged alliances amongst the persecuted, moderates and radicals alike, giving rise to agreement as to what was to be

---

[7] Just as afterwards, following the Restoration, his efforts for concord were ultimately aimed at promoting comprehension within a modified episcopacy. Baxter was not, as Hugh Martin argued, 'the Apostle of Christian Unity'. See Hugh Martin, *Puritanism and Richard Baxter*, 158-160. Nor, *contra* Morgan, was the fundamental problem Baxter was attempting to resolve a lack of church unity. See Morgan, *The Nonconformity of Richard Baxter*, 44-46. Paul Lim provides the best and most recent argument for viewing unity and purity as the primary concerns motivating Baxter's Worcestershire Association. Lim, 'In pursuit of unity, purity and liberty', 110-143. See A.L. Jukes's discussion of the implications of the Worcestershire Association for Baxter's later arguments against diocesan prelacy in his 'Gunning and the Worcester Agreement', in *MC*, 7 (1964), 184-86.

[8] See R.J. Acheson, *Radical Puritans in England 1550-1660* (London: Longman, 1990), 44.

undone, but producing an increasing lack of consensus as to what should be established in its place.[9] The puritan dream of completing the but-halfly-done Elizabethan reformation seemingly lay within reach. But the relatively limited objectives of a reformation of the Church of England seized upon in the early days of the Long Parliament in 1640 were soon overwhelmed by a steadily rising tide of political and religious radicalism as crown and parliament polarized. As John Morrill has observed, no one, at least publicly, set out to abolish monarchy or to undermine the authority of the established church, 'but as the political structures disintegrated under the sheer functional radicalism of a total war, so unthinkable thoughts began to be thought'.[10]

The way by which the long-desired reformation might be accomplished had seemed straightforward enough, at least at the beginning of the process. From 1641-1646, the Long Parliament was the locus of reforming zeal, content not merely to dismantle the old order, but to create the new.[11] And in 1641 Parliament called for a general synod to hammer out a settlement which would be 'more agreeable to God's Word and bring the Church of England into a nearer conformity with the Church of Scotland and other Reformed Churches abroad'.[12] But it took time for the Westminster Assembly's make-up and processes to be sorted. By the time the theological wranglings were over and the grand scheme for the puritan reformation of the Church of England was presented in 1646-7, England had changed, the moment had passed. The effects of the war, the army's seizure of political power and initiative in the summer of 1647 and the resulting collapse of political will to enforce a presbyterian settlement, not to mention growing popular distaste for the perceived excesses of the puritan/presbyterian minority and the crippling dissensions amongst the godly themselves, made the Presbyterian Church of England defunct on arrival.[13] Without sympathetic coercion from the centre, the Assembly's

---

[9] See Morrill, 'The Impact of Puritanism', 54; see also Morrill's more extensively developed argument in 'The Church in England 1642-9', 148-150.

[10] Morrill, 'Politics in an Age of Revolution 1630-1690', 373.

[11] This concern can be traced by the series of declarations, petitions and bills passed by parliament. See 'The Root and Branch Petition' of 11 December 1640, the 'Bill on Church Reform' of 3 July 1641, the 'Act for the Abolition of the Court of Star Chamber' of 5 July 1641, 'The Grand Remonstrance' of 1 December 1641, 'The Declaration of the Houses on Church Reform' of 8 April 1642, 'The Solemn League and Covenant' of 25 September 1643, for example. S. R. Gardiner, ed., *The Constitutional Documents of the Puritan Revolution*.

[12] On 22 November 1641, Commons passed by a narrow majority the Grand Remonstrance, calling for, among other things, a General Synod of the land's most learned and pious divines, to resolve the ecclesiastical question. After considerable delay, the Assembly of Divines finally met at Westminster on 1 July 1643. See Robert S. Paul, *The Assembly of the Lord: Politics and Religion in the Westminster Assembly* (Edinburgh: T. & T. Clark, 1985), 2-3; see also Vernon's 'The Sion College Conclave'.

[13] See Bolam and Goring's description of the reactions against Parliamentary

national Presbyterian Church became essentially voluntary (a contradiction in terms) and dependent upon local initiative.[14] The result was a stillborn reformation. What had begun under Charles I and Archbishop Laud as a political and religious crisis and then developed into an opportunity for long-suffering moderate puritans to reform the English Church was transposed through the trauma of civil war into a revolution that ultimately upended the three ancient buttresses of order in English society-the Church, the law and the monarchy itself.[15] In fact, England's new masters all but ignored the Westminster Assembly's proposed settlement, and instead made a virtue of the vice of no controlling ecclesiastical authority by promoting the *de facto* congregationalism of the one necessary ecclesiastical verity, freedom for tender consciences, or some of them, at least.[16]

Uniquely positioned as an observer of England's civil wars, Richard Baxter, who served first as chaplain to the parliamentary garrison in Coventry and then to Whalley's Regiment, perceived early on the danger posed by Cromwell and the army to Church, law and king.[17] While Baxter respected many of the

---

Presbyterianism in 'Presbyterians in the Parish Church', 41-45. See also Morrill, 'The Impact of Puritanism', 63; Hill, *The Century of Revolution*, 129; Anthony Fletcher, 'Oliver Cromwell and the godly nation', 216-228. See also Hughes, *Godly Reformation*, 1-8.

[14] Parliament instructed commissioners in each county to draw up proposals dividing the county into classes, which would be the primary units of ecclesiastical administration. But of 40 English counties (plus London), only 16 plans were produced, and in the end, only London, Lancashire and Essex established functional classical systems and provincial synods, while of the rest, only Suffolk, Middlesex, Shropshire, Somerset, Cheshire and Surrey (and later, Derbyshire and Nottinghamshire) made any attempt to erect a Presbyterian system of the parliamentary model. Counties where plans were produced but were either never approved by Parliament or implemented include Westmorland, Durham, Northumberland, Hampshire, Wiltshire and Yorkshire. See Morrill, 'The Church in England', 156-157.

[15] Acheson, *Radical Puritans*, 44.

[16] In light of these developments, the voluntary association movement, which we shall soon consider, arose not as a rival to parliamentary Presbyterianism, but as a response to the failure to enforce a nationwide church discipline. For a more sympathetic treatment of the emerging Cromwellian Church, see Tyacke, 'The "Rise of Puritanism"', 29-32. See also Claire Cross, 'The Church in England', 99-120.

[17] John Morrill and William Lamont's hesitation to depend upon Baxter's Restoration-era recollections for insights into the motives and inner workings of the Army is certainly a proper reflex, but a cautious use of *Reliquiae Baxterianae* will reward the scholar with valuable insights into the dynamics at work within Parliament's armies. See Morrill, 'Cromwell and his contemporaries', J. Morrill, ed., *Oliver Cromwell and the English Revolution*, 259-260; Lamont, 'The Religious Origins of the English Civil War', G. Schochet, ed., *Religion, Resistance, and Civil War*, 4-9. Of course Baxter was writing with the benefit of post-Restoration hindsight, but his predisposition against Cromwell and his circle is not the result of an attempt to make his writings palatable to Restoration

common soldiers in the New Model Army, he noted that 'a few proud, self-conceited, hot-headed Sectaries had got into the highest places, and were *Cromwell's* chief Favourites, and by their very heat and activity bore down the rest... and were the Soul of the Army'. Driven by a radical agenda, these leading men 'took the King for a Tyrant and an Enemy, and really intended absolutely to master him, or to ruine him; and they thought if they might fight against him, they might kill or conquer him' and that 'God's Providence would cast the Trust of Religion and the Kingdom upon them as Conquerors'. And with respect to the 'Trust of Religion', Baxter states that 'they were resolved to take down, not only Bishops, and Liturgy, and Ceremonies, but all that did withstand their way'. Uninterested in the contemporary, presbyterian-dominated parliamentary debates on the reform of Church government and discipline, they instead 'most honoured the Separatists, Anabaptists, and Antinomians'. And although Cromwell himself and his council 'took on them to joyn themselves to no Party', their stated religious policy was 'to be for the Liberty of all'. His information was not mere rumor, for 'Some orthodox Captains of the Army did partly acquaint me with all this, and I heard much of it from the Mouths of the leading Sectaries themselves. This struck me to the very Heart, and made me Fear that *England* was lost by those that it had taken for its Chieftest Friends.'[18]

Baxter's fears were well placed. What began as the puritan moment was now a reaction out of control.[19] Within a few years, the Army would be in command, Charles I would be executed, the Church would be effectively congregational

---

censors, but the result of his animosity towards anyone who used their authority to pursue a separatist or sectarian agenda. Diplomacy was not a particular strength of his, and Baxter was never known as one who would shade his meaning with an eye towards the approval of a particular audience (although he was not beyond projecting a currently held position back into a previous discussion, as we shall see). If anything, he erred in the opposite direction by being undiplomatic, if not outright reckless in his need to speak plainly about what he considered to be the truth of the matter, be it to Cromwell's face, in conference with assembled divines or even preaching before Charles II. Of course, Baxter, like everyone, learned to work with, and even grudgingly to appreciate the 'Usurper', not knowing how it might ultimately fall out, but Baxter's recorded antipathy has the ring of an original bias. See Tim Cooper's helpful analysis of aspects of Baxter's personality that made him prone to react unhelpfully over matters of controversy. Cooper, *Fear and Polemic*, 15-84; for an earlier treatment, see Nuttall, 'The Personality of Richard Baxter', in *The Puritan Spirit*; on Baxter's changing relationship with Cromwell, see 137; see also Cooper's 'Appendix A' for an overview of the complex issues involved in using *Reliquiae Baxterianae* as a source, 198-201. See also Hughes, *Godly Reformation*, 2.

[18] *Rel. Bax.*, I, §73, 50-51.

[19] 'The puritan moment' is taken from William Hunt's study, *The Puritan Moment: The Coming of Revolution in an English County* (Cambridge, MA: Harvard University Press, 1983).

and, with the proliferation of the sects, on the verge of utter fragmentation. In the growing chaos, however, the vision of a reformed Church of England was still uppermost in the minds of many of those ministers who had supported the parliamentary cause at the beginning of the Civil War.[20] But the promised land of legislated reformation was yet another mirage in the desert.

Even so, upon his return to Kidderminster in 1647 after illness forced his resignation from his army chaplaincy, Baxter discovered that not only had his parish changed, but the very framework within which pastors laboured had been altered. The failure to impose a top-down reformation legislatively had the effect of relegating the reform of the English Church to the local pastors.[21] Recognition of these new circumstances prompted him to reconsider the pastor's role in creating the context in which parish reformation might still be pursued and achieved.

Forging a Pastoral Agenda

Baxter's five-year absence from Kidderminster during the Civil War exposed him to a raft of increasingly contentious issues facing godly ministers across the nation. The chief threat to effective parish ministry, from Baxter's perspective, was the spread of a separatist agenda amongst pastors and laity who were impatient for reform. When escalating animosities against perceived supporters of Parliament's cause forced him to flee Kidderminster in July 1642, Baxter made his way to the godly stronghold of Gloucester, where he stayed for a month. 'Whilst I was at *Gloucester*', he writes, 'I saw the first Contentions between the Ministers and Anabaptists that ever I was acquainted with: For these were the first Anabaptists that ever I had seen in any Country'. This first hand experience of church discord made a striking impression, and as events unfolded he realized that such divisions were but 'the beginnings of the Miseries of *Gloucester*; for the Anabaptists somewhat increasing on one side, before I came away' two men came from Herefordshire and 'drew many to *Separation* on another side'. Obviously still closely following events after his departure in August, Baxter states that after this initial separation, a certain 'Mr. *Bacon*, a preacher of the Army' provoked a further separation 'to Antinomianism', the effect of which 'so distracted the good People, and eat out the Heart of Religion and Charity (the Ministers of the Place not being so able and quick as they should have been in...preserving the People)' that further effective ministry was fatally compromised.[22]

---

[20] Fletcher, 'Oliver Cromwell and the godly nation', 228.

[21] See Hirst, *Authority and Conflict: England 1603-1658* (London: Edward Arnold, 1986), 280-82. This eerily echoes the failure (though for very different reasons) of a similar press for structural reformation by an earlier generation of English Presbyterians in the 1570s and 80s and the subsequent modification of Elizabethan puritan tactics.

[22] *Rel. Bax.*, I, §58, 41. Nuttall has suggested that the 'Mr. *Bacon*' who so upsets the

Baxter attempted to return home, but he was forced to flee Kidderminster a second time in September 1642. This time he made his way to Coventry, where he was soon invited by the city's governor and committee of leading men to serve as preacher for the Parliamentary garrison.[23] However, in a replay of events in Gloucester, he states that 'one or two who came among us out of *New England*...had almost troubled all the Garrison, by infecting the honest Soldiers with their Opinions'. But Baxter, obviously a quick learner, asserts that 'they found not that Success in *Coventry*, as they had done in *Cromwel's* Army. In publick I was fain to preach over all the Controversies against the Anabaptists first, and then against the Separatists; and in private, some of my *Worcestershire* Neighbours, and many of the Foot Soldiers were able to baffle both Separatists, Anabaptists and Antinomians, and so kept all the Garrison sound', at least from his perspective.[24]

It was only in June of 1645 after the Battle of Naseby that the full extent of the danger from sectarians and separatists became evident to Baxter's mind. He traveled to the site of the battle in hopes of hearing word of several friends involved in the fighting. Unsuccessful, he went on to Leicester where the army had its headquarters in hopes of learning more. Upon finding his friends, he stayed with them overnight, evidently in the army camp itself. And there, he writes, 'I understood the state of the Army much better than ever I had done before.' Baxter explains:

> We that lived quietly in *Coventry* did keep to our old Principles,
> and thought all others had done so too, except a very few
> inconsiderable Persons... We believed that the War was only to
> save the Parliament and Kingdom from Papists and Delinquents...
> that the King might again return to his Parliament; and that no
> Changes might be made in Religion, but by the Laws which had his

scene in Gloucester is none other than Robert Bacon, a founder of what became the Broadmead Baptist church in Bristol who was also associated with the Lord and Lady Say & Sele, who themselves were closely involved with Cromwell and the circle of conspirators behind the revolution. Bacon, who later became a Quaker, and was eventually disowned by them, continued to exercise considerable influence on the fringes of English sectarianism for the mystical quality of his writing. See Nuttall's 'The Last of James Nayler: Robert Rich and the Church of the First-Born', in *FQ*, 23:11 (1985), 532-533. See also Gilbert's 'Richard Baxter's Visit to Gloucester, 1642,', *BNS*, 1:3 (1993), 14-16.

[23] Though he refused at this time to take a chaplain's commission, Baxter performed the duties of a chaplain, accompanying the Coventry regiment on its one major expedition, the siege of Banbury Castle in 1644. See Gilbert's 'Richard Baxter in Coventry-Again', in *BNS*, 3:3 (1995), 17. See also *Richard Baxter's Penitent Confession* (1691), 21.

[24] *Rel. Bax.*, I, §66, 45-46. For Henry Vane (1613-1662), former governor of Massachusetts who, after his return to England in 1637 became a prominent member of the Long Parliament, see *DNB*.

free consent.... And when the Court News-book told the World of
the Swarms of Anabaptists in our Armies, we thought it had been a
meer lye, because it was not so with us, nor in any of the Garrison
or County-Forces about us. But when I came to the Army among
Cromwell's Soldiers, I found a new face of things which I never
dreamt of: I heard the plotting Heads very hot upon that which
intimated their Intention to subvert both Church and State.[25]

Baxter was conscience-stricken that the progression he witnessed in
Gloucester might now be overtaking the army.[26] Moreover, he was well aware
that the situation was exacerbated because many orthodox ministers like
himself had previously refused to get involved to counter the spread of false
teaching. Therefore, when offered an opportunity to serve as chaplain to
Edmund Whalley's regiment, after consulting with a specially-called meeting
of ministers in Coventry (of which more anon), Baxter resolved to accept.[27]

---

[25] *Rel. Bax.*, I, §73, 50.

[26] I take a different view than Tim Cooper, who suggests that Baxter's primary concern
with the situation he found in the army after Naseby was the growing influence of the
Antinomians (Cooper, *Fear and Polemic*, 90). I do not argue Cooper's point that there
was a growing Antinomian influence in the New Model Army, nor that Baxter was
perhaps first exposed to the extent of its influence during his visit to the army's camp.
Baxter 'was provoked to enter the army as a chaplain in Colonel Whalley's regiment'
'[l]argely as a result of that one night's observation' (90); however the provocation came
not from Antinomianism, but from his alarm over the sectarian agenda of separation
from the mixed field of England's parishes and the plan of 'proud, self-conceited, hot-
headed Sectaries' who 'really intended absolutely to master [the king], or to ruin him'
and thus take upon themselves 'the Trust of Religion and the Kingdom...as Conquerors'
(*Rel Bax*. I, §73, 50-51). It is this radical agenda that, from Baxter's perspective,
threatened to 'subvert both Church and State'. Baxter's polemical description of an army
overrun by 'Swarms of Anabaptists' cleverly and deliberately connects his perception of
the growing religious chaos with the ultimate example of Anabaptist excess—Münster.
Cooper is right point out that at this time Baxter was not yet the 'anti-antinomian' he
was to become and that his soteriology was undergoing transition (Cooper, *Fear*, 87-90).
The sources Cooper cites are all written at least six or seven years later after this event,
after his perception of Antinomianism had changed and set. How much hindsight and
Baxter's tendency in polemic to overstate his concerns affects his recollection of this
event is unclear. What we do know is that at this time Antinomianism was neither
Baxter's only nor his greatest fear.

[27] In an example of his overconfidence, Baxter seems to feel that he was somehow
personally responsible for the radical drift of religion in Cromwell's New Model Army,
as he had refused on principle (and with an accompanying reproof!) an earlier invitation
to serve as pastor of a church gathered from Cromwell's troops when Cromwell was in
Cambridge before he had achieved national prominence. See *Rel. Bax.*, I, §74, 51. See
also Gilbert's suggestion that Baxter's close friend, James Berry, who had by then
become one of Cromwell's confidants, was probably behind Cromwell's invitation to

As he relates it, Baxter's efforts as chaplain over the next 18 months were those of a man on a mission: 'Here I set my self from day to day to find out the Corruptions of the Soldiers; and to discourse and dispute them out of their mistakes, both Religious and Political: My Life among them was a daily contending against Seducers, and gently arguing with the more Tractable'.[28] Not one given to understatement, Baxter goes on to claim that 'if the Army had but had Ministers enough, that would have done but such a little as I did, all their Plot might have been broken, and King, Parliament, and Religion might have been preserved: Therefore I sent abroad to get some more Ministers among them, but I could get none.'[29]

Baxter may have been persuaded of the rightness of his crusade against the separatists and sectaries of the army, and of the efficacy of his arguments, but upon his return to Kidderminster in June of 1647, he was confronted anew with the one point where both he and his separatist disputants knew he was vulnerable-the endemic lack of church discipline and the resulting profanation of the Lord's Supper. As we have seen in the previous chapter, this was not a new concern. The preceding generation of puritan pastors had attempted to devise comprehensive means to enable parishioners to participate in the sacrament in a worthy manner, but often the result was to raise standards so high as to make even the most godly fear profaning the sacrament in spite of their efforts.[30] Baxter himself had long wrestled with the issue, and his debates with the army separatists made obvious the necessity for resolution. In 1649, when asked about what behavior should exclude one from participating in communion, Baxter's advice, 'after long study of this point', was that a parishioner should be barred 'When hee will not be perswaded to confesse and bewaile his sinne, nor to give over practice of it.' But he admits that his views were only recently revised, 'For you know my former Judgement, and that I never administered the Sacrament, till within this year, and that I was then invited to it by an eminent wonder of providence'. He now realized he had been mistaken to withhold communion, and that in doing so he had exercised presumptuous judgement. Instead, one must 'beware how you deny to men the seales, till you have tried with them this way prescribed by Christ'.[31] Published

---

Baxter, in 'Richard Baxter and James Berry', in *BNS*, 6:1 (1998), 2-10. For Baxter's relation of the details of his entry into Army service as a chaplain, see *Rel. Bax.*, I, §§75-76, 51-53.

[28] Ibid., I, §77, 53.

[29] Ibid., I, §81, 56.

[30] See Robert Bolton's *The Saint's Selfe-enriching Examination. Or a Treatise concerning the Sacrament of the Lord's Supper. Which as a Glasse or Touch-stone, Clearly discovers the triall and truth of Grace; requisite to be looked into daily; chiefly before we come to the Lords Table.* (1634), whose 328 pages (the author died before he could complete the final five of seven points!) comes as close as anything does to proving that there can be too much of a good thing.

[31] Baxter, *Aphorisms of Justification*, 251-252. The 'eminent wonder of providence'

within eighteen months of his return to Kidderminster, this response indicates that Baxter already recognized the central role of an effective parish discipline. He agreed with the separatists that to countenance the *status quo* was to become party to an intolerable scandal within the church. But he had become convinced that their solution was even more ruinous to the Church's evangelistic task. For by gathering 'a few of the best together' and 'leaving the rest to sink or swim', England's separatists had consigned most of their neighbors 'to the Divel and their lusts' while 'scarce ever endeavoring their salvation'. Simple charity demanded that 'if any walk scandalously', their pastors should instead 'deal with them for their recovery'. Only if 'they prove obstinate after all, then avoid them and cast them off'. By arrogantly withdrawing to form their own churches, the separatists were pronouncing judgement upon whole parishes, effectively 'unchurching' their neighbors and arbitrarily separating them from the means of their recovery and salvation.[32]

We have seen in the previous chapter that the threat posed by the separatists to the church's evangelistic task compelled Baxter to refute their arguments justifying separation. But he nowhere contests their primary reason for separating.[33] Instead, he found their critique of the Church's lack of discipline to be all too true. It was their separating solution and its consequences that he found appalling, and he had ample experience, from Gloucester to the army, to confirm his observations. Moreover, the resulting fragmentation of the church had given rise to the proliferation of sects, who were nothing less than God's plague of judgment against England's separating brethren.

> The hand of God is apparently gone out against your waies of Separation and Anabaptism: It is your duty to observe it: You may see you do but prepare too many for a further progresse, Seekers, Ranters, Familists, and now Quakers, and too many professed Infidels do spring from among you, as if this were your Journeys end, and the perfection of your Revolt.... In one word, it is most evident that spiritual Pride doth turn most men from us to you, and that this is the very sinne that undoes such a multitude of Professors of Religiousness, and which hath let in all Gods Judgements upon us, and the sinne which he is now witnessing against from Heaven.[34]

---

which so influenced Baxter is not here mentioned.

[32] Baxter, *Saints Everlasting Rest*, 509. See also *Aphorisms of Justification*, 252.

[33] For 'the Separatists reproach [parish ministers] for suffering the Impenitent to continue members of their Churches, and make it the pretense of their separation from them; having little to say of any moment against the authorized way of Government, but only against our slackness in the Execution.' Baxter, *A Sermon of Judgement*, sig A9.

[34] Baxter, *The Quakers Catechism*, sigs B-B2v.

The dissolution of ecclesiastical authority and the failure of parliament's intended substitute had unleashed a puritan's nightmare of disorder that was threatening to engulf both church and state. Somehow order had to be restored, and basic biblical discipline reinstated. For Baxter, the key person against this onslaught of disorder was the parish minister. But a solitary parish minister attempting to reassert biblical church discipline faced enormous, if not insurmountable opposition. Baxter, as we have seen, had learned from experience that establishing discipline, even in a parish as 'tractable' as Kidderminster, was no easy thing. Writing to the Lord Mayor of London in a passage that rings of autobiography, Baxter sets forth the dilemma:

> Do you not perceive what a strait your Teachers are in! The Lord
> Iesus requireth them to exercise his Discipline faithfully and
> impartially... The work is, as to Teach the ignorant, and convince
> the unbelieving and gainsaying, so to admonish the disorderly and
> scandalous, and to reject and cast out of the Communion of the
> Church the Obstinate and Impenitent; and to set by the Leprous,
> that they infect not the rest, and to separate thus the pretious from
> vile, by Christs Discipline, that dividing separations, and soul-
> destroying Transgressions may be prevented or cured... If they
> obey him and do it, what a tumult, what clamours and discontents
> will they raise! How many will be ready to rise up against them
> with hatred and scorn!... If all the apparently obstinate and
> impenitent were cast out, what a stir would they make! And if
> Christ be not obeyed, what a stir will conscience make?[35]

Baxter was acutely aware from experience that the pastor labouring alone in his parish would not be able to affect the necessary reformation. Providentially, he did not have to look far before he came upon an already existing structure that, with some retooling, might just do the trick.

The Reformed Lecture

Protestant pastors in England had been gathering for preaching exercises, discussion and fellowship openly or in secret since Elizabethan days. Referred to in the early seventeenth century as 'exercises' or 'combination lectures', these gatherings formed wherever the evangelical emphasis on preaching began to make inroads in areas of more traditional religious practise. The lecture or exercise was a regularly scheduled event organized by local ministers intended to provide good preaching in a strategic place and at a strategic time, usually a market town on market day. Area ministers persuaded of the need for godly preaching organized a preaching rota (hence the term 'combination'), and often

---

[35] Baxter, *A Sermon of Judgement*, sigs A7v-A9.

attended even if they were not preaching. If the lecture was regularly attended by area ministers, there would often follow a time of conference for the ministers and even a meal, sometimes provided by the local magistrates or merchants, who appreciated the influence of good preaching on the local society as well as the crowds of potential customers such lectures would attract from the town and surrounding areas. Whereas formerly historians seized upon the subversive potential of these meetings of godly men with a godly agenda,[36] more recently Patrick Collinson has contended that these lectures were 'so characteristic of the Anglicanism of this epoch, of its settled life as much as of its tensions and divisions, and above all perhaps in their often successful containment of conflict, that there will be something at fault with any account of the Jacobean Church which overlooks them, or which treats the institution of lecturing too exclusively in the categories of opposition and disruption.'[37]

Collinson notes that the Jacobean combination lectures are essentially the generational adaptation of the same impulse in English Protestantism that produced the earlier Elizabethan prophesyings.[38] But it was an impulse that was concerned with more than just the provision of godly preaching. The evidence of lectures being organized in towns which already had adequate godly preachers suggests that ministers had additional reasons for coming together, reasons which Collinson has suggested include 'an interest in the associational character of the combination, as imparting some element of collegiality to its members'.[39] The prophesyings in Elizabethan England had been put down for just such a reason, the supplemental associational structures been viewed as subversive to the precariously balanced Settlement and as smacking too much of the presbyterianism of the more radical puritan agitators to which Elizabeth and Archbishop Whitgift seemed allergic. It is no coincidence that the associational impulse of the first generation of Elizabethan reformers can be located among those who fled to the Continent under Mary and experienced the workings of continental reformed ecclesiology in person. But the prolonged effort of the succeeding generation of increasingly impatient puritan clergy and gentry MPs to import a similar presbyterian system into the English context in the 1560s, 70s and 80s was ultimately quashed by an even more determined and anxious political and ecclesiastical hierarchy who were

---

[36] See, for example, Christopher Hill, *Society and Puritanism in Pre-Revolutionary England* (London: Secker and Warburg, 1964); Paul Seaver, *The Puritan Lectureships: The Politics of Religious Dissent 1560-1662* (Stanford: Stanford University Press, 1970); and Mark Curtis, 'The Alienated Intellectuals of Early Stuart England', in *P&P*, 23 (1962), 25-43.

[37] Collinson, 'Lectures by Combination: Structures and Characteristics of Church Life in 17th-Century England', in *Godly People*, 469.

[38] Collinson goes so far as to call the Elizabethan prophesyings the 'forerunners of the combination lectures and exercises of early Stuart England'. 'Lectures by Combination', 472.

[39] Collinson, 'Lectures by Combination', 472.

fearful of provoking an uncontrollable external and internal Roman Catholic backlash.

But before the presbyterian movement was perceived as a threat by Elizabeth, prophesyings had already been adopted and managed as a tacitly approved (or at least, not disapproved) English Protestant instrument of reform. Seeking to address the desperate need to improve clerical standards, growing circles of local godly clergy, and even reform-minded bishops adopted the device of regular meetings of area clergy as a stimulus for reforming the ministry, promoting preaching and converting the provinces. In 1564, Edward Gaston reported that 'the preachers from [Norwich] have taken in hand-both for their better exercise and also for the education of the people-prophecying, which is done once in three weeks, when one first interprets a piece of the scriptures...for an hour, and then two others reply for half an hour, when we end with prayer.'[40] Meeting regularly, these gatherings of clergy were a 'combination of public forum and literary society'.[41] Each minister was in turn assigned a certain Scripture passage of which they were to prepare an exposition. On the day of his turn, his public exposition would be followed by several other ministers who would offer their critique as well as provide further insights into the passage or doctrine being discussed. A moderator overseeing the proceedings would summarize the discussion. Afterwards, the ministers would retire in private for further mutual examination and censure.

Although these prophesyings were officially suppressed and some of the clergy were pressed by conscience into the margins of nonconformity or even into the beginnings of separatism, many pastors quietly shifted the same kind of meeting into a different guise. The practise of providing regular weekday lectures in strategic locations, as well as the reformed custom of periodic pulpit-centred fasts, continued in many places unaltered, with discrete associational aspects becoming increasingly prominent.[42] Indeed, Collinson argues that, despite the best efforts of the hierarchy, 'evidence survives to confirm the substantial continuity of prophesyings, exercises and combination lectures throughout the years from 1572-1636', a claim further verified by Tom Webster's study of Caroline clerical associations.[43] Webster observes that a regular gathering of clergy that maintained a disciplinary purpose continued in Arthur Hildersham's sphere of influence in south Leicestershire, but that for the

---

[40] *Calendar of State Papers, Domestic Series, of the Reign of Elizabeth, 1601-1603; with Addenda 1547-1565*, XII, M.A.E. Green, ed. (1870), 552.

[41] M.M. Knappen, *Tudor Puritanism: A Chapter in the History of Idealism* (Chicago: University of Chicago Press, 1939), 255.

[42] Collinson, 'Lectures by Combination', 475. See also Webster, *Godly Clergy*, 61-74.

[43] Collinson, 'Lectures by Combination', 477. Webster, *Godly Clergy*, 9-92. See also Bolam and Goring, 'English Presbyterian Beginnings', 33. It is interesting to note the similarities between meetings of clergy in prophesyings and lectures and meetings of clergy during episcopal and metropolitical visitations. See, for example, Fincham's *Prelate as Pastor*, especially 116-134.

most part clergy continued to gather for reasons that had less to do with presbyterian conspiracies and more to do with the need for fellowship and sociability.[44] Moreover, even after they were detached from overt Presbyterian aims, these regular lectures provided godly pastors with a powerful and adaptable mechanism which aided them in pursuing their local agendas of reform.[45] One Jacobean lecture participant has left the following nine reasons as to why these local gatherings of clergy were so valued by so many for so long: They provided for

1. First, the propagation of the Ghospell and edefieng of the Church.
2. Incouraging of the meaner sorte of preachers.
3. Exciting of sluggards to the studie of divinitie by means whereof their own parishes also shall be better served.
4. Increase of love and acquaintance among preachers.
5. Increase of religion and learning, by meeting and conference.
6. Varietie will more delighte the peoples attention.
7. Advauncement to the clergie man, when their guifts shalbe knowne.
8. People wanting preachers shall or maye be there taught.
9. Benefit also to the inhabitauntes for their markett by concurse of people.[46]

Against this backdrop, as we shall see, the origins of Baxter's Worcestershire Association become increasingly less of a mystery.

Baxter was, of course, no stranger to the godly conventions of both weekly and combination lectures. Sources indicate that there had been a regular lecture in Worcester since at least 1589, and for a time during the early seventeenth century Kidderminster apparently had a market day lecture, until it was suppressed under Archbishop Laud.[47] When the Long Parliament acted to remove Laud and then set about unworking his recent innovations, the 'godly' minority in Kidderminster perceived a window of opportunity and set about finding a preacher who would restore the weekday lecture and provide an alternative to the non-preaching ministry of their vicar George Dance and his allegedly scandalous curates. Securing Dance's permission (after threatening to report him to the parliamentary authorities as a grossly insufficient and scandalous minister), they proceeded to look for a suitable candidate. Baxter

---

[44] 'For most gatherings, even Richard Bancroft would have struggled to have found a Presbyterian plot.' Webster, *Godly Clergy*, 46.

[45] Webster's treats the early Stuart continuation of these ministerial 'conferences' in more fully in *Godly Clergy*, 43-59.

[46] Cited by Collinson, 'Lectures by Combination', 498.

[47] Gilbert, 'Richard Baxter's Ministry', 9.

was not their first candidate, but after bringing him from Bridgnorth where he was serving as a curate to Kidderminster to preach a trial market-day sermon, the local godly minority were persuaded they had found the right man. After negotiations, Baxter was hired as a lecturing curate with preaching responsibilities on Sundays and Thursdays.[48]

Although Baxter does not mention any associational aspects with fellow ministers that may have been part of his market day lectures during his initial ministry in Kidderminster, later actions show him well acquainted with the benefits and usefulness of ministers acting in conference with one another. Wartime Coventry was a haven for displaced ministers, and Baxter's position as regular garrison lecturer and town preacher placed him in the center of a company of his peers in ministry. During his fateful visit to Army quarters in Leicester after the Battle of Naseby, upon receiving the invitation from Colonel Whalley to become chaplain of his Regiment, Baxter requested 'a days time to deliberate, and would send him an Answer, or else come to him.' Baxter was 'loth to leave my Studies, and Friends, and Quietness at *Coventry,* to go into an Army so contrary to my Judgment', but given his experience among the Army sectaries, he felt that 'the Public Good commanded me' and was inwardly resolved to accept the invitation.[49] But before making a final decision, Baxter curiously returned to Coventry: 'As soon as I came home to *Coventry*, I call'd together an Assembly of Ministers... And I told them the sad News of the Corruption of the Army, and that I thought all we had valued was like to be endangered by them... The Ministers finding my own Judgment for it, and being moved with the Cause, did unanimously give their Judgment for my going.'[50]

Baxter resorted to his colleagues in Coventry yet again probably in 1643. After having served as chaplain for more than a year, a new crisis of decision prompted a reflexive return to Coventry for counsel. Baxter writes that, 'When *Worcester* Seige [sic] was over...my old Flock expected that I should return to them, and settle in Peace among them. I went to *Coventry*, and called the Ministers again together who had voted me into the Army'. 'I told them that the forsaking of the Army by the old Ministers, and the neglect of Supplying their Places by others, had undone us.... Though I knew it was the greatest hazard of my Life, my Judgment was for staying among them till the Crisis, if their Judgment did concur. Whereupon they all voted me to go, and leave

---

[48] Gilbert has provided the most detailed account of Kidderminster in the early 1640s, of the minority of puritans involved in Baxter's call and of the increasing local animosities between the godly and ungodly that would become increasingly politicized as national events moved toward civil war. See 'Richard Baxter's Ministry', 6-29. See Nuttall's account in *Richard Baxter*, 24-29. See Baxter's account in *Rel. Bax.*, I, i, §§29 & 129, 19-20, 80; III, §150, 71.

[49] Ibid., I, i, §75, 51-52.

[50] Ibid., I, i, §75, 52.

Kidderminster yet longer, which accordingly I did.'[51] There is no record to suggest that Baxter and, presumably, other ministers in Coventry were under a self-imposed obligation to make decisions in concert with a council of their peers. As Baxter relates the story, the impetus for both meetings is his own need for support in the face of what were life decisions for him.

As we have seen, broken health in the winter of 1647 put an end to Baxter's career as a chaplain and thus to his hopes of being a moderating influence in a radicalizing army. Returning to Kidderminster after convalescing at Rous Lench,[52] Baxter found that the parish had been fundamentally altered during the five years of war. Most notably, he discovered that his most implacable foes had, for the most part, joined the Cavalier army and been killed in the war, 'and so there were few to make any great Opposition to Godliness.'[53]

We have also seen that although he found a new attitude towards 'godliness' within the parish, Baxter found it exceedingly difficult to come up with a way to safeguard the celebration of communion from scandal. He struggled to devise a way to keep notoriously unrepentant parish members from communion, without at the same time alienating everyone else by appearing too heavy-handed and censorious. To that end, he was among those in Worcestershire who petitioned parliament to set up a presbyterian classis system, but for unspecified reasons, the attempt was never made.[54] Moreover, as we have seen in the previous chapter, Baxter indicates that he made at least one unsuccessful attempt to exercise some sort of discipline within the parish,

---

[51] Ibid., I, i, §84, 58. The 'Crisis' to which Baxter refers is the anticipated unveiling by the Army's leadership of their true revolutionary intentions.

[52] For Rous Lench, see E.A. Barnard, 'The Rouses of Rous Lench', in *TWAS,* ix (1933), 31-74.

[53] *Rel. Bax.*, I, i, §137, 86. This is the third of thirty 'Advantages' Baxter enumerates by which his 'Successes' as a pastor were effected.

[54] 'We in this county did seek for authority from the Parliament some years ago for the establishing of the Presbyterian Government; and all our endeavours were frustrate'. Baxter, *Christian Concord*, 'Explication', 31. This, along with Baxter's subsequent good relations with the London classis indicate that Baxter's intentions were not to set up an association that would rival the Presbyterians. Roger Thomas's contention that the Worcestershire Assembly 'was a clear break with Parliamentary Presbyterianism' thus cannot be sustained by the evidence, unless Baxter is made to be less than sincere. As Thomas himself points out, Baxter's own views on mid-seventeenth-century Presbyterianism are complex, owing to the fact that *English* Presbyterianism itself was defined by different advocates in different ways. It is possible that at some point, at least, in the evolution of his thought, Baxter could have lived with the Presbyterian system imposed by parliament, even if he had disagreed with the interpretation and application of that system by some of its advocates. The Worcestershire Association was not so much a statement against parliamentary Presbyterianism as it was a statement for discipline. See R. Thomas, 'The Rise of the Reconcilers', C. Bolam, *et al, The English Presbyterians*, 52-53, 48-49. For a discussion of how a classis functioned, see Nuttall, 'The Essex Classis (1648)', in *JURCHS,* 3:6 (1985), 194-202.

but was rebuffed by the congregation.[55]

Already in the habit of meeting with certain fellow ministers at the regular lecture in Worcester, Baxter describes how the seed of a new way of resolving the issue of discipline within the parish began to germinate: 'having determined of that way which was, I thought, most agreeable to the Word of God, I thought, if all the Ministers did accord together in one way, the People would much more readily submit, than to the way of any Minister that was singular.' Exploring his idea further, Baxter writes that 'At a lecture in *Worcester* I first procured a Meeting, and told them [the gathered ministers] of the Design, which they all approved: They imposed it upon me, to draw up a Form of Agreement.'[56]

Baxter's purpose for the association was clear from the start: 'According to their desire, I drew up some Articles for our Consent which might engage us to the most effectual practice of so much Discipline as might reduce the Churches to order, and satisfie Ministers in administering the Sacraments, and stop the more religious People from Separation, to which the unreformedness of the Churches through want of Discipline inclined them.'[57] He was obviously not alone in his vexation over the matter of discipline, for his proposals found an eager hearing:

> And I brought in the Reasons of the several Points: which after sufficient Deliberation and Examination (with the alteration of some few words) were consented to by all the Ministers that were present; and after several Meetings we subscribed them, and so associated for our mutual help and concord in our Work. The Ministers that thus associated were for Numbers, Parts and Piety, the most considerable part of all that County, and some out of some neighboring Counties that were near us.[58]

At the heart of Baxter's association was ministerial agreement on the fundamentals of Christian faith (and ministerial agreement to disagree on

---

[55] *Rel. Bax.*, II, §28, 148. For a discussion of the wider issues that Baxter was attempting to address locally, see Hughes, *Godly Reformation*, 4-5.

[56] *Rel. Bax.*, II, §28, 148. Powicke mistakenly claims that these events took place at the monthly meeting of ministers in Baxter's house. See Powicke, *A Life of the Reverend Richard Baxter*, 164. In a separate account, Baxter tells the same story from a different angle: 'When Discouragements had long kept me from mentioning a way of Church-order and Discipline, which all might agree in, that we might neither have Churches ungoverned, nor fall into Divisions among ourselves, at the first motioning of it, I found a readier Consent than I could expect, and all went on without any great obstructing difficulties'. *Rel. Bax.*, I, i, §136, 85.

[57] Ibid., II, §28, 148.

[58] Ibid., II, §28, 148. For the members of the Worcestershire Association, see Nuttall's article, 'The Worcestershire Association: its Membership', 197-206.

peripheral issues deemed divisive), combined with an adaptation of the church covenant ideas which, as we have seen, were advocated by Martin Bucer and currently in vogue among Congregational churches.[59] This made church membership and communion contingent upon members' agreement to take the minister as their pastor (that is, to submit to the pastor's authority and discipline where it was consistent with God's word). Securing his colleagues' agreement to doctrinal matters and operational procedures was an obvious necessity, and no small accomplishment given the contentiousness of the age.

But Baxter's purpose was more than creating a context for collegiality, ministerial accountability and 'ecclesiastical purity'; it involved a reinterpretation of the pastoral task itself, at least as practiced in the parishes of the Church of England. To isolate the concept of unity for unity's sake and precipitate out of Baxter's many comments on the issue of Christian concord a passion for unity and make this one of the major ends towards which he labored, especially with respect to the Worcestershire Association, is to read a modern ecumenical or theological agenda unhelpfully back into the seventeenth century and serves only to obscure Baxter's own *pastoral* agenda. Paul Lim is certainly correct to see 'unity' as a significant element of Baxter's mature theological motivation, or at least his rhetoric.[60] But one must be careful not to read Baxter's mature perspective back fully-formed into a situation such as the inauguration of the Worcestershire Association. Moreover, 'unity' is a notoriously slippery word, and in his use of the term Baxter slides too easily and unannounced into different meanings depending on the context he is addressing.[61] In the early 1650s, at least, concern for 'unity', as Baxter

---

[59] Baxter, *Christian Concord*, XVIII-XIX, sigs B2-B4; Bucer, *De Regno Christi*, 229-230. For the use of covenants among Congregational churches, see Nuttall, *Visible Saints*, 127-135.

[60] Lim, 'In pursuit of unity, purity and liberty', 112-113. I regret that the published edition of Lim's thesis is not yet available for me to interact with.

[61] Baxter often uses 'unity' in contexts that are decidedly non-ecumenical: 'And our *Unity and Concorde* was a great Advantage to us [in Kidderminster], and our freedom from those Sects and Heresies which many other Places were infected with. We had no private Church, though we had private Meetings; we had not Pastor against Pastor, nor Church against Church, nor Sect against Sect, nor Christian against Christian' (*Rel. Bax.*, I, §137, 8, 87). In Baxter's *Explication*, which is attached to *Christian Concord* (1653), for example, Baxter again uses 'unity' to mean the unity and integrity of the parish in the face of divisions threatened by separatists (see *Explication*, title page and 95-106). In a later Restoration reflection, Baxter states 'I have spent much of my Studies about the *Terms of Christian Concord*... [But] I am farther then ever I was from expecting great matters of Unity, Splendor or Prosperity to the Church on Earth, or that the Saints would dream of a Kingdom of this World, or flatter themselves with the Hopes of a Golden Age, or reigning over the Ungodly...And on the contrary I am more apprehensive that Sufferings must be the Churches most ordinary Lot, and Christians

understood it then, served pastoral, not ecclesiological ends. Tim Cooper has demonstrated with respect to Baxter's response to Antinomianism that he was quite adept at shifting his emphases in polemic, both from individual to individual and from year to year, depending on the needs of the moment.[62] Moreover, Baxter's *need* for unity, and his need to be seen in favor of unity evolves after the Restoration. Baxter himself admits that the Worcestershire Association never did attract the committed Presbyterians, Independents and Episcopalians that an association whose major priority was 'unity' might be expected to include. Those attracted to the Worcestershire Association were too busy being pastors to be party men and their reason for joining was not necessarily to make a statement about unity. That it achieved a degree of unity among its participants was more the happy result of their agreement on their pastoral predicament and on means to resolve it than the result of their signing up for a programme of unity for unity's sake.[63] Baxter's later recollections of his motives for the Association may make more of the potential for unity among the various factions than was actually the case. There may be more than a little hindsight at work in Baxter's own efforts to put his Kidderminster experience in the best possible light for a Restoration audience. Seen in context, the Worcestershire Association is primarily a pastoral response. [64]

---

indeed must be *self-denying Cross-bearers*, even where there are none but formal nominal Christians to be the Cross-makers' (*Rel. Bax.*, I, §212, 27, 132).

[62] Cooper, *Fear and Polemic*, chapter 3, for example.

[63] 'In our Association in this County, though we made our Terms large enough for all, Episcopal, Presbyterians and Independents, there was not one Presbyterian joined with us that I know of, (for I knew but of one in all the County, Mr. *Tho. Hall*) nor one Independent (though two or three honest ones said nothing against us) nor one of the New Prelatical way (Dr. *Hammond's*) but three or four moderate Conformists that were for the old Episcopacy; and all the rest were meer Catholics; Men of no Faction, nor siding with any Party, but owning that which was good in all, as far as they could discern it; and upon a Concord in so much, laying out themselves for the great Ends of their Ministry, the Peoples Edification' (*Rel. Bax.*, I, §140, 97).

[64] Thus I would disagree with Gilbert's conclusion that Baxter's frustrated desire for national unity was one of the major factors motivating his associational initiative. See Gilbert's otherwise helpful article, 'The Worcestershire Association of Ministers', *BNS*, 4:2 (1996), 7-8. See for example Nuttall's treatment of Baxter and unity in *Richard Baxter and Philip Doddridge*, 4, 7; see also Nuttall, *Richard Baxter*, 74-76 and the discussion of Baxter's relationship with the Scottish theologian John Dury. That Baxter could resonate with other people's revulsion over the spectacle of divided Protestants does not alter the fact that Baxter's own attempts to promote unity was motivated by very practical and pastoral ends. See for example, Baxter's initial letter to Dury, dated 7 May 1652, in DWL, BxL, iii, 272; *Calendar,* no. 83, 77-78. In this letter Baxter states, 'It is the Difference of the Godly & learned in matter of Discipline and Worship that so long hindered our peace; that caused & kept open our wounds. All the rest sprang out of that. Here <er>*go* must our Cure begin.' For a further treatment of the correspondence between Baxter and Dury over plans (never realized) for a conference between leading

Having secured his colleagues' commitment to associate and their agreement to use their association as a means to promote parish reformation, Baxter acknowledged that the foundation stone for the whole edifice lay in their parishioners' consent. By formally agreeing to have Baxter as a pastor (to obey his teaching and submit to his oversight), a parishioner confirmed his or her church membership and fitness for communion. This 'covenant' also allowed the pastor to enforce what he understood to be biblical standards of morality. Those unable to profess their faith adequately or unwilling to submit to the pastor's discipline were denied access to the Table. Under this system, if the proper biblical procedures (outlined in Matthew 18:15-18) were sensitively followed, the scandalously unrepentant could be kept from both Table and fellowship until they changed their ways.[65]

A covenantal basis for the relationships between Christian, church and pastor was not a new idea for Baxter, nor did his emphasis on parishioner consent in the organizing Articles of the Worcestershire Association and Explication published in *Christian Concord* (1653) mark a fundamental change in his own pastoral methodology. Baxter hints at a similar covenantal process that predicated his original coming to Kidderminster in 1641 when in *The Saints Everlasting Rest* (1650), he recalls his first days as their preacher: 'Do you not remember, that when you called me to be your Teacher, you promised me under your hands, that you would faithfully and conscionably endeavor the receiving every truth, and obeying every command, which I should from the Word of God manifest to you?'[66] Nevertheless, his associational initiative with his Worcestershire colleagues was a significant if consistent development of his pastoral philosophy coupled with its projection upon a wider, regional canvas.

Presbyterians, Independents and Episcopalians to attempt the resolution of their differences, see Nuttall's 'Presbyterians and Independents: Some Movements for Unity 300 years ago', in *JPHSE,* 10 (1952), 6.

[65] See the copy of the covenant that Baxter distributed to every parish member for their study and response in *Christian Concord*, sigs C2-C3v. One could question whether it is necessary to posit Bucer as the source of Baxter's ideas on parishioner consent when it was also a practise among certain separatists and Congregationalists. However, Baxter never cites the Congregationalists as being his source, and he certainly would not have wanted to be perceived as countenancing a strategy that was used to such divisive ends by the separatists. On the other hand as we have seen, he emphatically commends Bucer's proposals for 'Parish-Discipline, and pure Communion' in *De Regno Christi, De Vera Animarum Cura and Censura [De Caeremoniis Ecclesiae Anglicanae]*. See Baxter, *An Apology for the Nonconformists Ministry*, sig A3. However, the lack of definitive evidence either way makes any attempt to answer the question speculation.

[66] Baxter, *The Saints Everlasting Rest*, 601. Gilbert suggests that this was an engagement or covenant between Baxter and the godly circle responsible for calling him, rather than between Baxter and the congregation as a whole. Due to the lack of evidence, however, such a suggestion remains speculation. Gilbert, 'Richard Baxter's Ministry', 20.

The Association filled the vacuum caused by the absence of church courts or ecclesiastical structure (episcopal or presbyterian), providing the necessary wider context of spiritual authority in which the pastor's local call to teach and rule could take hold.[67] Baxter may have used associational and pastoral tools at hand, but the resulting composite struck many as the right idea at the right moment.

Baxter's dependence upon already existing models of ministerial association prominent in combination lectures as described by Collinson become increasingly obvious as he describes the Association's activities. The Worcestershire Association met as weekly gatherings of local clergy and monthly gatherings of the Association as a whole. The Association was initially subdivided into five weekly lectures meeting at Kidderminster, Worcester, Evesham, Bromsgrove and Upton-on-Severn, at which local minister members assembled to hear a sermon and to deal with disciplinary matters.[68] Monthly meetings of the whole Association were rotated around the various market towns during which time members arranged 'to keep up a publique Lecture for the common benefit.'[69] The Association agenda also included time for dinner, disputations, and 'for Conference about such Cases of Discipline as required Consultation and Consent'.[70]

The Association also resembled Lectures and Exercises in some of the responsibilities Baxter and his colleagues chose *not* to undertake. Responsibility for ordination and the placement of ministers was considered one of those issues over which agreement would not be achieved and was therefore not included as a function of the Association, even though this was a normal feature of the classis system approved by Parliament, and indeed of

---

[67] Baxter expounds his view of the pastor's ruling authority and the implications for church discipline, membership and sacraments in a significant exchange of letters between himself and Sir Ralph Clare, the polite but persistent leader of the Kidderminster remnant of prelatical opposition to Baxter's ministry, published in *Rel. Bax.*, II, §32, 150-162.

[68] 'Those meeting weekly at our lecture....' *Rel. Bax.*, I, i, §137, 91, #21;

[69] *Christian Concord*, sig B4.

[70] Rel. Bax., II, i, §§31-32, 149-150. Gilbert lists twenty examples of these 'Disputations' which were prepared by Baxter for use in Association meetings and remain either in their original manuscript form among the Baxter Manuscripts at DWL or were subsequently reworked and published. 'Richard Baxter's Ministry', 164-170. See Thomas, The Baxter Treatises: A Catalogue of the Richard Baxter Papers...in Dr. Williams's Library (London: Dr Williams's Trust, 1959). For a helpful discussion on the implications of 'godly' ministers' willingness to participate in disputations, not only in controlled settings such as the Worcestershire Association, but in the kind of public debates which Baxter held with separatists while in the army or with the Baptist John Toombes of Bewdley, or with certain Quakers, see Ann Hughes, 'The Meaning of Religious Polemic', F. Bremer, ed., Puritanism: A Transatlantic Perspective (Boston, MA: Massachusetts Historical Society, 1993), 204-05, 221-22, 228.

several other voluntary associations.[71] However, extensive networking and co-operation between ministers, patrons and other laypeople in particular parishes regularly occurred informally within the Association, resulting in the placement of many godly ministers in parishes throughout the county. In particular, Richard Baxter played a very active role behind the scenes and wielded great influence in many placement decisions.[72]

What *was* new was Baxter's incorporation of church discipline into the agenda of what might otherwise be viewed as a combination lecture writ large, as well as his efforts to comprehend as many of the 'godly', orthodox pastors in the county who would come.[73] The Association's role in the disciplinary process was not that of a court which decided the innocence or guilt of a defendant, but rather as a consultative body concerned to uphold the presenting pastor's authority and to use their combined gravity to persuade the offender of the seriousness of his or her offence and of the need to repent. As such, the Association provided direct assistance for pastors at the most difficult point of the disciplinary process, giving the pastor vital support at a moment when it might seem easier to avoid the discomfort of conflict. Baxter and his colleagues recognized that parish discipline would never survive unless pastors themselves

---

[71] William Shaw notes that on 13 April 1655, the thirteenth session of the sixteenth London Provincial Synod stipulated that a letter be sent to several voluntary associations about ordination (see the Minutes of the London Provincial Synod for 13 April 1655). Shaw concludes that, while evidence that the London Provincial Synod played a role in promoting the expansion of the voluntary association movement is negligible, this letter 'points to the fact that there was a distinctly felt need for some means of ordination in the counties and that that need is partly accountable for the genesis of these voluntary associations, as well as the second motive of a need for some disciplinary administration of the Sacrament.' Shaw, *A History,* ii, 157-58.

[72] Gilbert documents Baxter's success in securing positions near Kidderminster for many of his assistants and protégés. 'Richard Baxter's Ministry', 65-69. See also Webster's discussion of 'networks of patronage' in *Godly Clergy,* 36-38. Baxter's role as a patron will be explored in chapter 9.

[73] 'In our Association in this County, though we made our Terms large enough for all, Episcopal, Presbyterians and Independents, there was not one Presbyterian joyned with us that I know of (for I knew but of one in all the County, Mr. *Tho. Hall*) nor one Independent, (though two or three honest ones said nothing against us) nor one of the New Prelatical way (Dr. *Hammond*'s) but three or four moderate Conformists that were for the old Episcopacy; and all the rest were meer Catholicks; Men of no Faction, nor siding with any Party but owning that which was good in all, as far as they could discern it; and upon a Concord in so much, laying out themselves for the great Ends of their Ministry, the Peoples Edification.' *Rel. Bax.,* I, i, §140, 97. See also II, §28, 148. Thomas Hall (1610-1665) was from 1640 curate of King's Norton, Birmingham, and a member of the Kenilworth Classis, Warwickshire; see *CR,* 242-243. For Henry Hammond (1605-1660), a leader of the episcopal party and respected by Baxter, see *WR* and *DNB*.

were nerved by a group of supportive peers.[74] Even so, the emphasis on discipline further illustrates the intended pastoral function of the Association. Baxter himself makes it clear that he was much more concerned that the Association facilitate parish discipline than comprehend as many sorts of ministers as possible. Though the numbers of pastors participating in the Association was impressive, a majority of area ministers chose not to associate. These, not surprisingly, were marginalized by their more 'godly' brethren as 'all the weaker sort of Ministers, whose Sufficiency or Conversation was questioned by others, and knew they were of little esteem among them, and were neither able or willing to exercise any Discipline on their Flocks'.[75]

The Worcestershire Association, of course, was not a puritan combination lecture.[76] The times had changed and the issues faced by Baxter and his colleagues in Worcestershire were very different from those faced by the previous generations of godly pastors. That being said, there remains enough of a family resemblance to suggest a fairly direct genealogy between the two. Significantly, however, from generation to generation of godly pastors from Elizabeth to Cromwell, the core motivation remained the same: nothing less than the completed reformation of the English Church and the triumph of godliness in the English nation.

From Initiative to Movement

In September 1653, a letter from 'the Associating Ministers of Cumberland and Westmoreland' arrived in Kidderminster addressed 'to the Worcestershire Association and Richard Baxter'. Signed by seven ministers, the letter states:

> We, before we had heard of your Book [*Christian Concord*, 1653], had undertaken a Work of the like nature: Several of us…were convinced that for Reformation of our People, more ought to be done by us than bare Preaching, a brotherly Association of Ministers appeared to be the likeliest course for the attainment of our Desires… [Your book] was a great Encouragement to us to see that other godly and learned Men had walked much what in the same Steps, and had pleaded our Cause almost by the same Arguments wherewith we endeavoured to strengthen it.[77]

---

[74] See chapter 5 for an overview of Baxter's disciplinary process.

[75] *Rel. Bax.*, II, §28, 148.

[76] Nor was it, *contra* Ladell, a 'revival of the old Puritan "Exercises," or "Prophesyings," which Archbishop Grindal had approved'. Ladell, *Richard Baxter*, 62-63.

[77] Published in *Rel. Bax.*, II, §34, p. 162-163. See also *Calendar*, no 131, 106-107. The letter is dated 1 September 1653 and is signed by Richard Gilpin, pastor at Greystoke, Cumberland (for Gilpin, 1625-1700, who was the grand-nephew of Bernard Gilpin, see

Baxter had for several months already been receiving letters in response to the newly published *Christian Concord*.[78] Obviously delighted by the news of a sister association, and flush with the budding potential of the Worcestershire Association, Baxter responded to the ministers of Cumberland and Westmorland in a letter dated October 1653:

> We hear also that in many other Counties they are stirred up to Consultations for these Ends; and we perceive that the Excellency and Necessity of Unity, Peace and some Reformation, is a little more observable than it hath been heretofore: and that God begins

Nuttall, 'Congregational Commonwealth Incumbents', in *TCHS*, 14 [1944], 162; *DNB*; *CR*); John Macmillan of Edenhall; Roger Baldwin, minister of Penrith (for Baldwin, 1624-1695, who subsequently served as curate of Rainford, Prescot, Lancashire until 1662, see *CR*, 24-25); John Billingsley, minister of Addingham (for Billingsley, 1625-1683, see *DNB*; he removed to Chesterfield, Derbyshire, from which he was deprived in 1662; see *CR*, 53-54); Elisha Bourne, minister at Skelton; John Jackson, pastor of Hutton (Jackson later became scribe of the Association; see *CR*, 290); and Thomas Turner (see *CR*, 498), 'preacher of the gospel' and later vicar of Torpenhow, Cumberland.

[78] A letter from Richard Swayne, minister in Clyro, Radnorshire (27 January 1652/3, *Calendar*, no. 107, see also Thomas Richards, *Religious Developments in Wales (1654-1662)* (1923), 15, 499), indicates a further attempt independent of Baxter to establish some sort of local association of ministers. Other early responses to *Christian Concord* include a letter from Thomas Gataker, *'miles emeritus'* of Rotherhithe, Surrey (20 July 1653, *Calendar,* no. 124; see also *DNB*); and Thomas White of St Ann's, Aldersgate, London (16 July 1653, *Calendar,* no. 123; see also *CR*, 525, though Matthews indicates that there is some confusion as to which Thomas White the sources may be referring.). Baxter also corresponded with several people about the contents of *Christian Concord* before it was published. See the letter from Henry Bartlett (22 March 1652/3, *Calendar*, no. 113); from George Hopkins, vicar of All Saints, Evesham (3 February 1652/3, *Calendar*, no. 108; see *CR*, 275); as well as the correspondence with John Dury (*Calendar*, nos 83, 99, 104, 106, 109, 111, 114, along with a correspondence that continues through the early 1670s. For Dury, see *DNB*.). Baxter also carries on an extensive correspondence with Peter Ince, who would become a leader in the Wiltshire Association. In this correspondence, Nuttall & Keeble find corroborating evidence (in *Calendar*, i, 113-14, 117-18; no. 140 from Ince and Baxter's response in no. 148) of the existence of a voluntary association in Wiltshire alongside the already existing Wiltshire Classis. The existence of both a classis and a voluntary association in the same county is apparently unique, and raises questions about the relationship between the two groups and the circumstances behind the association's formation. Nuttall and Keeble state that 'The date of [Ince's] letter associates the origin of the Association with the excitement over the Barebones Parliament's move to abolish tithes' (i, 113), though the lack of further contemporary discussion qualifies such suggestions as speculation. For Ince's correspondence with Baxter, see *Calendar*, nos 103, 116, 140, 148, 152, 265, 199, 221, 236, 242, 274, 285. For Ince (1615-1683), see *CR*, 288-289.

to disgrace Divisions, and to put a zeal for Reconciliation into
many of his Ministers... These things give us hope, that God is
about the Restoring of his People, and that he is kindling that Zeal
for Unity and Reformation which shall overcome the Fire of
Contention that hath been wasting us so long.[79]

Indeed the response to Baxter's initiative and to *Christian Concord* proved to
be astonishing. By the time of Richard Cromwell's brief Protectorate, there
were seventeen county associations, most of which had taken the
Worcestershire Association as their inspiration and model.[80] The fact that
several were already pursuing an associational agenda independently of Baxter

---

[79] The letter is signed by Baxter and by Jarvis Bryan (Rector of Old Swinford,
Stourbridge, Worcestershire, and brother of John Bryan, whom Baxter knew from
Coventry; see *CR*, 82) 'in the Name and at the Appointment of the rest' of the
Worcestershire Association. *Rel. Bax.*, II, 164. See also *Calendar*, no. 143, 114-115.
Nuttall believes that the Cheshire Association which formed in October 1653 was one of
those mentioned here that formed independently of the Worcestershire Association.
Baxter also became aware in September of 1653 of ministers in Northampton who were
studying *Christian Concord*. See Nuttall, *Richard Baxter*, 72.

[80] There were associations of godly ministers in Worcestershire, Cumberland and
Westmorland (1653), Cheshire (1653), Northampton (1653), Wiltshire (which was the
first formed on the Worcestershire model, 1653), Hampshire (1653), Dorsetshire and
Somersetshire (1654), Kent (1654), Devonshire (1655), Cambridgeshire (1656),
Cornwall (1656), Sussex (1656), Shropshire (1656) Herefordshire (1658, though the
evidence merely suggests the possibility of an association here; see Shaw, *A History*, ii,
p. 452), Staffordshire (1658), Essex (1658), and Norfolk (1659). Evidence also exists of
a voluntary association in the County of Flint in north Wales (see Matthew Henry, *An
Account of the Life and Death of Mr. Philip Henry* [1698], 59-61, and M.H. Lee's
Diaries and Letters of Philip Henry [1882], 77), in Dublin (see *The Agreement and
Resolvtion of the Ministers of Christ Associated within the City of Dublin* [1659]), and
Cork (see *The Agreement and Resolvtion of Severall Associated Ministers in...Corke*
[1657]). See Nuttall, *Richard Baxter*, 71-74; also see Shaw, *A History*, ii, 152-165, 440-
456; Phil Kilroy, *Protestant Dissent and Controversy in Ireland 1660-1714* [Cork: Cork
University Press, 1994], 36-37); and Gilbert, 'Two Irish Ministerial Associations of the
1650s', in *BNS*, 4:2 (1996), 16-19. Along with the two Irish Associations mentioned
above, several other English Associations published Articles of Agreement and or
Exhortations: See [Richard Gilpin], *The Agreement of the Associated Ministers &
Churches of the Counties of Cumberland and Westmerland* (1656), *The Agreement of
the Associated Ministers of the County of Essex...with a word of Exhortation to
Brotherly Union* (1658), and *The Agreement of the Associated Ministers In the County
of Norfolk and City and County of Norwich, Concerning Publick Catechizing...* (1659).
For the Essex Agreement, see Susan Hardman Moore, 'Arguing for Peace: Giles Firmin
on New England and Godly Unity', R. Swanson, ed., *Unity and Diversity in the Church*
(Oxford: Basil Blackwell, 1996), 251-262. For Giles Firmin, leader of the Essex
ministers and correspondent of Baxter's, see *CR*, 197; *DNB*; *Calendar*, nos 192, 300,
306, 311, 660, 818, 850, & 852.

demonstrates the widespread existence of such an impulse among the godly, as well as the widespread perception that something had to be done to fill the ecclesiastical void before the godly hope was totally overrun by the separatists and the sects, and their resulting spiritual anarchy.[81]

Although the need for discipline was paramount for Baxter and the other members of the Worcestershire Association, the vacuum of ecclesiastical authority caused many other ministers outside the Presbyterian classis structure to be very concerned about the lack of available means for ordination.[82] And even though the members of Worcestershire Association intentionally chose not to pursue the practise of ordination as a function of the Association, many of other county associations made ordination as well as discipline a primary purpose for their associating.[83] Baxter was aware of the differing motives behind the various voluntary associations, but rejected the critique that the movement was compromised by such public divergences.[84]

---

[81] See the letter from William Mewe, Rector of Eastington, Gloucester, who wrote somewhat sourly, 'Tis well knowne...that my designe of association & accommodation of Dissenting partyes was on Foote certayne months if not years before I saw yours.' DWL, BxL, iv, 279. See also *Calendar*, no. 125, 103. Mewe was a member of the Westminster Assembly, and served in Eastington as Rector from 1635 until his death in 1669. See *CR*, 349.

[82] The Worcestershire Association was, in fact, very concerned with the issue of ordination, holding one of its disputations on whether 'those who Nullifie our present Ministry and Churches, which have not the Prelatical Ordination, and teach the People to do the like, do incur the guilt of grievous sin'. See Baxter, *Five Disputations of Church Government, and Worship*, Table of Contents. Tellingly, Baxter betrays the source of *his* primary concern-the Separatists-in the title page of the second disputation: *The Second Disputation: Vindicating the Protestant Churches and Ministers that have not Prelatical Ordination, from the Reproaches of those Dividers that would nullifie them. Written Upon sad complaints of many Godly Ministers in several parts of the Nation, whose Hearers are turning Separatists* (1658).

[83] Shaw, *A History*, ii, 152-153. Voluntary Associations for which exist records or reports of ordination include Cambridgeshire (see W.A. Shaw, ed., *Minutes of the Bury Presbyterian Classis, 1647-1657* [Manchester: Chetham Society, 1896], 193-194, 199-200, 202), Cheshire (see Henry Newcome's *The Autobiography of Henry Newcome*, Richard Parkinson, ed. [Manchester: Chetham Society, 1852], 44, 47, 57, 62-63, 67-68, 297. Newcome was the 'best known of Lancashire Presbyterians'. See *CR*, 362-63), Cornwall (see Shaw, *Minutes of the Bury Presbyterian Classis*, 181, 183), Cumberland (see Edmund Calamy, *Account of the Ministers and [Others] Ejected or Silenced after the Restoration in 1660* [2nd edition, 1713], i, 157, 159, 168), Devonshire (see R.N. North, 'Minutes', *Reports and Transactions of the Devonshire Association for the Advancement of Science* [1887], 279-281; also Calamy, *Account*, i, 227), Nottingham (see Shaw, *Minutes of the Bury Presbyterian Classis*, 153-174), and possibly Dorset (see Shaw, *A History*, ii, 451).

[84] 'And though some thought that so many Associations, and Forms of Agreement, did but tend to more Division, by shewing our diversity of Apprehensions, the contrary

Conclusion

The tortured frustration of godly hopes induced by the lingering death of the Long Parliament's reforms, combined with the proliferation and excesses of increasingly heterodox sects in the 1640s and 50s created an audience that found the solutions provided by Baxter in *Christian Concord* and the Worcestershire Association very compelling. Our own hindsight shows us that the this new structure, this 'practical piece of makeshift machinery' that evolved to promote the godly agenda was in fact the last and best effort of a puritanism that had outlived the church it was attempting to reform.[85] Stripped of its context by the political victories of Parliament and the military victories of the Army and the overthrow of the Church hierarchy, the godly minority, which had heretofore only played the role of the more-or-less loyal opposition within the Church of England, could never make the transition to power.[86] The reactionary habits which served puritans so well when they were being opposed and repressed continued unchanged when their moment of triumph came, and resulted in increasingly fractious internal division causing the fragmentation and collapse of the whole movement, resulting in a Restoration banishment to the margins of English church life as a defanged nonconformity.[87]

But we have gotten ahead of ourselves. What is significant for our purposes here is that Richard Baxter perceived an immediate threat from the separatists and the sects and acted to fill the vacuum of authority left by the overthrow of episcopacy and the subsequent failure of presbyterian reform. By modifying a godly commonplace, the combination lecture, Baxter was able to create an associational context in which the crucial issue of church discipline could be addressed. But it was always intended to be much more than a mechanism to promote ecclesiastical purity by enabling local church discipline. The resulting Association was, in Neil Keeble's words, his 'attempt to create by practical

---

proved true by Experience: for we all agreed on the same Course, even to unite in the practice of so much of Discipline as the Episcopal, Presbyterian, and Independents are agreed in, and as crosseth none of their Principles'. *Rel. Bax.*, II, §36, 167.

[85] Shaw, *A History,* ii, 163.

[86] See Acheson, *Radical Puritans,* 44.

[87] Commenting on the increasing dissonance between the puritan rhetoric of reformation and the fragmenting reality faced in the parishes, John Morrill states 'If this is where Puritan rhetoric had moved between 1641 and 1649, it is not surprising that the 1650s proved not a journey across the Desert to the Promised Land, but a dispirited trek back to Egypt.' Morrill, 'The Impact of Puritanism', 66. The natural question as to whether there is a continuity between the voluntary associations of the 1650s, and the associations which formed in the aftermath of Convention Parliament's limited toleration (1689) is beyond the scope of the present discussion. However, for an initial exploration, see Nuttall's 'Assembly and Association in Dissent, 1689-1831', G.J. Cuming and D Baker, eds. *Councils and Assemblies* (Cambridge: Cambridge University Press, 1971), especially 294-295.

Christianity...what force and politics had failed to achieve—reformation.'[88] And as we shall see in the next chapter, the Worcestershire Association also provided the context for Baxter to launch his most ambitious attempt to promote the long-sought reformation, his programme of parish-wide pastoral oversight and catechizing.

Geoffrey Nuttall argues that 'the Association was significant even more in that it existed at all than in what it did.'[89] A review of the evidence, however, begins to allow us to question that reading. Seen in its wider historical context, Baxter's associational initiative is nothing less than the capstone of his overarching strategy for pastor-led parish reformation. The Worcestershire Association thus reveals Baxter, not as a forerunner of the movement for the Enlightenment idea of toleration and unity (the thought of which would have made him blanche), nor as cantankerous and flawed leader of English Nonconformity (which, however apt a description it might later become, should not be read back into his days in Kidderminster), but as a parish pastor, making do as best he could with what was at hand in the remade world of Civil War and Interregnum England.

---

[88] Keeble, *Richard Baxter*, 155.
[89] Nuttall, *Richard Baxter*, 69.

CHAPTER 7

Baxter's Pastoral Initiative
and the Catalyst for Reformed Parishioners

Having considered the specifics of Baxter's practise of parish discipline in chapter 5 and traced the development of his Worcestershire association in chapter 6, we turn our attention to Baxter's strategy for engaging each person in his parish with the gospel through both a vigorous preaching ministry and the development of a scheme for the systematic catechizing of every family. In doing so, we will trace Baxter's own progress as he struggled with the shortcomings of the pulpit-centred pastoral ideal discussed in chapter 2 and ultimately reconfigured his ministry around evangelistic goals.[1] In combination with the consistent practise of an effective church discipline by pastors who were fortified by regular association and mutual encouragement, Baxter was convinced that these pastoral initiatives to engage parishioners personally with Christian truth would bring the long desired reformation, not only of England's parishes, but of the nation as a whole.[2]

Writing on 4 May 1655 on behalf of 'divers ministers' in Worcestershire, Richard Baxter put voice to their increasing alarm concerning the apparent failure of their preaching ministries. Despite the proliferation of preaching, 'to the grief of our souls... many thousands in this Land of light, do wilfully live in darkness'. Even in their own parishes, Baxter and his colleagues had been astonished to discover during conversation with 'some of our hearers', 'that they know very little of the Doctrine which we have been preaching to them so many years, as plainly as we could speak'. This lack of response brought Baxter and his colleagues 'to a deep Consideration of our own Neglects' as pastors and provoked a rethink of what they as pastors should do, 'perceiving that it must be a more familiar course that must help the extreamly ignorant to understand'.[3]

Seen in this light, Richard Baxter's strategy of pastoral oversight in

---

[1] Keeble, 'Richard Baxter's Preaching Ministry', 540-41; Lim, 'In pursuit of unity, purity and liberty', 22-23.
[2] See Baxter, *Gildas Salvianus*, sig (a6)v.
[3] [Baxter], *The Agreement of Divers Ministers*, 17-19.

Kidderminster was not merely a defensive reaction against the vacuum of spiritual authority and discipline confronting St Mary's parish and others like it in the unfolding religious chaos following the Civil Wars. Rather, he developed an aggressively evangelistic procedure to provide every member of his parish with the means to understand both the basic tenets of Christianity and the way one should live in response.

We have already argued that Baxter was making use of a pastoral strategy for parish evangelism and reformation that was first promoted in England by Martin Bucer. And we have seen that he was also revising the pastoral precedents of preceding generations of Protestant clergy such as prophesyings and lectures.[4] In the unsettling discord which followed the abolition of episcopacy and the frustration of national Presbyterianism, many parish ministers looking for effective models of ministry found Baxter's programme and supporting rhetoric both timely and attractive.[5] It was, for Baxter's Kidderminster, the Worcestershire Association members and nation as a whole, a pastoral synthesis that seemed almost to work. But first we must consider Baxter's experience of the insufficiency of the puritan pulpit in both matters of personal salvation and parish reformation.

The Inadequacy of Preaching

If we can take his word, Richard Baxter was ordained in the Church of England disinclined to be a pastor.[6] Instead, concerned that his poor health would lead to his early demise, his heightened awareness of approaching eternity made him 'exceeding desirous to Communicate those Apprehensions to such ignorant, presumptuous, careless Sinners as the World aboundeth with'.[7] While genuine, this rehearsal of motive marginalizes other more complex concerns behind his choice of vocation. His parents were not initially very keen on him becoming a minister.[8] Moreover, he struggled with the absence of any positive sense of call from God, and would later wonder aloud whether his Christian concerns resulted more from '*Education* and *Fear*' than from '*Regeneration* and *Love*'.[9] But perhaps his most consuming concern was his lack of a university education. Having taken the advice of his teacher John Owen, he chose a course of private

---

[4] One also hears the echo of the reforming emphases of pre-Reformation Christian humanists like Erasmus and Colet. See Margo Todd, *Christian Humanism and the Puritan Social Order* (Cambridge: Cambridge University Press, 1987); for an earlier example of the kind of reformation godly pastors had in mind, see David Underdown's study of seventeenth-century Dorchester in *Fire from Heaven: The Life of an English Town in the Seventeenth Century* (London: Harper-Collins, 1992).

[5] See Green, *The Christian's ABC*, 223.

[6] *Rel. Bax.*, I, i, §18, 13.

[7] Ibid., I, i, §16, 12.

[8] Ibid., I, i, §10, 11.

[9] Ibid., I, i, §6, 6.

tuition rather than a place at Oxford. His experience under his tutor was a tremendous disappointment. In a society overly concerned with one's place, his lack of a university degree had the immediate effect of relegating him to a position of lesser respect, not just with regards to colleagues and peers, but most importantly in his own eyes: 'I was conscious of my personal insufficiency, for want of that measure of Learning and Experience, which so great and high a Work required. I knew that the want of Academical Honours and Degrees was like to make me Contemptible with the most, and consequently hinder the Success of my Endeavours.'[10]

Baxter indicates, however, that his early understanding of call and ministry was influenced by several local 'godly' pastors and nonconformists. When Baxter returned from London after an internship at court proved disillusioning, he fell in with a group of Shrewsbury Nonconformists, whose godliness and zeal impressed him and whose complaints against the Church of England challenged him.[11] And though he found himself taking the Conformists' side in ongoing discussions with them, and found their arguments 'weak', his interaction with them provoked questions over certain requirements of conformity and pressed him to begin thinking through issues of church government and parish discipline. Such was the apparent influence of this small fellowship that Nuttall is persuaded that Baxter has them in mind when, in his *Gildas Salvianus,* he writes: 'Before the Parliament began, how frequent and fervent were we in secret... O the earnest prayers that I have heard in secret daies heretofore for a Painful Ministry, and for Discipline!... and [they] so preached and prayed for it, as if the setting up of Discipline, had been the setting up of the Kingdom of Christ.'[12]

So even though Baxter was 'conscious of a thirsty desire of Mens Conversion and Salvation', and though he was aware that he possessed 'some competent perswading Faculty of Expression, which fervent Affections might help to actuate', his actual transition from student to minister was more complex. He spent the two years following his mother's death mining the local network of 'godly' conformists and nonconformists, while preparing for some sort of preaching ministry and also for what he feared was his own imminent death, all the while (we can surmise) devoting an astonishing amount of energy to compensate for his academic shortcomings.

When asked in 1638 by 'old Mr. *Richard Foley* of *Stourbridge* in

---

[10] Ibid., I, i, §16, 12.

[11] 'At last at about 20 years of Age, I became acquainted with Mr. *Simmonds*, Mr. *Cradock*, and the other very zealous godly Nonconformists in *Shrewsbury,* and the adjoyning parts, whose fervent Prayers, and savoury Conferences and holy Lives did profit me much.' *Rel. Bax.,* I, i, §17, 13. Other members of this circle included George Fawler and Michael Old. For these Shrewsbury Nonconformists, see Nuttall, *Richard Baxter,* 11-14.

[12] *Gildas Salvianus* (1656), 378-79; Nuttall, *Richard Baxter,* 13.

Worcestershire' to serve as schoolmaster for the new grammar school in Dudley, the young Baxter saw it as 'not an inconvenient' opportunity, especially as it allowed him scope to 'Preach up and down in Places that were most ignorant'.[13] Baxter traveled to Worcester with Foley and his friend James Berry, who would later become one of Cromwell's associates, and was ordained a deacon by the Bishop of Worcester on 23 December 1638, and licensed to teach.[14] Baxter himself gives few clues as to what induced him to seek ordination and to become a preacher, or how, in fact, he learned to preach. Many of the formative ministerial examples he mentions in his *Reliquiae Baxterianae* are negative, the common refrain for almost all of them being that they 'never preached'.[15] He does, however, gratefully mention the influence of 'three or four constant competent Preachers [who] lived near us', and he was later to acknowledge the influence of another, Francis Garbett, minister at Wroxeter. In a letter of thanks to Baxter for the gift of his first three books, Garbett protests: 'I know not why you should acknowledge your self so much beholden to me as in your letter you have done'.[16] In the absence of direct attributions, the formative influences encouraging Baxter both in godliness and towards ministry are most likely found in the network of relationships which he pursued with local ministers like Francis Garbett who impressed him as being serious about religion.

He is also reticent when referring to his first year of teaching school and preaching in Dudley: 'I there Preached my first publick Sermon in the upper Parish Church; and afterward Preached in Villages about'.[17] In his recollection of this formative year, he is much more interested in charting the development of his position on issues identified with nonconformity. The people of Dudley were responsive to Baxter's first efforts. Baxter describes them as 'a poor tractable People, lately famous for Drunkenness, but commonly more ready to hear God's Word with submission and reformation, than most Places where I

---

[13] *Rel. Bax.*, I, i, §18, 13. For Baxter's relationship with the Foleys, see Nuttall, *Richard Baxter*, 15-17; H.E. Palfrey, 'The Foleys of Stourbridge', *TWAS*, new series, 21 (1945), 1-15.

[14] The certificate itself, along with the license to teach are in DWL, BT, iv, 120-21. Nuttall argues that circumstantial evidence suggests that Baxter was also ordained a priest. See *Richard Baxter*, 18; Nuttall, *The Holy Spirit in Puritan Faith and Experience*, 10; F. J. Powicke, *The Reverend Richard Baxter Under the Cross*, 218-220. For Baxter's increasingly complicated relationship with James Berry, see Nuttall, *Richard Baxter*, 14-16; Gilbert, 'Richard Baxter and James Berry', in *BNS*, 6:1 (1998), 2-10.

[15] *Rel. Bax.*, I, i, §1, 1-2. Baxter goes into much greater detail in *A Third Defence of the Cause of Peace* (1681), 38-40.

[16] DWL, BxL, vi:120; iii:165. Garbett's letter to Baxter is dated 17 January 1650[1]. For the several godly preachers 'near us', later identified as Humphrey Barnet, Curate of Uppington, Samuel Smith, Curate of Cressage in Cound, and George Baxter, Rector of Little Wenlock, see Nuttall, *Richard Baxter*, 8-9.

[17] *Rel. Bax.*, I, I, §19, 13.

have come'. Baxter did not forget them. When he returned to Kidderminster after the Civil War, he preached in Dudley often, arranging a monthly lecture which he found 'usually as much crowded within, and at the Windows, as ever I saw any *London* Congregations'.[18]

Baxter had not been nine months in Dudley when in 1639 he was invited to serve as curate in Bridgnorth under William Madstard, a 'grave and severe Ancient Divine' 'afflicted' with a 'dead-hearted unprofitable People'.[19] Unencumbered by other pastoral responsibilities such as baptisms and celebrating the Lord's Supper, he nevertheless found preaching in Bridgnorth an exercise in frustration. 'Though I was in the fervour of my Affections, and never anywhere preached with more vehement desire of Mens Conversion...yet with the generality an Applause of the Preacher was most of the success of the Sermon which I could hear of; and their tipling and ill company and dead-heartedness quickly drowned all.'[20]

When in 1681 Baxter published *Compassionate Counsel to all Young Men* as a guide book for those young men attending university and considering Church of England ministry,[21] much of his counsel bears striking resemblance to his own experience and may illuminate the reasons behind his own earlier choice of positions:

> By Preaching some years to a small ignorant people where you fear not critical judgments, you will get boldness of speech, and freedom of utterance, without that servile Study of words, and learning your written notes without Book, which will be *tiresome, time-wasting* and *lifeless*. And when freedom and use hath brought you to a habit of ready speaking of the great and necessary things, and acquaintence with ignorant Countrey people hath taught you to understand their case, you will have a better preparation for more publick places... than you were ever like to get either in Universities, among Schollars, or in great mens Houses.[22]

---

[18] Ibid., I, i, §20, 14.

[19] Ibid., I, i, §21, 15. Bridgnorth's unusual ecclesiastical arrangements, being exempt from episcopal jurisdiction except for the Archbishop's triennial visitation, ironically provided shelter for both Madstard's and Baxter's nonconformity. For Madstard, see Nuttall, *Richard Baxter*, 19-21.

[20] *Rel. Bax.*, I, i, §21, 15. See W.G. Clark-Maxwell, 'Baxter at Bridgnorth', in *TSAS*, 4th series, 9 (1923), 66-75.

[21] Baxter's title for chapter IX, 'Additional counsel to Youngmen, who are bred up to Learning, and Publick work, especially to the Sacred Ministry in the Universities and Schools', indicates a continuing concern to influence pastoral ministry within the Church of England, as Nonconformists were barred from the universities. See *Compassionate Counsel*, 108.

[22] Ibid., 158.

Baxter's opportunity for a more public place of ministry came in March 1641 when he received two letters signed by fourteen leading parishioners inviting him to become lecturer of St Mary's, the parish church of Kidderminster.[23] The position offered Baxter was the result of a compromise between the parish vicar, George Dance, and a group of puritan townsmen scandalized by Dance's non-preaching ministry and the allegedly scandalous behaviour of his two curates. Threatened with citation before the Long Parliament's Committee for Scandalous Ministers, which had been established the previous year to deal with the flood of local complaints against insufficient incumbents, Dance agreed to dismiss one of his curates and to provide £60 per annum from his own living to cover the salary of a replacement who would serve as preacher and would be chosen by a committee of fourteen parishioners selected to oversee the arrangement.[24] Baxter preached a trial sermon in Kidderminster on Sunday, 4 April. The Monday following a document was drafted and signed by the committee along with thirteen additional parishioners affirming that Baxter was hereby 'chosen, elected and nominated... preacher and Lecturer'.[25]

'I preached before the Wars twice each Lord's Day', wrote Baxter, as well as on Thursdays, Kidderminster's market day.[26] Although he had the unwavering support of Kidderminster's 'godly' minority, Baxter became the focus of increasing controversy as various local factions polarized in the drift towards civil war. His insistence on conversion, holiness and discipline (as well as his 'eagerness and dogmatism'[27]), while refreshing to some, caused great offense to others.[28]

Baxter's initial tenure as Kidderminster lecturer ended in confusion and apparent failure when, less than 18 months after his arrival he was forced to flee out of concern for his safety, first to Gloucester for a month, and then after an unsuccessful bid to return home, to Coventry. Though Baxter supposed 'that a very few days or weeks by *one other* Battel, would end the Wars' and allow him to resume his ministry, five years would pass and England would be remade before a convalescing Baxter, forced by illness from his army chaplaincy, would heed the petitions of his former congregation to resume his ministry.[29] The situation which met him upon his return was very different from the one he had left. As we have seen, Kidderminster had changed, for 'most of the bitter Enemies of Godliness in the Town, that rose in Tumults against me

---

[23] See DWL, BxL, i:212; vi:45.

[24] See Nuttall, *Richard Baxter*, 22-28. The bond for £500 which Dance signed as a guarantee of good faith is still extant. See Roger Thomas, ed., *Baxter Treatises,* 5a.

[25] DWL, BxL, iii:111.

[26] *Rel. Bax.*, I, i, §135, 83. Baxter mentions that after the wars, he preached 'once on Sundays, and once every Thursday, besides occasional Sermons.'

[27] Nuttall, *Richard Baxter*, 29.

[28] *Rel. Bax.*, I, i, §56, 40.

[29] Ibid., I, i, §61, 43.

before, in their very Hatred of Puritans, had gone out into the Wars, into the King's Armies, and were quickly kill'd, and few of them ever returned again'.[30] The context for preaching and parish ministry, too, had changed. The abolition of episcopacy and the inability of parliament to enforce a Presbyterian alternative left a vacuum of ecclesiastical authority increasingly exploited by separatists and sects which left many pastors in a defensive scramble to salvage order and reformation.[31] And Baxter, himself, had changed. Extensive preaching experience, incessant debates with a spectrum of ecclesiastical, theological and political opponents as well as the attempt to cope with the new, fluid religious and political situation upon his return to Kidderminster precipitated a reevaluation of the pastoral means necessary to promote parish and national reformation. And along with his concerns over discipline, Baxter was also wrestling with his changing assessment of the received commonplace of the sufficiency of preaching.

Tom Webster states that 'It is a truism to suggest that the ministry as conceived of by the godly focused on the act of preaching almost to the exclusion of all else.'[32] Yet despite their official rhetoric to the contrary,[33] England's Protestants had long had a conflicted view of the efficacy of preaching. Their reading of the New Testament taught them that preaching was the God-appointed means to call forth faith in God's elect (Romans 10:8-15).[34] Their understanding of history taught them that lack of (Protestant) preaching and the resulting unavailability of the light of God's word meant that untold thousands of men and women lived their lives in darkness, ignorant of the only means by which they might be reconciled with God and saved.[35] Their understanding of the loving providence of God taught them that England's reformation was in fact God's hand at work to restore God's word and the faithful preaching thereof, so that the darkness of England's ignorance of the gospel might be banished and the way made by the increasing number of preachers for England to become, in Baxter's phrase, 'a Land of light'.

But the fruits of this preaching ministry had been uneven at best. As early as 1584, the lack of expected progress led the Cambridge puritan William Fulke

---

[30] Ibid., I, i, §137, 86. See also I, i, §59, 42.

[31] See chapters 5 and 6.

[32] Webster, *Godly Clergy*, 96.

[33] Defensive reaction against Roman Catholic and then Laudian critique of the centrality and sufficiency of preaching served to ossify the 'godly' stance on preaching. See chapter 2 for a survey of puritan rhetoric on the sufficiency of preaching.

[34] See Richard Sibbes, 'Lydia's Conversion', in *Works of Richard Sibbes*, VI, 526-27. 'Lydia's Conversion' was published as the first of two short treatises under the title *The Riches of Mercy* (1638).

[35] [William Fulke] (attributed by Wing), *A Brief and plain declaration, concerning the desires of all those faithfull Ministers* (1584), 36-37. For Fulke, controversial colleague of Thomas Cartwright and later master of Pembroke Hall, Cambridge, see Porter, *Reformation and Reaction*, 119-135.

(1538-1589) to complain, 'We may be ashamed, now that our church hath had rest and peace, with free preaching of the gospel this 25 or 26 years... to be [still] unfurnished of learned pastors as we are: whereas, if that diligence had been used of all partes...that unfaignedly seeke the kingdome of God..., almost in halfe the time, this necessitie might have been well supplied.'[36] Another candid Elizabethan minister observed that while faithful preaching of God's word in 'sinceritie and plaines' should continue to be promoted, 'yet in many yeares wee come but to a small measure of knowledge, and reformation of life'. Yet, he continues, this apparent frustration of protestant hopes ought not surprise anyone, however, since 'the Apostles of Christ, hearing their master preach so often, & so familiarly, by the spane of three yeres and more, yet for all his paines and travaile in that time, they knew not well the vertue of his death, and resurrection.' Even so, the lack of return for all their efforts was confusing. 'Yea, we heare say, that many painefull preachers, both in townes & cities, exercising the word three or foure times a weeke, yet do they complaine of the small profiting of the flocke.'[37] Richard Greenham, rector of Dry Drayton near Cambridge, is reported to have bewailed the fact that 'the lord offereth the myne of his mercy to be divided to them, that wil but hear, and beleev it, and no man almost regardeth it.'[38] The widespread nature of these complaints on the part of ministers lends credence to Christopher Haigh's assertion that the preaching-focused programme of Elizabethan Protestant evangelism was not nearly as effective as its own rhetoric and later historians have implied.[39] Even so, it is difficult to discern how much all this whinging on the part of godly clergy concerning the effectiveness of their preaching was a reflection of actual short-comings or merely standard rhetorical posturing.

Whatever its source, this rhetoric of complaint persisted among preaching ministers for decades. Richard Baxter, in a statement with which fifty-seven of his fellow Worcestershire Association colleagues could concur, declared that 'We finde by sad experience, that the people understand not our publike teaching, though we study to speak as plain as we can, and that after many years preaching, even of these same fundamentals, too many can scarce tell anything that we said'.[40] Even though Baxter affirmed that 'publike preaching' was 'the most excellent' part of a pastor's work, 'because it tendeth to work on many', his own pulpit shortcomings had convinced him that even the most plain and 'painful' preaching was insufficient for the goals of conversion and

---

[36] [Fulke], *A Brief and plain declaration* (1584), 38.

[37] 'A brief answere to the principall pointes of the same [Archbishop's] articles, written an. 1583', in *A Parte of a register* (1593), 207-08.

[38] Parker and Carlson, *'Practical Divinity'*, 112.

[39] See Haigh, 'The Church of England, the Catholics and the people', P. Marshall, ed., *The Impact of the English Reformation 1500-1640* (London: Arnold, 1997), 235-256; and Haigh, 'Puritan evangelism in the reign of Elizabeth I', in *EHR*, 72 (1977), 30-58.

[40] [Baxter], *The Agreement of Divers Ministers*, 11.

reformation it was intended to effect.[41] 'I am daily forced to admire, how lamentably ignorant many of our people are, that have seemed diligent hearers of me this ten or twelve years, while I spoke as plainly as I was able to speak! Some know not that each person in the Trinity is God; nor that Christ is God and man; Nor that he took his humane nature into heaven; Nor many the like necessary principles of our faith.'[42]

If the insufficiency of preaching had long been unofficially recognized, so the apparent solution had long been attempted. By the early seventeenth century, catechizing was a Protestant commonplace regardless of one's stand on ecclesiastical or theological issues, ubiquitous in terms of emphasis if not always in practise. Ian Green suggests that one of the greatest benefits attributed to catechizing, by 'godly' ministers especially, was as a means of helping parishioners understand sermons.[43] The Word-centred focus of much Elizabethan and early Stuart ministry caused many to view careful and constant catechizing as a necessary supplement to 'painful' preaching, lest the entire thrust of Protestant ministry be undermined.[44] Much has been made of Green's observations concerning the avoidance of theological controversies in most of the more popular catechisms which he examines in greater depth. While some have found that Green's evidence calls into question the 'penetration of Calvinism, the appeal of Protestantism and even the very success of the Reformation in England', it is probably better understood as representing the concern of convinced Protestant pastors for the eternal well-being of those parishioners under their spiritual care whose salvation was in doubt.[45] This concern, however, suggests that a broader role was envisaged for catechizing than simply as a means to prepare young parishioners for confirmation and

---

[41] Baxter, *Gildas Salvianus*, 78. Earlier overviews of Baxter's preaching fail to acknowledge Baxter's concerns over the effectiveness and sufficiency of preaching. See Keeble, 'Richard Baxter's Preaching Ministry', 539-42; J.R. Knott, Jr., *The Sword of the Spirit: Puritan Responses to the Bible* (Chicago: University of Chicago Press, 1980), 73-74, 176-77; Nuttall, *Richard Baxter*, 48-49, 57-58; Eayrs, *Richard Baxter*, 40-45; Grosart, 'Richard Baxter: Seraphic fervour', 112-13, 143-44. In *Richard Baxter*, Keeble acknowledges that, 'Despite his own success [in the pulpit], [Baxter] knew how ineffectual preaching alone could be with many individuals'. While rightly stating that Baxter 'regarded the personal care of individual parishioners...as important as preaching', he does not then go on to explain why (82).

[42] Baxter, *Gildas Salvianus*, sig (a5).

[43] Ian Green, *The Christian's ABC*, 31.

[44] Green, *The Christian's ABC*, 31. That is not to say that godly ministers in Elizabethan and Stuart England were devoid of concern for the sacraments. See Hunt, 'The Lord's Supper', 39-83.

[45] John Spurr, '[Review of] *The Christian's ABC. Catechisms and Catechizing in England c. 1530-1740.* By Ian Green', in *JTS*, 48 (1998), 333.

admission to the Lord's Supper.[46] Indeed the evidence cited by Green indicates that many catechists assumed catechizing was not only appropriate for adults, but because of the self-examination required for a right participation in the Lord's Supper, it would for most be a necessity.[47] In 1588, Thomas Sparke declared, 'It is impossible for any man, without the knowledge of the first and necessary principles of religion, to make due examination of himself' before participating in the Lord's Supper.[48] And later in the 1640s, William Lyford urged that adult parishioners who were deemed unready for participation due to their ignorance be taken through a three-year course of catechizing, to enable even the most simple to make an adequate profession of faith and obedience into which they had been baptized as infants.[49]

Thus when Baxter suggested that one of the principle reasons that 'godly' ministry languished and reformation tarried was the absence of diligent catechizing, he had not stumbled upon some lost secret of reformation truth, but was merely highlighting an oft-promoted pastoral mechanism and pointing out that it had too often not been practiced.[50] 'It is a well known duty', he confessed. Indeed, by urging his fellow ministers to resume catechizing, Baxter echoed his Elizabethan predecessors by viewing it not as a Protestant novelty, but as 'the restauration of the antient Ministerial work'.[51] Even so, while Green's research skillfully sorts through the torrent of catechetical material which poured from the pens of concerned Elizabethan and early Stuart ministers, and provides historically informed insight into the evolution of early modern English catechetical ideals and the range of various practises, the

---

[46] Green acknowledges that confirmation during this period was often 'flawed...in execution', though 'it seems to have struck a chord, and if most of those who participated were in fact able to say the Creed, they were at least in a position to make a bare profession of their faith, as the catechists who had taught them had intended.' *The Christian's ABC*, 34.

[47] Green, *The Christian's ABC*, 35-6.

[48] Thomas Sparke, [preface], *A catechisme, or short kind of instruction* (1588), 16-17. Quoted in Green, *The Christian's ABC*, 36. For Sparke (1548-1616), rector of Bletchley in Buckinghamshire, see *DNB*.

[49] William Lyford, *Principles of faith* (1642), sigs A2v-3. Cited by Green, *The Christian's ABC*, 36. See Green's discussion of the reasons why ministers found it consistently difficult to maintain adult participation in catechizing, 96-97. Though Lyford was *'a maintainer of Episcopacy'*, Baxter strongly recommends a later work of his, *William Lyford his Legacy* (1656) on admission to the Lord's Supper. See *Gildas Salvianus*, sig (b6). For Lyford (1598-1653), vicar of Sherborne, Dorset, see *DNB*. See also William Fulke, *A Briefe and plaine declaration* (1584), 51, 52. While Fulke mentions the pastor's responsibility to instruct families, it is unclear whether or not he has catechizing specifically in mind.

[50] For examples of published exhortations warning against the neglect of catechizing in favour of preaching, see Green, *The Christian's ABC*, 128-29.

[51] Baxter, *Gildas Salvianus*, 309.

nature of such a broad survey of catechetical material and practise and the categories by which he interprets his evidence limit his ability to appreciate the particular catechetical composite which evolved during Baxter's Kidderminster ministry. Baxter understood the difficulties ministers would face when they attempted to introduce a new programme of catechizing in their parishes. But he was convinced that certain alterations in traditional catechetical practise would allow him and his colleagues to press more effectively for the conversion of their parishioners and the reformation of their parishes. Because of his alterations in the purpose for catechizing and its subsequent practise, Baxter's method does not easily fit the ideals and technique of his Elizabethan and Stuart predecessors.[52] Baxter's concern over the insufficiency of preaching, his high estimation of catechizing, his practise of personal oversight house by house, and his complaints over the effects of a non-catechizing ministry all find precedents in Green's research and in other primary sources. Nevertheless, his incorporation of systematic parochial catechizing as part of a wider strategy for systematic parish evangelism and pastoral oversight appears to be unique.

Public Preaching and Private Dealing

The outlines of Baxter's evolving pastoral strategy began to emerge with the publication of a dedicatory epistle *'To my dearly beloved Friends... of Kederminster'* prefacing *The Saints Everlasting Rest* (1650). In this letter, Baxter gives his flock *'ten directions'*, *'my best advice for your immortal souls,... the legacy of a dying man, that you may here read it, and practice it, when I am taken from you'*.[53] His second direction exhorts them to *'Do the utmost you can to get a faithful Minister, when I am taken from you'* and to *'acknowledg him your Teacher, Overseer, and Ruler'*. *'Especially,'* he continues, *'submit to his private over-sight, as well as publick Teaching.'* With characteristic emphasis by overstatement, Baxter expounds the heart of his strategy of pastoral initiative among them: *'It is but the least part of the Ministers work, which is done in the Pulpit... To go daily from one house to another, and see how you live, and examine how you profit, and direct you in the duties of your families, and in your preparation for death, is the great work.'*[54]

---

[52] Green considers the absence of an adequate category or precedent for Baxter's work to be a 'moot point', and continues instead to describe the particulars of Baxter's catechetical practise (Green, *The Christian's ABC*, 223-24). But while all of the particulars of Baxter's *pastoral* practise have godly precedent (and can, in fact, be traced to the pastoral emphases of Martin Bucer), his way of fashioning them into a coherent, workable strategy is new.

[53] Baxter, *The Saints Everlasting Rest*, sig A3v. His letter is dated 15 January 1649/50.

[54] Baxter, *The Saints Everlasting Rest*, sig A4. See Nuttall's comment on Baxter's overstatement in *Richard Baxter*, 48.

Baxter had by now been back in Kidderminster nearly three years, though he writes this direction as if it had been his practise for some time. But if his words reflect his changing ideas about pastoral ministry, they also reflect the changed role he was playing within the parish itself. Prior to the civil wars, Baxter was hired as a lecturer and viewed himself primarily as a preacher. Upon his return in 1647, despite pleas for him to take over as vicar from the sequestered Dance, Baxter insisted on his old position as lecturer.[55] Nonetheless, the man addressing the parish in this letter is doing so, not as a lecturer, but as their pastor. His own changing ideas about pastoral ministry met with a vacuum of pastoral leadership in the parish upon his return, giving him the opportunity to take on broader pastoral responsibilities.[56] His status amongst the 'godly' of the parish (mainly from his powerful preaching), the attrition of his most vocal opponents during the wars, and the absence of any sizeable separatist faction provided him with a context of 'tractable' parishioners rare in such a fractious time. With Kidderminster providing perhaps the closest thing to laboratory conditions for seventeenth-century ministry, Baxter was able to embark on what proved to be one of the most notable experiments of pastoral practise Protestant England had heretofore seen.[57]

Reflecting later on his decision to modify the way he practiced parish ministry, he states that 'Experience in my Pastoral Charge convinced me that publick Preaching is not all the ordinary Work of a faithful Minister, and that personal Conference with every one about the State of their own Souls, together with Catechising, is a Work of very great Necessity.' But Baxter here is conflating a process that did not result in a settled pastoral strategy until after 1655. Although Baxter's published commitment to 'house to house' pastoral oversight predates by at least five years the adoption by the Worcestershire Association of his specific plan for parish-wide catechizing in *The Agreement of Divers Ministers of Christ In the County of Worcester... For Catechizing or Personal*, exactly *when* he decided to include a general programme of catechizing as part of his own practise of oversight is unknown.[58] The earliest

---

[55] A group of parishioners petitioned the Committee for Plundered Ministers and had Baxter appointed to the living without his approval or knowledge. See Nuttall, *Richard Baxter*, 40-41.

[56] This included responsibility for the Sacraments, which proved to be one of the factors which forced him to rethink the connection between participation in the Sacraments and the necessity of discipline and pastoral oversight. See Baxter's *Aphorisms of Justification*, 248-255, 258-59.

[57] See Duffy's critique of Baxter's pastoral efforts in 'The Long Reformation', 51-52.

[58] Baxter corresponded with at least one other minister who was already seeking to implement his own programme of house-to-house oversight. Richard Swayne, 'my old Friend', formerly 'Reader' and 'School-master at *Bridgnorth*, and since a godly fervent Preacher in Radnor-shire' (see *Rel. Bax.*, I, i §26, 17; III, §208 (15), 98.), wrote to Baxter on 27 January 1652/3: 'I appointed at such an house, every Friday to come to such neighbours houses most convenient to speake to them & pray with them...to finde

extant reference to Baxter's catechetical concerns is second-hand. Writing to Baxter on 17 November 1653, Abraham Pinchbecke, then chaplain to Edmund Sheffield, 2nd Earl of Mulgrave, mentions a letter recently received from Baxter 'while My Lord & I were discoursing about chattechizing... & upon that occasion I sayd to him My Lord! I have received a letter from Mr. Baxter, wherein he puts mee on very much to duty diligent, & frequent, whereupon he asked me to shew him the letter (that which indeed was my designe)... <and> desired mee to write to you, to know your judgm*ent* concerning the way of putting that in practise.' Pinchbecke then points to some of the difficulties Baxter's suggestions seem to raise, even within a single family: 'some of the family are high, & proud, some profane, some not able to read, and exceedingly ignorant, some old, & some young, & some inclined to goodnesse, & I hope some really good'.[59] Such opposition by adults to catechizing was widespread, if not universal, at least beyond puritan circles.[60] Despite the insistence of many catechists concerning the necessity of adult participation in catechesis, Baxter, like Pinchbecke, was aware of a different reality: 'For the Custom in *England* is only to catechise the younger sort, and that but by teaching them the Words of the Catechism in the Liturgy'.[61] Even so, while Pinchbecke's letter provides evidence of Baxter's high estimation of catechizing, especially within the family, it does not provide any evidence that a more general programme of all-parish catechizing had begun under Baxter's leadership in Kidderminster. At this stage, Baxter was firmly persuaded of the value of parish-wide pastoral oversight; the thought of imposing a catechetical component to his practise of

---

out by proposing sometimes questions to them, their present p*a*rticular condition, & so to apply myselfe to them both my publik & privately accordingly that they might first receive Christ into their hearts & then receive the seale of the Covenant in the lords supper.' Swayne would assemble groups of parishioners at centrally located houses for these exercises 'because I could not (according to me desire) goe to every p*a*rticular house in the p*a*rish...because... the p*a*rish is large....' DWL, BxL, vi:212, folio 2; *Calendar*, no. 107, 90-91.

[59] DWL, BxL, v:50; *Calendar*, no. 146, 116. For Pinchbecke (d. 1681/2), who would later be appointed rector of Mashbury in Essex, and ultimately assistant to Thomas Manton at St Paul's Covent Garden in London, from which he would be ejected in 1662, see *Calendar*, no. 120, 100. For Sheffield (1611?-1658), see *DNB*.

[60] Green comments on the large number of Elizabethan catechisms that were written with adults specifically in mind, produced undoubtedly in part because 'older members of a congregation may have resisted instruction in the children's catechism of 1549 as beneath their dignity' even though many were probably unable to digest the more theologically sophisticated versions produced by Alexander Nowell and others like him. *The Christian's ABC*, 73-75. See Nowell's *Catechismus, sive prima institutio* (1570) and its English translation (by Thomas Norton) *A Catechism, or first instruction of Christian religion* (1570) and *The Christian's ABC*, 690-693 for further variations in Nowell's catechisms.

[61] *Rel. Bax.*, II, §40, 179.

house-to-house oversight proved, as we shall see, still daunting even to Baxter.

Abraham Pinchbecke had already found interaction with Baxter on the practical aspects of ministry to be helpful, and when offered the living of Mashbury in Essex in the Spring of 1654, he immediately wrote Baxter two letters explaining both his opportunity and his concerns about the parish: 'I can call none a church their yet <,> I can \not/ give to any the Lords Supper & for baptisme I can not tell what to thinke well, but I shall incline to the most charitable & mercifull side till I be better satisfyed.'[62] In his reply, Baxter recognized that Pinchbecke's main challenge came from his lack of pastoral experience in a parish context, and so he sketched for him a model of parish ministry based upon his own experience till then.[63]

Baxter tells Pinchbecke that pastoral ministry is essentially an exercise in trust and persuasion, and must have both public and private components if it is to be effective in accomplishing reformational ends. While acknowledging the necessity of prayer, Baxter assumes that the pastor's efforts themselves will be the means by which God achieves his purposes ('the Glory of the redeemer [and] the winning & saving of soules'). Moreover, Pinchbecke must 'let them *per*ceive by all your dealing wit them that your very heart is set uppon them for their salvation, & studiously [avoid] whatever may hinder it or may bring them to other thoughts of you.'[64] Baxter's particular instructions assume the complementary roles of both preaching and personal oversight. In public preaching, the pastor must stick to fundamentals and modify his presentation of truth to 'make all so evident to them in their owne way of reasoning that they may be forced to confess that its all reasonable which you require of them.' The act of preaching must itself be active, engaging, moving, even dramatic, and the pastor must 'drive home every truth to resolution & practice & to that end sett them as home as you can to the very quicke of their affections. be as serious & deeply affected yourself as is possible. to weep \over/ them sometimes will doe more than to speake to them, let them se that you meane as you speake'.[65]

At the heart of Baxter's counsel, he exhorts Pinchbecke, 'in *pr*eaching & private dealing, [to] be sure to manifest as much love to your hearers as you can: *pr*each rather with tender melting affec*ti*on, than with anger & disdaine. speake to them as loveingly as if they were your owne brethren.' Pinchbecke must explain to them their 'duty' of resorting to him as their 'teacher & guide',

---

[62] DWL, BxL, vi:156 (6 May 1654); *Calendar*, no. 178, 138. See also *Calendar*, no. 176, 136 (22 April 1654). For his earlier correspondence with Baxter, see nos 120, 122, 127, 129, 134, 146, 155 & 163. See also Nuttall, 'Congregational Commonwealth Incumbents', 166.

[63] Others have recognized the practical value of Baxter's directions. See Nuttall, 'Advice to a Young Minister by Richard Baxter', 231-35.

[64] DWL, BxL, iv:168; *Calendar*, no. 190, 145-46.

[65] DWL, BxL, iv:168; *Calendar*, no. 190, 146. For the dramatic nature of godly preaching see Bryan Crockett, 'The Act of Preaching and the Art of Prophesying', in *SR*, 105 (1997), 39-52.

and 'how much of the ministeriall worke lyeth in such private instructions & solutions, & other oversight'. And those parishioners that 'will not, do you go oft to them, & se how they live & set them in a way of duty in families & private; & deale seriously yet prudently with them for the matter of their salvation...specially when you heare of any that live in scandalous sin or gross omissions.'[66]

Throughout this letter, Baxter assumes that the greatest expenditure of pastoral effort in a parish such as Mashbury will be evangelistic in nature, and that the most significant pastoral need of most of the parishioners is for their conversion. He defers giving advice concerning 'the more godly of your flocke' until he learns more of the 'quallity' of the congregation, except that Pinchbecke should 'keep a private meeting once a weeke', thereby providing for their edification and quietly disarming arguments for separation.[67]

The absence in this letter of any directions concerning catechizing beyond its expected place as a family 'duty' is striking, given that Baxter is writing in July of 1654. But the lack of mention does not imply disinterest. Indeed, Baxter had long toyed with somehow incorporating catechetical methods into his own pastoral oversight, but had been put off by the bother he feared such an innovation would cause. In a scant 21 months, Baxter would write in the dedicatory epistle of *Gildas Salvianus*: 'I do admire at my self, how I was kept off from so clear and excellent a duty so long.... I was long convinced of it, but my apprehensions of the difficulties were too great, and my apprehensions of the duty too small, and so I was hindered long from the performance.' Usually keen to explode the hindering excuses of others, Baxter reveals a list of his own that held him back from parish-wide catechizing: 'I thought that the people would but have scorned it, and none but a few that had least need would have submitted to it: and the thing seemed strange: and I stayed till the people were better prepared; and I thought my strength would never go through with it... and thus I was long detained in delayes, which I beseech the Lord of mercy to forgive.'[68]

Though *when* Baxter was finally persuaded to attempt a more systematic catechetical effort remains unclear, as well as the particular catalyst which prompted it,[69] later in 1654 or early 1655 he began a 'tryal' of a reworked

---

[66] DWL, BxL, iv:168; *Calendar*, no. 190, 147.

[67] DWL, BxL, iv:168; *Calendar*, no. 190, 147-48. Patrick Collinson observes that 'Another strategy of Puritan ministers concerned to find a prophylactic for the bacillus of separation was the semi-separated, semi-gathered group, the church within the church realized in private meetings of the godly minority. Such house meetings were so commonplace as to make it appear that they were always related to a perceived separatist threat.' 'Sects and the Evolution of Puritanism', in F. Bremer, ed., *Puritanism: Transatlantic Perspectives*, 159-60.

[68] Baxter, *Gildas Salvianus*, sig (a6)v. Baxter's letter is dated April 16, 1656.

[69] Gilbert, following Powicke, states that Baxter's 'sudden enthusiasm for catechising was probably acquired during his visit to London in December 1654 and January 1655'.

system of pastoral oversight that made systematic catechizing the focal point of a private meeting between family and pastor.[70] Writing to Thomas Wadsworth, the rector of Newington Butts, Surrey, in late January 1656, Baxter described how he began the new work: 'I first breifly explained to the reasons of our undertakinge in the open Congregation, & reade them over the Agreement, Exhortation & Catechism [*The Agreement of Divers Ministers* (1656)]. And then I Preached 2 or 3 dayes (from Heb. 5.11.12.) to shew the necessity of it, even to the aged and ancient *professours'*. After laying the groundwork, 'I caused my Assistant himselfe with one of the Deacons, to goe from house to house through towne & Parish (neere 20 miles Compasse) and deliver to every family [a copy of *The Agreement*]'. After six weeks to allow families time to learn the catechism, 'I cause one of the Clarkes to goe every weeke, weekly before their time comes & give notice to the familyes that are to come in, which

---

He also suggests that Baxter's meetings with James Ussher could very well have provided the catalyst prompting him to action. Without further evidence, however, this remains speculation. Gilbert, 'Baxter and the Work of Catechizing', in *BNS*, 6:2 (1998), 4-5; F.J. Powicke, *A Life of the Rev. Richard Baxter,* 128-133. Although Baxter may certainly have received encouragement to proceed with his catechizing programme while in London, as we have seen, his awareness of the need for some kind of personal and systematic instruction for the entire parish certainly predates his London trip. There was no 'sudden enthusiasm'.

[70] On 21 April 1655, Peter Ince, rector of Donhead St Mary, Wiltshire, states in a letter to Baxter that Baxter's parish was more willing to submit to catechizing than his own. Baxter must have mentioned his new catechetical work and its progress to Ince in a previous letter not extant. See DWL, BxL, iii: 179; *Calendar*, no. 242, 177-78. For Ince, see *Calendar*, no. 103, 88. In a joint letter dated 12 August 1655 from Baxter and several other leaders of the Worcestershire Association to the newly formed 'Ireland Association', Baxter writes, 'We are now upon a joint Agreement to bringe all the ancient *persons* in our Parishes (who will not doe it in the Congregation) to our houses on certaine dayes every weeke, by turnes, to be Catechized or Instructed, as shall be most to their Edification: A worke...wherein we are like to meet with soe much resistance, & yet doth appeare to us of soe great necessity & use, we earnestly crave your prayers.' DWL, BxL, v:110; *Calendar*, no. 262, 188. As to published material that may have influenced him, Baxter writes, 'I could here produce a heap of testimonies, of Fathers and Reformed Divines that charge this duty with great importunity'. But he goes on to cite two contemporaries whose works were of particular help to him: William Lyford (*William Lyford his Legacy* [1656]; see also *An Apologie for our Publick ministerie and infant Baptism* [1653]) and Thomas Ball (1590-1659) ('in his late Book for the Ministry': *A Letter of Many ministers in old England* [1643]; see also Ποιμηνοπυργοσ. *Pastorum propugnaculum*). Lyford was 'a maintainer of Episcopacy'. Ball studied at Queens' College, Cambridge under John Preston and lectured in Northampton for 27 years. For both, see *DNB*. Baxter, *Gildas Salvianus*, sigs (b3)-(b3)v, (b6), (b7). Ian Green provides the most substantive overview of Baxter's catechetical method. See *The Christian's ABC*, 222-26. See also Keeble, *Richard Baxter*, 81-82, 86-88; Nuttall, *Richard Baxter*, 57-58.

is 3 familyes a day: the first have order to come at one a clock, the 2d at two a clock & the 3d at 3. Two dayes a weeke (munday & Tuesday) from one a Clock till night we spend in it, & take 6 familyes a weeke.[71] Elsewhere, Baxter states that 'those in the Town came to us to our Houses'.

Once a family arrived at their appointed hour, they first 'recited the Catechism to us' after which Baxter 'first helpt them to understand it, and next enquired modestly into the State of their Souls'. At the end of their hour, he 'endeavoured to set all home to the convincing, awakening, and resolving of their hearts according to their several Conditions'. It was an interview which took 'about an Hour' and which cost him 'the Labour of a Sermon' with each family.[72]

Baxter came to regard these hours with his parishioners as the most significant aspect of his ministry. His efforts took great skill and patience, and received no public applause. Furthermore, few if any younger ministers had received training for this kind of ministry. The puritan emphasis on preaching produced young ministers who understood ministry in terms of preaching. Baxter himself had to train his own assistants in the practise of personal catechizing.[73] His first assistant, Richard Sargent, proved so adept at personal catechizing that Baxter later wrote to a friend two weeks after Sargent had left Kidderminster to become the vicar of Stone:

> One of my Assistants is now goinge from me: And I can have my choice amonge many, & many of younge men, that will Preach to the Congregation with greater applause than he: but where to gett one, that is able & willinge to deale with persons one by one in advise & personally instructinge the Ignorant, reprovinge the offendours, convincinge gainsayers, guidinge in Discipline, visitinge the sicke, comfortinge the troubled minds &c. I cannot yet heare: & can sooner find 40 of the former than one of these.[74]

To his surprise, parishioners' initial response to his experiment defied his fears and bucked the national trends. 'All Men thought that the People especially the ancienter sort, would never have submitted to this Course, and so

---

[71] DWL, BxL, ii: 249; *Calendar*, no. 290, 202. Compare Baxter's numbers here with those of *Gildas Salvianus*, sig (a6)v-(a7) ['about 15 or 16 families in a week'], and *Rel. Bax.*, II, §41, 179, where Baxter says 'my (faithful unwearied) assistant [Richard Sargent] and myself, took fourteen Families every Week'.

[72] *Rel. Bax.*, II, §41, 179-80.

[73] DWL, BxL, iii: 188; *Rel. Bax.*, I, i, §§79, 88, 137; Nuttall, *Richard Baxter*, 62; for further discussion of Baxter's efforts to train young men for pastoral ministry, see chapter 9 below.

[74] Letter to John Bryan (12 November 1656), DWL, BxL, i:253; *Calendar*, no. 333, 231. For Bryan (1628/9-99), son of Dr. John Bryan of Coventry and at this time vicar of Holy Cross, Shrewsbury, see 230. For Baxter's assistants, see Nuttall, *Richard Baxter*, 61-63.

that it would have come to nothing.'[75] But in his initial attempts to 'set upon Personal Conference with each Family, and Catechizing them, there were very few Families in all the Town that refused to come'.[76] Though Baxter admits that 'the first time they came with Fear and Backwardness, after that they longed for their turn to come again'. Best of all, Baxter found that it was 'effectual': 'few went away without some seeming Humiliation, Conviction, and Purpose and Promise for a holy Life'.[77] He was amazed to discover that those things which 'were spoken to them personally, and put them sometime upon Answers, awakened their Attention, and was easilier applyed than publick Preaching, and seemed to do much more upon them.'[78] 'I find more outward signs of sucess with most that come, then of all my publike preaching to them.'[79] Moreover, the relationships that Baxter had with nearly everyone in the parish as a result of his taking time with each household paid rich dividends for both his preaching and counseling ministries. He *knew* the people of his parish, and he was able to speak directly to their needs and address their issues. Baxter found such knowledge invaluable in his efforts to feed his flock, if not always comfortable. In a letter of September 29, 1658 to Thomas Lambe who lived with his wife Barbara near St Bartholomew the Great in London, Baxter confides

> If you were with me, I could tell you quickly where to find Forty Families of humble godly Christians, that are as bare and poor as you would With [sic], and need as much as you can give them or procure them: that scarce lose a Day's Work by Sickness, but the Church must maintain them. And I could send you to Sixty Families that are as poor, and yet so Ignorant as more to need your spiritual Help. When they have sat by me to be instructed in my Chamber, they sometimes leave the Lice so plentifull that we are stored with them for a competent space of time.[80]

Deflecting criticism that systematic parochial catechizing was an innovation, Baxter claimed that this was not 'a new invention, where envy might charge [us] as innovators.... It is but the more diligent and effectual management of the Ministerial work, and the teaching of our Principles, and the feeding of babes with milk.'[81]

Regular meetings of the Worcestershire Association throughout these

---

[75] *Rel. Bax.*, II §41, 179.

[76] Ibid., I, i, §136, p. 85; see also *Gildas Salvianus*, sig (a6)v.

[77] *Rel. Bax.*, II, §41, 180.

[78] Ibid. I, i, §137, 91.

[79] Baxter, *Gildas Salvianus*, sig (a7).

[80] *Rel. Bax.*, III, 63.

[81] Baxter, *Gildas Salvianus*, 309.

formative months guaranteed that many of Worcestershire's 'godly' ministers were well aware of Baxter's initial ideas for systematic parochial catechizing, as well as the advent of his programme and its progress.[82] Such awareness would go far to explain the speed at which Baxter's programme for St Mary's, Kidderminster in 1654/5, became *The Agreement of Divers Ministers of Christ In the County of Worcester...For Catechizing or Personal Instructing All in their Several Parishes, that will consent thereunto* in 1655/6.[83]

As his own enthusiasm for the new method began to increase, Baxter never lost sight of the long held goals for the reformation of individuals, parish and even nation around which he had formulated his pastoral practise in general and which this new method sought to further. In the sermon intended for his Worcestershire Association brethren which became *Gildas Salvianus* he exclaimed, with all the uncautious zeal of a new convert: 'How long have we talkt of Reformation, how much have we said and done for it in general, and how deeply and devoutly have we vowed it for our own parts... And after all this, how shamefully have we neglected it, and neglect it to this day!' This reformation, however, would not supernaturally descend from God's hand and transform England's churches. And in an indictment of his own puritan heritage, he asserted: 'They thought of a Reformation to be given by God, but not of a Reformation to be wrought on and by themselves. They considered the blessing, but never thought of the means of accomplishing it.' 'Little did they think of a Reformation that must be wrought by their own diligence and unwearied labours, by earnest preaching, and catachizing, and personal instructions, and taking heed to all the Flock, whatever pains or reproaches it should cost them.'[84] Furthermore, the heart of reformation was not for Baxter the abolition of ceremony or a change in structures, or an external change in societal manners, or the mere adoption of religious behavior. 'Alas, can we think that the Reformation is wrought, when we cast out a few Ceremonies, and changed some vestures, and gestures, and forms! O no Sirs! It is the converting and saving of Souls that is our business: Thats the chiefest part of the Reformation that doth most good, and tendeth most to the salvation of the

---

[82] Nuttall states that 'Catechizing and discipline together were...the basis for the Association of ministers which he formed in Worcestershire' (*Richard Baxter*, 57), but the inroads of separatists and the need for discipline were Baxter's primary motives for the Worcestershire Association (see chapter 6). Catechizing, as we see here, did not become an issue until the Association had been meeting for several years.

[83] Having committed themselves to appropriate Baxter's plan for systematic parochial catechizing in their own parishes, the Association set apart a day (4 December 1655) for fasting and prayer to ask God's blessing on their efforts, and requested that Baxter preach. Unable to preach on the appointed day due to illness, Baxter instead expanded the exposition of Acts 20:28 which he had prepared and published it under the title *Gildas Salvianus, The Reformed Pastor*. See chapter 4. See also J.I. Packer, 'Introduction', in Baxter, *The Reformed Pastor*, 13.

[84] Baxter, *Gildas Salvianus*, pp. 341-43. See Duffy, 'The Long Reformation', 48-49.

people.'[85]

Reformation for Baxter was fundamentally local and personal.[86] It began in individuals whose hearts were changed, who were, in his words, 'converted'. Accordingly, most of a minister's time and efforts should be spent, especially in a parish system where most parishioners were decidedly not godly, labouring for their conversion. Preaching was, of course, the biblically mandated means to promote conversion and draw forth faith. But preaching alone, as we have seen, had proven insufficient for the task. Voluntary catechizing of young people, servants and the 'grossly ignorant', was effective only for those who were motivated to participate. House to house 'private dealing' had proven a competent supplement, and served to involve the minister in the lives of his parishioners in a way that furthered the effect of his preaching. But such personal conferences lacked a consistent and systematic means to constrain the parishioner to grapple with biblical truth. For Baxter, systematic parochial catechizing brought together in the same room biblical truth represented by the catechism, a minister who could explain and apply that truth simply, plainly and affectionately, and every parishioner, who each had a mind endowed with the ability to understand and a will that needed to be persuaded. Since, as he was fond of repeating, God ordinarily works through means,[87] Baxter was persuaded that it was a technique that could not but help produce reformational results. It was, essentially, casuistry on a grand scale. Margo Todd has observed that such 'Puritan casuistry from Perkins and William Ames to Richard Baxter should thus be interpreted as evidence of the consensus among humanists and protestant reformers that since individual sin is the root of England's troubles, individual reform will assuage the turmoil.'[88] This seemingly protestant approach was, according to Todd, a continuation of the 'Erasmian requirement for spiritual self-examination' which served both humanists and committed protestants as a 'technique of social control.' Todd concludes that 'Elizabethan protestants and puritans of the next century were in full agreement with humanists that the problem of order in the commonwealth was to be approached at the level of individual conscience.'[89] The early response Baxter witnessed in Kidderminster convinced him that he had come upon the 'means' that was in fact producing the very conversions and reformation for which generations of 'godly' pastors had labored so long. If later events were to prove him over-optimistic, his recorded early enthusiasm for these means must also be seen in light of the overall distortion of his perspective induced by the bitter

---

[85] Baxter, *Gildas Salvianus*, 387.

[86] For a full discussion of Baxter's understanding of reformation, see chapter 3.

[87] See Baxter, *Gildas Salvianus*, sig (a6)v.

[88] Todd, *Christian Humanism*, 194. See Peter Lake's discussion of this concern for the 'reformation of manners' in 'Defining Puritanism—Again?', F. Bremer, ed., *Puritanism: Transatlantic Perspectives*, 10-12.

[89] Todd, *Christian Humanism*, 194-95.

experience of his Restoration banishment from ministry.

It is perhaps in this light that Baxter's oft-cited list of pastoral results should be considered.[90] Most significant for Baxter were the growing number of parishioners professing conversion: 'when I first entered upon my Labours in the Ministry, I took special notice of every one that was humbled, reformed or converted; but when I had laboured long, it pleased God that the Converts were so many, that I could not afford time for such particular Observations'.[91] St Mary's Church, which could hold 1000, was also regularly thronged with people eager to hear Baxter preach, necessitating a building programme to accommodate the burgeoning congregation. With the benefit of Restoration-induced hindsight, Baxter claims that the town itself experienced such a measure of reformation that it became a standard of godliness and helped shape the hopes of fellow clergy throughout the Commonwealth:

> On the Lord's Days there was no disorder to be seen in the Streets, but you might hear an hundred Families singing Psalms and repeating Sermons, as you passed through the Streets. In a word, when I came thither first, there was about one Family in a Street that worshipped God and called on his Name, and when I came away there were some Streets where there was not past one Family in the side of a Street that did not so...by professing serious Godliness give us hopes of their Sincerity. And those Families which were the worst, being Inns and Alehouses, usually *some persons* in each House did seem to be Religious. [92]

From Baxter's perspective, parochial catechizing played the pivotal role in the transformation of his parish: 'When I set upon Personal Conference with each Family, and Catechizing them... few families went from me without some tears, or seemingly serious promises for a Godly Life.' Baxter acknowledged that his efforts did not meet with total success, as ' many ignorant and ungodly Persons there were still among us: but most of them were in the Parish, and not in the Town; and in those parts of the Parish which were furthest from the Town.' But his eagerness to promote what he felt was an effective pastoral means led him to downplay the difficulties and trumpet the perceived

---

[90] See *Rel. Bax.*, I, i, §136, 84-86.

[91] Ibid., I, i, §31, 21. ' O what am I, a worthless Worm, not only wanting Academical Honours, but much of that Furniture which is needful to so high a Work, that God should thus abundantly encourage me, when the Reverend Instructors of my Youth, did labour Fifty years together in one place, and could scarcely say they had Converted one or two of their Parishes!' *Ibid.*, I, i, §136, 85.

[92] Ibid., I, i, §136, 84-85. Baxter's recollection of Kidderminster's reformation became the standard by which other successful godly ministries were measured and expressed. See Samuel Clarke's account of Samuel Fairclough's ministry, *Lives of Sundrie Eminent Persons*, 169; Duffy, 'The Long Reformation', 50-51.

successes.

Baxter indicates that the publication of *Gildas Salvianus* in 1656 generated a significant amount of attention nationwide. Later he would write, 'I have very great Cause to be thankful to God for the Success of that Book, as hoping many thousand Souls are the better for it, in that it prevailed with many Ministers to set upon that Work which I there exhort them to. Even from beyond the Seas, I have had Letters of Request, to direct them'.[93] A number of pastors did write for advice. On 25 August 1656, Stephen Streete, the rector of Buxted, Sussex, wrote to Baxter: 'ever since I was with you, I have laboured to my utmost, to promote that most excellent worke of Catechising & personal instructing of whole ffamilies; & through Gods goodness have at last (though with much difficulty) prevailed with many godly Ministers in our County of Sussex to subscribe to that worke.'[94]

Despite his initial optimism, however, it became increasingly apparent that Baxter's success in Kidderminster was not being reproduced in other parishes.[95] Peter Ince wrote on 7 January 1656: 'Wee have bin in our association [Wiltshire] very earnest upon the busynesse of catechisinge, and account beinge called for at our last meetinge what had bin done; some said they could not get a family; but wee have not yet thought of your way of goinge to them, which shall be suggested and presst the next time we meete'.[96] One of Baxter's Worcestershire Association colleagues, a very discouraged Richard Eedes, wrote in December 1657: 'When I first associated with you and subscribed the *Agreem<ent> for catechizing*, and familiar instruction of families in their order, I promised myselfe much comfort from the benefitt that would thereby accrew to soules; but I find that the old Adam is too strong for young

---

[93] *Rel. Bax.*, I, i, §177 (22), 115.

[94] DWL, BxL, v:105; *Calendar*, no. 320, 210-20. Streete also tells Baxter, 'I have dispersed many of your Reformed Pastors.... We give your little booke, the Agreement, to all the ffamilies in our Parishes.' For Streete, see *CR*. See Fletcher, *A County Community in Peace and War*, 111. For other letters requesting Baxter's advice or containing his counsel on systematic catechizing, see *Calendar*, nos 242, 262, 285, 290, 293, 320, 324, 333, 345, 348, 357, 403, 405, 407, 408, 410, 459, 462, 674, 712, 768, 910.

[95] This appraisal must be qualified by acknowledging that, while several letters survive which indicate that parish-wide catechizing was being attempted by individual ministers (*Calendar*, nos 262, 345, 408) and sometimes whole associations (nos 285, 320), the reality of exactly how widespread and how successful such attempts were remains beyond our grasp. I would assume that most of the pastors who read *Gildas Salvianus* would have been daunted from even attempting such a work, while those who did and for whatever reason failed in the attempt, would not have marked their failure by a letter to Baxter.

[96] DWL, BxL, v:77; *Calendar*, no. 285.

Melancthon'.[97] Perhaps the two most significant problems that worked against a wider effectiveness of Baxter's method of parochial catechizing and oversight were first, not all parishes were like Kidderminster; and secondly, not all pastors were like Baxter. Moreover, Baxter's catechetical programme came as the culmination of a seven-year process during which Baxter, building on the foundation of a potent preaching ministry, successfully initiated a programme of parish-wide visitation, a covenant-based procedure for participation in the Lord's Supper, a workable system for church discipline and a broader context for pastoral identity and support through the Worcestershire Association. The parish to which Baxter introduced systematic parochial catechizing was a well-tended garden. Without the benefit of such strategic pastoral oversight, other parishes would not surprisingly find such a system hard to swallow. Ian Green may be correct in suggesting that the uniqueness of Baxter's 'enormous drive and vision' goes far to explain why 'the further from the epicenter of Kidderminster, the weaker the vibrations became.'[98]

Conclusion

Richard Baxter entered the ministry persuaded that the most significant *pastoral* need of most of the people listening to him preach was that they be converted. And as a pastor, he was persuaded that God had given him the responsibility to use whatever means necessary to effect the conversion of the men, women and children of his parish. Though allowing that individuals were converted by the effective workings of God's grace, Baxter behaved as though individuals could be converted by the effective workings of God's pastors. His assumptions about the plight of the people around him as well as the nature of his call as a pastor compelled him to seek practical ways that the people under his care could be *made* to understand their desperate straits as sinners under threat of God's judgment and the way of escape through the cross to a new life of faith, godliness and blessed hope. Moreover, the accumulation of individual transformations would of a course provide the basis for progressive community transformation-reformation would occur not as a gift bestowed from on high, but as a result of the house by house conversion of the parishes. These

---

[97] Eedes admits that, living in Gloucestershire, he is 'at too great distance to receive the Comfort, and Countenance of the Associations influence, my body being so weake, and my distempers so pressing, that I can not visit their neerest meeting, with is at Evesham.' Eedes is among the subscribers to *The Agreement of Divers Minsters of Christ* (1656), 14. For Eedes (1626-86), vicar of Beckford, Gloucestershire, see *DNB* and *CR*. Baxter's response is not extant. Interestingly, Baxter uses a similar phrase, 'and that old *Adam* is too strong for young *Luther* (as he said)', in *Rel. Bax.*, I, i, §15, 12.

[98] Green, *The Christian's ABC*, 226. However, the letters which Baxter preserves, which demonstrate both the successes and the difficulties in applying Baxter's programme in other parishes, provide too small a sample on which to base a definitive statement as to Baxter's overall impact on pastoral practise in English parishes prior to the Restoration.

assumptions enflamed his preaching, and he was astonished to find that others could preach apparently without regard for their listeners eternal well-being: 'What! speak coldly for God! and for mens Salvation! Can we believe that our people must be converted, or condemned, and yet can we speake in a drowsie tone! In the name of God, Brethren, labour to awaken your hearts, before you come, and when you are in the work, that you may be fit to waken the hearts of sinners. Remember that they must be wakened or damned; and a sleepy Preacher will hardly wake them.'[99]

Francis Bremer has observed that [t]hroughout the seventeenth century the primary method used by clergymen to disseminate their ideas remained the sermon.... Believers were urged to take written notes of the preacher's arguments, which were meant to be reviewed and savored afresh by the individual alone and also with his family and friends.'[100] But Baxter was increasingly aware that even a lively, 'godly' and painful preacher armed with his most powerful sermon may struggle to awaken a spiritually drowsy auditory. Sermons were not enough. Hence his search for the 'means' by which his pastoral task might be accomplished and the sheep brought safely to the fold. He devised an increasingly involved aggregate of pastoral tasks intended to supplement the steady diet of sermons, from personal oversight to rightly ordered sacraments and discipline, and finally, crowning all, a system of catechizing designed to confront every single parishioner with his or her danger and the way of salvation. This combination, by Baxter's account, transformed the parish and transfixed the 'godly' pastors of first Worcestershire, and then the nation. Reports of his great success were matched by his claims of even greater implications:

> I find by some experience that this is the work that must Reform indeed; that must expel our common prevailing ignorance; that must bow the stubborn hearts of men; that must answer their vain objections; and take off their prejudice; that must reconcile their hearts to faithful Ministers; and help on the success of our publike preaching; and must make true godliness a commoner thing, through the Grace of God, which worketh by means. I find that we never took the rightest course to demolish the Kingdom of Darkness till now.[101]

Baxter was never allowed to witness the long-term results of his pastoral method. Writing to the Massachusetts missionary John Eliot in January 1669, he sadly recalls: 'And this course was just set up, and beginning to spread all over England (8 or 9 Counties had begun by agreement to attempt it) at 1659

---

[99] Baxter, *Gildas Salvianus*, 211.
[100] Bremer, *Shaping New Englands*, 18-19.
[101] Baxter, *Gildas Salvianus*, sig (a6)v.

when confusion buryed all'.[102] After disastrous attempts to influence the course of the Restoration settlement, he was forbidden in 1661 by George Morley, the new Bishop of Worcester, to return to Kidderminster under any ministerial pretence.[103] Baxter was thus deprived of his pastoral charge, ending his pastoral career as he had begun it, as a preacher, this time in London until 1662. Two weeks after the Bill for Uniformity received royal assent on 19 May 1662, he preached a farewell sermon at St Anne's, Blackfriars, and ceased all public preaching.[104] His pastoral efforts may have ended in premature frustration and failure. But even in the laboratory of Kidderminster, achieving the reformation of both individuals and the community had proven problematical. Not everybody in Kidderminster was as enthusiastic about their pastor's zeal for reformation and the pastoral means devised to attain them as he was. Even so, subsequent events would indicate that Richard Baxter's pastoral initiative in Kidderminster was in fact the last and best effort to reform the English Church and nation, fittingly attempted by England's last Reformation pastor.

---

[102] DWL, BxL, iv:6; *Calendar*, no. 768, 70.

[103] For Baxter's efforts to influence the Restoration settlement, see Nuttall, *Richard Baxter*, 85-93.

[104] A full account of Baxter's subsequent career in London has yet to be told. For an earlier attempt, see Powicke, *The Reverend Richard Baxter Under the Cross*.

PART THREE

A Reformed Heritage

CHAPTER 8

Martin Bucer, Richard Baxter, Samuel Clarke and the Remaking of a Tradition

Up to this point, I have observed that the sixteenth- and early seventeenth-century published rhetoric of England's 'godly, learned, and faithful ministers' focused on the minister's pulpit responsibilities almost to the exclusion of all other forms of pastoral ministry except catechising. I have also observed that nearly all of England's Elizabethan and early Stuart 'puritan' ministers and authors assumed an understanding of 'reformation' that betrays Genevan priorities and attempted both legislated and pulpit-centred means to promote it. On the other hand, Richard Baxter perceived 'reformation' as the natural consequence of the conversion of a given parish's *unsound Professors* and formulated a pastoral strategy that combined preaching with house-to-house pastoral oversight and catechising, confirmation and church discipline to achieve evangelistic ends.[1] I have demonstrated the striking correspondence between Baxter's strategy and that described by Martin Bucer and later published in his posthumous *Scripta Anglicana* (1577). Based on their close similarities in emphasis and strategy, and also on Baxter's commendation of Bucer's pastoral regime in *An Apology for the Nonconformists Ministry* (1681)[2], I have argued that familiarity with Bucer's works on reformation and pastoral ministry may have been decisive (though not exclusively so) in the development of Baxter's own Kidderminster ministry.

One of the difficulties with this argument, however, is that its depictions of Elizabethan and early Stuart ministry is dependent upon published accounts of pastoral practise, often written with polemic intent.[3] While the small number of

---

[1] Baxter, *Gildas Salvianus*, 68.

[2] Baxter, *An Apology for the Nonconformists Ministry*, sig A3.

[3] See Tim Cooper's analysis of the dynamics of seventeenth century polemic, specifically the role of 'binary opposition', where 'positive values are reinforced by denouncing their opposites'. Cooper states that this polemic strategy served 'not so much as to destroy an opponent's position as to reinforce and conserve one's own values to which that opponent was seen as a threat.' Cooper, *Fear and Polemic*, 5-7; see also Ann Hughes, 'The Meanings of Religious Polemic', F. Bremer, ed., *Puritanism: Transatlantic Perspectives*, 201-229.

contemporary accounts and clergy diaries from this period generally affirm that the published rhetoric of a pulpit-centred ideal was widely held, efforts by ministers over many years to encourage catechising, association and discipline indicate that, despite their rhetoric, pastors were concerned about more than simply preparing for the next sermon. I have already shown that Baxter's Worcestershire Association was related to a long line of attempts to gather clergy together for associational purposes, from Elizabethan prophesyings to Jacobean combination lectures. Is there evidence that other aspects of Baxter's pastoral strategy that I have labeled 'Bucerian' (such as his programme for parish discipline and adult confirmation, or individual oversight and catechising, as well as his emphasis on pastor-led, parish-centred reformation) also have precedence in the practise of his predecessors? This chapter will explore the extent of Bucer's influence on pastoral practise in Elizabethan and Stuart England and will seek to determine whether there exists a more likely source of influence behind Baxter's pastoral strategy than Martin Bucer's *Scripta Anglicana*. Three lines of investigation suggest themselves. First is to trace Bucer's direct influence on the way English Protestants practiced pastoral ministry. Second is to consider whether particular Bucerian pastoral emphases can be found in Elizabethan and Stuart descriptions of pastoral practise. And a third is to look more closely at the extant responses generated by Baxter's pastoral programme in general and *Gildas Salvianus* in particular, sifting his correspondence for clues as to whether his colleagues perceived a shift in English pastoral strategy or were simply responding to the rhetorical hiding resulting from Baxter's incandescent exhortations to get on with what everyone already knew they should be doing.

The Vanishing Trail

As we have seen, in the immediate aftermath of Elizabeth's Protestant settlement, Bucer's direct influence in England was overshadowed by the controversies surrounding the attempts to further a Presbyterian vision of reformation. Basil Hall states that Bucer's own 'master plan for reforms in church and state faded' as new issues dominated the Elizabethan Church's attention.[4] Moreover, his relevant works on ministry and reformation were not widely available in England until a generation after his death, and their appearance in the bulky Latin folio *Scripta Anglicana* appears to have limited access to his ideas to a small set of university-trained scholars. Bucer's personal influence upon a circle of Cambridge students and colleagues was much more profound.[5] Several of his students outlasted Mary's reimposition of Roman

---

[4] Hall, 'Martin Bucer in England', 157.

[5] Amongst his students and sympathetic colleagues were Matthew Parker (Master of Corpus Christi College and first Archbishop of Canterbury under Elizabeth), Walter Haddon (Master of Trinity College and Vice Chancellor of the university), Roger

Catholicism and returned from exile to take up positions of authority in Elizabeth's restored Protestant Church. Edmund Grindal, who in Collinson's words 'personified the memory of Bucer in England', consciously modeled his own pastoral undertakings on Bucerian lines.[6] Grindal, who was consecrated as Elizabeth's bishop of London in 1559, translated to York in 1570, and finally chosen to succeed Parker as archbishop of Canterbury in 1575, was widely respected for his attempts to maintain a moderating and evangelical episcopal policy. The fact that Grindal was willing to run afoul of Elizabeth because of a principled stand on prophesyings demonstrates his sensitivity to pastoral issues and is perhaps an untallied legacy of Bucer's impact.[7]

But Grindal was not the only Elizabethan divine for whom Bucer was an authority. In the debates between Cartwright and Whitgift on episcopacy and vestments, Whitgift vigorously enlisted Bucer's support wherever he could. This prompted Cartwright to complain that by citing Bucer against him, Whitgift was giving the misleading impression that Bucer and other continental reformers were 'against us in these matters' when in fact, 'if they have spoken one word against us, they have spoken two for us.'[8] Nevertheless, Whitgift's use of Bucer against the 'precisionist' position on the question of vestments and church structure made Bucer appear unhelpful to the younger generation of puritans who were increasingly influenced by a Genevan model of reformation.[9]

Ascham, John Cheke, Edmund Grindal (Elizabeth's second Archbishop of Canterbury, to whom Conrad Hubert, Bucer's secretary, dedicated *Scripta Anglicana*), Edwyn Sandys (later Bishop of London and Archbishop of York) and John Bradford, the Marian martyr.

[6] Collinson, *Archbishop Grindal*, 51, 53. See Collinson's 'The Reformer and the Archbishop', 38-44; *The Elizabethan Puritan Movement*, 159-61.

[7] See Wright, 'Martin Bucer and England-and Scotland', 528. For Edmund Grindal and his relationship with Martin Bucer, see Collinson, *Archbishop Grindal*, 49-55. For Grindal's letter refusing Elizabeth's order to prohibit 'prophesyings' (dated December 20, 1576), see Edmund Grindal, *The Remains of Archbishop Grindal*, W. Nicholson, ed. (Cambridge, 1843), 382-84.

[8] John Whitgift, *The Works of John Whitgift*, J. Ayre, ed. (Cambridge, 1851), i, 258-59. In his 'For Direction in the Study of Divinity' that Cartwright sent to Arthur Hildersham in 1583, Cartwright identifies Bucer along with Calvin, Beza and Luther as 'new writers' that could be emulated. See *Cartwrightiana*, eds. A. Peel and L.H. Carlson, *Elizabethan Nonconformist Texts*, 1 (London: George Allen and Unwin, 1951), 112-115.

[9] However, later use of Bucer's position in Elizabethan polemic failed to take into consideration the complexities of the context in which Bucer wrote. While Bucer did say 'I think that such ministers of the English Churches may with the grace of God use those vestments which are prescribed at this day', MacCulloch observes that 'it was not that Bucer especially approved of vestments in themselves; in his almost contemporary comments on revising the Prayer Book, he made it clear that he wanted them abolished. However, evidently he had accepted Cranmer's arguments about timing and authority; he trusted his friend to choose the moment properly.' MacCulloch, *Thomas Cranmer*,

Elizabeth's sequestration of Grindal in 1577 effectively removed the primary conductor of Bucer's pastoral perspective from any further influence in the English Church. Even so, Parker and Carlson describe Richard Greenham's ministry as motivated by 'the Bucerian commitment to foster a parish life centred around the word of God, read, preached and taught.'[10] Such a connection is plausible, as Greenham was at Pembroke College in Cambridge during the masterships of Grindal (1559-1562) and Matthew Hutton (1562-1567), through whom he would have become familiar with Bucer's legacy.[11] But the argument for Bucer's influence on Greenham is made on the basis of this association alone, and, in a separate study, John Primus finds Bucer's influence on Greenham to be negligible. Surprisingly, neither Primus nor Parker and Carlson make any mention of Bucer's *Scripta Anglicana*.[12] While it is possible that echoes of Bucer's programme for a pastor-led reformation of the English Church can be discerned from the likes of Greenham, in reality with the passing of those who had known Bucer and his generation of English reformers directly, evidence for his direct influence on Elizabethan pastoral practise evaporates.[13] Thus while William Whitaker could in 1595 remind his Cambridge auditory of their theological indebtedness to Bucer and Peter Martyr,[14] and though Bucer was increasingly requisitioned as an authoritative proof text as the English Church became embroiled in controversies over Calvin's theology and polity, his pastoral programme appears to have been largely forgotten.[15]

481; for Bucer's comments on vestments, see also Bucer, *Martin Bucer and the Book of Common Prayer*, 18-19.

[10] Parker and Carlson, '*Practical Divinity*', 84.

[11] For Matthew Hutton (1529-1606), subsequently bishop of Durham and Archbishop of York, see *DNB*.

[12] Parker and Carlson, '*Practical Divinity*', 9-11, 84, 116-17, 119. See Primus, *Richard Greenham*, 24-54.

[13] Bucer is cited as an authority in the debates on church government throughout the sixteenth- and seventeenth-centuries. And Barbara Coulton suggests that Thomas Ashton, the Cambridge-educated godly schoolmaster and preacher of Early Elizabethan Shrewsbury was influenced by Bucer, in particular Bucer's views on the propriety of plays. See 'The Establishment of Protestantism in a Provincial Town: A Study of Shrewsbury in the Sixteenth Century', in *SCJ*, 27:2 (1996), 315. However there is as yet no direct evidence to suggest that any Elizabethan and early Stuart ministers intentionally adopted Bucer's programme of pastoral ministry and discipline.

[14] William Whitaker, *Cygnea Cantio* (Cambridge, 1599), 8, 15-16. See the English translation in William Prynne's *Anti-Arminianisme* (2nd edition, 1630), 261-62. See also Hopf, *Martin Bucer and the English Reformation*, 260.

[15] Tom Webster notes that in the backlash against the Presbyterians, the 'Whitgiftian reaction' also swept away particular aspects of Bucer's programme for the reform of church structures that had for a time in the 1570s seemed possible. Webster, *Godly Clergy*, 314. Note the focus on externals and the absence of Bucerian evangelistic emphases in the description of ministry and its reformation in Albert Peel, ed., *The*

A Question of Influence

There may, however, be indirect evidence of Bucer's continuing influence that has survived in the work of the nonconformist hagiographer Samuel Clarke.[16] Clarke's accounts of exemplary English Protestants betray a special interest in both pastoral practise and local instances of 'reformation', especially in his 1683 *Lives of Sundry Eminent Persons of the Later Age*. In this last collection, Clarke's pastors range far beyond the conventional ideal of pulpit-centred ministry and are found engaged in catechising,[17] visitation,[18] co-operating with local magistrates sympathetic with godly discipline,[19] restricting sacraments to those who adequately profess and live their faith,[20] all with the goal of overseeing local reformation.[21] But do these later accounts reflect actual early Stuart pastoral practise and thus provide an indication of a Bucerian model of

---

Seconde Parte of a Register, ii, 199-202. A similar lack of Bucerian emphases is found in Peter Marshall's description of pastoral ministry in *The Face of Pastoral Ministry in the East Riding, 1525-1595* (York: Borthwick Institute of Historical Research, 1995), 16-22.

[16] The difficulties attendant upon dependence on Clarke's compilations of godly lives have been previously flagged by Patrick Collinson and Jacqueline Eales. But even if caution is necessary before using Clarke as a reliable source for biography and history, Clarke's hagiographies provide an invaluable window on godly priorities and concerns. It is in this second sense that this study makes use of Clarke's work. See Collinson, '"A Magazine of Religious Patterns"', 499-526; Eales, 'Samuel Clarke and the "Lives" of Godly Women', 365-376; see also Eamon Duffy' comments on Clarke's motives in 'Wesley and the Counter-Reformation', J. Garnet and C. Matthew, eds., *Revival and Religion Since 1700: Essays for John Walsh* (London: Hambledon, 1993), 3-4.

[17] See Clarke's account of Maidstone's pastor Thomas Wilson, who 'took up *Catechising* in the Week-days in publick; and this he continued till he had gone through all the Town'. *The Lives of Sundry Eminent Persons*, 33.

[18] See Clarke's account of Richard Blackerby, who 'used much to Ride about from Family to Family...and only alight and pray with them, and give them some heavenly exhortation, and then away to another Family'. *The Lives of Sundry Eminent Persons*, 57-64, here 59.

[19] See Clarke's account of Maidstone under the ministry of Thomas Wilson, where 'when the *Mayor* hath searched the Inns, and Ale-houses, he hath scarce found one Townsman there'. *The Lives of Sundry Eminent Persons*, 35.

[20] See Clarke's account of Samuel Fairclough below, and also Clarke's 1662 account of William Gouge's efforts to establish an effective discipline in his London parish of St Annes Blackfriars, in *A Collection of the Lives of Ten Eminent Divines, famous in their Generations for Learning, Prudence, Piety, and painfulness in the Work of the Ministry* (1662), 107. For Gouge (1578-1653), longtime pastor of St Anne's, Blackfriars, and member of the Westminster Assembly, see Barker, *Puritan Profiles*, 35-38. See also Webster, *Godly Clergy*, 56-57, 85-86. 131, 139.

[21] See Clarke's marginal note 'Reformation in the Town' beside the paragraph describing the impact of Thomas Wilson's ministry in Maidstone. *The Lives of Sundry Eminent Persons*, 35.

pastoral ministry operating underneath the rhetorical ideal, or might these accounts reflect a Baxterian perspective on ministry which has been read back into the practise of more conventional 'godly' pastors? The relevant data is both patchy and complicated, but an examination of what evidence remains provides an opportunity to clarify the ministerial context from which Baxter emerged as well as give an indication as to the surprising impact his *Gildas Salvianus* had, not just on how certain ministers undertook their ministry, but also on the way pastoral ministry itself was perceived in subsequent discussion.

The most exemplary pastor of all in Clarke's *Lives of Sundry Eminent Persons* is Samuel Fairclough (1594-1677), under whose thirty-three year ministry Kedington in Suffolk was said to be 'yet *more and more* reformed' and 'a *pattern* to all his Neighbour Towns'.[22] The 'great design' of Fairclough's ministry 'was first to awaken the Consciences of obstinate sinners; and then to make known to them the way of salvation.' Fairclough 'clearly saw that souls were eternally lost' if they remained unconverted. He therefore pursued evangelistic themes in his preaching, making use of whatever 'he judged most properly conducing thereunto'.[23] Even so, Fairclough's evangelistic efforts are explained almost entirely in terms of his pulpit ministry. His manner of preaching contained all of those elements 'which do properly *influence* the mind of man, and are *apt to perswade*'. In due course, his sermons 'became very *effectual*, multitudes being wrought upon, and *turned from the errour of their ways*', with scarce anyone 'since the Apostles days' 'more *visibly instrumental* in saving Souls than he'.[24]

---

[22] Clarke, *The Lives of Sundry Eminent Persons*, 169. Fairclough was born in Haverhill in 1594, his father Lawrence being the vicar of Haverhill parish. Fairclough matriculated at Queens' College, Cambridge, and took BA in 1615. He was a protégé of Richard Blackerby, whose daughter Susan he married. He was lecturer in Kings Lynn in 1619, and later in Clare, before coming to the attention of the local 'puritan' patron, Sir Nathaniel Barnardiston, who presented Fairclough to the small parish of Barnardiston in 1623. In 1629, Sir Nathaniel presented Fairclough to the much larger parish of Kedington, where Fairclough ministered until he was ejected in 1662. Webster uses Fairclough's story as an example of the importance of early Stuart ministerial conferences, through which opportunities for ministry for the likes of Fairclough often came. Webster, *Godly Clergy*, 36-37. See *DNB*, which is heavily dependent upon Clarke's *The Lives of Sundry Eminent Persons*.

[23] Clarke, *The Lives of Sundry Eminent Persons*, 165.

[24] Ibid., 166. A second anonymous testimony appended to the author's account states that 'his Church was so thronged, that (though for a Village, very large and capacious, yet) there was no getting in, unless by some hours attending before his Exercise began; and then the outward Walls were generally lined with Sholes and Multitudes of People, which came (many) from afar, (some above twenty Miles) so that you should see the Church Yard (which was likewise very spacious) Barricadoed with Horses, tyed to the outward Rayles, while their Owners were greedily waiting to hear the word of Life from his mouth.' *The Lives of Sundry Eminent Persons*, 187. Fairclough's pulpit, a 'triple-decker' evidently installed by Sir Nathaniel shortly after Fairclough's arrival in 1629,

Fairclough's success is also attributed to the close co-operation that existed between the minister and the local magistrate, Sir Nathaniel Barnardiston, and to the system of adult confirmation, which the two were able to devise and enforce.[25] Fairclough 'also set up the great duty of *Catechising* of young and old'. Moreover, 'Neither did he *content* himself with publick Preaching alone', but, in a practise established first while he was in Barnardiston, 'he went to all the Houses...*once every moneth*, and *discoursed* there with his People about the *State* of their Souls'. The effect of Fairclough's ministry was such that a Suffolk town described as 'very *ignorant* and *prophane*', where 'not one Family in twenty' were demonstrably Christian (according to the author's standards), was 'in a short time after his coming' so transformed by his preaching that 'there was not one Family in twenty but *professed godliness*'.[26]

Immediately obvious are the parallels between this account of Fairclough's pastorate and the way Richard Baxter describes his own Kidderminster ministry. Both Baxter and Fairclough made evangelism their primary pastoral concern. Both were gifted preachers. Both practiced catechising and house-to-house visitation, though the account is unclear whether Fairclough, like Baxter, intentionally used visitation and catechising as means to further his evangelistic goals. Both exercised a form of adult confirmation. Both had the co-operation of local magistrates (though in contrast to Sir Nathaniel Barnardiston's helpfulness to Fairclough, Baxter was frustrated by Sir Ralph Clare's resistance to various aspects of his pastoral programme). And both indicate that a huge number of their parishioners experienced a remarkable transformation under their ministries. Even Baxter's description of the Kidderminster reformation finds its echo in Kedington.[27]

---

survives in the nave of Kedington's parish church of Sts Peter and Paul. See H. Munro Cautley, *Suffolk Churches and their Treasures*, 4th edition (Ipswich: n.p., 1975), 171, 182.

[25] Nathaniel Barnardiston (1588-1653) 'encouraged in his parish catechetical instruction in religion; and he attended with his children the religious classes held by Samuel Fairclough'. He was knighted by James I on 15 December 1618, elected a member of the Short Parliament for Suffolk on 14 April 1640, and re-elected to the Long Parliament the following October. 'Shortly after the execution of the King, [his] health broke down, and he returned to Ketton to prepare for death. He devoted himself unceasingly to religious exercises during his last two years (1651-1653) and read constantly Baxter's Saints Everlasting Rest.' See *DNB*. See also Samuel Fairclough's, Ἅγιοι ἄξιοι or *The Saints worthinesse and the worlds worthlessnesse, Both opened and Declared in a Sermon preached at the Funerall of that Eminently Religious and highly honoured Knight Sr. Nathaniel Barnardiston. Aug.26.1653* (1653). Fairclough goes to great lengths describing Sir Nathaniel's character, but his provision of historical details is unhelpfully thin, and there is no mention at all of their partnership in parish affairs.

[26] Clarke, *The Lives of Sundry Eminent Persons*, 161-62, 166, 169.

[27] Compare Fairclough's Kedington with Baxter's Kidderminster. Baxter writes: 'In a word, when I came thither first, there was about one Family in a Street that worshipped

At first glance, it would appear that this account provides evidence that many of the pastoral practises advocated first in England by Martin Bucer and later amplified in Richard Baxter's ministry and writings, also survived in the day-to-day ministries of 'godly' pastors like Samuel Fairclough. Eamon Duffy has suggested that Fairclough's ministry, as presented by Clarke, was a 'spectacularly successful example of a not uncommon type of godly ministry', which made catechising the basis of parish discipline, the goal of which was 'awakening, conversion and Christian formation and reformation'.[28] That being the case, it would also seem that nearly twenty years before Baxter's return to Kidderminster, Fairclough was undertaking a pastoral strategy that exhibited nearly all of the main emphases that Baxter would later highlight in *Gildas Salvianus*. Thus it could be argued that Baxter's ministry in Kidderminster was itself hardly unique, and part of an ongoing tradition of Bucerian pastoral practise that continued on quietly beneath the pulpit-centred rhetoric of the 'puritan' pastoral ideal. Our search for pastoral antecedents need not look any further than Baxter's immediate predecessors and colleagues to find adequate explanations for his own strategy. However, a closer examination of this account of Fairclough's ministry raises at least three issues which begin to cast doubt on such a straightforward interpretation.

First, the Fairclough piece as we have it is actually anonymous, as Clarke himself states that he is not the author.[29] It was also most likely composed after Fairclough's death in 1677, though it is possible that some of the material may have been composed beforehand. Sensitive to the charge that such a complimentary piece celebrating the life of a dissenter could only have been written by someone *'of like Spirit'* and *'Interest'*, the author claims that he 'was never ejected for *Non-conformity*.'[30] Instead, he vouches for the accuracy of his account and claims to be acquainted with 'the *full History of [Fairclough's] Life'* and to have 'seen his *Diary'*, which, unfortunately, is no longer extant.[31] Even so, the fact that fifty years separates the author from the onset of Fairclough's Kedington ministry, and that he is writing twenty years after Baxter's *Christian Concord* (1653), *Gildas Salvianus* (1656) and *Confirmation and Restauration* (1658) reoriented the discussion over pastoral ministry among England's 'godly' and later Nonconformist clergy, raises the question of who is being influenced by whom.

God and called on his Name, and when I came away there were some Streets where there was not past one Family in the side of a Street that did not so...by professing serious Godliness give us hopes of their Sincerity' (*Rel. Bax.*, I, i, §136, 84-85). Compare with the description of Fairclough's Kedington above on 201. Clarke, *The Lives of Sundry Eminent Persons*, 161-62, 166, 169.

[28] Duffy, 'The Long Reformation', 45.

[29] Clarke, *The Lives of Sundry Eminent Persons,* 169.

[30] Ibid., 186-87.

[31] Ibid., 187.

Secondly, while Fairclough uses many of the same pastoral tools prominent in Bucer's strategy for Strasbourg and Baxter's strategy for Kidderminster, he does not reflect the same strategic focus that one finds in either Bucer or Baxter. Fairclough achieves his evangelistic goals primarily through preaching, though the author allows that 'he did compare *publick Preaching* to *sowing* of Seed, and *private discourse* he compared to the Plow-mans *harrowing, healing,* or *covering* the Seed, without which the *Fowls of the air*, that is, a multitude of diverting thoughts, and the *Prince of the Air* also, the Devil, (by his *temptations*) would soon *pick* up the word, without *fruit or benefit.*'[32] Curiously, however, the description of the results of Fairclough's ministry is, as we have seen, almost identical to those results ascribed to Baxter, though their means and emphases differ. The Fairclough account appears to be an example of the 'puritan' ideal of pulpit-centred ministry at its best. But if the account is accurate, it also indicates that many of the pastoral practises such as visitation, confirmation covenants and catechising, reconfigured by Baxter in the 1650s were being used as early as the 1630s. Fairclough's ministry, as presented in this account, not only reflects the standard 'godly' emphasis on effective preaching present in the published rhetoric of the treatises and sermons examined in chapter 2, but also more fully reveals those supplements to preaching such as catechising and the concern to tie participation in the sacraments with pastoral oversight only hinted at in the writings of his contemporaries and predecessors. Moreover, in conjunction with these hints, seen in Herbert's *Priest to the Temple*, Rogers' *True Convert*, Bernard's *Faithfull Shepheard,* and in the surviving anecdotes about Richard Greenham's Dry Drayton ministry, this account may indicate the ongoing survival within English Protestant pastoral practise of many of the pastoral tools recommended by Bucer and later reconfigured by Baxter.[33] Thus while there is little evidence offered here of Fairclough having adopted an intentional Bucerian pastoral *strategy*, the evidence, if accurate, may shed light on the vigorous efforts undertaken by many 'godly' pastors which were intended to supplement the preaching ideal.

A third issue, which also makes the attribution of Bucerian influence in Fairclough's ministry difficult to sustain, is the fact that there are so few chronological markers in the account. Thirty-three years of ministry are telescoped into a list of highlights. The events described can be fairly easily dated up until Fairclough moved in 1629, at the age of 35, from the 'small and

---

[32] Ibid., 162.

[33] See Nehemiah Rogers, *The True Convert* (1632), 'To the Reader', upn.; Richard Bernard, *The Faithfull Shepheard* (1607), 9; George Herbert, *A Priest to the Temple*, 'Table of Contents', sigs A8-A8v. See the discussion of each one in chapter 2. The concern of Fairclough and Sir Nathaniel to bar unworthy receivers from participating in the Lord's Supper is simply the flip side of the contemporary concerns to help parishioners become worthy receivers.

straight' Suffolk parish of Barnardiston to the nearby 'capacious and receptive' parish church in Kedington.[34] Sir Nathaniel Barnardiston's death in 1653 puts a bracket on those aspects of Fairclough's ministry such as his schemes for catechising and adult confirmation that benefited from a partnership with the parish's most prominent member.[35]

The chronological ambiguities allow several possible interpretations. It could be that Baxter was, in fact, dependent, not upon his familiarity with Bucer, but upon the examples of predecessors like Fairclough who perpetuated Bucerian priorities for the main thrust of his pastoral strategy and practise. As we have seen, Baxter publicly perceived himself as continuing the same pastoral tradition as his 'godly' predecessors.[36] Baxter also uses many of the same pastoral tools used by Fairclough such as visitation, catechising, discipline and adult confirmation. But as we have seen, though they shared many of the same tools, they did not share the same pastoral strategy. It is striking that when Fairclough preaches before the Long Parliament in 1641, he makes an utterly conventional call for a Genevan-style partnership between minister and magistrate as the formula for reformation.[37] However, the circumstances faced by Baxter in the aftermath of the civil wars necessitated a strategy which took into account the vacuum of ecclesiastical authority, the opposition of the local gentry, the failure of legislated reformation, and the inability of the inherited pastoral ideals to address the unprecedented circumstances faced by pastors with any measure of effectiveness. The *strategy* that Baxter adopted to address the challenges he faced upon his return to Kidderminster in 1647 marks the

---

[34] Samuel Clarke, *The Lives of Sundry Eminent Persons*, 161-163b. The notice on the title page continues: 'To which is added His [Clarke's] own Life..., Mr. Richard Blackerby, and Mr. Samuel Fairclough, drawn up by other Hands.' Throughout this biography, the author's use of 'Ketton' in place of 'Kedington' reflects local pronunciation. This could indicate that the account was composed by a local associate, or even by his successor in Kedington.

[35] Fairclough himself makes the same attribution in this 1641 dedicatory epistle to Sir Nathaniel: 'Sir, So remarkable and conspicuous, in the view of all the neighbouring parts of our Country, are the expressions of your noble patronage, and support, both of my selfe, and ministry, that each eye (almost) observes it; and more tongues speake of it; yet every pious heart, that ever reaped any profit from my poore and unworthy labours (next under the free grace of God) acknowledge your selfe the chiefe and grand instrument of the same...I should have an opportunitie hereby offered, to make publique confession how much both my selfe, and all the Angle where you live, are obliged to your selfe and Familie, for planting and supporting the ministrie of the word and power of the Gospell amongst us'. Samuel Fairclough, *The Troublers Troubled, or Achan Condemned, and Executed. A Sermon, Preached before sundry of the Honourable House of Commons at Westminster, April, 4.1641.* (1641), sigs A3-A3v. For a further example of the cooperation between magistrate and minister, see Underdown, *Fire From Heaven*, 128-130.

[36] Baxter, *Gildas Salvianus*, 150-154.

[37] See Fairclough, *The Troublers Troubled*.

primary point of difference between his ministry and that of Samuel Fairclough. The distinction that I am making here is between the survival of pastoral techniques and the survival of a particular pastoral strategy. As we would expect, Baxter is drawing on elements of puritan pastoral practise, but he is interpreting them in a distinctively Bucerian way. Clearly, the limited evidence that survives indicates that Protestant pastors in England made use of a similar range of pastoral techniques in furthering their ministries. It is the configuration of particular techniques couched in a distinctively Bucerian rhetoric and strategy that makes Baxter's efforts unique.

A second explanation that would account for the similarities between Fairclough's ministry and Baxter's is that Fairclough himself was influenced by Baxter's *Gildas Salvianus*, and that the account's description of Fairclough's pastorate reflects his mature and *Baxterian* perspective on parish ministry. Apart from the full description of those supplemental pastoral practises which Fairclough employed to augment his preaching, the most significant deviation from the 'puritan' ideal, and one which resonates most with Baxter's emphases is the explicit description of an evangelistic purpose for his pastoral ministry and the accompanying claims of community reformation that result from his efforts.[38] It is possible that Fairclough found Baxter's arguments compelling and experienced an untroubled transition to a Baxterian perspective on the primacy of evangelism in the pastor's task, and that his subsequent recollections of his ministry read an explicit evangelistic intent back into all his previous pastoral efforts. The difficulty with this explanation is that it is speculation, there being no tangible evidence upon which to base it. Moreover, Fairclough was sixty-four when Baxter published *Gildas Salvianus*, and it is difficult to imagine an elderly man twenty-seven years into a celebrated ministry making strategic changes in his pastoral approach however much he may have approved of what he read.

A third explanation for the similarities between Fairclough's ministry and Baxter's is that the author himself was decisively influenced by Baxter's writings on ministry and read explicit evangelistic motives back into Fairclough's pastorate while he was compiling information for his account. Moreover, as we shall see in relation to Samuel Clarke himself, the way Fairclough and his ministry is portrayed is strikingly more detailed than earlier accounts of Fairclough's contemporaries and predecessors. With the exception of Herbert's *Priest to the Temple* (1652, though written in 1632), such a detailed presentation of Protestant pastoral practise beyond the pulpit does not make its appearance in the literature on ministry until Baxter's descriptions and counsel appear in his *Aphorisms of Justification* (1649) and *The Saints Everlasting Rest* (1650). Freed from the need to defend the 'puritan' emphasis on preaching from the sacramentalist critique of the Laudians, Baxter provides a succession of realistic glimpses into the day-to-day realities of 'godly'

---

[38] Clarke, *The Lives of Sundry Eminent Persons*, 165, 169.

ministry, culminating in *Christian Concord* (1653), *Gildas Salvianus* (1656) and *Confirmation and Restauration* (1658). The Fairclough account has the same focus on the details of pastoral practise that are found in Baxter's accounts. The multi-faceted reality of 'godly' ministry only hinted at previously in earlier pre-civil war attempts to bolster the pulpit-centred ideal is strikingly obvious in both narrations. And while Fairclough himself is obviously presented as an ideal, it is a presentation, which may bear witness to the impact Baxter had on the way pastoral ministry was both understood and communicated by the author.

Of the three explanations discussed, this third suggestion of Baxter's influence on the author of the Fairclough account seems most plausible. Once again, however, the lack of direct evidence makes resolution of the issues raised by the account of Fairclough's ministry provisional at best. Yet there is additional evidence relating to the evolution of Samuel Clarke's understanding and presentation of pastoral ministry which suggests that Baxter was not so much influenced by a surviving tradition of Bucerian pastoral emphases (the existence and influence of which is faithfully recorded in Clarke's 1683 *Lives of Sundry Eminent Persons*) as he was himself the primary influence behind the way 'godly' ministry was understood and written about following the Restoration. In other words, Clarke's *Lives*, the Fairclough account included, may indicate just how much Baxter's reconfiguration of pastoral ministry influenced later Nonconformity, affecting even the preservation of its tradition and collective memory.

Samuel Clarke himself knew Baxter well. Baxter was Clarke's guest in his Alcester pulpit on the day of the early civil war battle in nearby Edgehill.[39] After the Restoration, both Baxter and Clarke lived in the London area. When Baxter married Margaret Charlton on 10 September 1662, Clarke presided over the service.[40] After Margaret's death some 19 years later, Clarke edited Baxter's account of her life and their marriage for his last collection of lives alongside that of Fairclough.[41] Though one can only speculate as to whether Baxter influenced the anonymous author of the Fairclough account, his influence on Clarke's perspective on ministry is more clearly discernible.

As we have suggested, Clarke's accounts of ministers such as Fairclough, Thomas Wilson and Richard Blackerby in *The Lives of Sundry Eminent Persons* give a picture of Elizabethan and Stuart pastoral practise that is of an

---

[39] *Rel. Bax.*, I, i, §61, 43; see also Baxter's letter 'To the Reader', in Clarke's *The Lives of Sundry Eminent Persons*, sigs a3v-a4.

[40] 'Richard Baxter of St Buttolphs Aldersgate' and 'Margaret Charlton of Christ Church' Newgate were given a marriage license on 29 April 1662. See Nuttall, *Richard Baxter*, 94. After 'many changes and stoppages...and long delays', they were married 'at last' in St Benet-Fink Church by Clarke. See Packer, *A Grief Sanctified*, 100-101.

[41] See Clarke, *The Lives of Sundry Eminent Persons*, 181-191. See Eales's 'Samuel Clarke and the "Lives" of Godly Women', 375.

entirely different dimension from descriptions in his earlier published collections of exemplary lives. Writing in his 1651 *A Generall Martyrologie*, Clarke is altogether conventional in his profiles of 'godly' ministers and their ministries, reflecting concerns that mirror those of the many published treatises and sermons on pastoral ministry surveyed in chapter 2.[42] Summarizing Hugh Clark's ministry in Woolstone, Warwickshire, Clarke focuses on his preaching and depicts his heroic efforts to supply his two congregations with the Word of God, for 'he rode foure times a [Sunday] winter and summer between the two Churches, read the Word, and preached foure times a day, administered the Sacraments'. Almost as an afterthought, Clarke concludes, 'and [he] performed all other ministerial duties in the both.'[43] In the same volume, Richard Sedgwick (1574-1643) is described by Clarke as being 'abundant in labours, preaching constantly thrice a week, and Catechizing on the Lord's day besides.'[44] Even Clarke's fulsome description of Herbert Palmer's ministry in Ashwel, Hertfordshire is entirely routine in its recital of his prowess in the pulpit and his efforts to catechise not only the young but the ignorant as well.[45]

Unexpected, however, is a remarkable digression in the midst of Clarke's description of Palmer's ministry, as he attempts to explain why pastors like Palmer were so troubled over the matter of discipline and the right celebration of the sacraments. The 'difficulty' was not so much the 'manner of administration', but 'concerning the persons that might be judged fit to be admitted thereunto'. With clergy uncertain how the issue of discipline and sacraments could be resolved, Clarke reports that 'many...have apprehended a necessity of a total intermission, and almost an impossibility of administering it in any tolerable manner'. Baxter, as we have seen, scrupled the same issue and attempted when he returned to Kidderminster in the year of Palmer's death to resolve it in the same way. 'They durst not promiscuously admit all' parishioners to the communion table because 'the great ignorance of many, and the profanenesse or loosenesse of others' would cause serious scandal. And yet Clarke admits that pastors such as Palmer 'saw not how they might be able, (for want of authority) to debar any: waiting still for the settling of a Government in the church'. However, withholding communion began to have the adverse effect of causing the 'profane and carnal' to 'slight and scorn it, and those of better principles do much abate in their affections to it'. Parliament's 'remedy',

---

[42] Ann Hughes has these earlier works in mind when she writes that 'In his biographical works...Samuel Clarke...constructed a 'moderate-Puritan' tradition of sober, godly reformers from the sixteenth to mid-seventeenth century who were forced into nonconformity by the errors of the established Church but who consistently argued against separation.' See Hughes, *Godly Reformation*, 26, note 3,.

[43] Clarke, *A Generall Martyrologie* (1651), 391.

[44] Ibid., 398.

[45] Ibid., 422-23. Clarke does note the increasing concern of pastors like Palmer to insure the integrity of the Lord's Supper, acknowledging that no one has yet been able to provide an adequate solution. See 432.

the Westminster Assembly's 'late' and diluted Presbyterian settlement, was 'so much defective in want of power, and so much opposed to scorn and reproach' that it was perceived as totally inadequate. Clarke candidly acknowledges that 'the matter is now almost grown desperate, unlesse God will be pleased in special favour, to afford some unexpected remedy.'[46] Ironically, as Clarke was preparing this piece for publication, Richard Baxter was wrestling with these same issues in Kidderminster, and in the process of putting his reconfigured pastoral strategy into practise. But there is no hint in Clarke's 1651 *A Generall Martyrologie* that he was aware of any pastor who had answers for the unprecedented challenges facing the nation's parishes.

Later, in Clarke's 1662 *Collection of the Lives of Ten Eminent Divines*, accounts of the ministries of such worthies as Samuel Crooke, William Gouge and Thomas Gataker, the pastoral ideals that they embody are of 'painfulness' in preaching, diligence in catechising and holiness in 'conversation'.[47] When compared with these earlier accounts, it becomes increasingly apparent that Clarke's 1683 representation of pastoral ideals, as well as that of his anonymous contributor, reflects more the wholesale adoption of Baxterian pastoral priorities which brought accounts of earlier ministries more up to date with contemporary priorities than historically accurate accounts of pastoral practise in the 1630s and 40s. Certainly if the pastorate described in the Fairclough account were representative of 'godly' ministry in the 1630s and 40s, or even exemplary, one would not expect quite the desperate tone one hears in Clarke's 1651 digression over discipline. Far from being the pastoral antecedents for Baxter's ministry, it is perhaps more likely that these 1683 accounts of men such as Wilson, Blackerby and Fairclough are themselves presented from a post-*Gildas Salvianus* perspective.[48]

---

[46] Ibid., from the biography of Herbert Palmer (1601-1647), 432.

[47] Clarke, *A Collection of the Lives of Ten Eminent Divines*, for Crooke, see 25-54; for Gouge, see 96-125; for Gataker, see 126-159. See also Clarke's account of Richard Stock's ministry in *A Martyrology Containing A Collection of all the Persecutions Which have befallen the Church of England* (1652), in which is contained *The Life of Jasper Coligni...Together with the Lives of some of our English Divines* (1652), 142. A marginal note states 'His [Stock's] character by Mr. Gataker'.

[48] In Baxter's letter 'To the Reader' prefacing Clarke's *The Lives of Sundry Eminent Persons*, he states *'I have not read over this book... But I know so many of the Persons and Histories myself, as makes me not doubt but the Reader will have no cause to question the Historical truth.'* Baxter then reminisces: *'Dr. Sam. Bolton, Mr. Vines, Mr. Robinson, Mr. Machin, Dr. Staunton, Mr. Wadsworth, Mr. Stockton, I knew: Dr Twisse was so well known (whose worthy Daughter Mrs. Corbet hath lived with me formerly, and this year and half) that the History hath full evidence. Judge Hales and the Countess of Warwick (my great Friends) need no testimony of mine. I knew not of his Epitomizing my Wives life; but the manner of that tells me he is like to be faithful in the rest.'* In all this, Baxter, however, appears not to have known, or known of Samuel Fairclough. It is

Samuel Clarke never wrote directly about Richard Baxter or his ministry. But it appears that his interaction with Baxter and, more significantly, his reading of Baxter's *Gildas Salvianus*, progressively influenced what aspects of pastoral ministry he considered most important and began subsequently to highlight.[49] Later generations of historians and commentators on 'puritan' ministry can perhaps be excused for presenting a seamless garment of 'puritan' ministry from the Elizabethan Settlement to Charles II's Restoration and beyond into Nonconformity. As one of the primary sources for biographical information on many of these 'puritan' worthies, Clarke's Collections and Lives have provided historians a unique vantage point from which to understand Elizabethan and Stuart pastoral ministry, but from an increasingly Baxterian perspective. The difference between the 1651 Hugh Clark and the 1683 Samuel Fairclough is most likely explained by 1650s Kidderminster. At the very least, it calls into question the propriety of using Clarke's later 'biographies' uncritically as evidence of a *Bucerian* pastoral tradition prior to Baxter.

Apart from Clarke's accounts, it is possible that further evidence for the survival of Bucer's influence on English pastoral practise is seen in the survival of an evangelistic emphasis in the ministries of Elizabethan and early Stuart puritan pastors. Bucer, we have seen, articulated a parish-centred strategy to promote the conversion of the parish's nominal majority. Bucer's recommendation of combining regular house-to-house pastoral oversight and instruction, adult confirmation, and effective discipline with a strong pulpit ministry was England's earliest and most comprehensive pastoral strategy, the goal of which was conversion and parish reformation. Eamon Duffy has found a continuity of evangelistic concern in the emphasis on preaching throughout Elizabethan and early Stuart England. While this preaching was instrumental 'in the forming of a devout Protestant culture', it was also missionary in its intent. Duffy further observes that 'such ministry, easily categorized as a process of consolidating and servicing a Puritan consensus, was rarely described or conceived by those who practiced it in isolation from the language of awakening, conversion.'[50]

Though Duffy highlights an important aspect of Protestant pastoral rhetoric, the examples he cites are those like Bernard Gilpin and Samuel Fairclough, ministers that were held up as examples by George Carleton and Samuel Clarke precisely because their ministries were exceptions to the rule of prevailing

---

likely that the Fairclough account was one of those 'now newly added, at least which I never saw.' Baxter, 'To the Reader', sigs a4-a4v.

[49] After Clarke was ejected, Baxter states that he moved from Benet Fink parish in London to Thistleworth where he 'lived privately' till his death. 'I never saw him since, nor heard that he came to *London*, but by a Letter from him a year before he died he told me he was 82 years old.' Baxter, 'To the Reader', in Clarke's *The Lives of Sundry Eminent Persons*, sig a4.

[50] Duffy, 'The Long Reformation', 39.

apathy and inaction among the majority of Protestant clergy. While the 'language of conversion' may appear to have been 'a ubiquitous feature of Protestant discourse',[51] it was more accurately perhaps a ubiquitous concern of that minority who earned the pejorative label 'puritan'. If we removed Clarke's galleries of godly heroes from consideration, one wonders if the same level of evangelistic concern and effort could be found among Laudian clergy, for example? Duffy's evidence indicates an ongoing remnant of ministers motivated by evangelistic zeal, but there is no documentation that Elizabethan and early Stuart evangelistic strategies moved beyond the 'painful' efforts by these ministers to communicate the gospel from their pulpits as plainly and clearly as possible. Clarke's hagiographies aside, a comprehensive, parish-centred, pastoral strategy for evangelism and reformation does not reappear in England until Richard Baxter's Kidderminster ministry.

The Immediate Response

Clues to how some of Baxter's contemporaries perceived his pastoral strategy can be found in his surviving correspondence with several of his ministerial colleagues who wrote after reading his *Gildas Salvianus*. If his correspondents were simply stirred up to take their gospel duty seriously, then a case could perhaps be made that Baxter was not suggesting anything particularly novel in terms of pastoral practise, and that his purpose for writing was to exhort ministers to undertake a closer application of already known tactics. But if his correspondents imply they are undertaking something new both for them and their parishes, it may be an indication that Baxter was in fact initiating a shift in prevailing emphasis and practise.

The response which greeted *Gildas Salvianus* upon its publication late in the summer of 1656 gave Baxter reason to hope his exhortation would succeed in motivating his colleagues throughout the Protectorate to restore church discipline, to associate with their fellow pastors for the sake of unity, and most of all to undertake the practise of personal oversight and catechising. Two early letters, while munificent in their praise of Baxter and *Gildas Salvianus*, are more ambiguous when it comes to identifying precisely how their ministries were affected. In August 1656, Samuel Corbyn wrote from Trinity College, Cambridge, to relate 'what god hath wrought in mee, by converse formerly & of late by your works', especially *Gildas Salvianus*, which 'stirred mee up to a more thorough examinacion & selfe condemnacion'.[52] Young Matthew Meade, lecturer at St Dunstans, Stepney, also wrote Baxter to say 'I blesse God for your precious booke', for 'your *Gildas Salvianus* so severely summoned mee to a more conscientious diligence in my duty.'[53] Thomas Wadsworth, who had

---

[51] Duffy, 'The Long Reformation', 40.

[52] DWL, BxL, v:220; *Calendar*, no. 321, 220.

[53] DWL, BxL, v:59; *Calendar*, no. 322, 221. The letter is undated, though Keeble and

engaged Baxter in an extended correspondence over ways to apply Baxter's ideas about church discipline, is more direct. Writing on 3 January 1657, Wadsworth exclaims, 'Your exhortatorie letter to catechizing [*The Agreement of Divers Ministers of Christ in the County of Worcester...for Catechizing* (1656)] awakened me first to personall instructing of my flock', and 'your *Reformed Pastour* hath now... engaged me to a dealing with my whole parish family by family'.[54]

But the responses were not all laudatory and encouraging. Even negative responses provide insight into how Baxter's programme was perceived. In 1657, Baxter produced a second edition of *Gildas Salvianus* which included an appendix 'in answer to some Objections which I have heard of, since the former Edition.'[55] While acknowledging Baxter's remarkable success in Kidderminster, there were those who were persuaded that his achievements were not simply the result of pastoral zeal and right technique: 'You cut us a shoo too narrow for our foot: You judge all our Congregations by your own: we have stubborn people that will not be instructed.... Had we a tractable people, we would yield to all [your suggestions].'[56] Baxter, of course, read the situation differently: 'If I understand this, the meaning of it is, we are resolved not to suffer the hatred...of our Neighbours: if we had a people that would take it well, and put us to no such suffering...then we would do it. If this be [your] meaning, it sounds not well'![57]

But unfriendly critics were not the only ones to have trouble with Baxter's regimen. Many who were sympathetic to Baxter's ideas and others who made a genuine attempt to adjust their own practise of ministry accordingly, found implementation of these ideas ultimately unfeasible and subsequently gave up. In March 1657, Thomas Gouldstone, Rector of Finchley, Middlesex, wrote: 'Sir I thanke you for your *Gildas Salvianus* &... wish I were able to putt it in practise...but the truth is that was calculated aright for the meridian of Kederminster and not of ffinchly. I buckle under the burthen.'[58] Adam Martindale, vicar of Rostherne in Cheshire, left perhaps the most detailed

---

Nuttall suggest August 1656 because of the mention of *Gildas Salvianus*. Meade (d. 1699) would in 1658 become curate of Shadwell, Stepney, Middlesex. After his ejection in 1660, he became minister of the Congregational church in Stepney, and became prominent leader among the London nonconformists. See Nuttall, 'Stepney Meeting: The pioneers', in *CHST*, 18 (1956), 17-22.

[54] DWL, BxL, ii:245; *Calendar*, no. 345, 236. See also the letter from Stephen Street (*Calendar*, no. 320), quoted in the previous chapter.

[55] *Gildas Salvianus* (1657), sig Oo. Future citations from this second edition will include (1657).

[56] *Gildas Salvianus* (1657), sig Oo5.

[57] *Gildas Salvianus* (1657), sig Oo5.

[58] DWL,BxL, v:121; *Calendar*, no. 438, 296-97. Gouldstone also mentions that 'My 2d birth, if yet borne againe, I owe to (you, you are my ffather,) your *S[aints] Rest* I meane which I read 3 times in the year 51.'

account of the frustrations endured by the many pastors who may have attempted to put Baxter's plan into practise:

> in the yeare 1656, the ministers of our classis...agreed upon...the worke of personal instruction.... But when we actually set upon the worke, [we] met with great discouragements, through the unwillingness of people (especially the old ignoramusses) to have their extreame defects in knowledge searched out, the backwardnesse of the prophane to have the smart plaister of admonition applied (though lovingly) to their sores, and the businesse (reall or pretended) left as an excuse why the persons concerned were gone abroad at the time appointed for their instruction. Besides these, [we] had such vast parishes to go through, that multitudes of the people would be dead, in all probability, ere we could goe once over them.[59]

Yet, even when one takes these criticisms into account, Baxter's *Gildas Salvianus* generated a remarkable amount of soul-searching and led many pastors to modify their practise.[60] While Baxter's contemporaries would have been familiar with the issues pertaining to discipline, oversight and catechising, it seems that the effect of *Gildas Salvianus* was to encourage pastors to *alter* their practise rather than simply try harder with respect to familiar duties. Those pastors who bothered to correspond with Baxter (and whose letters are extant) write as though Baxter's programme of catechising, at least, was a new idea. And when one views Baxter's catechetical programme in its Kidderminster context as one part of a unified strategy for parish evangelism utilizing well developed systems of discipline, oversight, and association, it becomes evident fairly quickly that, apart from those influenced by his example, Baxter is a seventeenth-century pastoral singularity.

We have seen that Baxter's ministry was developed in the laboratory of post-civil war Kidderminster. Baxter's pastoral genius was that he devised or adapted a strategy that addressed the particular circumstances and needs that met him upon his return in 1647 and best utilized his own abilities. Whether pulling ideas from Bucer's *Scripta Anglicana,* or long standing traditions of

---

[59] Adam Martindale, *The Life of Adam Martindale, written by himself,* R. Parkinson, ed. (1845), 122. See also letters from Peter Ince (*Calendar* no. 285) and Richard Eedes (*Calendar*, no. 408), quoted in the previous chapter.

[60] The assumption is that those ministers who would actually take the time and write Baxter himself about their successes or failures was a small percentage of those others who made similar attempts. That Adam Martindale's entire classis undertook a regimen of personal instruction and catechizing, while only Martindale himself bothered to write about it illustrates the point that Baxter's influence may have been more widespread than the available evidence found in letters and memoirs would indicate.

association, the examples of older ministers or from the undocumented free-for-all sharing of ideas in conference with colleagues, Baxter fashioned them into a unified programme that worked for St Mary's parish. But what was his greatest strength also proved his wider ministry's most significant weakness. Using a strategy rooted in the particular circumstances of 1650s Kidderminster and dependent upon the force of his own indefatigable persona, his correspondence indicates that it was transferred to other contexts and circumstances only with difficulty. Later Baxter tacitly acknowledged that his model for pastoral ministry was indeed context-specific. Despite the 'Success' which *Gildas Salvianus* enjoyed, Baxter gloomily reflected that 'since Bishops were restored, this Book is useless, and that Work not medled with.'[61]

While there were precedents to particular aspects of Baxter's ministry, recognizing the contextual nature of Baxter's approach solidifies our contention that Baxter's Kidderminster ministry was unparalleled as a deliberate pastoral strategy in England. Moreover, this aspect of his ministry goes far to explain why he never sought to reproduce his successes in another pastoral position after 1660. So context-specific is his ministry that Baxter offers the readers of *Gildas Salvianus* not so much a proper strategy for pastoral ministry, as his own experience as a model of 'godly' ministry. Keith Wrightson observes that constant critical reflection upon his own experience made Baxter 'one of the most sensitive analysts' not only of the relationship between seriously-practiced Protestant religion and 'customary culture', but of the crucial role which clergy played in the decline or advance of religion at the local level.[62] Baxter is self-consciously the Reformed Pastor. Indeed, the purpose driving Baxter in *Gildas Salvianus* is arguably the same which Keeble ascribes to his *Reliquiae*, that of personal apologetic.[63] The entire piece is haunted by his experiences of the dreadful shortcomings of an unconverted and inadequate ministry and threats of divine judgement, relieved only by the counter-example of his experiences in Kidderminster. For Baxter, any converted minister using the God-ordained means of preaching, personal instruction, discipline and association, could experience the same success that had characterized his Kidderminster ministry. He refused to see anything exceptional in what he had done and was determined that his ministry not be taken as a singularity. He writes with the confidence that he speaks for the majority of England's 'godly' pastors, that his cause is that of England's Protestants, and that his example is worthwhile precisely because his experience has been merely representative of the godly consensus.[64] Baxter uses autobiography in the same way he uses history-his experiences illustrate the vindication of godly ministry over and against that of the diocesan prelates and their Laudian sacramental emphases as well as that of

---

[61] *Rel. Bax.*, I, i, §177, 115.
[62] Wrightson, *English Society*, 184.
[63] Keeble, *Richard Baxter*, 149.
[64] Ibid., 149.

the separatists. In contrast with the Kidderminster of his predecessor (and successor) George Dance where the 'godly' were embattled and Christ's interests frustrated, in Baxter's Kidderminster the 'godly' flourished and he could even boast to Thomas Wadsworth that 'we never hitt the way of pulling downe the Kingdome of the Devill till now'.[65] Tellingly, once Baxter was removed from Kidderminster in 1660, the Reformed Pastor drops from view as well.[66] The refusal of Dance and Bishop Morley to be impressed by the evidence of his pastoral successes as typical of the majority of non-partisan godly ministry helped persuade Baxter that factors other than the 'interests of Christ' were driving Restoration ecclesiastical policy.[67] However, perhaps they were simply being realistic.

The New Tradition

Baxter's pastorate was an impossibility beyond its Interregnum context. Baxter's revisions of local parish discipline were dependent upon the devolution of ecclesiastical authority for discipline from bishop to parish minister, which could not have happened apart from the removal of English episcopacy. Unharrassed by Laudian polemic, he could take the unprecedented step of publicly questioning the sufficiency of preaching, which opened the possibility of implementing all-parish oversight and catechising. Only with the failure of Presbyterian reforms could he undertake setting up an alternative voluntary association. Those admirers and historians, beginning with Samuel Clarke and his *Lives of Sundry Eminent Persons*, who have assumed continuity between the ministries of Elizabethan and early Stuart puritans and the pastoral zenith of that tradition in Richard Baxter have neglected to recognize the even more substantial evidence for discontinuity.

Only when Baxter's practise is set alongside Martin Bucer's recommendations does the mystery of Kidderminster begin to clarify. Baxter's pastoral ministry has far more in common with Bucer's *De Vera Animarum Cura* and *De Regno Christi* than it does with anything Perkins, Greenham Bernard, Sibbes or even Calamy suggested.[68] Puritan ministry had, in fact, exhausted itself with the failure of the Westminster Assembly. Having achieved political power, the movement could not make the transition from repressed opposition to the give-and-take of political reality, and in the end was undone in the main by its own internal inconsistencies. At the parish level, with the proliferation of

---

[65] DWL, BxL, ii:249; *Calendar*, no. 290.

[66] As Wrightson observes, 'their withdrawal into nonconformity represented also a retreat from the ideal of national reformation. The emotional exhaustion of the Interregnum experiment and its failure had left their mark.' *English Society*, 219.

[67] Keeble, *Richard Baxter*, 150, 153.

[68] Greenham's case is unusual as he never entered the public discussion about ministry, his *Workes* having been gathered and published posthumously.

sects and the absence of any centrally co-ordinated discipline, even Clarke admitted, as we have seen, 'the matter is now almost grown desperate' apart from 'some unexpected remedy.'[69] Barry Reay asserts that the 'single most important aspect of the religious history of this period is the shattering of both Puritanism and the Church of England, and the emergence of hundreds of independent and semi-independent congregations.'[70] The effect of this unprecedented religious and social chaos on the guardians of the nation's existing religious and social structures, structures that were never intended to withstand such pressure, cannot be overstated. It would seem that in responding to this crisis, Baxter, with the help of Martin Bucer, provided Clarke's 'unexpected remedy' and demonstrated a challenging but feasible way out of the disasters that had overcome the English Church and attempts to reform it in the 1640s. It would also appear that Baxter's pastoral vision was swallowed in its entirety by many of England's 'godly' ministers, even if they were later forced to modify their application of it or even abandon it altogether as unworkable in their local context. Of course, this is not to say that all Nonconformists were persuaded by Baxter's perspective or that the older, preaching-centred focus of 'puritan' ministry was totally displaced. The vast majority of England's clergy conformed to the re-imposition of pre-1640s episcopacy and ministry. Even so, due to the sheer force of *Gildas Salvianus*, England's pastors were now discussing pastoral ministry on Baxter's terms. The older, pulpit-centred rhetoric is heard less and less.

As there were no published discussions of the relative merits of competing pastoral strategies, we are left to speculate as to why such a major transformation in pastoral priorities and strategy seemed to pass by so silently, given that related areas of theology and ecclesiology were among the most fiercely debated concerns of the day. At least seven reasons for this unmarked transition come to mind. The first reason is because the received pastoral ideal of a pulpit-centred ministry buttressed by catechising simply did not work. After episcopacy was brought down and the parish system itself teetered on the verge of disintegration through the separatists' challenge, the old assumptions about the sufficiency of right preaching were demonstrated to be inadequate in the face of the new realities confronting parish ministers. The absence of an immediate threat from Roman Catholicism and the removal of the Laudian sacramentalist regime eliminated the polemical necessity to maintain the cause of Protestant preaching. The old arguments were abandoned with surprising haste, and it was not too long before pastors like Baxter began to articulate publicly what had only a few years earlier been *Laudian* critiques of pulpit-

---

[69] Clarke, *A Generall Martyrologie*, 432.

[70] Reay, *The Quakers and the English Revolution* (London: Temple Smith, 1985), 15.

centred ministry, though with a different end in mind.[71] Baxter's arguments were persuasive because he simply articulated what many of his colleagues had already experienced in their parishes: the old ideal was insufficient for the new reality.

A second reason for the quiet displacement of the puritan pastoral tradition was the collective weariness of England's 'godly' pastors in the aftermath of their 1640s failure to follow through with the reformation of the Church of England.[72] No study has yet done justice to the acute trauma inflicted by the civil wars themselves on ministers of all sorts in general, and 'puritan' pastors and their ministries in particular. Barbara Donagan breezily asserts that 'All in all, it was a disappointing war for ministers.'[73] The real impact for the individuals involved is more likely to be measured in terms like 'devastating' and 'disastrous'. Communities divided. Ministers were forced to flee.[74] Baxter was probably not the only one to return to find that 'home' was now a different place from when he had left.[75] English puritanism emerged from those years a spent force, unable to adapt, with only old ideas and parliamentary politics to commend itself. And in the end, both were badly outflanked-by Independents, by separatists, by the army, and by Cromwell himself. The frustration of the Westminster Assembly reforms was a crushing blow. The puritan movement's 'strenuous, determined and protracted effort' to 'transform England' ended in confusion, and the long press for a reformation by legislated settlement proved ultimately illusory.[76] The result was not so much a conscious shift from one system of pastoral ministry to another, as much as it was a void needing desperately to be filled.

A third reason contributing to the abandonment of the puritan pastoral tradition was the genuine alarm felt with respect to the centrifugal forces of separatism and sectarianism unleashed by the absence of an enforceable religious settlement.[77] The pulpit-centred strategy had always assumed the

---

[71] See, for example, John Cosin, 'A Sermon at the Consecration of Dr. Francis White, Bishop of Carlisle', in *The Works of the Right Reverend Father in God John Cosin, Lord Bishop of Durham*, vol. 1 (1843), 95-96.

[72] For Baxter's discussion of the Westminster Assembly, see *Rel. Bax.*, I, i, §117, 72-74.

[73] Barbara Donagan, 'Did Ministers Matter? War and Religion in England, 1642-1649', in *JBS*, 33 (1994), 156.

[74] See Baxter's harrowing description in *A Holy Commonwealth* (1659), William Lamont, ed. (Cambridge: Cambridge University Press, 1994), 211-12.

[75] See *Rel. Bax.*, I, §137 (3-4), 86-87.

[76] Webster, *Godly Clergy*, 338.

[77] See Baxter's discussion of 'the Vanists', 'the Seekers', 'the Ranters', 'the Quakers', 'the Behmenists' and 'the Socinians', *Rel. Bax.*, I, i, §§19-127, 74-79. In this case, it was the *perception* of social and religious disorder, of the 'world turned upside down', that was sufficient to motivate consternation among clergy and others who felt their social standing and authority was threatened. As was the case with recent arguments asserting that the middling sort supported parliament during the civil wars while the Catholics

stability of the parish system, and at least the potential for co-operation between minister and magistrate to insure that order was maintainable. And with attendance at sermons legally enforced, ministers could at least guarantee that most parishioners were within earshot during service times, thus giving the Word of God preached the opportunity to perform its converting and sanctifying work, under God's sovereign pleasure, of course. But civil war England convulsed into an altogether different world from the relatively stable societies of previous generations.[78] Church, king and law were upended. And the weaknesses of the parish system, particularly its ministers' inability to exercise meaningful discipline, were used as provocations justifying the radical step of abandoning one's parish church and forming instead a local society of saints more capable of pleasing God than the mixed field of the parish ever had been.[79] The old puritan ministry, though it was an unhappy minority within the episcopal system, had nevertheless gotten by under the previous regime of ecclesiastical justice, such as it was. But once removed from its sheltered position under episcopacy and prevented from enforcing the Presbyterian alternative, the old puritan pastoral ideal had no answer to the critiques of those 'godly' parishioners who found the integrity of the sacraments hopelessly compromised through lack of discipline. More than any other factor, it was England's untethered separatists who confirmed the bankruptcy of the old puritan ideal during and after the civil wars.

A fourth factor contributing to the shift from the defunct puritan pastoral

---

went to the Royalist side, what was presented as such in the blizzard of propaganda about the separatists and sects, and widely accepted by most people, was not necessarily reflected in reality. See Morrill, *The Revolt of the Provinces: Conservatives and Radicals in the English Civil War 1630-1650* (London: Longman, 1980), 47-51; Reay, *The Quakers and the English Revolution*, 62-78.

[78] See, for example, Fletcher, 'Oliver Cromwell and the godly nation', 229, 231.

[79] 'But our trouble (next to the ignorance and badness that we found most Parishes in) was Antichurches, or Separatists, that in great Towns and where they found Entertainment, did gather Congregations out of the Parochial Congregations; which being gathered on pretence that the Communion of our Churches was unlawful, employed so much of their Preaching and converse in labouring to prove it so, and in magnifying their own Opinions and Ways, and vilifying others, as made many Towns become places of meer strife, that I say not of almost hostility. These separating Antichurches were of divers sorts: But of these it was two Parties that most hindered our Concord and Success. The Laudian Prelatists, and the rigid Independents: the former set up mostly in Great mens Houses, that had been against the Parliament.... The other sort pretended sometimes faultiness in our Churches, as not so pure as they; and sometime Liberty to gather the willing into Churches of their Conduct, because Parish Bounds were not of Divine Right. The Anabaptists also made us no small trouble; But the Quakers that made the loudest noise, by railing at us in our Assemblies and Markets, did little harm, being contemned because of the grossness of their Behaviour: especially when we had admitted them to publick Disputes, and showed them before all the People.' Baxter, *Church Concord* (1691), sigs A2v-A3.

synthesis to Baxter's revised strategy was the inherent pragmatism of most parish ministers, burdened by the rhetoric of an impossibly high calling, equipped with limited resources and confronted by the reality and trials of day to day parish ministry. Overwhelmed by preaching responsibilities, sacraments, catechising, visiting the sick, burials, counseling the troubled, and with too little time to be much bothered by the pamphlet wars on ecclesiology and doctrine in London, these pastors were more concerned with an idea's practicality than with its pedigree. It is perhaps these sorts of pastors that Baxter had in mind when he described his colleagues in the Worcestershire Association as 'wholly addicted to the winning of Souls...adhering to no Faction; neither Episcopal, Presbyterian, nor Independent, as to Parties', and 'for Numbers, Parts and Piety, the most considerable part of all that County'.[80] Baxter's strategy was tailor-made for just such a constituency because he knew from his own experience the sort of issues each one faced. And out of his own struggles, he had devised an answer to the need for church discipline, and a solution to the problem of maintaining the integrity of the sacraments. Moreover, he found a way to supplement pulpit work by arranging a regular conference with every parishioner for the evangelistic purpose of discussing the weighty issues raised in the catechism. Baxter's obsessive thoroughness in *Gildas Salvianus* may come across to modern readers as overkill. But to the hundreds, if not thousands of his fellow pastors who read it, who themselves were trying desperately to cope with an impossible calling, the fact that one could so clearly address their situation and provide them with specific and practical ideas must have seemed immensely encouraging.

A fifth reason why England's 'godly' pastors so quietly adopted Baxter's perspective on ministry was due to Baxter's own efforts to present himself as continuing the long-term emphases of his Stuart and Elizabethan pastoral predecessors. This was no intentional act of deception on his part. We have already noted how Baxter viewed England's Protestant history in dualistic terms as an ongoing conflict between 'godly' Abel and 'prelatical' Cain. Baxter's historiography allowed him to build a case against those English churchmen who supported the cause of diocesan prelacy and would restore episcopacy and end his pastoral reforms if given the chance. While concentrating on the long-term conflict between the 'prelates' and the 'puritans', the subtler but no less profound shifts in emphasis from Edwardian to Elizabethan understandings of reformation were overlooked, or at least remained unnoted. Moreover, by delivering the most systematic exposition of his pastoral vision in the exhortatory format of *Gildas Salvianus*, Baxter avoided the necessity of a formal defense of his views and was able to focus his attention on uncontroversial aspects such as repentance and right motivation as well as careful application. And by stressing those areas of concern shared by all 'godly' pastors, such as the need for discipline, the value of association and

---

[80] *Rel. Bax.*, I, §137 (21), 90; II, §28, 148.

the efficacy of catechising, the fact that many of his solutions to these concerns were unprecedented and served to reconfigure pastoral duties around the explicit goal of parochial evangelism passed through without anybody catching on.

A sixth reason why pastors were inclined to abandon the old puritan emphases and take Baxter seriously was because published accounts of his Kidderminster ministry indicated that his strategy was a stupendous success. Not only did *Gildas Salvianus* provide seemingly up to the minute reports on the astonishing results Baxter's methods were achieving, the growing network of voluntary ministerial associations provided Baxter with an immediate and influential audience of ministers who were already sympathetic with previously published aspects of his pastoral agenda. After the Restoration, Baxter's polemical attempts to demonstrate the disastrous effects of 'Prelatical' ministry insured that coverage of his own pastoral efforts would continue to focus on his successes. It is not surprising, in light of the demonstrable shortcomings of the older puritan ideal, that pastors would have been attracted to Baxter's ideal instead, which held out the prospects of accomplishing the same reformational goals and added to the equation verifiable evidence that such goals could actually be achieved.

A seventh reason why Baxter's pastoral strategy became identified in later Nonconformist minds with the puritan pastoral tradition was because Baxter's Kidderminster experiment was overtaken and dismantled by the Restoration in the flower of its success before it had a chance to prove its viability as a long-term system.[81] We have seen that Baxter's correspondence indicates that other pastors were having difficulties implementing aspects of both discipline and parochial catechising. And within St Mary's parish itself, the majority of Baxter's parishioners had opted to remain out from under his pastoral oversight. Given the immense workload generated by Baxter's recommendations, it would not be surprising if most pastors who attempted to modify their ministries found their experiences more like those of Richard Eedes, Adam Martindale, and Thomas Gouldstone, who found Baxter's reformed pastor 'calculated aright for the meridian of Kederminster' but not necessarily 'of ffinchly'.[82] But however tempted one might be to suggest that Baxter's pastoral programme was doomed to collapse of its own weight, the historical record shows that Baxter's new ideal did not fail, but was in fact put

---

[81] I disagree with the implications which Derek Hirst draws from Baxter's frustration with his own parishioners' hesitation to submit to his pastoral oversight that Baxter's 'reformation' was not working. Though Baxter's strategy may have eventually proven unviable, Hirst is too quick too use this as evidence in support of his own argument for the failure of national reformation. Hirst, 'The Failure of National Reformation', 53.

[82] DWL, BxL, v:121; *Calendar*, no. 438, 296-97.

down with the reimposition of episcopacy.[83] This allowed Baxter's martyred method to enjoy a glorious afterlife in the minds of subsequent Nonconformists as the pinnacle of *puritan* pastoral prowess. And it is a myth that has been perpetuated since.

Conclusion

In this chapter, I have asked whether the Bucerian emphases evident in Baxter's ministry could have been picked up by Baxter through an intermediate source. More specifically, I have attempted to follow the trail of Bucer's influence through the writings of his Elizabethan successors, only to discover that the evidence for his continuing impact on English pastoral practise is slight to begin with, and vanishes altogether after Grindal's fall. Moreover, there was no 'rediscovery' of Bucer after the 1577 publication (in Basle) of his posthumous *Scripta Anglicana*. His voluble folio appears to have served mostly as a source for proof texts in the ongoing debates over ecclesiology and theology.

However, the anonymous portrayal of Samuel Fairclough's ministry during the 1630s and 40s in Kedington unexpectedly contains many of those pastoral practises and emphases this study has labeled 'Bucerian'. But the Fairclough account was not written until after Fairclough's death in 1677. Moreover, the fact that that it appeared in Samuel Clarke's final collection of exemplary 'godly' lives, a collection that shows tale-tell signs of having been influenced by his long friendship with Richard Baxter, raises questions as to whether the pastoral practises utilized by Fairclough actually date from the 1630s, or whether their presentation was influenced by the publication of Baxter's *Gildas Salvianus* in 1656. If it is an accurate record of a genuine ministry, then the Fairclough account preserves a unique example of a sophisticated, almost-Bucerian concept of ministry for which no precedent appears to exist. If that is the case, however, no one seems to have picked up on Fairclough's success, or the system that produced it, all the more amazing given Kedington's relative proximity to Cambridge. In fact, in a time when ministers were increasingly casting about for ways to cope with a serious separatist threat to the status quo, the absence of any 1640s recourse to Fairclough's example is remarkable. The fact that the first published mention of Fairclough's pastoral achievement occurred more than two decades after the Restoration begins to look suspicious. Fairclough no doubt had an exemplary ministry. But the evidence suggests that a Restoration author updated a successful Caroline puritan ministry to bolster a subsequent agenda.

---

[83] See Hirst, 'The Failure of National Reformation', 53. Hirst is correct to note the many problems confronting efforts to promote reformation in the 1650s. He is, however, premature in his claim that such efforts had resulted in failure. The Restoration killed all hope of reformation. Prior to 1660, though in serious decline, hopes for reformation were not dead yet.

Thus it would appear that the best explanation for close correspondence between Martin Bucer's recommendations for furthering the English Reformation through a reconfigured pastoral ministry and Richard Baxter's reformed pastor is that Baxter was influenced directly by Bucer through his reading of *Scripta Anglicana*. It was in fact the only time in the century following Bucer's death that the political and ecclesiastical circumstances were such that his pastoral strategy ideas could actually be put into practise. In Bucer, Baxter found a fellow pastor responding to similar challenges, whether it was the need to devise a discipline that worked in the mixed field of the parish, or pressure from separatists, or the desperate need to facilitate the conversion of the unregenerate majority. And he was pragmatic enough to recognize that what worked in Strasbourg could, with some updating, make a difference in Kidderminster as well.

Secondly, I have argued that Baxter's Reformed Pastor supplanted the long-standing ideal of the godly preacher as the dominant pastoral model informing 'puritan' ministry after 1656. It was a transformation that occurred quietly and without debate, as clergy found that the older, pulpit-centred ideal required too many exceptions to continue as a useful model in the remade religious world after the civil wars. Baxter's *Reformed Pastor* was a daunting challenge for even the most enthusiastic ministers, but it had both the force of Baxter's formidable rhetoric and the advantage of appearing to work to commend itself. As it turned out, Baxter, who perhaps did more than anyone else to discredit the old puritan ideal of the preaching pastor by simply being honest in public about its shortcomings, ironically became identified by many even within the puritan tradition as the apogee of puritan pastoral prowess, much to the confusion of later admirers and historians. But Baxter was never a 'puritan' pastor, in the sense of combining a preaching-centred ministry with attempts to bring the ceremonies and government of the Church in line with Reformed (read Genevan and Scottish practise). Instead, Baxter resurrected the earlier, Bucerian emphasis on pastor-led, evangelism-centred parochial reformation, which strategically supplemented preaching with discipline, oversight and instruction for evangelistic ends. And though the Restoration insured that Baxter's method as published in *Gildas Salvianus* would dominate the pastoral agenda nationwide for only four or five years, the Restoration also insured that the Reformed Pastor would be the dominant ideal many pastors would take with them into Nonconformity and Dissent.[84]

---

[84] There is no modern study of Dissenting clergy and their ministries. For studies around the edges, see Richard Greaves, *John Bunyan and English Nonconformity* (London: Hambledon, 1992) and *Saints and Rebels: Seven Nonconformists in Stuart England* (Macon, GA: Mercer University Press, 1985); David L. Wykes, *'To revive the memory of some excellent men.' Edmund Calamy and the early historians of nonconformity* (London: Dr Williams's Trust, 1997); Keeble, *The Literary Culture of Nonconformity in later Seventeenth Century England* (Leicester: Leicester University Press, 1987);

As a result, Baxter's *Gildas Salvianus* influenced the way even pre-civil war 'puritan' ministry was perceived by his contemporaries and subsequent Nonconformists. Samuel Clarke's earlier biographies of Elizabethan and early Stuart luminaries are utterly conventional in their reflection of puritan pulpit priorities. But his later collections, particularly his 1683 *Lives of Sundry Eminent Persons*, carry descriptions of ministries that sound suspiciously Baxterian in terms of emphasis. Because of this, the true extent of the inadequacy of the puritan pastoral tradition in the wake of the civil wars was obscured, as were the real reasons for Baxter's own influence on pastoral practise in the Interregnum and in subsequent Nonconformity. If his ongoing influence in later Nonconformist, Reformed and Evangelical circles has seemed inordinate, at least we are now in a better position to understand why.

Having considered the rather intangible questions of Baxter's influence in the way ministry was both practiced and perceived by his contemporaries and successors, it remains to consider a more intimate view of Baxter's influence upon one individual who followed him into ministry to become one of the leading Nonconformist pastors and tutors in London, Thomas Doolittle.

Nuttall, et al, *The Beginnings of Nonconformity* (London: James Clark and Company, 1964). There are only a few studies that examine Restoration clergy and their ministries. See Spurr, *The Restoration Church,* and John H. Pruett, *The Parish Clergy under the Later Stuarts: The Leicestershire Experience* (Urbana, IL, and London: University of Illinois Press, 1978), 23-28.

CHAPTER 9

Richard Baxter, Thomas Doolittle, and the Making of a *Reformed Pastor*

Richard Baxter's efforts to reform English Protestant ministry extended beyond his published attempts to influence pastoral practise. Within a very short time of his return to Kidderminster in 1647, overshadowed perhaps by his more public labours, the evidence indicates that Baxter was methodically building relationships with certain young men in his parish in an effort to recruit and train them for ministry. Moreover, Baxter provided opportunities for a series of other young graduates from Cambridge and Oxford to gain practical experience in Christian ministry under his direction before moving on to positions of leadership, often in neighbouring parishes. And in at least one case, as we shall see, Baxter was the long-time mentor of a young man who would go on to become an influential London pastor, not only by example and through his writings, but by correspondence as well. By this sort of intentional involvement in the lives of young men preparing for ministry in the Church of England, Baxter was not initiating anything new. Efforts like his were part of a long tradition among England's more zealous Protestants both to supplement their university education with a more practical preparation for parish ministry and to seek patronage from respected ministers for future placement.

The need for an educated ministry had been recognized from the earliest days of the English reformation. Bishops charged by Elizabeth to maintain the 1559 Settlement agreed with their puritan antagonists that an uneducated clergy was a serious detriment to the proper reformation of the English church, however differently they might define proper.[1] Moreover, the Protestant emphasis on preaching, with the corresponding de-emphasis on the sacerdotal role of the minister, transformed the ministry from a mediatorial office to an interpretative task.[2] Not surprisingly, both bishops and puritans looked to the universities as

---

[1] See Wenig, *Straightening the Altars*, chapters 1-2.

[2] William Perkins characterizes ministers as primarily messengers (*'Angels'*) and interpreters in *Of the Calling of the Ministrie*, sigs A2v-B. Also see Rosemary O'Day, 'The reformation of the ministry, 1558-1642', 67-75. What O'Day describes as 'the religious impetus' should not be overlooked in the rush to consider other sociological factors feeding into the Elizabethan emphasis on clergy education. Whatever roles played by patron preference for university graduates, increasing opportunities for higher

the obvious context in which to further their educational agenda for the rising generation of clergy.[3] That the universities were often the battleground in the struggles between the various factions along the Protestant spectrum in the Elizabethan and then Stuart Church underscores how important the education of future clergy was to all parties.[4]

This sustained emphasis on educating clergy brought about a remarkable change in the makeup of the Church of England ministry. Nevertheless, by the time James became king, it had been apparent in some circles for some time that something more than a university education was needed to equip a young man for the pastoral ministry.[5] Grammar school and a university education might make him more learned, but the curriculum as such afforded little if any practical training that might prepare the future parish pastor for the 'burthen of the ministrie'.[6] Though university-educated men were pouring into church vacancies, it became increasingly clear that a learned clergy was not necessarily a 'godly' clergy. For many, having 'time-serving hirelings' or 'educated wolves' leading the flock was just as bad as 'dumb [nonpreaching] dogs', if not worse.[7] A university education was important, but a university education did not guarantee an effective preaching pastor.

For England's ardent Protestants, the presence of a 'godly' and 'painful' preaching pastor was viewed as God's chief means of blessing his people and effecting personal and national righteousness.[8] The absence of such a minister was viewed as a curse, and a principal reason behind the deplorable state of

---

education, or recognition of the better placement opportunities more education provided, the original push for a better educated clergy was driven by *Protestant* convictions.

[3] New rules overseeing ordination requirements in 1571 and 1575 pointedly encouraged those seeking a clerical career to the universities for education. See O'Day, *Education and Society*, 136-137; and also Doran and Durston, *Princes, Pastors and People*, 147-148.

[4] See Porter, *Reformation and Reaction in Tudor Cambridge*.

[5] There was a general recognition that however effective a university education might be in making future clergy learned, there was nothing in the university curriculum that provided training in scriptural hermeneutics or the practical aspects of preaching and pastoral practise. O'Day, *Education and Society*, 140. John Twigg states that, in Cambridge, 'Religious ideals were propagated among students mainly through university sermons, which they were required to attend, and by their college tutors, for there was no formal religious instruction in the undergraduate course.' John Twigg, *The University of Cambridge and the English Revolution* (Cambridge: Cambridge University Press, 1990), 14; see also W.T. Costello, *The Scholastic Curriculum at Early Seventeenth Century Cambridge* (Cambridge, MA: Harvard University Press, 1958).

[6] The title of John Holmes's book on the pastor's call, *The burthen of the ministrie* (1592). See Mark Curtis, *Oxford and Cambridge in Transition 1558-1642* (Oxford: Clarendon, 1959), 185-186.

[7] See Collinson's critique of the puritan pastoral agenda in his 'Shepherds', 185-187.

[8] See Packer, *A Quest for Godliness*, 38-39.

ungodliness prevalent throughout the land.[9] Reflecting on several generations of Protestant effort, Richard Baxter could conclude that 'All Churches either rise or fall as the Ministry doth rise or fall, (not in Riches and worldly Grandure) but in Knowledge, Zeal and Ability for their Work.'[10]

Yet 'godly' ministers did not come from nowhere. By their own testimony, as we shall see, they were *made*. A 'godly' perspective was not assumed by the rising generation of ministers as if it were merely a school of thought to be absorbed. Such things could not be taught in grammar school lessons or at university. Rather this chapter will argue that a 'godly' perspective on ministry was passed, informally but not unintentionally, from person to person, as a matter of personal nurture or mentorship. Recent overviews of clerical education, such as the one found in Tom Webster's *Godly Clergy in Early Stuart England* (1997) have gone far to advance our understanding of how young men in godly circles prepared themselves for ministry as well as the associational context in which their training often occurred.[11] Francis Bremer notes that '[I]t became commonplace for a Puritan graduate who aspired to the ministry to continue his training in the home of an established clerical figure.'[12] Nevertheless, the way this occurred—the relational manner by which this 'godly' agenda was passed down to the new generation of ministers—has not been fully explored, especially with respect to the clergy following the civil wars. The purpose of this chapter, therefore, is to build on the work of scholars like Collinson, Bremer and Webster and carry the discussion of 'godly' clerical education into the experience of ministers after the civil wars and into Restoration Nonconformity. I will illustrate the reflex among many young men preparing for parish ministry to supplement their university education by examining Richard Baxter's efforts to provide for a series of graduates an intermediate opportunity for practical ministry experience under supervision. I will also underscore his role as a patron, and highlight his use of the 'godly' network within the Worcestershire Association to secure placements for his assistants when they were ready for parish of their own. And finally I will explore his mentoring relationship with one young man in particular, his parishioner Thomas Doolittle.

Early Modern English clergy education seems, at first glance, to be a well-ploughed field from an historiographical perspective. Mark Curtis's *Oxford and*

---

[9] Richard Baxter states,'If God would but reform the Ministry, and set them on their Duties zealously and faithfully, the People would certainly be reformed'. *Rel. Bax.,* I, i, §177 (22), 115.

[10] *Rel. Bax.,* I, i, §177 (22), 115 .

[11] Webster, *Godly Clergy*, 15-59. For the network of relationships developed at the University of Cambridge, see Bremer, *Congregational Communion: Clerical Friendship in the Anglo-American Puritan Community 1610-1692* (Boston, MA: Northeastern University Press, 1994), 17-40; for the Elizabethan puritans, see Collinson, *The Elizabethan Puritan Movement*, 127-130.

[12] Bremer, *Shaping New Englands*, 16.

Cambridge in Transition 1558-1642 (1959) has for a generation provided the standard point from which all other studies depart. Rosemary O'Day's own studies of the English clergy have led her to explore the transformation in clergy roles and identity that occurred with reformation. The change from a mostly unlearned to a mostly graduate clergy that occurred in the century following Henry VIII's break from Rome forever transformed the way in which the English understood the church and perceived its ministers, a transformation that is documented by O'Day's helpful analysis.[13] Several recent studies have provided valuable insight into more specific questions, concerning both the students who were to become pastors and the institutions that educated them. John Twigg's *The University of Cambridge and the English Revolution* (1990) carefully examines the context in which so many of the Elizabethan and Stuart puritans studied towards their B.A. and M.A. degrees. And John Morgan's *Godly Learning: Puritan Attitudes toward Reason, Learning and Education, 1560-1640* (1986) is a searching study of the various puritans' use of the educational means at hand. Although others, such as O'Day, make note of the increasing practise among puritan graduates to go first to the household of a prominent puritan pastor for additional preparation before moving to a cure of their own, Morgan was the first to examine the phenomenon in more depth.[14] Webster's subsequent analysis of puritan graduates' 'period of tuition in the household of a godly minister' (which was 'plainly intended to be a temporary arrangement') has gone far to update our understandings of the dynamics of a significant means of puritan discipleship.[15]

Even so, the finished product of puritan pastoral education is greater than the sum of the parts described in the historiography. After having examined different aspects of the formal education which a young man of puritan persuasion would have received from childhood through his participation in a 'household seminary', the present literature points to but still has not explained the last, and in many respects most crucial, step: how upon finishing his course of formal academic training a young man was then equipped to climb the steps of a pulpit as the *Boanerges* and then climb down and live among the people as the *Barnabas* to which the more 'godly' sort of ministers aspired.[16] Or to

---

[13] See O'Day's 'The reformation of the ministry', and *Education and Society*. See also O'Day's *The English Clergy*. For more broadly based studies content to summarize the conclusions drawn by others in the area of clergy education, see Doran and Durstan's *Princes, Pastors and People*; see also Robert Towler and A.P.M. Coxon's *The Fate of the Anglican Clergy: A Sociological Study* (London: MacMillan, 1979).

[14] See O'Day, *Education and Society*, 143-147. See also John Morgan's discussion of 'household seminaries' in *Godly Learning: Puritan Attitudes toward Reason, Learning and Education, 1560-1640* (Cambridge: Cambridge University Press, 1986), 290-300.

[15] Webster, *Godly Clergy*, 36.

[16] To be known by your peers as a 'Boanerges' and or a 'Barnabas' was high praise in puritan circles. These Biblical phrases were stock terms of pulpit prowess, especially in the application of the bad news that a right understanding of the Old Testament law

transpose the discussion into the decade following the Civil Wars, how did one become, according to Baxter's revision, a *reformation* pastor? For the conscientious young graduate, it was no small thing to be called to be the pastor of a parish. The intimidating responsibilities of spiritual leadership caused many to recognize that, despite their learning, they were, practically speaking, unprepared and ill-equipped to undertake their calling. This next section gives an overview of how many sought to make up their lack. As with most excursions, we must start out on what has become a well-traveled path. But the view in the end will, I think, repay our effort.

'At the feet of *Gamaliel*'

Motivating the desire for extracurricular training on the part of 'puritan' students preparing for pastoral ministry was their awareness of the awesome responsibility that a call from God to pastor his flock entailed.[17] Tender 'puritan' consciences were vexed enough by the introspective gymnastics undertaken to ascertain the status of their own souls. But what made post-Reformation ministry in England so radically different from what had passed for Christian ministry before was the emphasis of the minister as *primarily* preacher and teacher of the Bible.[18] By virtue of his charge to preach the gospel, William Perkins states that God had given to the minister the '*Commission* and authority' '*to redeeme* a man penitent, from hell & damnation: not that he is the *meanes* of working out this redemption, for that wholy and onely is Christ himselfe; but hee is *Gods instrument, and Christs instrument*, first, *to apply* those meanes vnto him'. Such a calling 'is the greatest that euer was

---

brought so that the good news of the New Testament Gospel could be comprehended. For example, see Samuel Clarke's description of Thomas Wilson in his *The Lives of Sundry Eminent Persons*, 20. For a later example, see Daniel Williams's funeral sermon for Thomas Doolittle in which he calls Doolittle a 'Boanerges' because of his powerful manner of presenting the claims of the law and the terrors of God's judgement. See Daniel Williams, *Christian Sincerity; Described in a Funeral Sermon June 1. 1707. Occasioned by the death of T. Doolittle.* (1707), sig B8.

[17] Perkins, *Of the Calling of the Ministrie*, sigs C-C10v, 5-13. Baxter writes in his *Gildas Salvianus*, 78: 'One part of our work, and that the most excellent, because it tendeth to work on many, is the publicke preaching of the word. A work requireth greater skill, and especialy greater life and zeal then any of us bring to it. It is no small matter to stand up in the face of a congregation, and to deliver a Message of salvation or damnation, as from the living God, in the name of our Redeemer. It is no easie matter to speak so plain, that the ignorant may understand us; and so seriously, that the deadest hearts may feel us; and so convincingly, that the contradicting Cavillers may be silenced.'

[18] Nearly a century later, John Owen echoes Perkins in his *The True Nature of a Gospel Church* (1689), writes: 'The first and principal duty of a pastor is to *feed the flock* by diligent preaching of the word.' (his emphasis) *The Works of John Owen*, 16 (Edinburgh: The Banner of Truth Trust, 1968), 74.

vouchsafed to any creature, Man or Angell'. Ministers are the agents of God's saving grace and must therefore 'doe the *dutie* of redeemers'. The 'end that they must ayme at, must be to winne soules'. In practical terms, their call meant that ministers should '*pray* earnestly for the people', '*mourne* for the impenitent when they will not turne to God', and '*priuately conferre, visite, admonish, and rebuke*'. But despite the apparent range of pastoral tasks encouraged by Perkins, the real focus of his strategy for ministry is preaching: 'principally they must *preach*, and that in such good manner, and in so diligent measure, as that they may redeeme and winne soules'.[19] This, for the godly, was both the glory and the 'burthen' of the pastor's calling. To do it well was the pastor's *raison d'être*. Not to do it well was to fail God and become a hindrance to the salvation of lost souls. Thus, in the puritan universe the call to be a pastor was an unfathomably great privilege, but the corresponding stakes were terribly high.[20]

With 'godly' rhetoric having set the expectations for puritan ministry so high, it is little wonder that young graduates available for placement were intimidated. Moreover, successive generations of students at Cambridge (for example) would have been exposed to the preaching of some of the most widely acclaimed preachers in the kingdom. Men like Richard Greenham (1535?-1594?), William Perkins (1558-1602), Paul Baynes (d. 1617), John Preston (1587-1628), Richard Sibbes (1577-1635), Thomas Hill (d. 1651), Richard Vines (1600?-1656) and John Arrowsmith (1602-1659) all had positions in or near Cambridge that enabled them to undertake preaching

---

[19] Perkins, *The call of the ministrie*, sigs C7v-C9.

[20] Collinson, in 'Shepherds' is certainly correct in noting the gap that existed between puritan pastoral ideals and rhetoric and the reality that 'must' [his word] have existed in the parish, though he admits the difficulty in reconstructing the realities of day-to-day life in a puritan parish from the sources available (189). But his criticism of puritan books on pastoral ministry (such as Perkins *Of the Calling of the Ministrie*, Samuel Crooke's *The ministeriall husbandry and building*, George Downame's *Commending the ministrie*, Richard Bernard's *The Faithful Shepherd*, etc.) as giving a skewed perspective of what pastors actually did or were supposed to do misses the point of the authors' intent. These authors were not intending to offer *descriptions* of puritan pastoral practise, rather they were offering *prescriptions* to correct what they saw as a deplorable lack at the parish level. It is true that these prescriptions are based on a pulpit-centred ideal of pastoral ministry. But the fact that these puritans hardly mention other aspects of the ministerial calling such as prayer, visitation, sacraments, and other regular pastoral duties does not mean that these were of no concern (199). It may mean that, from the authors' perspective, these aspects were not broken and thus did not need their attention. If preaching was the most important aspect of puritan pastoral ministry, as I have argued elsewhere, and if inadequate preaching seems to have been the bane of the English Church (as these authors so forcefully argued), then it makes sense for their manuals to focus on those things that would enable the Protestant ministry to strengthen its weaknesses and thereby make progress in achieving its highest priorities.

ministries that were widely influential, especially among students. And the evidence suggests that the high view of the pastor's call, combined with the powerful examples of 'puritan' ministry, began to convince at least some of those preparing for a clerical career in the Church of England that their academic training had not adequately prepared them to be a good shepherd, at least by 'godly' standards. Many of these young men began to seek out respected ministers for counsel and advice.

As we have seen, Richard Greenham was an early magnet for concerned students.[21] Himself a student and then fellow of Pembroke Hall in Cambridge, he then accepted the call to serve as pastor in the village parish of Dry Drayton, about five miles west of the University. After commenting on the various strengths of Greenham's ministry, Samuel Clarke mentions that 'He was a special instrument and meanes under God to incourage and train up many godly and learned young men in the holy service of Christ, in the Work of the Ministry'.[22] Henry Holland, the compiler of Greenham's 'Graue Covnsels and Godlie Observations' states that 'he feared much the preposterous zeale and hastie running of young men into the Ministerie; because as iudgement, so also stayednesse, and moderation, vse, experience, grauity in ordering affections, and the hauing some masterie ouer corruption, was needfull in him that should teach others.' Greenham observed that, unlike the procedure of the early church where potential leaders underwent a long period of preparation before being given responsibility in the church, the present practise seemed to run to the opposite extreme: 'But now our education being bettered, they are too soone imployed. Too hastie a triall must not be made of mens giftes to their hurt that vse them, and that haue the vse of them.' Greenham's solution was that 'before we come to the complet function of the Ministerie, there should be some training vp by degrees in the schooles of the Prophets...it is good, first, to be of the children of the Prophets; then a Prophet, then a Pastor.'[23] Greenham therefore suggested that 'it were a happy nourcery for this church if every grounded pastor would train up both in lyfe, learning, doctrine, and discipline

---

[21] 'That we know so much of his parish ministry is due almost entirely to the household seminary which sprouted in Dry Drayton. It was the first of its kind and a truly significant innovation in clerical education, filling a crucial gap: the absence of any *practical* training for the ministry.' Parker and Carlson, *'Practical Divinity'*, 21. See also Carlson, '"Practical Divinity": Richard Greenham's Ministry', 180-181; John Primus, *Richard Greenham*.

[22] Samuel Clarke, *A General Martyrologie* (1677), 14. Clarke evidently got much of his material on Greenham from Henry Holland's letter 'To the Reader' preceding Greenham's *Works* (1598). Holland writes that Greenham was often asked to 'traine up some younger men to [the ministry], and communicate his experience with them' (sig A5). This indicates that he actively maintained relationships with many of the tutors in the University.

[23] Richard Greenham, *The Works of... Richard Greenham*, 3rd edition, Henry Holland, ed. (1601), 24.

some toward schollar to be his assistant in the ministry', and that after training
'he may commend him to the church government, and being happily discharged
of one, to draw some other out of the university, to be framed in like manner fit
for the work of the lord.'[24] Given his standing among the following generations
of 'godly' pastors, it is evident that Greenham practiced what he preached.

Clarke's account of Richard Blackerby's ministry more fully explores the
informal but intentional nature of this extracurricular 'puritan' education.
Converted while he was a student at Trinity College, Cambridge under the St
Andrew the Great preaching ministry of William Perkins, Blackerby (1574-
1648) left Cambridge intending to become a minister, but either was unable to
secure a living or was not yet ready to shoulder the burden. Instead, he lived for
two years 'with his Reverend Father-in-law, Minister of *Denham*, and from
thence was called to be Minister at *Feltwell* in *Norfolk*'.[25] Blackerby was soon
forced from his parish 'by reason of his Non-conformity', moving from
Feltwell to Ashdon, a village in Essex, where, further prevented from
undertaking a parish ministry, he instead hired a house and began to board
young men and prepare them for the university. Blackerby led this informal
academy for twenty-three years while also preaching weekly in neighboring
towns. Such was his reputation that 'Divers young Students (after they came
from the University) betook themselves to him to prepare them for the
Ministry, whom he taught the Hebrew Tongue, to whom he opened the
Scriptures, and read Divinity, and gave them excellent advice for Learning,
Doctrine and Life'. Clarke records that 'many eminent persons proceeded from
this *Gamaliel*'. Among Blackerby's disciples were 'Dr. *Bernard*, afterwards
Dean and Bishop in *Ireland*..., Mr. *Prosse*, Minister of two *Dutch*
Congregations, first in *Colchester*, then in *London*; Mr. *Stone*, afterwards
famous in *New England*; holy and learned Mr. *Fairclough*, and Mr. *Burrel*, and
many others.'[26]

'Holy and learned Mr. [Samuel] *Fairclough*' (1594-1677) sought out
Blackerby on the recommendation of 'his spiritual father, Mr. *Ward*'.[27]
Fairclough remained at Blackerby's house, drawing not only on Blackerby's
experience as a preacher, but finding his eldest daughter suitable for a wife as
well (and thereby following Blackerby's example in more ways than one).[28]

---

[24] Parker and Carlson, *'Practical Divinity'*, 230.

[25] Clarke, however, doesn't divulge whether Blackerby's real motivation was to get
further training or to get a bride. The ambiguity leads us to believe that he indeed
received both before he then moved to a cure of his own in Feltwell. Clarke, *The Lives
of Sundry Eminent Persons*, 58.

[26] Ibid., 58. For Nicolas Bernard (d. 1661), ordained by Archbishop Ussher in 1626 and
presented by him to the Deanery of Kilmore, see *DNB*. For Samuel Stone (1602-1663),
who emigrated to New England in 1633 with John Cotton and Thomas Hooker, see
DNB; Webster, *Godly Clergy*, 30-31.

[27] Clarke, *The Lives of Sundry Eminent Persons*, 159-160.

[28] Ibid., 161.

Indeed, in Fairclough, we see the cycle of puritan influence carried yet another generation further. Clarke observes that 'There are divers *Ministers* yet alive that will *acknowledge*, that unto some of them he [Fairclough] was the *sole founder*, and many others confess him their greatest Benefactor, as to the University maintenance.'[29]

Thomas Gataker (1574-1654) is another who sought to provide training for a circle of young men who were attracted by the example of his ministry. Evening meals at the Gataker table were evidently opportunities for discussions and 'lectures' in divinity based on a catechism that he published for the benefit of his parishioners. His parlor, says Clarke, had the reputation of being

> one of the best Schooles for a young Student to learn Divinity in; and indeed his house was a private Seminary for divers young Gentlemen of this Nation and for more Forreigners, who did resort to, and sojourn with him, to receive from him direction, and advancement in their studies, and many who afterwards were eminent in the Churches, both here and abroad, were brought up under his eye, at least, as *Paul* was at the feet of *Gamaliel.* [30]

Moreover, Clarke informs us of Gataker's habit of taking on assistants to help him in his ministry, who then went from under his wing to serve their own parishes.[31]

Perhaps the most striking example in Clarke's accounts of this supplemental education at work is the experience of Thomas Wilson (1601-1654?). In an episode that also demonstrates the informal network that existed between parish and university, Joseph Mead (1586-1638)[32], fellow of Christ's College in Cambridge who was also Wilson's tutor, received a letter from John Bristow, who was the minister at 'Chauswod' [Charlwood] in Surrey, requesting Mead to send him 'an able and Religious Scholar, to teach School in his House.'[33] Mead suggested that Wilson, who had just completed B.A., would be suitable for the position. And so the way was opened for Wilson to join Bristow's household, where 'he continued about four years, instructing the Youths

---

[29] Ibid., 179.

[30] Clarke, *A Collection of the Lives of Ten Eminent Divines* (1662), 145-46.

[31] Ibid., 146. Among those Clarke lists as having served as Gataker's assistants are 'Master *Young*, Master *Goodal*, Master *Symonds* (of whom yet in these latter times of Division, Mr. Gataker hath been heard to say, *It was pity that our Church had lost him,* intimating his turning aside to wayes of separation) Master *Grayle* and others who are yet living labourers in God's Vineyard.'

[32] After he was elected fellow in 1613, Joseph Mead was appointed to the Greek Lectureship founded by Sir Walter Mildmay. The master of Christ's College, Valentine Carey, prevented further advancement in spite of Mead's considerable reputation as a scholar because he 'looked too much towards Geneva.' *DNB*, vol. XIII, 178.

[33] Clarke, *The Lives of Sundry Eminent Persons*, 19.

committed to his charge with great diligence and faithfulness'. Though Wilson was officially employed as a teacher, under Bristow it became an intermediate position. Having observed Wilson's 'fitness, and Ability for a greater and higher employment than that of instructing Children, and taking notice that his Heart was set on the work of the Ministry', Bristow 'judged it not convenient to deprive the Church any longer of so able and worthy a Labourer'. Bristow thus 'advised Mr. *Wilson* wholly to betake himself to Preaching'.[34] After a short while preaching in the village church of Capel in Surrey, Bristow's influence on Wilson's behalf opened a further opportunity at Farlington in Hampshire.[35] Bristow may have brought Wilson into his household to serve as schoolmaster; but while under Bristow's supervision, it is clear that Wilson also developed both a heart and aptitude for ministry.

To summarize, the evidence from Clarke's gallery of 'puritan' exemplars suggests a considerable concern among the 'godly' to ensure that the rising generation of pastors receive the practical and spiritual preparation for pastoral ministry that the university curriculum did not provide.[36] Webster rightly states that '[t]he godly household integrated the young minister into godly society.'[37] But the godly household seminary did much more. In it a young man was able to observe from the inside the techniques of godly ministry, and he was given a safe place to practice those techniques until they were mastered. But even more importantly, he was able to observe and experience the day-to-day rhythms of godly spirituality in the contexts of family and parish, a much different reality than life in college. There were certainly connectional advantages to be obtained by becoming part of a godly clerical household, and the associational aspects of these seminaries are by far easier to trace. But I would suggest that it was the more intangible desire for spiritual growth and training that was the engine driving the proliferation of the household seminaries we find described by Clarke.

As yet there were no formal attempts to set up schools for young men aspiring to the ministry to replace what the universities provided, as happened following the Restoration Act of Uniformity (1662), which effectively barred nonconformists from the universities altogether.[38] And at no time were those

---

[34] Ibid., 19.

[35] Ibid, 19.

[36] In *Godly Clergy*, Webster cites the additional examples of 'household seminaries' led by Thomas Hooker (31-33) Samuel Wharton (33-34), Samuel Collins, John Rogers and Stephen Marshall (34).

[37] Ibid., 35.

[38] Nonconformist academies were built on the already established puritan pattern of household schools and seminaries, only now the purpose was not to prepare for a university education or to make up for its insufficiencies. It was instead the *only* education a Nonconformist minister in training would receive. H. McLachlan, *English Education Under the Test Acts: Being the History of the Nonconformist Academies 1662-1820* (Manchester: Manchester University Press, 1931).

labeled 'puritans' ever against the universities or the education they provided. While, as John Morgan observes, there were at various times 'godly' attempts to reform the undergraduate curriculum, the reform had to do with what academic subjects to emphasize *within* the system as opposed to *changing* the system.[39] Simply because they were also concerned about vocational training as well does not mean that the more committed Protestants lightly esteemed the academic preparation provided by the universities. On the contrary, grounding in the classical languages and literature, logic, rhetoric and philosophy was viewed as a necessary prerequisite to the 'puritan' pastoral task.[40] Even so, however necessary a university education was considered to be, the evidence suggests that among the 'godly' at least, something more was needed.

As we see even in our limited sample, there was no set pattern governing attempts to remedy this perceived need. Indeed, household seminaries were one a number of different ways various individuals attempted to make up for the lack.[41] This 'godly' reflex to supplement a future minister's education was a long-established commonplace when, late in his life, Richard Baxter undertook to publish his own advice to young men who were preparing for the ministry.

Richard Baxter's *Compassionate Counsel*

Some forty-three years after he himself was ordained into Church of England ministry, Richard Baxter published a hurriedly written piece hoping it would be of some use to young men as they pondered their future careers, his *Compassionate Counsel to All Young Men* (1681). Of particular concern to Baxter were those men who were hoping to become ministers. In a chapter entitled 'Additional counsel to Young men, who are bred up to Learning, and Publick work, especially to the Sacred Ministry in the Universities and Schools', Baxter begins to tap into the wealth of his own experience, giving his perspective on what makes an effective minister.[42] Although John Spurr states that at this time Restoration clergy 'were on the defensive', both from prevalent anti-clericalism and the decay of national piety, Baxter nowhere suggests that his 'counsel' is addressed to the national situation.[43] Instead his tone is pastoral

---

[39] Morgan, *Godly Learning*, 103.

[40] Twigg provides a helpful outline of the universities' curriculum during our period. See *The University of Cambridge and the English Revolution*, 207-10.

[41] Prophesyings, conferences and lectures also played an important role in the supplemental education of 'godly' clergy.

[42] Baxter, *Compassionate Counsel*, 108-59.

[43] Spurr, *The Restoration Church*, 225. Given the scrutiny he and his works were constantly under, it is unlikely that he would have endeavored even a veiled critique of Anglican ministry in this format. Moreover, the heated controversies generated by books such as John Eachard's *The Grounds and Occasions of the Contempt of the Clergy and Religion Enquired Into. In a Letter Written to R.L.* (1670) were by now a decade old. Furthermore, the ministry is not the only vocation or profession discussed by Baxter. It

and fatherly throughout. For Baxter, given that matters of eternal life and death were at stake, it was impossible to overestimate the importance of the '*Quality of the Clergy*', both 'to the Church and to mens salvation'. And 'of what importance the Quality of Scholars and Young Candidates, is to the soundness of the Clergy, I need not many words to make men of reason and experience know.'[44] Drawing attention first to those 'Impediments' to a worthy ministry, Baxter proceeds to dissect the failures of contemporary ministry. Of particular concern was the patronage system governing the placement of clergy within the Church of England, which he viewed as being both corrupt and corrupting.[45] But the greatest plague upon God's Church was the distressing number of clergy who were 'Hypocrites, Ungodly, Unexperienced, Proud, Worldly, Fleshly, Unskilful, unfaithful and Malignant Pastors'. Such were a curse 'to the Prince and States that have and follow such Counsellors, and to the Souls that are subverted by them.' It was in fact an alarmingly successful Satanic plot to corrupt the ministry 'by getting HIS SERVANTS INTO RULE and MINISTRY, TO DO HIS WORK AS FOR CHRIST, and his Church and by his authority and in his name.' Baxter took the contemporary church to task with biting sarcasm. He granted that 'Our natural enmity with the Serpent disswadeth him from speaking or sending to us in his own name. Should one say in the pulpit *[Thus saith the Devil, hate Christs servants; silence his Ministers, call serious Godliness Hypocrisie,]* I should not much fear his success with any.' But there was biblical precedent to expect a more diabolical route of attack: for 'if he be a lying Spirit in the mouth of *Ahabs* Prophets, and can get a Prophet to smite *Michaiah* for pretending to more of the Spirit than he had; or if he can get men in the Sacred Office to say (thus saith the *Lord)* when they speak for sin or against the Lord, this is the Devils prosperous way.'[46]

In contrast, Baxter sets out 'what Blessings...*Able and Faithful Ministers* are.'[47] The glory of a pastor's ministry is his leading role in God's evangelistic agenda: 'Christ maketh them the cheif [sic] instruments for the propagating of his Truth and Kingdom in the World, for the gathering of Churches, and preserving and defending contradicted Truth.'[48] A minister's true status is thus derived from the exalted nature of the gospel with which he is entrusted. Therefore, aligning one's motives with God's revealed agenda is the foundational task of those who undertake to be pastors. For the pastor who

---

seems most likely that Baxter intended his work as practical advice for young men making decisions about their future direction, perhaps in response to correspondence requesting his guidance. For John Eachard (1636-97), Master of Catherine Hall, Cambridge, see Spurr, *The Restoration Church*, 220-23; *DNB*.

[44] Baxter, *Compassionate Counsel*, 110.

[45] Ibid., 115-21.

[46] Ibid., 129, 132-33.

[47] Ibid., 133.

[48] Ibid., 133.

serves out of lesser motives occupies his position under false pretences and cannot be anything but a false shepherd.

Having thus set the context, Baxter proceeds to give his counsel. There are three qualifications that are absolutely essential for the young man who hopes to become a pastor. First, he must be intelligent. Secondly, he must be able to communicate effectively. Thirdly, he must be converted.[49] A deficiency in any of these areas should cause one to steer clear of the ministry as a vocation. But Baxter is particularly concerned to warn away those whose lives reflect an unconverted heart, for 'if your unfitness be not in your *disability* but in your *ungodliness*, whether you be Ministers or not, you will be for ever miserable unless you consider well the great things that should change your Hearts and Lives, and turn unfeignedly to God: and when that is done, I am no discourager of you.' For Baxter, 'it is far better to be a Cobler, or Chimney sweeper, or to beg your bread, than to be an *ungodly Clergy man*, with greatest preferments, riches and applause.'[50]

For those who set themselves to prepare for the ministry, Baxter's counsel runs the spectrum from warnings on morals (*'abhor sloth and idleness'*, *'Fear and fly from sensuality, and Fleshly lusts'*, *'Watch with great fear against Pride, Ambition and Worldly ends, in your hearts and lives'*),[51] advice on the choice of friends ('Be sure to make *a prudent choice of your Companions, especially of your bosom Friends.'*),[52] to practical suggestions on what and how to study.[53] But of most interest to this study is Baxter's final word of advice:

> Lastly, I advise you, *that you begin not the exercise of your Ministry too boldly, in publick, great or judicious Auditories....* But (if you can) at first *settle a competent time in the house with some ancient experienced Pastor, that hath some small Country Chappel that needs your help.* And 1. There you may *Learn* as well as *Teach*, and learn by his practice what you must practice.... 2. By Preaching some years to a small ignorant people where you fear not critical judgements, you will get boldness of speech, and freedom

---

[49] Ibid., 143-44.

[50] Ibid., 146.

[51] Ibid., 147-53.

[52] Ibid., 150.

[53] *'Begin then with your Catechism and practical Divinity, to settle your own Souls in a safe condition for Life or Death.* And deal not so foolishly as to wast many years in inferior Arts and Sciences before you have studied how to please God and to be saved. I unfeignedly thank God that by sickness and his Grace, he called me early to learn how to Die, and therefore to Learn what I must be and how to live, and thereby drew me to study the Sacred Scriptures, and abundance of practical spiritual English Books, till I had somewhat setled the resolution, and the peace of my own Soul, before I had gone farre in humane Learning: and then I found more leisure and more capacity to take in subservient knowledge it its proper time and place.' Ibid., 155-56.

of utterance, with out that servile Study of words, and learning your written notes without Book, which will be *tiresome, time-wasting* and *lifeless*. And when freedom and use hath brought you to a habit of ready speaking of the great and necessary things, and acquaintance with ignorant Countrey people hath taught you to under-stand their case, you will have a better preparation for more publick places (when you are clearly called to them) than you were even like to get either in Universities, among Schollars, or in great mens Houses.[54]

As we shall see, Richard Baxter knew whereof he spoke.

A Seminary for Reformed Pastors

England's Civil Wars cut short Richard Baxter's initial and tumultuous preaching ministry as lecturer in the town of Kidderminster. When Baxter returned in 1647 to resume his duties, the earlier sequestration of the vicar George Dance thrust Baxter into the role of *de facto* pastor.[55] Baxter undertook his responsibilities with a perspective refined by the experience of five years of uncertainty, war, and awareness of his own mortality. Though these years are documented only by his reminiscences, it is clear that much occurred that was never recorded which nevertheless had a substantial impact on his subsequent pastoral ministry. We do know that he was able to interact with a large number of his puritan colleagues while in Coventry.[56] We know that he continued to be an active preacher, preaching weekly at the Governor's invitation to soldiers garrisoned in Coventry and once on Sundays 'to the people'.[57] His army chaplaincy bears witness to a growing drive to take a leadership role in resolving controverted issues, motivated by a pastor's concern that the New Model flock be rescued from error and rightly fed and led.[58] And we know that his subsequent Kidderminster ministry was prosecuted with such deliberateness

---

[54] Ibid., 157-58.

[55] Baxter understood himself to be returning in the same capacity as he had left, as a lecturer and as curate to St Mary's Vicar Dance. The parishioners, however, had secured the sequestration of Dance and offered Baxter his position as Vicar. Baxter refused, scrupling over the questionable legality of the sequestration process. A compromise was reached, and Baxter returned to what he thought was his former position. The parishioners, however, secured Baxter's official appointment to the living without Baxter knowing it for several more years. Nuttall, *Richard Baxter*, 40-41.

[56] See *Rel. Bax.*, I, i, §§61 & 63, 43-44.

[57] Ibid., I, i, §61, 43.

[58] Baxter was in fact aghast at how far the leaders and members of the New Model Army had drifted into the errors of the separatists and Anabaptists and the extremes of Antinomianism. *See Rel. Bax.*, I, i, §§73 & 77, 50-51, 53-54; Cooper, *Fear and Polemic*, 87-121.

and enjoyed such success that he quickly began to attract national attention. The evidence that remains does not allow one to say with certainty if Baxter returned to Kidderminster with a preconceived pastoral strategy which he then proceeded to implement, or if, as seeming more likely, the elements of his strategy came into focus shortly after his arrival once the nature of his ministry there and the reality of the situation there became clear. What is clear, however, is that although no early blueprint remains, shortly after his return Baxter was armed with a clear sense of what his pastoral goals were, of what steps he needed to take to get there, and an awareness of the unprecedented new religious and political reality, produced by the war's outcome, that gave him the relative freedom to make it so.[59]

Though Baxter later candidly acknowledged the shortcomings of the 'puritan' overemphasis on preaching and would soon begin to implement supplemental means to accomplish his evangelistic agenda for St Mary's parish, his initial success and reputation came as a result of his preaching ministry.[60] Baxter's effectiveness in the pulpit provided the platform from which to launch his further initiatives. And it was the renown generated by his preaching ministry that gave him the standing that allowed him to mobilize the area ministers into what became the Worcestershire Association. And as the people of Kidderminster began to respond to Baxter's preaching, he could then feed their response by providing practical ways to apply the implications of biblical truth.

It was in this context of his growing stature as a preacher as well as the implementation of an aggressively evangelistic pastoral strategy that opportunities began to arise for Baxter to interact with a growing circle of boys and young men who evidenced both academic and spiritual promise, making them in Baxter's eyes, potential candidates for future pastoral ministry. Within Kidderminster itself, Baxter found many young people responding eagerly to his evangelistic efforts from the pulpit: 'Many Children did God work upon at 14, or 15, or 16 years of Age: And this did marvelously reconcile the Minds of the Parents and Elder sort to Godliness.'[61] Baxter would have been aware of the scope of this response because of his intentional efforts to meet yearly with every family through his scheme of pastoral oversight. Moreover, Baxter's resulting awareness of the personal circumstances of most of the individuals and families in his parish provided him with many opportunities to provide not just pastoral counsel but financial help, which came from his own salary and,

---

[59] This is based on my reading of Baxter's later recollections in his *Rel. Bax.*, his 'Dedication' to *Gildas Salvianus*, and from Baxter's correspondence with other pastors such as Thomas Wadsworth (see, for example, *Calendar*, nos 287, 290 and 293).

[60] See Baxter, *Gildas Salvianus*, 78. Earlier overviews of Baxter's preaching fail to acknowledge Baxter's concerns over the effectiveness and sufficiency of preaching. See chapter 7.

[61] *Rel. Bax.*, 1, i, §137 (18), 89.

later, from the profits from his books.[62] But from his earliest days back in Kidderminster, he also took an active role in creating opportunities for young men to further their education, especially those who otherwise had neither the means or the connections that made a university education possible:

> I took the aptest of their Children from the School, and set divers of them to the Universities; where for 8*l.* a year, or 10*l.* at most, by the help of my Friends there I maintained them. Mr. *Vines* [Master of Pembroke Hall] and Dr. *Hill* [Master of Trinity College] did help me to Sizars places for them at *Cambridge*: And the Lady *Rous* allowed me 8*l.* a year awhile towards their Maintenance, and Mr. and Col. *Bridges* also assisted me. Some of them are honest able Ministers, now cast out with their Brethren: But two or three, having no other way to live, turned great Conformists, and are Preachers now.[63]

This interest in and provision for the young men in his parish in the hopes of their future readiness for the ministry was a direct result of his own evangelistic mindset and followed naturally from his preaching and systematic oversight. However, Baxter's efforts to train future ministers were undertaken in uncharacteristic silence, at least with respect to material he published. But even if he was not concerned to bring public attention to his work among young men, the evidence suggests a tremendous amount of intentional effort on his part, hidden from public view, that went into preparing a new generation for pastoral ministry.[64]

Baxter's concern to prepare men for the ministry was not limited to his work among the boys of his parish or to his helping promising teenagers attend the university. Baxter regularly took university graduates on as his assistants, who then usually lived with him in his home and helped him in the various aspects

---

[62] 'Another help to my Success, was that small relief which my low Estate enable me to afford the Poor: though the Place was reckoned at near 200*l. per Annum*, there came but 90*l.* and sometimes 80*l. per Annum* to me: Besides which, some years I had 60*l.* or 80*l.* a year of the Booksellers for my Books: which little dispersed among them, much reconciled them to the Doctrine which I taught'. *Rel. Bax.*, I, i, §137 (13), 89.

[63] Ibid., I, i, §137 (13), 89. Those young men from Kidderminster known to have received this help from Baxter include Joseph Read, (possibly) Edward Boucher, Simon Potter and Thomas Doolittle. See Powicke, *A Life of the Reverend Richard Baxter*, 154-56.

[64] See Baxter's participation in Matthew Poole's scheme to raise funds for the support of godly students preparing for the ministry at the universities, evidenced by his commendatory epistle in Poole's *Model for the Maintaining of Students* (1658), as well as his extensive correspondence with Poole about the scheme (among other issues). See Poole's letters to Baxter in *Calendar*, nos 393, 410, 425, 434, 476, 485, 551, & 565. Unfortunately, Baxter's letters to Poole commenting on the scheme have not survived.

of his ministry for a year or so until they were ready for a pastoral charge of their own. Richard Sargent (1621-1696) was Baxter's first assistant upon his return to Kidderminster.[65] With a characteristic lack of tact, Baxter describes him as being 'Very honest, but of no extraordinary Learning, and of no taking utterance'.[66] Nevertheless, Baxter saw potential. Rather than dismiss Sargent, Baxter undertook to train him. Initially, he writes, Sargent 'was always present while I did my work; and he helped me in hearing them repeat the words [catechisms], and then sat by while I discoursed with them: by which means he quickly perceived the way that I took'.[67] Helped by this personal nurture, Baxter writes that Sargent 'so increased in Ability, that he became a solid Preacher, and of so great Prudence in Practical Cases, that I know few therein go beyond him: but none at all do I know that excelleth him in Meekness, Humility, Self-denial and Diligence.'[68] Baxter eventually gave Sargent the responsibility of traveling from house to house in the parish to catechize those who were unable to come to Baxter's house in town.[69] When the living at Stone (not far from Kidderminster) became available, Sargent was chosen as vicar. And though no direct evidence exists, we can surmise that Baxter had a hand in his placement.

Humphrey Waldron, who graduated B.A. from Balliol, Oxford in 1654, succeeded Sargent as Baxter's assistant. Baxter comments that he was much like Sargent in character, and was soon able to continue the work that Sargent had done.[70] Within a year, Waldron, too, was chosen to fill a vacant living, this one at Broom.[71]

Baxter made use of his Cambridge connections to find a graduate who would assist him by being Master of the Kidderminster school. When queried by Baxter in the early summer of 1649 if he knew of any among his students that he could recommend as schoolmaster in Kidderminster, Richard Vines at Pembroke eventually sent him Thomas Baldwin.[72] Baldwin (1628?-1693) lived with Baxter and, in addition to teaching school, learned Baxter's version of shorthand and transcribed the sermon notes that were eventually published as *A treatise of conversion* (1657).[73] In 1654, Baldwin was chosen to become pastor

---

[65] Richard Sargent (or Sargeant) studied at Pembroke in Oxford and preached at St Mary's, Kidderminster, in Baxter's absence during the Civil War. He was therefore not altogether inexperienced when Baxter returned. Nonetheless, he evidently readily submitted to Baxter's leadership and the opportunity to serve as his assistant. *CR*, 433.
[66] Baxter, *Rel. Bax.*, I. i, §137 (11), 88.
[67] DWL, BxL 3:188. Also quoted by Nuttall, *Richard Baxter*, 62.
[68] *Rel. Bax.*, I, i, §137 (11), 88.
[69] Ibid., I, i, §137 (11), 88.
[70] Ibid., I, i, §137 (11), 88.
[71] *CR*, 506.
[72] *Calendar*, nos 15, 64.
[73] *Rel. Bax.*, I. i, §173, 114; III, i, §202 (22), 92. *CR*, 25.

at nearby Wolverley.[74]

Joseph Read (1635?-1712), who had grown up in Kidderminster and been sent by Baxter to Trinity College in Cambridge, returned in 1657 to be Baxter's assistant. Rather than living with his family, Read lived in Baxter's house where he benefited from Baxter's supervision for a year until he was called to become the pastor at Witley.[75] Another of Baxter's Trinity students and a friend of Read's, Simon Potter (b. 1633), apparently benefited from Baxter's Worcestershire Association network by being called to serve as pastor at Wolverley in 1656 (where he succeeded Thomas Baldwin). It is not known whether he also spent any postgraduate time under Baxter's direct tutelage.[76] Another young man from Kidderminster whom Baxter mentions with great respect, Edward Boucher, was appointed to be pastor at nearby Churchill. But unlike the others, no record remains either of his being sent by Baxter to the university or of his assisting Baxter in his ministry.[77]

Richard Baxter did not at the beginning of his Kidderminster ministry set out to form a 'seminary' in the modern sense or even in the sense that Samuel Clarke uses when describing Thomas Gataker's household. But because of the number of young Kidderminster men who responded to his preaching, because of his desire to provide educational opportunities for those who might make good pastors, because of his network of connections at Cambridge and Oxford, because of the success of his Kidderminster ministry and his growing reputation as preacher and pastor, and because of his need for help, a growing number of young men learning from, living with and working alongside him were thereby trained to undertake pastoral ministries that reflected his pastoral priorities.[78] Baxter never refers to his ministry with these young men as being a 'seminary for reformed pastors', but that was its effect.

With the exception of Simon Potter's 1660 letter to Baxter and Joseph Read's preface to Baxter's posthumously published *Universal Redemption* (1694),

---

[74] *CR*, 25. In 1656, Baldwin was appointed vicar of Chaddesley Corbett, where he served until he was forced out in 1660. He settled in Kidderminster and was licensed to preach there in 1672. He preached as opportunity allowed there until his death in 1693.

[75] *CR*, 406. Read also transcribed several of Baxter's Worcestershire Association lectures, which were published posthumously as *Universal Redemption* (1694); see sig A3v.

[76] *CR*, 396. John Arrowsmith, who succeeded Thomas Hill as Master of Trinity College, mentions both Read and Potter in a letter to Baxter dated 18 January 1656, in which he discusses their progress and hopes for future preferment. DWL BxL iii. 173. See *Calendar*, no. 289. See also Potter's Latin and Greek letter to Baxter, written in September 1660. DWL, BxL, iv. 151; *Calendar*, no. 654.

[77] *Rel. Bax.*, I. iii, §92; *CR*, 66; Powicke, *A Life of the Reverend Richard Baxter*, 154.

[78] Each of the young men whom Baxter helped to place in the Worcestershire area joined Baxter as ministers of the 'Worcestershire Association', submitting under its discipline and adopting its priorities. See Nuttall, 'The Worcestershire Association: its Membership', 197-206.

there is little direct contemporary evidence that might shed light on the nature of his relationships with these young men or give us more than circumstantial evidence concerning his hopes for their future effectiveness as pastors. The one exception is found in his relationship with Thomas Doolittle. Though as we shall see, Doolittle's experience was different from those young men who came to live with Baxter following their university education, the evidence that survives reveals Baxter's profound influence on Doolittle's ministerial formation and provides insight into the mentoring relationships that often supplemented a 'godly' young man's preparation for ministry.[79]

'My Son and fellow-servant in the work'

Most likely, Thomas Doolittle was born in Kidderminster, Worcestershire, and baptized on 12 September 1633, the son of Humphrey Doolittle and his wife Anne.[80] Doolittle's family was active in the affairs of St Mary's parish, and was evidently part of a larger extended family of Doolittles influential in the church.[81] Nathaniel Brokesby oversaw Doolittle's early education at the

---

[79]Ironically, Doolittle is the only one of Baxter's Kidderminster circle (of whom we are aware, save Simon Potter) who did *not* spend some time in an intermediate position (whether with Baxter or elsewhere) before proceeding to a cure, although Baxter had made arrangements for such a position for Doolittle. Of this more anon.

[80] Alexander Gordon, in his article on Doolittle in the *DNB*, states that Thomas Doolittle was born in Kidderminster in 1632, the son of Anthony Doolittle, a glover. While I am hesitant to contradict Gordon, there is no evidence for this 1632 birth date in the St Mary's Kidderminster parish register. See *CR*, 167-168; see also *DNB*. However, in his funeral sermon for Doolittle, Daniel Williams gives Doolittle's age at the time of his death as 77, which would make the year of his birth 1630. Daniel Williams, *Christian Sincerity*, sig B8. 'The source of the error is that another Thomas, son of William and Jane Doolittle, was baptised at Kidderminster on 20 October 1630.' (*DNB*, 1142). See the Parish Register, St Mary's Church, Kidderminster, Hereford and Worcestershire Records Office. For an exhaustive discussion of the complexities involved in determining Doolittle's birthdate and family, see J. William Black, 'Thomas Doolittle', in *ODNB*. The subsequent biographical information follows the same article.

[81]Humphrey Doolittle is one of eleven Doolittles whose names are among the 265 affixed to 1647 letter from the parish to Baxter inviting him to return and become 'our Minister', '[o]ur place being now vacant' by the recent sequestration of George Dance. DWL, BxL, i. 213; *Calendar*, no. 9. Another Thomas Doolittle, an uncle or grandfather perhaps, played a leading role in parish affairs and was one of the eleven parish members who signed the second letter sent from the parish in March of 1641 making the original attempt to secure Baxter's services for the parish. See DWL, BxL, iii, 111; *Calendar*, no. 4. However, in their reference to Thomas Doolittle in no. 651 (July 1660), Keeble and Nuttall confuse the elder Thomas Doolittle, who remained in Kidderminster and who is one of the signatories of Letter 651, with the younger Thomas Doolittle, whom we shall see was still rector at St Alphage in London at this time. Also note 5 of no. 238 (20 April 1655) which numbers 'Thomas Doelittle' as one of Baxter's

Kidderminster grammar school, which met in a converted chapel of St Mary's Church.[82] Upon his return to Kidderminster, Baxter would have known Doolittle, both because of the Doolittle family's prominence in the parish and also from Doolittle's work as a student in the local school, since Baxter was keen to encourage students of ability. But it was Baxter's preaching that initially caught the teenager's attention and provided the context for the decisive event in Doolittle's life. Jeremiah Smith states in his 1723 'Memoirs' that while he was a student in Kidderminster, Doolittle 'heard Mr. Baxter preach those sermons, which were afterwards printed in his book of *the saints rest*: some of which discourses were blessed of God to his saving conversion, which was the grounds of that peculiar esteem and affection which he would often express for that holy man, as whom God had made his spiritual father.'[83]

There was evidently some early conflict in Doolittle's mind as to what vocation to undertake. At the encouragement of 'Some of his friends', Doolittle was 'put upon trial to an attorney in the country, with whom he did not long stay'. Ordered to 'copy some writings' on a Sunday, Doolittle 'obeyed his master with great reluctance'. His conscience smarting, Doolittle promptly returned home the next day. According to Smith, this event galvanized within him a sense of call to the ministry, for he subsequently 'could no more think of returning to his place, or of applying himself to anything else as the business of his life, but serving Christ in the work of the Gospel.'[84]

Baxter's intervention at this point in Doolittle's life proved critical. Seeing his academic potential, he encouraged Doolittle to attend university and gave the money enabling him to do so. Making use of his connections, Baxter arranged for Doolittle to attend Pembroke Hall in Cambridge, whose master was Baxter's friend Richard Vines. Admitted June 7, 1649 as a sizar, Doolittle attained B.A. in 1652/3, and M.A. in 1656.[85]

One letter survives from these university years from Doolittle to Baxter. Written on 12 November 1652 at the end of his undergraduate studies, Doolittle's letter is significant in that it presupposes an earlier and extensive

---

Kidderminster assistants attending meetings of the Worcestershire Association is mistaken. Doolittle was elected rector of St Alphage in 1653, proceeding there directly from Cambridge. There is no evidence that Doolittle ever served as one of Baxter's Kidderminster assistants.

[82] See C.D. Gilbert, *A History of King Charles I Grammar School Kidderminster* (Kidderminster, UK: Kenneth Tomkinson, Ltd, 1980), 5-7, 31-35, 51-58, 64-65; Gilbert, 'Richard Baxter and Nathaniel Brokesby', in *BNS*, 5:2 (1997), 3-7.

[83] Jeremiah Smith, 'Some Memoirs of the Author's Live and Character' prefacing Thomas Doolittle's posthumously published *Complete Body of Practical Divinity: Being a New Improvement of the Assembly's Catechism* (1723), sig a1.

[84] Smith, 'Memoirs', in Doolittle's *Complete Body*, sig a1.

[85] Smith, 'Memoirs', sig a1; see also Venn, 215. We can assume that Baxter's relationship with Richard Vines, Master of Pembroke Hall, was instrumental in securing a place for Doolittle there. *Rel. Bax.*, I, i, 89, §137 (13). For Vines, see *DNB*.

correspondence. But it also demonstrates that Baxter involved not only with Doolittle's maintenance, but as a mentor as well. Doolittle writes:

> Lo: sir
> I received your last 2° by Dr Hills servants; I would now willingly understand your pleasure concerning my Batchlors degree, the time draws very neere, and hastens apace, I send yours sooner for I was afraide your letter like an *individuum vagum* may wander long before it come into my hands, & so might bee too late before you could acquainte mee concerning it.[86]

Doolittle desired to continue his studies towards a Master of Arts, but was concerned about the expense and what his patron might think of his staying on.[87] But Baxter was more than just a lifeline of financial support for Doolittle at Cambridge; he was a father figure as well, serving as a kind of confessor, as Doolittle's long confession of his shortcomings at the letter's conclusion indicates.[88]

After completing B.A. in Cambridge, Doolittle began looking for a pastoral position and was given the opportunity to preach a series of trial sermons in London. On 14 August 1653, the St Alphage parish account book records that Doolittle was paid 1 pound, 6 shillings and 8 pence 'for preachinge fouer tymes' before the congregation of St Alphage, London Wall, a parish within London's 6th Classis which was then without a minister.[89] On 13 September 1653, the St Alphage vestry chose Doolittle 'by a generall consent' to become their minister.[90] Meanwhile, Baxter had utilized his own network to secure Doolittle a chaplaincy 'with an ample salary'.[91] However, Baxter's letter notifying Doolittle of the opportunity arrived after he had already committed himself to serve as minister over St Alphage parish in London. Doolittle received Presbyterian ordination and began his ministry later that Autumn, his signature, 'Thomas Doelittle Minister', first appearing in the vestry minutes on 1 November 1653.[92]

Doolittle's early success in ministry was also the occasion of an episode of anxiety and depression. Writing Baxter on 3 June 1654 from 'Alphage', Doolittle unburdens his heart:

---

[86]DWL, BxL, vi. 128. The 'Dr. Hill' to which Doolittle refers is Thomas Hill, master of Trinity College, another of Baxter's Cambridge friends. For Hill, see *DNB*.

[87]DWL, BxL, vi. 128. Also *Calendar*, no. 101.

[88]DWL, BxL, vi. 128. Doolittle concludes his letter to Baxter, '[your] (hard: hearted) friend Tho. Doelittle'.

[89] LGL, MS 1432/4, unp.

[90] LGL, MS 1431/2, fol. 230.

[91] Thomas Doolittle, *The Lord's Last-Sufferings* (1681), sig C3v.

[92] LGL, MS 1431/2, fol. 231.

I must acknowledge [my gratitude] But specially for the care you
have of my soule... Yet upon serious search of my own heart & by
a due watchfulness over my soule I find a more tendency in me to
sit down in despondency at the sight of the smallest of my parts and
graces to carry on and goe through my worke that some times I am
thinking to preach noe more, because of the sight of my great
Ignorance. They may see my best but you cannot know my worst.
They may see wt I have but I see more what I want.[93]

The source of Doolittle's internal conflict with pride becomes apparent as he
gives Baxter an account of his preaching and of the extraordinary response his
ministry has met with:

I did much delight in Preaching to men.... god hath done it...that I
have many...weeping and bemoaning in my congregation that now
I doe apply my selfe frequently to them.... I can see many weeping
eyes and I hope here ie many bleeding hearts in my congregation....
I am now & have beene about 10 weeks in answering O joyful
Question. what things I must doe to be saved...[94]

Even at this beginning stage of his ministry in London, Doolittle recognized
that Baxter had played a formative role in his life. He ends this letter with this
benediction: 'I bless god for You & I hope this will encourage you to do the
like for others you have done for me & god grant that your Labour of love
might not go without this reward that you might obtain the ends you aim at in
wt you doe.'[95]

The few surviving letters between the two represent only a fraction of the
total that were exchanged. The first surviving letter from Baxter to Doolittle
again assumes a continuing conversation between the two, and is in response to
a previous letter from Doolittle (not extant) containing questions about Baxter's
stance on universal redemption. On 6 March 1657, Baxter writes: 'Sir I thanke
you for your pains &c. As to your Questions I suppose you expect me to
answer'.[96] After dealing with Doolittle's objections to his views, Baxter
concludes this theological seminar on parchment with these hurried comments:
'And thus I have briefly, but I conceive sufficiently, answered your Arguments;
with enough in hast from   Your Brother   Ri: Baxter'.[97]

Doolittle penned his response to Baxter on 9 May 1657. And though he picks

---

[93]DWL, BxL, vi. 28. *Calendar*, no. 185.
[94]DWL, BxL, vi. 28.
[95]DWL, BxL, vi. 28.
[96]DWL, BxL, i. 121; *Calendar*, no. 363.
[97]DWL, BxL, i. 121.

up the discussion on universal redemption, his concerns are far deeper than simply furthering a theological disputation. Once again, he turns to Baxter for counsel, revealing that his struggles with depression and pride continue unabated:

> I hope, sir, I have still a share in your prayers at the throne of grace, that I who have beene soe much cared for by you shall not be turned out of your prayers. Especially still that god would keepe mee from pride & despondency, to both wch I have temtation at severable times... But God hath given mee abundant encouragement in my work, by giving mee roome in the hearts & affections of the people. to wm he hath sent me & others in the city... Oh yt this might bee the end of my living to love god & to win & build up soules, that I may not make sure only of my own salvation, but alsoe may get as many to heaven along with me as I can...[98]

Baxter's response, still extant, comes a little more than a month later. Answering Doolittle's questions and arguments against his position on universal redemption was obviously the central issue on Baxter's mind, as his letter to Doolittle is wholly taken up with a detailed theological argument. Even though he is a very busy man (writing 'in great hast & *[er]go* curt & imperfect'), he still finds the time to respond promptly to Doolittle's questions.[99]

Several later letters indicate the respect Baxter had for Doolittle and for his abilities as a pastor. On 25 August 1658, Baxter responded to a letter from the London teenager George Maynard asking for help to know how he might be assured of his conversion, and for advice on someone Baxter could refer him to for further counsel.[100] Baxter's letter gives Maynard the practical counsel he was seeking, prescribing eight steps to follow to ensure a sound conversion.[101] In the last of these directions, Baxter urges Maynard 'to choose some godly able Minister, & in every doubt have recourse to him, & open your case to

---

[98] DWL, BxL, i. 125; *Calendar*, no. 372. Doolittle concludes this wide-ranging letter with a request of his mentor, one that Baxter was to receive from others who valued his perspective: 'I remember in one of your letters you told me you had a catalogue lying by you of good authors, wch if it bee not to troublesome to have them written forth (by any) I wish I had. Because I intend to furnish my self more...' DWL, BxL, i. 125. Baxter did eventually respond to Doolittle's (and other's) request by publishing in *A Christian Directory* (1673) the astonishing list of books which he introduces by saying to those desiring to be students of divinity, 'I will name you the Poorest library that is tolerable...' (922-928).

[99] DWL, BxL, i. 123; *Calendar*, no. 382.

[100] For Maynard's letter, see DWL, BxL, iv. 263; *Calendar*, no. 474.

[101] DWL, BxL, iv. 264; *Calendar*, no. 488.

him'. He encourages Maynard to approach his parish minister, 'if he be godly'.
But 'If your owne be unfitt or unwilling goe to old Mr. Cross in ffryday street
neere you, or to young Mr. Doelittle at Alphage Parish not farr from you, &
either shew them this letter or tell them it is my desire that they would be your
Directours, & I dare warrent you they will do it to your advantage.'[102]

The following year, Baxter received another letter from Francis Youell,
'apprentice to a Stationer living on Snow Hill [London]', who, having recently
been persuaded against his prior interest in the Quakers after reading Baxter's
Sheet against the Quakers (1657), wanted Baxter's recommendation as to
which London church he might attend.[103] In his response, Baxter suggests that
Youell look for a church that is led by a pastor 'in a scripture way, by officers,
in concord with other Churches, & not in a way of separation & division'.[104] To
that end, Baxter points Youell to the ministries of 'Mr. Thomas Doelittle, Mr.
Poole, Mr. Crosse, [and] Mr. Ash or any godly able minister that you have at
hand'.[105]

Baxter's approval of Doolittle and his ministry in these private
recommendations is high praise indeed, coming from a man at the height of his
own celebrated ministry in Kidderminster. Reflecting later in his *Reliquiae* on
his relationship with Doolittle, Baxter gives his unstinting approval of him and
his pulpit abilities directly and in terms that perhaps display his own quiet
satisfaction: 'Mr. *Thomas Doolittle*, born in *Kidderminster* is a good Schollar, a
godly man, of an upright Life, and moderate Principles, and a very profitable,
serious Preacher.'[106]

But it is later, in two published letters, that the full extent of Baxter's
involvement with Doolittle, and the impression it made on him as a young man,
becomes clear. The first passage, though brief, not only gives insight as to
Baxter's perspective on his relationship with Doolittle, but it also humanizes
the process whereby vision for pastoral ministry was transferred to the rising
generation. In his 'Epistle to the Reader' prefacing Doolittle's *The Protestants
Answer* (1678), Baxter writes, 'And I may say, that this short discourse of Mr.
Thomas Dolittle (*My Son and fellow-servant in the work and patience of the
Gospel*) *hath performed much*, and will not fail the Readers sober
expectation....'[107] By using this Biblical term of endearment, Baxter

---

[102] DWL, BxL, iv. 264; *Calendar*, no. 488. Baxter signs his letter, 'A desirer of your
soules everlastinge Happiness. Rich: Baxter'.

[103] DWL, BxL, iv. 229; *Calendar*, no. 587.

[104] DWL, BxL, iv. 231; *Calendar*, no. 590.

[105] DWL, BxL, iv. 231; *Calendar*, no. 590.

[106] *Rel. Bax.*, III, §205 (8), 95. Doolittle is here described by Baxter as one of those 'few
who by Preaching more openly than the rest, and to greater Numbers, are under more
Men's displeasure and censure'.

[107] Baxter, 'Epistle to the Reader' prefacing Thomas Doolittle's *The Protestants Answer
to that Question, Where was your Church before Luther? Wherein Popery is proved a
Novelty: and That the Protestant Doctrine was not only before Luther, but the same that*

intentionally evokes the relationship that existed between the Apostle Paul and his associate Timothy.[108] In doing so, Baxter intimates that there is a good deal more to his relationship with Doolittle than simply financial sponsorship to the university. With these words he acknowledges his instrumentality in Doolittle's spiritual rebirth, but he also recalls the pivotal role he played in Doolittle's spiritual maturation and preparation for ministry.

That Doolittle felt a resulting debt of gratitude towards Baxter has been seen already in Doolittle's private correspondence with him. But in 1681, Doolittle made that debt public by publishing an *'Epistola Dedicatoria'* to Richard Baxter as the preface to *The Lord's Last-Sufferings Shewed in the Lords Supper*. Doolittle focuses the final pages of this discourse on his relationship with Baxter. He first credits Baxter with being his spiritual father, the human means used by God to draw him to Christ. Doolittle then acknowledges that it was Baxter who 'transferred me from ordinary school to the academy of Cambridge and took care to add me to the studious men of Pembroke Hall.' He recalls that while he was at Pembroke, Baxter 'saw fit to send letters distinguished by marks of love and filled with advice about the method of study and to supply help in many ways'. And here is where we learn that Baxter used his connections to secure for Doolittle a chaplain's living 'with an ample salary' at the completion of his studies at Cambridge. Though as we have seen, Baxter's letter informing Doolittle arrived too late, Doolittle was obviously grateful for Baxter's initiative on his behalf. He then mentions his gratitude for three of Baxter's works of particular significance to him: *The Saints Everlasting Rest* (1650), *Catholick Theology* (1675), and *Methodus christianae theologiae* (1681). Indeed, so influential had Baxter been in his life, says Doolittle, that his own writings could almost be considered an extension of Baxter's work, and could, in fact, even call Baxter their 'grandfather', though he modestly adds that he did not presume to put his works on the same level as Baxter's.[109]

Thomas Doolittle was converted under Baxter's preaching. His initial Christian experience was under Baxter's pastoral care. Through Baxter's encouragement, he determined to prepare for the ministry. With Baxter's help, he was given the opportunity to attend university, and proceeded to M.A. at Pembroke Hall in Cambridge. With Baxter as confessor and casuist, he navigated the trials of faith and insecurity induced by the transition to

---

was taught by Christ and His Apostles (1678), sig A4v; *Calendar*, no. 1021.

[108] See I Timothy 1:2; II Timothy 1:2; Philippians 1:1; see also I Peter 5:13 for Peter's description of John Mark in similar terms and Philemon 10 where Paul refers to the runaway slave Onesimus as 'my son'.

[109] Doolittle, *The Lord's Last-Sufferings*, sigs A3, C3-C4, my translation. It is interesting that Doolittle does not include *Gildas Salvianus* in this list. Perhaps he also recognized just how specifically contextualized Baxter's prescription for the Interregnum ministry was.

adulthood. Under Baxter's example, he became a pastor. And with Baxter as sounding-board and tutor, he wrestled with the controversial theological issues of his day. And although he had the benefit of the finest educational opportunities that were available while at Cambridge, when he reflects on the most formative influences that shaped his life and ministry, his focus rests squarely on his relationship with Baxter.

Baxter's influence can be seen not only from the words of Doolittle's own correspondence with Baxter, but can be traced through the course of his career. While at St Alphage, Doolittle possessed a growing reputation as a preacher. And like Baxter, his primary concern was the salvation of sinners who heard him preach.[110] But his career took an unexpected turn when the Protectorate collapsed after Cromwell's death, opening the way for the restoration of monarchy and episcopacy.

Doolittle was nearly twenty-nine, with a pregnant wife and three small children, when he was ejected from his living as rector of St Alphage on 24 August 1662 under the terms of the Act of Uniformity.[111] Doolittle moved to nearby Moorfields, where he opened a boarding school in his house.[112] An increasing number of students necessitated a move to a larger house in Bunhill Fields. Doolittle also enlisted Thomas Vincent, the ejected minister of St Mary Magdalene, Milk Street, as his assistant. With the outbreak of the plague during the summer of 1665, Doolittle moved his family and school to Woodford Bridge, Essex, while Vincent remained behind to minister to plague victims.

In the chaos following the London fire in September 1666, Doolittle and his family moved back to Bunhill Fields where in open defiance of the Clarendon Code he opened a meeting house and continued in public the preaching

---

[110] See DWL, BxL, vi. 28, quoted above at note 95.

[111] Doolittle married Mary Gill on 13 July 1655. See John Shower, *Death a Deliverance. Or, A Funeral Discourse, Preach'd (in Part) on the Decease of Mrs.Mary Doolittle, (Late Wife of Mr. Thomas Doolittle, Minister of the Gospel in London.) Who Departed this Life the 16th of Decemb. 1692* (1693); *CR*, 167-68. Her influence appears to have been felt immediately, as vestry minutes record on 5 September 1655 that 'It is this day mewtually agreed vpon that new riuer water shalbe laid into Mr. Doelittle's house our present minester by a leaden pipe & Coxke of Brase'. See G.B. Hall, *Records of St Alphage, London Wall: Compiled from its ancient documents* (London: J.H. Woodley, 1882), 37. Thomas and Mary Doolittle had at least six children, five of whose names have survived: a son Samuel, and four daughters: Mary Sheafe, Tabitha Hearne, Martha Taylor, Susannah Roades, and a fifth daughter who married Anthony Dawson. See also Smith's 'Memoirs', 20.

[112] The primary sources for the following chronology include Daniel Williams's funeral sermon, *Christian Sincerity* (1707); Jeremiah Smith's 'Memoirs' (1723); *CR*; Walter Wilson's *The History and Antiquities of Dissenting Churches and Meeting Houses in London, Westminster and Southwark: including the Lives of their Ministers*, 3 (1810), 190-199; *DNB* and Black, 'Thomas Doolittle'. See also C.E. Whiting, *Studies in English Puritanism from the Restoration to the Revolution* (London: SPCK, 1931), 55, 457.

ministry he had previously more discretely undertaken. This facility was quickly outgrown. To accommodate his burgeoning congregation, Doolittle had a new meeting house constructed in Monkwell (Mugwell) Street near Cripplegate. Having thus become a provocation that could no longer be ignored, Doolittle was summoned privately by the Lord Mayor who attempted to dissuade him from preaching. When Doolittle refused, soldiers were sent to his home the following Saturday night to arrest him. As they were breaking down the door, he managed to escape. His congregation was harassed and the meeting house was requisitioned for use as a chapel for the Lord Mayor. Doolittle later quietly returned to his home and school, and by 1669 was reported to be preaching again at his house in Monkwell Street.

Upon Charles II's Declaration of Indulgence in March 1672, Doolittle was licensed to hold Presbyterian services in 'a room adjoining his dwelling' in Monkwell Street.[113] At this time, Doolittle also established an academy at a house in Islington, Middlesex. However, when the King's Indulgence was revoked on 3 March 1673, Doolittle was forced to move to Wimbledon, Surrey. At some point before 1680, he was able to return to Islington. However, on 16 November 1682, he was convicted for preaching at Monkwell Street the previous September 15 and was fined £40. The following April, he was convicted of having repeated the same offence three times and fined £100, but by this time he had fled to Battersea, Surrey. The authorities located him in Battersea, however, and seized his possessions. At this point, Doolittle was forced 'to disperse his pupils into private Families at Clapham'.[114] In 1687, Doolittle was forced to move yet again to St John's Court, Clerkenwell, Middlesex.

After the Toleration Act of 1689, Doolittle moved back to Monkwell Street where he re-established both his ministry and academy. Despite frequent interruptions, Doolittle's academy was reputedly the 'leading Presbyterian academy in London', educating as many as 28 students at a given time.[115] Among those taught by Doolittle were the Nonconformist leaders Edmund Calamy and Matthew Henry, the Unitarian Thomas Emlyn, and Nonconformist tutors John Ker and Thomas Rowe.[116]

---

[113] The license is dated 2 April 1672. See *CR*, 167. The original license granted to Doolittle after Charles II's Declaration of Indulgence in 1672, once a prized possession of the Monkwell Street vestry and later of Dr Williams's Library, was inadvertently destroyed during an unauthorized attempt to clean it prior to an exhibition at Whitehall in 1989.

[114] William Tong, *An Account of the Life and Death of the Late Reverend Mr. Matthew Henry Minister of the Gospel at Hackney, who died June 22nd, 1714, in the 52nd Year of his Age* (1716), 29.

[115] McLachlan, *English Education Under the Test Acts*, 10.

[116] See the references to Philip Henry's interactions with Thomas Doolittle in Matthew Henry's *The Life of the Rev. Philip Henry, A.M. with Funeral Sermons* (1698), 125, 143-144, 274; and Matthew Henry's life as a student in Doolittle's academy in J.B.

Doolittle's wife, Mary, died on 16 December 1692.[117] Afterwards, Doolittle apparently quit taking students. Within several years, however, Doolittle married another woman named Mary, who assisted him in his ministry. The second Mary Doolittle, 'my dear and loveing wife', survived her husband by only five months, dying in November 1707.[118]

As a pastor, Doolittle combined preaching with a rigorous catechetical ministry. Preaching two sermons each Sunday, Doolittle was also noted for his regular Wednesday lecture series on the Westminster Assembly's catechism. A popular author, Doolittle published 23 treatises, tracts and sermons, though peers valued most his five works on catechizing.[119]

As we have seen, Doolittle's surviving correspondence with Baxter demonstrates that he carefully followed the rancorous theological debates between Anglicans and Nonconformists and amongst the Nonconformists themselves. In his own published works, however, Doolittle consistently chose to address pastoral and evangelistic concerns.[120] His later reputation as one 'not eminent for compass of knowledge or depth of thought' is undeserved, as it is based on patronizing comments by his student Thomas Emlyn, whose rejection of 'the narrow schemes of systematical divinity' and later drift into

---

Williams's *Memoirs of the Life, Character, and Writings of the Rev. Matthew Henry* (1828), 9-13, 203; reprinted together as *The Lives of Philip & Matthew Henry* (Edinburgh: The Banner of Truth Trust, 1974). See Nuttall, 'Philip Henry in London', *JURCHS*, 5:5 (1994), 263-64. See also Edmund Calamy's remembrances of his studies with Doolittle as a student in his academy in *An Historical Account of My Own Life*, I (1829), 44, 105-108. Of Thomas Doolittle's son, Samuel, Calamy writes that he 'died some years since, pastor of a congregation of Dissenters, at Reading, in Berkshire' (108). See Samuel Doolittle, *A Sermon Occasioned by the Late Earthquake* (1692); S. Doolittle, *The Righteous Mans Hope at Death* (1693). See also James Waters, *The Christian's Life, a Hidden Life. Being a Sermon, Lately Preached at Reading: Occasion'd by the Death of the Reverend Mr. Samuel Doolittell, who Departed this Life on the 10th Day of April last past* (1717).

[117] See John Shower, *Death a Deliverance* (1693). In response to his grief, Doolittle published *The Mourner's Directory* (1693). Doolittle's son Samuel also published *The Righteous Mans Hope at Death* (1693) in response to his mother's death.

[118] PRO, Thomas Doolittle's will: PROB 11/495, sig 138; PRO, Mary Doolittle's administration: Probate 6/83, sig 180v/213v. Certain oblique statements in Doolittle's will lead one to believe that the relationship between Doolittle's children and his second wife caused him some concern.

[119] Doolittle's *A Treatise Concerning the Lord's Supper* (1667) reached 27 English editions, 22 Scottish editions and 26 New England editions, as well as translations into Welsh and German.

[120] Exceptions being Doolittle's anti-Roman Catholic polemic 'Popery is a Novelty', Nathaniel Vincent, ed., *The morning-exercise against popery* (1675), which was also published separately in 1675 as *The Protestants Answer to that Question, Where was your Church before Luther? Wherein Popery is proved a Novelty.* (To which is prefixed an epistle to the reader by Richard Baxter).

Unitarianism did not incline him to think favourably of his former teacher.[121]

Though Doolittle suffered chronically from stone and other ailments, his final illness was brief. Daniel Williams reports that the Sunday before his death 'he preach'd, and Catechized with great vigour'.[122] Late the following week he became ill. He signed his will on Friday, and died the following day, Saturday, 24 May 1707.[123] He was the last surviving London clergyman who had been ejected for Nonconformity in 1662. He was buried in Bunhill Fields cemetery.

For nearly three decades, Thomas Doolittle and Richard Baxter shared the status of persecuted London Nonconformists, during which time Doolittle managed to reproduce many of the emphases that characterized Baxter's own pastoral ministry. Doolittle was respected for his preaching, for his emphasis on catechizing, for his published books and sermons and for his training of young men for the ministry. While it could be argued that these were all hallmarks of nonconformist ministry in general, it cannot be disputed that Doolittle learned his nonconformity in the context of his relationship with the 'mere Nonconformist' Baxter.[124] Baxter's influence can be further discerned by the striking similarities in both content and style found in many of Doolittle's published works. For example, Doolittle's sermon 'How Should We Eye Eternity' (1683) reproduces Baxter's attempts in *Gildas Salvianus* (1656) to persuade fellow ministers concerning the value of a church-wide catechetical ministry. Both Doolittle and Baxter produced several catechisms intended for use in local churches.[125] Both Doolittle and Baxter produced anti-Catholic

---

[121] 'Memoirs of the Life and Writings of Thomas Emlyn', in *Works of Mr. Thomas Emlyn* (1746), vi-vii. Cotton Mather later comments that 'though a Doolittle may not pass for one of our greatest men, yet having in his book on the Catechism, given us the body of divinity all in a flame, I am willing that it should be...a fire-kindler for you and put you in the way, after an awakening manner, to set conscience about its work, when you come to that application with which your sermons are still to be enlivened'. Cotton Mather, *Student and Preacher; or Directions for a Candidate of the Ministry* (1789), 188. See also Charles E. Hambrick-Stowe comments on Doolittle in 'The Spirit of the Old Writers: The Great Awakening and the Persistance of Puritan Piety', F. Bremer, ed., *Puritanism: A Transatlantic Perspective*, 282-83. Usually very judicious, Hambrick-Stowe must have gotten his wires crossed when he later states that Baxter was 'known for his irenic temperment'! (285). For an alternative perspective, see Cooper, *Fear and Polemic*, 46-59.

[122] Daniel Williams, *Christian Sincerity: Described in a Funeral Sermon* (1707), 32.

[123] See Thomas Doolittle's will, PRO, PROB 11/495, sig 138.

[124] The label is Baxter's own, and may be found in his 25 October 1672 letter to a person at Court requesting the King's license for preaching, without any sectarian denomination. See Roger Thomas, *Baxter Treatises: A Catalogue of the Richard Baxter Papers...in Dr. Williams's Library*, 15a; Nuttall, *Richard Baxter*, 103.

[125] See Doolittle's *Plain Method of Catechizing* (1698), *Catechizing Necessary for the Ignorant* (1692), *The Young Mans Instructer and the Old Mans Remembrancer* (1673) and *A Complete Body of Practical Divinity* (1723); and see Baxter's *The Poor Mans Family Book* (1674) and *The Catechizing of Families* (1683), for example.

polemic.[126] Both Doolittle and Baxter produced tracts to call the unconverted to repentance and faith.[127] Not surprisingly, Doolittle reproduces the same concern to train young men for the ministry that marked Baxter's own ministry.[128]

Their relationship, however, matured. Doolittle was not above taking a critical view of some aspects of Baxter's legacy, even if obliquely. Seven years after Baxter's death, when reflecting on his recovery from his own near-fatal illness the previous year in 1697, Doolittle still perhaps has his mentor in mind (if in a negative way) when he writes: 'After my recovery, I set my thoughts on work, what had God for me to do? ...I was resolved I would not Contribute any thing in making Divisions amongst such as feared God, or spend the little remaining part of my days in wrangling with others in little things, nor in engaging with any party in Needless Disputes, to which I saw too many were inclined...'[129]

Conclusion

Richard Baxter's uncharacteristic reserve over his efforts to *make* reformed pastors (as opposed to his broadcast exhortation to already practicing pastors to *be* reformed in his *Gildas Salvianus*), reflects a broader silence on this issue across the Protestant spectrum. Contemporary biographers such as Samuel Clarke note how certain ministers gathered about themselves young men who were seeking further training in preaching and ministry, but there was hardly any published guidance indicating the kind of supplemental education future ministers needed or of the means by which it might be facilitated. Absence of printed advice on pastoral apprenticeships or other means to ensure 'godly'

---

[126]See Doolittle's *The Protestants Answer* (1675).

[127]Compare Doolittle's *A Call to Delaying Sinners* (1683), *Captives bound in Sin Made Free By Christ* (1674) and *Love to Christ Necessary* (1672) with Baxter's *Call to the Unconverted* (1658), *Now or Never* (1662), *Directions and Persuasions to a Sound Conversion* (1658), &c.

[128] 'This Eyeing of Eternity would stir us up to improve our Interest in God and Men for a continual Sucession of Men in the Ministerial Function: in God, by prayer, that the Lord of the Harvest would send forth Labourers into his Harvest: In men, whether such as have Children of pregnant parts, studious and bookish, serious in Religion, and inclined to this Imployment, that they would give them to God, and give them Education in order to it, which would be the Honour of Parents to have such proceed from their loins that shall be Embassadors to call the blind ungodly World to mind Eternity, to escape Everlasting Damnation, and obtain Eternal Life; or whether they be such as have no Children so qualified, or disposed, yet have riches to be helpful to such as have such Children, but not an Estate to bring them up.' Doolittle, 'How Should We Eye Eternity', Samuel Annesley, ed., *A Continuation of Morning Exercise Questions* (1683), 1007. See also *The Mourners Directory* (1693), sigs A3- A4. Here Doolittle sounds eerily Baxteresque in a passage that could have been lifted straight from *The Saints Everlasting Rest*.

[129] Thomas Doolittle, *A Plain Method of Catechizing* (1698), sig A8.

successors to the present generation of ministers does not indicate a lack of action, however. It seems that, in Baxter's case at least, he was more intent on doing the training than writing about it. The one exception, in Baxter's case, is his *Compassionate Counsel to All Young Men* (1681), though it was written more than two difficult decades after he himself exercised a pastoral charge.

Baxter's relationship with Thomas Doolittle occurs at the height of his pastoral work in Kidderminster and at a time when his broader pastoral concerns were coming to fruition with the Worcester Association and the popularity of his books. In the early 1650s, neither Baxter nor anyone else was in a position to anticipate the eventual unraveling of the new order. However chaotic the religious scene was becoming nationally, it was a time when the future still held great promise locally, though not without the necessary hard work of pastor-led reformation. Baxter's overall pastoral strategy was taking shape in the form of an evangelistically-oriented parish ministry based on preaching, discipline and systematic catechizing.[130] But Baxter's pastoral vision looked beyond the boundaries of St Mary's parish. The Worcestershire Association not only enabled Baxter more effectively to enforce his regime of parish discipline, it also enabled him to pursue a ministry of encouragement, mutual accountability and discipline among his colleagues. Baxter's vigorous pursuit of a writing ministry must also be viewed as an intentional effort to project his pastoral agenda onto a nation-wide screen. His published efforts to promote association, parish discipline and systematic catechizing, along with his ground-breaking efforts to evangelize the masses through the press mirror his strategy in Kidderminster.[131] As part of this wider application of his pastoral strategy, Baxter's pains to raise up and train young men for the ministry ensured a godly succession that would maintain and build upon the present successes. Moreover, his efforts also enabled a geographical spread of his pastor-based reformation as an increasing number of parishes experienced the pastoral leadership of men who had been influenced by his example. Even his polemic can be seen as having a pastoral intent.[132] Taken altogether, Baxter's efforts at the parish, county and national level suggest nothing less than an intentional strategy both to redefine pastoral ministry and remake England's pastors. While the original coherent vision of this pastor-led reformation may have been suggested a century earlier by Martin Bucer during his final months in Cambridge, it was Richard Baxter who devised its application and promotion. And to his credit, he nearly pulled it off.

Richard Baxter's pastoral ministry ended when he left Kidderminster in 1660,

---

[130] See T.R. Cooke's discussion of Baxter's pastoral emphases in 'Richard Baxter, Puritan Churchman' (University of Western Ontario PhD thesis, 1991), 100-106.

[131] See Nuttall's discussion of the Worcestershire Association in the context of Baxter's concern for Christian unity in his *Richard Baxter*, 65-71. See Keeble's chapter 'A Pen in God's Hand' for an overview of Baxter's literary ministry in his *Richard Baxter*, 1-21.

[132] Cooper, *Fear and Polemic*, 51-53.

arguably at the peak of his pastoral career. Though he continued to have opportunities to preach, and though he continued to address an even wider audience through the multitude of practical and polemical pieces that flowed from his pen, it is tempting to say that his most lasting contribution occurred as a result of his input in the lives of the young men who gathered around him in the last fourteen years of his ministry in Kidderminster and learned from him the art of being a pastor. Unfortunately, no record survives of the inner workings of any of his relationships with the likes of Richard Sargent, Humphrey Waldron, Thomas Baldwin, Joseph Read, or Simon Potter. If our purpose here was to demonstrate the supplemental input that transformed a university graduate taking clerical orders into a reformed pastor, then we have not quite succeeded. Nevertheless, though Thomas Doolittle never assisted Baxter as a preparatory step for his own ministry, in their long relationship one comes as close as the available evidence will allow to observing the mentoring and nurturing core of this 'godly' supplement. If, however, the exact nature and content of Baxter's input remains elusive, its impact is clear. Even so, this kind of relationship between Baxter and Doolittle is hardly unique in the broader context of 'godly' pastoral practise. And it is in tracing this personal network of intentional, mentoring relationships that one begins to uncover the elusive dynamic that lay at core of the transmission of belief and practise at the puritan and then nonconformist end of the spectrum of seventeenth-century English Christianity. For Baxter and his colleagues, pastors, like Christians, were not born but *made*. The intellectual and political issues facing the godly in Baxter's century may have evolved, but the efforts by pastors to fashion the new generation of leaders in their own image ensured that England's 'godly' remnant, however marginalized, would not be without reformation pastors to lead them.

CHAPTER 10

Richard Baxter and Reformation Pastors

Richard Baxter's pastoral ministry was shaped primarily by his response to three crises that confronted him upon his return to Kidderminster in 1647. The first crisis was the unfulfilled evangelistic mandate of England's 'godly' pastors. This Baxter diagnosed as the inability of the inherited 'puritan' ideal of pulpit-centred ministry to facilitate the conversion of the vast majority in the nation's parishes, or to cope adequately with the new pastoral realities in the aftermath of the civil wars. The second crisis was the failure of parliament's legislated reformation and the absence of a feasible government and discipline for the Church. The third and related crisis was the subsequent proliferation of separatists and sectarians, who took advantage of local pastors' struggles to maintain effective ministries in the absence of functioning structures for ecclesiastical discipline. The resulting divisions at the parish level, often over issues of sacramental integrity, threatened to shipwreck what Baxter perceived as God's evangelistic design for the Church and her ministers. This concluding chapter will draw together the observations concerning these crises made during the course of this investigation, consider Baxter's responses, and finally summarise the findings of this study.

The Frustrated Mandate

To the Inhabitants of the Burrough and Forreign of *Kiderminster*....
I believe God, and therefore I know that you must every Soul of you be converted or condemned to everlasting punishment. And knowing this, I have told it you over and over again: I have showed you the proof and Reasons of it, and the certain misery of an Unconverted state: I have earnestly besought you, and begged of you to return... and if I had but time and strength (as I have not) I should have made bold to have come more to you, and sit with you in your houses, and entreated you on the behalf of your souls, even twenty times, for once that I have entreated you. The God that sent me to you knows, that my soul is grieved for your blindness, and stubbornness, and wickedness, and misery, more then for all the losses or crosses in the World, and that my hearts desire and prayer

for you to God, is, that you may yet be converted and saved.[1]

Richard Baxter became lecturer in Kidderminster in 1641, and later the town's *de facto* pastor in 1647, utterly persuaded of the reality of heaven and hell and of the efficacy of the Christian gospel for salvation. Since all people were separated from any hope of heaven due to their wilful rebellion against God and his just laws, Christian ministers were given the astonishing task of declaring God's way of salvation in Christ. As such, ministers were given the responsibility to shepherd those under their spiritual care to heaven. Therefore ministers also had the burden of insuring that their parishioners understood both their plight and the means of escape. Since a person's eternal destiny was determined by her or his response to that gospel, and since God held negligent ministers responsible for the blood of those in their parish who were never evangelised and who were eternally condemned, Baxter as a minister could not rest until he had ensured that his parishioners both understood the gospel and were given the opportunity to respond. For Baxter, the minister's job was primarily evangelistic. Parish pastors were ambassadors sent by God to entreat parishioners 'on behalf of your souls' to repent and be reconciled with God. Sacraments, ceremonies, even spiritual feeding from the Scriptures could not do a soul a bit of good unless he or she was first converted. Compelled by the logic of this desperate need and clear call, Baxter undertook his pastoral charge.

Once decided, Baxter was both relentlessly consistent and tenacious in his attempt to apply the most effective pastoral means to his evangelistic end.[2] Firmly persuaded of his evangelistic mandate, he made every effort to facilitate the conversion of those under his care. Although Baxter fulfilled in every way the inherited ideal of the 'godly' pastor, he found that ideal an insufficient means to accomplish his evangelistic task. He excelled as a preacher and consistently addressed congregations crammed with auditors, both in his own parish of St Mary's and wherever he travelled to lecture.[3] And though he recorded the conversions of increasing numbers of people responding to his evangelistic appeals, by his own admission the vast majority of his parish remained unmoved and unconverted. Baxter considered his primary ally in his evangelistic efforts the incontrovertible logic of the biblical diagnosis of the human situation and its accompanying prescription. But even if the logic was divine, the necessity of presenting that logic in an intelligible and persuasive manner lay at the heart of the pastor's task. Even so, Baxter found that 'it is no

---

[1] Baxter, *A Treatise of Conversion. Preached and now published for the Use of those that are strangers to a true Conversion* (1657), sigs A1v-A2.

[2] Whether it be his anti-Laudian position on episcopacy, or his anti-antinomianism with respect to the doctrine of salvation, or his absolute refusal to countenance separation, Baxter maintained and ferociously defended those positions he was firmly convinced of until his death.

[3] See Baxter's account of his regular lecture in Dudley in *Rel. Bax.*, I, i, §20, 14.

easie matter to speak so plain, that the ignorant may understand us, and so seriously, that the deadest hearts may feel us; and so convincingly, that the contradicting Cavillers may be silenced.'[4] And the more he tried, the more he realised that the inherited, pulpit-centred, 'puritan' formula to facilitate conversion and reformation could not deliver the intended outcome. Most people failed to comprehend even the plainest, most forceful presentations of gospel danger and deliverance that came at them from the pulpit. Recognition of this shortcoming led Baxter to experiment with alternative 'means' that might supplement a pastor's pulpit efforts.

The Failure of Puritan Reformation

The army's failure to enforce parliament's Westminster Assembly reforms was a sore blow to many of the nation's 'godly' clergy and presented a particular challenge to clergy like Baxter who were located in those areas where the Presbyterian settlement failed to take hold. Rather than having the issues of church government, discipline and ceremonies resolved in a way that brought fulfilment and closure to the long 'puritan' effort to finish England's reformation, the vast majority of England's pastors were thrust into a no-man's-land of spiritual anarchy, and each one was forced to devise his own solutions to contentious questions of discipline which had been suppressed for most of England's Protestant history. The sense of confusion and despair is palpable as Samuel Clarke writes in 1651 that the

> remedy, which though late, began at length to be applyed, in beginning to establish the Presbyterian Government, hath been yet so much defective in want of power, and so much exposed to scorn and reproach, which men of profane or turbulent spirits cast upon it, either from principles of profanenesse, or of separation, or from some other bitter root which renders men unwilling to have their lusts, errors, unlawful liberties, or licentious courses in any kind whatsoever to be checked or contradicted, that the matter is now almost grown desperate, unless God will be pleased in special favour, to afford some unexpected remedy.[5]

For Baxter, however, the crisis provided an opportunity to return to what he felt to be the New Testament model of local pastors exercising authority in matters of discipline and excommunication, responsibilities that had been usurped by the territorial bishops of the unreformed government of the Church of England.[6] By identifying parish priests (presbuteroi) with Pauline and Lukan

---

[4] Baxter, *Gildas Salvianus*, 78.

[5] Clarke, *A Generall Martyrologie* (1651), 432.

[6] Baxter, *The Unreasonableness of Infidelity*, 150-52; *Gildas Salvianus*, 48-53.

overseers and bishops ("episkopoi), Baxter was able to resolve the problem of ecclesiastical authority that had arisen with the overthrow of episcopacy, but in a way that also skirted concerns over certain rigidities of structure in the Westminster Presbyterian alternative. Armed with this biblical justification, he was free to improvise a structure for discipline and oversight that responded to the particular circumstances in St Mary's parish. As we have seen, this relocation of ecclesiastical authority to the parish level provided the theological foundation for his subsequent reconfiguration of the pastor's tasks.

Moreover, with national, government-led reformation motivated by law fatally stuck in the birth, Baxter's vision of a pastor-led, parish-centred reformation motivated by conversion could be attempted in its place. Responding swiftly to the debacle that had befallen the 'puritan' reformation, Baxter had already added the systematic visitation of his parish to his pastoral routine and experimented with at least one programme of parish discipline by the time he published *The Saints Everlasting Rest* in 1650. By the time *Christian Concord* was published in 1653, Baxter had successfully resolved the issue of parish discipline and oversight, and had created a voluntary association of like-minded ministers to provide a structure in which parish discipline could be enforced and further reforming steps could be resolved upon and jointly undertaken. By 1655, Baxter had supplemented his annual parochial visitation with a programme for the systematic catechising of every family in the parish. *Gildas Salvianus* (1656) exhorted his fellow pastors to revise their pastoral practise by using evangelistic means to achieve reformational ends. By calling his colleagues to bring their lives in line with their professed beliefs, offering his own strategy as a model and pointing to his own astonishing results, Baxter transformed the discussion and practise of pastoral ministry among England's 'godly' pastors by suggesting that such reformed pastors making use of reformed means could at last effect the reformed parishioners and reformed parishes that would bring the goal of a reformed nation within reach. With his 1658 publication of *Confirmation and Restauration*, Baxter further refined his thinking on confirmation, adult membership and church discipline.

The Separatists' Goad

It is altogether unlikely that any of Baxter's prodigious efforts to reform the ministry would have occurred apart from the crisis provoked by the disorienting proliferation of separatists and sectarians. What had begun as a rebellion in the 1640s quickly overheated in the reformational ferment, and was transformed into a revolution which succeeded in overturning the previous order of church, monarchy and law, but which was much less successful in finding effective substitutes with which to fill the resulting vacuum of authority. While parliament, the army, and Cromwell struggled to create a workable synthesis of authority from the center, the full brunt of the resulting disorder was played out in the localities, and in particular, the nations parishes. With Episcopacy banished, and sectarian fragmentation appearing to gain momentum, the old models of Protestant ministry were faced with predicaments for which they had no answers. Every parish was affected. The extraordinary scope and nature of the challenge necessitated a pastoral response that superseded the older, failing pastoral ideals. Local upheaval left ministers overwhelmed and despairing. One pastor who had already attempted some of Baxter's suggestions, but who was still facing the imminent partition of his parish wrote to say:

> (though I know your hands are other wise full) yet, I am bold to crave your counsel, & Direction in a case or two. Sir, God was pleased to call mee to a people amonge which there are many hopfull and Godly; but they were inlininge much to Separation: which to prevent I endeavoured (accordinge to our agreement at our Association) to settle some Discipline among them, and fixed uppon the Worcestershire agreement which Modell was at first well approved by my People, & I was in hope of doinge much good amonge them; but in a short space, through the Levity of one, or two younge ones, helped much forward by some Adjacent Ministers, who Preached upp Separation; my people became unsettled, and Headstronge, soe that now I am full of trouble.[7]

Baxter later admitted that these separatists had in God's providence been the means to awaken him and other pastors to the need to reform parish discipline. 'They are his messengers, calling aloud to *England*...to keep the doore, and repaire the hedge'. God 'did permit' these 'Anabaptists' to 'make such a stirre among us'. But 'it will prove a mercy to us in the End, if we have the wit and grace to learn this, upon this troublesome occasion; and then the Reformation will do us more good, then ever the Anabaptists did us harm.'[8]

Reforming the Ministry

Baxter's response to these crises was to abandon the inherited model of 'godly' ministry and attempt a comprehensive reformation of pastoral practise. He was, however, not the only one who recognised the need or who was experimenting with alternative strategies. After the publication of *Christian Concord* in 1653, he discovered that a group of pastors in Cumberland and Westmorland had also established a voluntary association of ministers quite independent of his own

---

[7] DWL, BxL, iii: 171. From John Dolphin to Richard Baxter on 31 January 1655. Dolphin was vicar of Church Honeybourne, then in Worcestershire, and a member of the Worcestershire Association. He matriculated at Pembroke College, Oxford, in 1640. It is possible that this letter is from another John Dolphin who was instead the rector of Broadway, Worcestershire (see *WR*, 387). See *Calendar*, no. 216.

[8] Baxter, *Confirmation and Restauration*, 249.

Worcestershire Association efforts.[9] Others had also wrestled with the problem of insufficient parish discipline.[10] Still others had experimented with catechising.[11] But while most of these attempts were efforts to shore up the old 'puritan' pastoral ideal, Baxter introduced a completely new strategy. He had a similar reformational goal, and the means he used, such as catechising, visitation, preaching, discipline, were all familiar components in the Protestant pastoral arsenal. But Baxter acknowledged the failure of 'puritan' assumptions that 'godly' preaching and the legislated reform of Church ceremonies, government and discipline would be sufficient to effect England's long-delayed reformation. Instead, reformation would occur as the cumulative result of the conversion of the unsaved, professing majority of every parish. Baxter's reformation was thus parochial, pastor-led, and evangelistic in intent, and was accomplished by pastoral means. Preaching remained crucial 'because it tendeth to work on many'.[12] But because it was insufficient on its own as a means of parish evangelism, Baxter supplemented a vigorous pulpit ministry with a regime of all-parish visitation, into which he later incorporated his scheme for parochial catechising. The purpose of this Herculean attempt to catechise every parishioner was not simply to get everyone to learn the basics of Christian doctrine, though that was obviously one of several helpful consequences. Instead, Baxter used the opportunity to 'enter into a prudent enquiry into their state'. Once he found out their 'spiritual state', he was able to respond in a manner appropriate to their need.[13] It was this 'plain close dealing' with individual parishioners 'in private' 'about their sin and misery and duty' that Baxter found so evangelistically effective.[14]

But Baxter's pastoral strategy was also intended to silence the critique of the separatists over the lack of discipline and the resulting profanation of the Lord's Supper. In an effort to prevent notorious sinners within the parish from participating in 'Church Priviledges' such as communion, Baxter instituted a kind of church covenant whereby those who made a credible profession of faith and agreed to submit to Baxter's pastoral authority were allowed to participate in the privileges of adult church membership. While those who were found to be 'ignorant' of basic Christian teaching were prevented from participating in communion (though not from attending services), Baxter made sure that they were given the opportunity to make up their lack and enabled to profess their

---

[9] *Rel. Bax.*, II, §34, 162-163.

[10] See Samuel Clarke's 1662 account of William Gouge's efforts to establish an effective discipline in his London parish of St Annes Blackfriars, in *A Collection of the Lives of Ten Eminent Divines*, 107.

[11] See Clarke's account of Maidstone's pastor Thomas Wilson, who 'took up *Catechising* in the Week-days in publick; and this he continued till he had gone through all the Town'. *The Lives of Sundry Eminent Persons*, 33

[12] Baxter, *Gildas Salvianus*, 78.

[13] Ibid., 436-442.

[14] Ibid., 426.

faith with comprehension. And for those under his pastoral oversight who fell into scandalous sin, Baxter implemented a painstaking process to warn them of their danger, and if no repentance was forthcoming, to remove them from the church's communion and fellowship.[15]

As a further help to promote effective parish discipline, Baxter modified the existing associational model of the combination lecture by making it also a body of referral for particular disciplinary cases. By establishing regular meetings of like-minded clergy, he also created the context for mutual spiritual nurture through preaching, intellectual stimulation through organised disputation, opportunities for 'conference', fellowship and mutual encouragement through shared meals, and a forum in which local clergy could address contentious issues and circumstances while still maintaining unity on the basics. As such, his Worcestershire Association provided a practical and portable structure that allowed for easy replication in other parts of the country still languishing in the vacuum of ecclesiastical authority. Such associations also made use of positive peer pressure to maintain a reforming agenda among those pastors whose circumstances or constitution might incline them to compromise their calling. Voluntary associations provided the context in which Baxter's reformed pastor could thrive, while allowing associating pastors the freedom to modify the structure to meet the needs of their local circumstances.

Though Baxter obviously drew inspiration from existing structures (such as combination lectures) and particular individuals (such as the Shrewsbury Nonconformists and the other local 'godly' pastors he mentions as influences in his *Reliquiae*)[16], his pastoral strategy is remarkable for its lack of affinity with any prior pastoral model published by English Protestant clergy. But as we have seen, even more striking is its almost complete consonance with the strategy for reformation and parish ministry presented a century earlier by Martin Bucer and published in his *Scripta Anglicana* (1577). Baxter's conception of a parish-based, pastor-led, conversion-induced reformation, of the evangelistic purpose of parish ministry, of supplementing preaching with systematic visitation and instruction, of limiting access to communion to those who could credibly profess Christian faith and submit to the pastor's oversight, and of confirmation as a opportunity both to evangelise and to re-establish the notion of both privileges and responsibilities in adult church membership—all of these were hallmarks of Bucer's published advice to the English reformers and of his own pastoral practise in Strasbourg. Baxter's systematic implementation of what essentially is a Bucerian strategy raises the possibility that he was not only aware of Bucer's writings on reformation and ministry, and found them relevant to his circumstances upon his return to Kidderminster in 1647, but that he also used them as the basis for his own pastoral strategy.

Initial successes convinced him that he had finally 'hitt the way of pulling

---

[15] Baxter, *Christian Concord*, sigs A4-B.

[16] See *Rel. Bax.*, I, i, §17, 13; Nuttall, *Richard Baxter*, 11-14.

downe the Kingdome of the Devill'.[17] Further encouragement from his Worcestershire Association colleagues persuaded him to broadcast his pastoral method and the results which they produced. And though pastors who read *Gildas Salvianus* when it was published in 1656 were aware that Baxter was urging them to modify their own pastoral practise, no one seems to have recognised that Baxter was not simply getting pastors to do more, but urging them to adopt an entirely new paradigm for their ministry.

Gildas Salvianus motivated many 'godly' ministers across the nation to reform their pastoral practise. Though some found Baxter's strategy impossible to implement due to their particular circumstances, no one seems to have questioned his arguments. It appears that Baxter's reformed pastor provided the 'unexpected remedy' for which the despairing Samuel Clarke pled in 1651. And though not all of England's soon-to-be Nonconformist ministers adopted Baxter's pastoral programme, the Restoration ensured that Baxter's reconfiguration of 'godly' ministry would be the starting point for subsequent discussions. So pervasive was the impact of Baxter's *Gildas Salvianus* that his model appears even to have coloured the way earlier 'puritan' ministry was remembered and subsequently recorded. The portrayal of 'godly' ministry in Samuel Clarke's 1683 *The Lives of Sundry Eminent Persons* suggests a development in Clarke's own understanding of the means and goals of effective ministry when compared with his earlier collections of ministers' lives taken from the same period. And the fact that these changes in ministerial ideals are in a uniformly Baxterian direction is probably best explained by Baxter's direct influence on Clarke and other authors rather than mere coincidence.

However, the difficulties met by those who would attempt to discern the relative influence of one person's ideas upon another through means of their published and private writings are illustrated in the long relationship between Baxter and the London Presbyterian Thomas Doolittle. Baxter clearly was the dominant influence in Doolittle's life. But without the opportunity to see them interact or hear them converse, the precise mechanism of his influence remains hidden and subject to a degree of speculation. And as is the case with Bucer's influence upon Baxter, or Baxter's influence upon Clarke, the argument for Baxter's influence upon Thomas Doolittle is limited to what the evidence allows. Nevertheless, the strength of the evidence examined in this study allows us to assert that through Richard Baxter a new pastoral strategy, remarkably similar to that of the Strasbourg and Cambridge reformer Martin Bucer, was articulated and implemented during the course of his Kidderminster ministry. And through *Gildas Salvianus*, Baxter's reformed pastor displaced the failed 'puritan' ideal of the 'godly' pastor and became the starting point in future discussions of evangelical ministry in England.

---

[17] DWL, BxL, ii, 249. See *Calendar*, no. 290.

Bibliographies

Manuscripts

Dr Williams's Library, London
      MS 59
                 Baxter Letters, volumes i-vi
                 Baxter Treatises, volume iv

Guildhall Library, London
      MS 1432/4
                 St Alphage, London Wall, parish account book
      MS 1431/2
                 St Alphage, London Wall, vestry minutes

Hereford and Worcester Records Office, Worcester
      St Mary's Church, Kidderminster, Parish Register

Public Records Office, London
      PROB 11/495
                 Thomas Doolittle's will
      PROB 6/83
                 Mary Doolittle's administration

Works by Richard Baxter arranged Chronologically

- *Aphorisms of Justification.* 1649.
- *The Saints Everlasting Rest.* 1650.
[Baxter], *The Humble Petition of Many Thousands...of the County of Worcester... In behalf of the Able, Faithful, Godly Ministry of this Nation.* 1652.
- *Christian Concord.* 1653.
- *True Christianity.* 1655.
- *Making Light of Christ and Salvation.* 1655.
- *A Sermon of Judgement.* 1655.
- *The Quakers Catechism.* 1655.
- *Richard Baxter's Confession of his Faith.* 1655.
- *The Unreasonableness of Infidelity.* 1655.
   Humble Advice...Offered to Many honourable members of Parliament. 1655.
[Baxter], *The Agreement of Divers Ministers of Christ In the County of Worcester...For Catechizing or Personal Instructing.* 1656.
- *Gildas Salvianus; The Reformed Pastor.* 1656.
- *Gildas Salvianus; The Reformed Pastor*, 2nd edition. 1657.
- *A Treatise of Conversion. Preached and now published for the Use of those that are strangers to a true Conversion.* 1657.

- *Confirmation and Restauration, The necessary means of Reformation and Reconciliation.* 1658.
- *Certain Disputations of Right to Sacraments.* 1658.
- *A Call to the Unconverted to Turn and Live.* 1658.
- *Directions and Persuasions to a Sound Conversion.* 1658.
- Commendatory epistle in Matthew Poole, *Model for the Maintaining of Students.* 1658.
- *Five Disputations of Church-government and Worship.* 1659.
- *A Holy Commonwealth.* 1659.
- *A Holy Commonwealth* [1659], W. Lamont, ed. Cambridge: Cambridge University Press, 1994.
- *Universal Concord.* 1660.
- 'To the Reader', Samuel Clark, *Ministers Dues and Peoples Duty.* 1661.
- *Now or Never.* 1662.
- *A Christian Directory.* 1673.
- *The Poor Mans Family Book.* 1674.
- 'Epistle to the Reader', Thomas Doolittle, *The Protestants Answer to that Question, Where was your Church before Luther? Wherein Popery is proved a Novelty: and That the Protestant Doctrine was not only before Luther, but the same that was taught by Christ and His Apostles.* 1675.
- *A Treatise of Justifying Righteousness.* 1676.
- *The Nonconformists Plea for Peace.* 1679.
- *A Treatise of Episcopacy.* 1680.
- *Church History of the Government of Bishops.* 1680.
- *The Second Part of the Nonconformists Plea for Peace.* 1680.
- *A Breviate of the Life of Margaret Baxter.* 1681.
- *Compassionate Counsel to All Young Men.* 1681.
- *An Apology for the Nonconformist Ministry.* 1681.
- *A Third Defence of the Cause of Peace.* 1681.
- *The True History of Councils Enlarged.* 1682.
- *The Catechizing of Families.* 1683.
- 'To the Reader', Samuel Clarke, *The Lives of Sundry Eminent Persons in this Later Age.* 1683.
- *Whether Parish Congregations Be True Christian Churches, and the Capable Consenting Incumbents, be truly their Pastors, or Bishops over their Flocks.* 1684.
- *Cain and Abel Malignity.* 1689.
- *The English Nonconformity.* 1690.
- *Richard Baxter's Penitent Confession.* 1691.
- *Church Concord.* 1691.
- *Universal Redemption.* 1694.
- *Reliquiae Baxterianae*, Matthew Sylvester, ed. 1696.

Works by Richard Baxter arranged Alphabetically

[Baxter], *The Agreement of Divers Ministers of Christ In the County of Worcester...For Catechizing or Personal Instructing.* 1656.
- *Aphorisms of Justification.* 1649.

- *An Apology for the Nonconformist Ministry.* 1681.
- *A Breviate of the Life of Margaret Baxter.* 1681.
- *Cain and Abel Malignity.* 1689.
- *The Catechizing of Families.* 1683.
- *Certain Disputations of Right to Sacraments.* 1658.
- *Christian Concord.* 1653.
- *A Christian Directory.* 1673.
- *Church Concord.* 1691.
- *Church History of the Government of Bishops.* 1680.
- Commendatory epistle in Matthew Poole, *Model for the Maintaining of Students.* 1658.
- *Compassionate Counsel to All Young Men.* 1681.
- *Confirmation and Restauration, The necessary means of Reformation and Reconciliation.* 1658.
- *Directions and Persuasions to a Sound Conversion.* 1658.
- *The English Nonconformity.* 1690.
- 'Epistle to the Reader', Thomas Doolittle, *The Protestants Answer to that Question, Where was your Church before Luther? Wherein Popery is proved a Novelty: and That the Protestant Doctrine was not only before Luther, but the same that was taught by Christ and His Apostles.* 1675.
- *Five Disputations of Church-government and Worship.* 1659.
- *Gildas Salvianus; The Reformed Pastor.* 1656.
- *Gildas Salvianus; The Reformed Pastor,* 2nd edition. 1657.
- *A Holy Commonwealth.* 1659.
- *A Holy Commonwealth* [1659], W. Lamont, ed. Cambridge: Cambridge University Press, 1994.
- *Humble Advice...Offered to Many honourable members of Parliament.* 1655.
- [Baxter], *The Humble Petition of Many Thousands...of the County of Worcester... In behalf of the Able, Faithful, Godly Ministry of this Nation.* 1652.
- *Making Light of Christ and Salvation.* 1655.
- *The Nonconformists Plea for Peace.* 1679.
- *Now or Never.* 1662.
- *The Poor Mans Family Book.* 1674.
- *The Quakers Catechism.* 1655.
- *Reliquiae Baxterianae,* Matthew Sylvester, ed. 1696.
- *Richard Baxter's Confession of his Faith.* 1655.
- *Richard Baxter's Penitent Confession.* 1691
- *The Saints Everlasting Rest.* 1650.
- *The Second Part of the Nonconformists Plea for Peace.* 1680.
- *A Sermon of Judgement.* 1655.
- *A Third Defence of the Cause of Peace.* 1681.
- 'To the Reader', Samuel Clark, *Ministers Dues and Peoples Duty.* 1661.
- 'To the Reader', Samuel Clarke, *The Lives of Sundry Eminent Persons in this Later Age.* 1683.
- *A Treatise of Conversion. Preached and now published for the Use of those that are strangers to a true Conversion.* 1657.
- *A Treatise of Episcopacy.* 1680.
- *A Treatise of Justifying Righteousness.* 1676.

- *True Christianity.* 1655.
- *The True History of Councils Enlarged.* 1682.
- *Universal Concord.* 1660.
- *Universal Redemption.* 1694.
- *The Unreasonableness of Infidelity.* 1655.
- *Whether Parish Congregations Be True Christian Churches, and the Capable Consenting Incumbents, be truly their Pastors, or Bishops over their Flocks.* 1684.

Editions of Baxter's *Gildas Salvianus: The Reformed Pastor*

Gildas Salvianus; The First Part: i.e. The Reformed Pastor. By Robert White for Nevil Simmons at Kederminster. 1656.

Gildas Salvianus; The First Part: i.e. The Reformed Pastor. By Robert White for Nevil Simmons, and are to be sold by William Raybould. 1656.

Gildas Salvianus; The Reformed Pastor . Second edition. By Robert White, for Nevil Simmons, to be sold by Joseph Nevil. with apendix in answer to some objections. 1657.

Practical Works of the late Reverend and Pious Mr. Richard Baxter, 4 vols. 1707.

The Reformed Pastor...Abridged and reduced to a new method, Samuel Palmer, ed. London: J. Buckland, 1766.

The Reformed Pastor, Thomas Rutherford, ed. 1806.

The Reformed Pastor; a discourse on the pastoral office. To which is added, an appendix, containing Hints of advice to students for the ministry, and to tutors of academies. 2nd edition. Abridged by Samuel Palmer. London: William Baynes, 1808.

The Reformed Pastor; a discourse on the pastoral office. Designed principally to explain and recommend the duty of personal instruction and catechising. To which is added an appendix, containing some hints of advice to students for the ministry, and to tutors. Washington, PA, 1810.

The Reformed Pastor; a discourse on the pastoral office. Designed principally to explain... Cincinnati, OH: J.W. Browne & Co., 1811.

The Reformed Pastor; shewing the nature of the pastoral work. New York: J.C. Totten, 1821.

Gildas Salvianus; The Reformed Pastor. Printed for Richard Edwards. 1825.

The Reformed Pastor, William Brown, ed. Introduction by Daniel Wilson. Glasgow, 1829.

The Works of Richard Baxter, 23 vols, William Orme, ed. 1830.

Gildas Salvianus. Baxter's Refomed Pastor, Abridged and arranged by Samuel Palmer. 1845.

Practical Works, 4 vols, reprint of 1707 edition. 1847.

The Reformed Pastor. New York: American Tract Society, 1850?

Gildas Salvianus. The Reformed Pastor, reprint of the 1657 edition with appendix. London, 1860.

The Reformed Pastor, William Brown, ed. 5th abridged edition, 1862.

Gildas Salvianus: the Reformed Pastor, John T. Wilkinson, ed. London: Epworth Press, 1939.

As Silver is Tried. Maxims and Meditations for Ministers and Other Christians. An anthology from The Reformed Pastor of...R. Baxter, C.E. Surman, ed. Introduction by G. F. Nuttall. London: Independent Press, 1947.

Gildas Salvianus: the Reformed Pastor, John T. Wilkinson, ed., 2nd edition. London: Epworth Press, 1950.

The Reformed Pastor, Hugh Martin, ed. London: SCM Press, 1956.

Gildas Salvianus.. In Thomas Wood, *Five Pastorals*. London: SPCK, 1961.

The Reformed Pastor, William Brown, ed. (5th abridged edition reprinted). Introduction by J.I. Packer. Edinburgh: The Banner of Truth Trust, 1981, c. 1974. Currently in print.

'The Reformed Pastor': A Pattern for Personal Growth and Ministry, James Houston, ed. Portland, OR: Multnomah Press, 1986.
Currently in print.

The Ministry We Need: An Abridged and rewritten version of 'the reformed pastor' by Richard Baxter...together with the Life of Richard Baxter 1615-1691, W. Stuart Owen, ed. London: Grace Publications Trust, 1997. Currently in print.

The Reformed Pastor, Introduction by J.I. Packer, 2nd edition, in *The practical works of Richard Baxter: with a preface, giving some account of the author....* 4 volumes. Morgan, PA: Soli Deo Gloria Publications, 2000. Currently in print.

The Reformed Pastor, Preface by Jay Green. N.p.: Sovereign Grace Trust Fund, 2000. Currently in print.

There are also online editions of *Gildas Salvianus, The Reformed Pastor*.

This list is not exhaustive.

Primary Sources

Note: Anonymous works are listed here alphabetically according to the title.

The Agreement and Resolvtion of the Ministers of Christ Associated within the City of Dublin. 1659.

The Agreement and Resolvtion of Severall Associated Ministers in...Corke. 1657.

The Agreement of the Associated Ministers In the County of Norfolk and City and County of Norwich, Concerning Publick Catechizing. 1659.

The Agreement of the Associated Ministers of the County of Essex...with a word of Exhortation to Brotherly Union. 1658.

Ames, William, *Medulla Theologiae*, 3rd edition. 1629.

Ball, Thomas, *A Letter of Many ministers in old England.* 1643.

- Ποιμηνοπυργος. *Pastorum Propugnaculum. Or, the Pulpits Patronage Against the Force of Un-Ordained Usurpation, and Invasion*. 1656.

Bates, William, *A Funeral Sermon for the Reverend, Holy and Excellent Divine, Mr. Richard Baxter*. 1692.

Bayly, Lewes, *The Practice of Pietie: Directing a Christian how to walke that he may please God*, 30th edition. 1632.

Bayly, Richard, *The Shepheards Starre, or the Ministers Guide*. 1640.

Bedingford, Robert, *Cura pastoralis, concio ad clerum*. 1629.

Bernard, Richard, *The Faithful Shepheard*. 1607.

- *Two Twinnes: or Two part of one portion of Scripture. I. Is of Catechising. II. O the Ministers maintenance*. 1613.

Bolton, Robert, *Instructions for a Right Comforting Afflicted Consciences*. 1631.

- *The Saint's Selfe-enriching Examination. Or a Treatise concerning the Sacrament of the Lord's Supper. Which as a Glasse or Touch-stone, Clearly discovers the triall and truth of Grace; requisite to be looked into daily; chiefly before we come to the Lords Table*. 1634.

Bowles, Oliver, *De pastore evangelico tractatus*. 1649.

- *Zeal for Gods House Quickned: Or, A Sermon Preached before the Assembly of Lords, Commons, and Divines at their solemn Fast July 7.1643. In the Abbey Church at Westminster. Expressing the Eminencie of Zeale requisite in Church Reformers*. 1643.

Bradshaw, William, *The Unreasonableness of the Separation*. 1614.

Brown, William, 'Preface', Richard Baxter, *The Reformed Pastor*, W. Brown, ed. 1829.

Browne, Robert, *A treatise of reformation without tarying for anie*. 1582.

- *The Writings of Robert Harrison and Robert Browne*, A. Peel and L. Carlson, eds. London: George Allen and Unwin, 1953.

Bucer, Martin, *Censura De Caeremoniis Ecclesiae Anglicanae*. 1551.

- *Concerning the True Care of Souls and Genuine Pastoral Ministry and how the latter is to be ordered and carried out in the church of Christ*, P. Beale, tr. [Strasbourg, 1538] n.d.

- *De Regno Christi, Melanchthon and Bucer*, Wilhelm Pauck, ed. and tr. *Library of Christian Classics*, XIX. London: SCM Press, and Philadelphia: Westminster Press, 1969.

- *De Regno Christi, Scripta Anglicana fere omnia*. Basle, 1577.

- *De Vera Animarum Cura, Scripta Anglicana fere omnia*. Basle, 1577.

- *Martin Bucer and the Book of Common Prayer*, E.C. Whitaker, ed. Great Wakering: Mayher-McGrimmon, 1974.

- *Scripta Anglicana fere omnia*, Conrad Hubert, ed. Basle, 1577.

- *A treatise declaryng and shewing...that pyctures and other ymages...ar in no wise to be suffred in...churches*. 1535.

Calamy (senior), Edmund, *Englands Looking-Glasse, Presented in a Sermon Preached before... Commons... December 22, 1641*. 1642.

- *Gods True Mercy to England... In a Sermon Preached before... Commons Feb.23.1641[2]*. 1642.

Calamy, Edmund, *Account of the Ministers and [Others] Ejected or Silenced after the Restoration in 1660*, 2nd edition. 1713.

- *An Historical Account of My Own Life*. 1829.

Calderwood, David, *The Pastor and the Prelate*. Edinburgh, 1843.

Calvin, John, *Institutes of the Christian Religion*, F.L. Battles, tr. *Library of Christian Classics*, XX. Philadelphia: Westminster Press, 1960.

Carleton, George, *The Life of Bernard Gilpin*. 1629.

Cartwright, Thomas, *Cartwrightiana*, A. Peel and L.H. Carlson eds. *Elizabethan Nonconformist Texts*, 1. London: George Allen and Unwin, 1951.

Chaderton, William, 'Letter to the Earl of Leicester, 8 August 1580', in *Calendar of State Papers Domestic Series, Elizabeth and James, 1580-1625, Addenda*, 12, XXVII, M.A.E. Green, ed. London,1872, 11-12

Clark, Samuel, *Ministers Dues and Peoples Duty*. 1661.

Clarke, Samuel, *A Collection of the Lives of Ten Eminent Divines, famous in their Generations for Learning, Prudence, Piety, and painfulness in the Work of the Ministry*. 1662.

- *A Generall Martyrologie...whereunto is added the lives of Thirty Two English Divines, Famous in their generation for Learning and Piety, and most of them Sufferers in the Cause of Christ*. 1651.

- *A General martyrologie...whereunto is added the lives of Thirty Two English Divines, Famous in their generation for Learning and Piety, and most of them Sufferers in the Cause of Christ*. 1677.

- *The Lives of Sundry Eminent Persons in this Later Age*. 1683.

- *A Martyrology Containing A Collection of all the Persecutions Which have befallen the Church of England*. 1652.

Cosin, John, 'A Sermon at the Consecration of Dr. Francis White, Bishop of Carlisle', *The Works of the Right Reverend Father in God, John Cosin, Lord Bishop of Durham*, I. Oxford: John Henry Parker, 1843.

Crofton, Zachary, *Catechising Gods Ordinance*. 1656.

Crooke, Samuel, *Three Sermons, viz. The Waking Sleeper, The Ministeriall Husbandrie, The Discourse of the Heart*. 1615.

Crowley, Robert, *The Confutation of xiii articles whereunto n. Shaxton subscribed*. 1548.

A Directory for the Publique Worship of God Through out the Three Kingdoms of England, Scotland, and Ireland. 1644, repr. Bromcote, Nottinghamshire, 1980.

Dod, John, *A Treatise or Exposition upon the Ten Commandments*. 1603.

Doolittle, Samuel, *The Righteous Mans Hope at Death*. 1693.

- *A Sermon Occasioned by the Late Earthquake*. 1692.

Doolittle, Thomas, *A Call to Delaying Sinners*. 1683.

- *Captives bound in Sin Made Free By Christ*. 1674.

- *Catechizing Necessary for the Ignorant*. 1692.

- *Complete Body of Practical Divinity: Being a New Improvement of the Assembly's Catechism*. 1723.

- 'How Should We Eye Eternity', Samuel Annesley, ed., *A Continuation of Morning Exercise Questions and Cases of Conscience, Practically Resolved by Sundry Ministers in October 1682*. 1683.

- *The Lords Last-Sufferings Shewed in the Lords Supper*. 1682.

- *Love to Christ Necessary*. 1672.

- *The Mourner's Directory*. 1693.

- *A Plain Method of Catechizing*. 1698.

- *The Protestants Answer to that Question, Where was your Church before Luther? Wherein Popery is proved a Novelty: and That the Protestant Doctrine was not only before Luther, but the same that was taught by Christ and His Apostles*. 1678.

- *A Treatise Concerning the Lord's Supper*. 1667.

- *The Young Mans Instructer and the Old Mans Remembrancer.* 1673.

Downame, George, *Commending the ministrie.* 1608.

Eachard, John, *The Grounds and Occasions of the Contempt of the Clergy and Religion Enquired Into. In a Letter Written to R.L.* 1670.

Emlyn, Thomas, *Works of Mr. Thomas Emlyn.* 1746.

Fairclough, Samuel, 'Αγιοι ἀξιοι, *or The Saints worthinesse and The worlds worthlessnesse, both opened and Declared in a Sermon preached at the funerall of that Eminently Religious and highly honoured Knight Sr. Nathaniel Barnardiston. Aug.26.1653.* 1653.

- *The Troublers Troubled, or Achan Condemned, and Executed. A Sermon Preached before sundry of the Honourable House of Commons at Westminister, April, 4.1641.* 1641.

Favour, John, *Antiquities triumphing over Novelties.* 1619.

Fenner, Dudley, *A Defence of the godlie ministers against the slaunders of D. Bridges.* 1587.

[Field, John and Thomas Wilcox], *An Admonition to Parliament.* 1572.

Fincham, Kenneth, ed., *Visitation Articles and Injunctions of the Early Stuart Church,* II. Woodbridge, Suffolk: The Boydell Press, 1998.

Foxe, John, *Acts and Monuments,* J. Pratt, ed. London: G. Seeley, 1853-8, 1870.

- *De censura sive exommunicatione ecclesiastica rectoque eius usu.* 1551.

Frere, W.H. and C.E. Douglas, eds., *Puritan Manifestoes.* London: Church Historical Society, 1907, repr. London: SPCK, 1954.

Fulke, William, *A Brief and plaine declaration, concerning the desires of all those faithfull ministers, that haue and do seeke for the discipline and reformation of the Churche of Englande.* 1584.

Fuller, Thomas, *The Appeal of Iniured Innocence: unto The Religious Learned and Ingenuous Reader.* 1659.

Gardiner, Richard, *Concio ad clerum habita in templo beatae Oxon.* 1631.

Gardiner, S.R., ed., *Constitutional Documents of the Puritan Revolution, 1625-1660.* Oxford: Clarendon Press, 1906, 1979 printing.

The Geneva Bible. 1602. Facsimile reprint, New York, 1989.

Gilby, Anthony, *A Pleasaunt Dialogue...between a Souldier of Barwick, and an English Chaplain.* 1573.

- *To my louynge brethren that is troublyd abowt the popishe apparrell, two short and comfortable Epistles.* 1566.

Gildas, *De Excidio et Conquestu Britanniae,* Michael Winterbottom, ed., *Gildas: The Ruin of Britain and Other Works.* London: Phillimore, 1978.

Gillespie, George, *Aarons Rod Blossoming.* 1646.

[Gilpin, Richard], *Agreement of the Associated Ministers & Churches of the Counties of Cumberland and Westmerland: With something for Explication and Exhortation Annexed.* 1656.

Green, M.A.E., ed., *Calendar of State Papers Domestic Series, Elizabeth and James, 1580-1625, Addenda,* 12, XXVII. 1872.

- *Calendar of State Papers, Domestic Series, of the Reign of Elizabeth, 1601-1603; with Addenda 1547-1565,* XII. 1870.

Greenham, Richard, *The Workes of the Reverend and faithful servant of Iesus Christ M. Richard Greenham, Minister and Preacher of the Word of God,* first edition, Henry Holland, ed. 1599.

- *The Workes of the Reverend and faithful servant of Iesus Christ M. Richard Greenham, Minister and Preacher of the Word of God,* third edition, Henry Holland, ed. 1601.
- *The Workes of the Reverend and faithful servant of Iesus Christ M. Richard Greenham, Minister and Preacher of the Word of God,* fourth edition, Henry Holland, ed. 1605.

Gregory the Great, *The Book of Pastoral Rule,* J. Barmby, tr., *Nicene and Post-Nicene Fathers, Second Series, 12.* Peabody, MA: Hendrickson, 1995.

Grindal, Edmund, *The Remains of Archbishop Grindal,* W. Nicholson ed. Cambridge, 1843.

Grotius,Hugo, *De Imperio Summarum Potestatum Circa Sacra.* Paris, 1647.

Hall, G.B., *Records of St Alphage, London Wall: Compiled from its ancient documents.* London: J.H. Woodley, 1882.

Hammond, Henry, *Of the Power of the Keyes.* 1647.

Harrison, William, *The Difference of Hearers. Or, an exposition of the Parable of the Sower.* 1614.

Harward, Simon, *Two Godlie and learned Sermons, preached at Manchester in Lancashire, before a great Audience, both of Honor and Worship. The first containeth a reproofe of the subtill practices of dissembling Neuters, and politique Worldlings. The other a Charge and Instruction , for all unlearned, negligent, and dissolute Ministers.* 1582.

Herbert, George, *A Priest to the Temple: Or, The Country Parson: his Character, and Rule of Holy Life,* 2nd edition [containing a life of Herbert by Barnabas Oley]. 1671.
- *A Priest to the Temple, Or, The Parson, his Character, and Rule of Holy Life.* 1652.
- *Works of George Herbert,* Hutchinson, F.E., ed. Oxford: Clarendon Press, 1941, repr. 1978.

Henry, Matthew, *The Life of the Rev. Philip Henry, A.M. with Funeral Sermons.* 1698.

Hieron, Samuel, *Aarons Bells A-sounding. In a sermon, tending chieftly to admonish the ministerie, of their charge, & duty.* 1623.
- *All Sermons of Samuel Hieron.* 1614.
- *The Preachers Plea: Or A Treatise in forme of a plain Dialogue, making known the worth and necessary vse of Preaching.* 1604.
- *The Spirituall Fishing. A Sermon Preached in Cambridge.* 1618.

Holme, John, *The Burthen of the Ministerie. Gathered out of the sixt chapiter of the Epistle of S. Paul to the Galathians, the first verse.* 1592.

The Holy Bible. Authorized Version. 1611.

Hooker, Richard, *On the Laws of Ecclesiastical Polity,* J. Booty, ed. London: Belknap Press, 1982.

Hooker, Thomas, *The Soules Preparation for Christ.* 1632.

Hooper, John, *A Declaration of Christ and His office.* Zurich, 1547. *Early Writings,* S. Carr, ed. 1843.

James VI, *BASILIKON DWRWN. Or His Maiesties Instrvctions to His Dearest Sonne, Henry the Prince.* Edinburgh, 1603.

James, Richard, *Concio habita ad clerum Oxoniensem de ecclesia.* 1633.

Josselin, Ralph, *The Diary of Ralph Josselin,* A. MacFarlane, ed. Oxford: Clarendon Press, 1991.

Jus divinum ministerii evangelici. 1654.

Keating, W., ed., *Book of Common Prayer* (1559), *Liturgical Services: Liturgies and Occasional Forms of Prayer set forth in the Reign of Queen Elizabeth.* Cambridge: Cambridge University Press, 1847.

Lancaster, Thomas, *The Right and True Understanding of the Supper of the Lord.* 1550.

Lee, M.H., *Diaries and Letters of Philip Henry, of Broad Oak, Flintshire, A.D. 1631-1696.* 1882.

Lyford, William, *An Apologie for our Publick ministerie and infant Baptism.* 1653.

- *Principles of faith.* 1642.

- *William Lyford his Legacy, or a Help for young People to Prepare them for the Sacrament.* 1656.

Mandevill, Robert, *Timothies Taske: or A Christian Seacard.* Oxford, 1619.

Marshall, Stephen, *Reformation and Desolation: or A Sermon tending to the Discovery of the Symptomes of a People to whom God will by no meanes be reconciled.* 1642.

Martindale, Adam, *The Life of Adam Martindale, written by himself, and now first printed from the original manuscript in the British Museum,* R. Parkinson, ed. 1845.

Mather, Cotton, *Student and Preacher; or directions for a Candidate of the Ministry.* 1789.

Melanchthon, Philip, *The thre bokes of Cronicles whych John Carion...gathered,* Walter Lynn, tr. 1550.

Myrc, John, *Instructions for Parish Priests, Early English Text Society,* Original Series, 31. 1868.

Newcome, Henry, *The Autobiography of Henry Newcome,* R. Parkinson, ed. Manchester: Chetham Society, 1852.

Nowell, Alexander, *A Catechism, or first instruction of Christian religion,* Thomas Norton, tr. 1570.

- *Catechismus, sive prima institutio.* 1570.

Orme, William, *The Life and Times of Richard Baxter: with a Critical Examination of his Writings.* 1830.

Owen, John, *The True Nature of a Gospel Church.* 1689.

- *The Works of John Owen.* Edinburgh: The Banner of Truth Trust, 1968.

Palmer, Samuel, 'The Preface', Richard Baxter, *The Reformed Pastor; A Discourse on the Pastoral Office,* S. Palmer, ed. 1766.

Parker, K.L. and E.J. Carlson, 'Practical Divinity': The Works and Life of Revd. Richard Greenham. Aldershot: Ashgate, 1998.

Parr, Richard, *Concio ad clerum habita Oxoniae Jul.12.1625.* 1625.

A Parte of a register, contayninge sundrie memorable matters written by diuers godly and learned in our time, which stande for, and desire the reformation of our church, I discipline and ceremonies, accordinge to the pure worde of God, and the lawe of our lande. 1593.

Peel, Albert, ed., *The Seconde Parte of a Register: being a calendar of manuscripts under that title intended for publication by the Puritans about 1593.* Cambridge: Cambridge University Press, 1915.

Penry, John, *A defence of that which hath bin written in the questions of the ignorant ministerie.* 1588.

Perkins, William, *Of the Calling of the Ministerie: two Treatises, describing the Duties and Dignities of that Calling.* 1605.

- *A Reformed Catholic.* 1611.

Phillips, George, *The good Sheapeheardes dutie.* 1597.

Phillips, Jerome, *The Fisher-man. A Sermon Preached at a Synode held at Southwell in Nottinghamshire.* 1623.

Poole, Matthew, *Model for the Maintaining of Students.* 1658.

Porter, H.C, ed., *Puritanism in Tudor England.* London: MacMillan, 1970.

Potter, Christopher, *A Sermon preached at the Consecration of the Right Reverend Father in God Barnaby Potter D.D. and L. Bishop of Carlisle.* 1629.

Preston, John, *The Cuppe of Blessing: Delivered in Three Sermons upon 1 Cor.10.16.* 1634.

- *Life Eternal: or, a Treatise of the Knowledge of the Divine Essence and Attributes,* 3rd edition. 1632.

- *Three Sermons upon the Sacrament of the Lords Supper.* 1631.

Prynne, William, *Anti-Arminianisme,* 2nd edition. 1630.

Pykeryng, Peter, *A Myroure or glasse for all spiritual Ministers to behold them selues in; wherein they may learne theyr office and duitie towardis the flocke comitted to their Charg.* 1551.

Rogers, Nehemiah, *The True Convert: or an exposition upon three Parables. The lost sheep. The lost groat. The lost sonne.* 1632.

Salvian, *A Treatise of God's Government and of the justice of his present dispensations in this world,* 1700.

- *The Writings of Salvian, the Presbyter,* J.F. O'Sullivan, tr. New York: Cima Publishing Company, 1947.

Shaw, W.A., ed., *Minutes of the Bury Presbyterian Classis, 1647-1657.* Manchester: Chetham Society, 1896.

A short Catechism or Plain Instruction containing the sum of Christian learning. 1553.

Shower, John, *Death a Deliverance. Or, A Funeral Discourse, Preach'd (in Part) on the Decease of Mrs. Mary Doolittle, (Late Wife of Mr. Thomas Doolittle, Minister of the Gospel in London.) Who Departed this Life the 16th of Decemb. 1692.* 1693.

Sibbes, Richard, *The Works of Richard Sibbes,* A. Grosart, ed. 1862-64, repr., Edinburgh: The Banner of Truth Trust, 1983.

Smith, Jeremiah, 'Memoirs', in Thomas Doolittle, *Complete Body of Practical Divinity: Being a New Improvement of the Assembly's Catechism.* 1723.

Some, Robert, *A Godly Treatise containing and deciding certaine questions, moued of late in London and other places, touching the Ministerie, Sacraments and Church.* 1588.

Sparke, Thomas, *A catechisme, or short kind of instruction.* 1588.

Spurgeon, C.H., *Autobiography, Volume I: The Early Years 1834-1859.* Edinburgh: The Banner of Truth Trust, 1962 (revised edition of 4 volume autobiography first published in 1897-1900).

Strype, John, *Annals of the Reformation.* Oxford, 1824.

Taylor, John, *A Swarme of Sectaries, and Schismatiques.* 1641.

Tong, William, *An Account of the Life and Death of the Late Reverend Mr. Matthew Henry Minister of the Gospel at Hackney, who died June 22nd, 1714, in the 52nd Year of his Age.* 1716.

Twittee, Thomas, *Ad Clerum proforma concio habita Marii 13 1624.* 1624.

Ussher, James, *A briefe declaration of the universalitie of the church of Christ.* 1624.

- *The Reduction of Episcopacie unto the Form of Synodical Government received in the Antient Church.* 1656.

- *Veterum episotlarum hibernicarum sylloge.* 1632.
Vincent, Nathaniel, ed., *The morning-exercise against popery.* 1675.
Wall, George, *A Sermon at the Lord Archbishop of Canterbury his Visitation Metropolitical, held at All-Saints in Worcester.* 1635.
Waters, James, *The Christian's Life, a Hidden Life. Being a Sermon, Lately Preached at Reading: Occasion'd by the Death of the Reverend Mr. Samuel Doolittell, who Departed this Life on the 10th Day of April last past.* 1717.
Whately, William, *The New Birth.* 1618.
- *The Redemption of Time.* 1606.
Whitaker, E.C., tr., *Martin Bucer and the Book of Common Prayer.* Great Wakering, Essex: Mayher-McGrimmon Ltd, 1974.
Whitaker, William, *Cygnea Cantio.* Cambridge, 1599.
Whitgift, John, *The Works of John Whitgift*, J. Ayre, ed. Cambridge, 1851.
Widdowes, Giles, *The Schysmatical Puritan.* 1630.
Wigmore, Michael, *The Meteors. A Sermon preached at a visitation by Michael Wigmore, Rector of Thorseway in Lincolnshire, and sometimes Fellow of Oriel college in Oxford.* 1633.
Williams, Daniel, *Christian Sincerity; Described in a Funeral Sermon June 1. 1707. Occasioned by the death of T. Doolittle.* 1707.
Williams, J.B., *Memoirs of the Life, Character, and Writings of the Rev. Matthew Henry.* 1828.
Williams, J.B. and Matthew Henry, *The Lives of Philip & Matthew Henry.* Edinburgh: Banner of Truth Trust, 1974.
Wilson, Walter, *The History and Antiquities of Dissenting Churches and Meeting Houses in London, Westminster and Southwark: including the Lives of their Ministers.* 1810.

Secondary Sources

Acheson, R.J., *Radical Puritans in England 1550-1660.* London: Longman, 1990.
Amos, N.S., ' "It is Fallow Ground Here": Martin Bucer as Critic of the English Reformation', *Westminster Theological Journal*, 61 (1999), 41-52.
Adair, John, *Founding Fathers: The Puritans in England and America.* London: J.M. Dent, 1982.
Ashton, Robert, *Reformation and Revolution 1558-1660.* London: Granada, 1984.
Aston, Margaret, *England's Iconoclasts*, i. Oxford: Clarendon Press, 1988.
- *Faith and Fire: Popular and Unpopular Religion 1350-1600.* London: Hambledon, 1993.
Bainton, Roland, 'The Ministry in the Middle Ages', *The Ministry in Historical Perspectives*, R.N. Neibuhr and D.D. Williams, eds. New York: Harper, 1956.
Ball, R.M., 'The Education of the English Parish Clergy in the Later Middle Ages with Particular Reference to the Manuels of Instruction', Ph.D., University of Cambridge, 1976.
Barker, W.S., *Puritan Profiles.* Fearne, Scotland: Mentor, 1996.
Barnard, E.A., 'The Rouses of Rous Lench', *Transactions of the Worcestershire Archeological Society,* ix (1932), 31-74.

Baskerville, Stephen, *Not Peace But a Sword: The political theology of the English Revolution*. London: Routledge, 1993.

Benn, Wallace, *The Baxter Method: Guidelines for Pastoring Today*. Lowestoft, 1993.

Binfield, Clyde, 'Profile: Geoffrey Nuttall: The Formation of an Independent Historian', *The Epworth Review*, 25 (1998), 79-106.

Black, J. William, 'From Martin Bucer to Richard Baxter: "Discipline" and Reformation in Sixteenth and Seventeenth Century England', *Church History*, 70:4 (2001), 644-673.

- 'Richard Baxter and the Ideal of the Reformed Pastor', Ph.D., University of Cambridge, 2000.

- 'Richard Baxter's Bucerian "Reformation" ', *Westminster Theological Journal*, 63 (2001), 327-349.

- 'Thomas Doolittle', in *Oxford Dictionary of National Biography, in association with the British Academy,* Brian Harrison and Colin Matthews, eds. Oxford, Oxford University Press, forthcoming 2004.

Blaikie, W.G., *Richard Baxter*. London, 1885.

Boersma, Hans, *A Hot Pepper Corn: Richard Baxter's Doctrine of Justification in Its Seventeenth-Century Context of Controversy*. Zoetermeer, Netherlands: Boekencentrum, 1993.

Bolam, C.G., and J. Goring, 'Presbyterians in the Parish Church: English Presbyterian Beginnings', C.G. Bolam, *et al., The English Presbyterians, from Eliazbethan Puritanism to modern Unitarianism*. London: Allen and Unwin, 1968.

Bornert, René, *La Réforme Protestante du Culte à Strasbourg au XVIe Siècle (1523-1598): Approche Sociologique et Interprétation Théologique* in *Studies in Medieval and Reformation Thought*, xxviii. Leiden: Brill, 1981.

Bossy, John, *Christianity in the West 1400-1700*. Oxford: Oxford University Press, 1985.

Bottrall, Margaret, *Every Man a Phoenix: Studies in seventeenth century autobiography*. London: John Murray, 1958.

Boyle, G.D., *Richard Baxter*. London, 1883.

Boyle, Leonard E., 'Robert Grosseteste and the Pastoral Care', *Pastoral Care, Clerical Education and Canon Law, 1200-1400*, L.E. Boyle, ed. London: Variorum Reprints, 1981.

Brachlow, Stephen, *The Communion of Saints: Radical Puritan and Separatist Ecclesiology 1570-1625*. Oxford: Oxford University Press, 1988.

Bremer, Francis J., *Congregational Communion: Clerical Friendship in the Anglo-American Puritan Community 1610-1692*. Boston, MA: Northeastern University Press, 1994.

- *Shaping New Englands: Puritan Clergymen in Seventeenth-Century England and New England*. London: Prentice Hall International, 1995.

Breward, Ian, 'Introduction', *The Work of William Perkins*. Abingdon, Berkshire: Sutton Courtenay Press, 1969.

Brown, John, *From the Restoration of 1660 to the Revolution of 1688*. London: National Council of Evangelical Free Churches, 1904.

Brown, John, 'Richard Baxter, the Kidderminster Pastor', *Puritan Preaching in England: A Study of Past and Present*. London: Hodder and Stoughton, 1900.

Burnett, Amy Nelson, 'Church Discipline and Moral Reformation in the thought of Martin Bucer', *Sixteenth Century Journal*, XXII (1991), 439-456.

- 'Confirmation and Christian Fellowship: Martin Bucer on Commitment to the Church', *Church History*, 64:2 (1995), 202-217.

- 'Martin Bucer and the Anabaptist Context of Evangelical Confirmation', *Mennonite Quarterly Review*, 68:1 (1994), 95-122.

- *The Yoke of Christ: Martin Bucer and Church Discipline*. Kirksville, MO: Sixteenth Century Journal Publishers, 1994.

Butterfield, Herbert, *The Whig Interpretation of History*. London: G. Bell and Sons, 1931; repr. New York: Norton, 1965.

Caldecott, Stratford, 'Conclusion: Eternity in Time', *Eternity in Time: Christopher Dawson and the Catholic Idea of History*, S. Caldecott and J. Morrill, eds. Edinburgh: T&T Clark, 1997.

Caldwell, Patricia, *The Puritan conversion narrative: The beginnings of American expression*. Cambridge: Cambridge University Press, 1983.

Cameron, Euan, 'Frankfurt and Geneva: the European Context of John Knox's Reformation', *John Knox and the British Reformations*, R.A. Mason, ed. Aldershot: Ashgate, 1998.

Cameron, James, 'Godly Nurture and Admonition in the Lord: Ecclesiastical Discipline in the Reformed Tradition', *Die danishe Reformation vor ihrem internationalen Hintergrund*, L. Grane and K. Hørby, eds. Gottingen: Vandenhoeck and Ruprecht, 1990.

Carlson, Eric Josef, 'Cassandra Banished? New Research on Religion in Tudor and Early Stuart England', *Religion and the English People, 1500-1640: New Perspectives New Voices*, E.J. Carlson, ed. Kirksville, MO: Thomas Jefferson University Press, 1998.

- '"Practical Divinity": Richard Greenham's Ministry in Elizabethan England', *Religion and the English People, 1500-1640: New Perspectives New Voices*, E.J. Carlson, ed. Kirksville, MO: Thomas Jefferson University Press, 1998.

Cautley, H. Munro, *Suffolk Churches and their Treasures*, 4th edition. Ipswich: n.p., 1975.

Clark, H.W., *History of English Nonconformity*. London: Chapman and Hall, 1913.

Clark-Maxwell, W.G., 'Baxter at Bridgnorth', *Transcripts of the Shropshire Archeological Society*, 4th series, IX (1923), 66-75.

Clebsch, W.A. and C.R. Jaekle, *Pastoral Care in Historical Perspective*. New York: Harper and Row, 1967.

Cohen, Charles, 'Two Biblical Models of Conversion: An Example of Puritan Hermeneutics', *Church History*, 58:2 (1989), 182-196.

Collinson, Patrick, *Archbishop Grindal 1519-1583: The Struggle for a Reformed Church*. London: Cape, 1979.

- 'The Cohabitation of the Faithful with the Unfaithful', *From Persecution to Toleration: The Glorious Revolution and Religion in England*, O. Grell, J. Israel and N. Tyacke, eds. Oxford: Clarendon Press, 1991.

- 'Comment on Eamon Duffy's Neale Lecture and the Colloquium', *England's Long Reformation, 1500-1800*, N. Tyacke, ed. London: UCL Press, 1998.
- *The Elizabethan Puritan Movement*. Oxford: Clarendon Press, 1990, c. 1967.
- *Godly People: essays on English Protestantism and Puritanism*. London: Hambledon Press, 1983.
- *The Religion of Protestants: The Church in English Society 1559-1625*. Oxford: Clarendon Press, 1982.
- 'Sects and the Evolution of Puritanism', *Puritanism: Transatlantic Perspectives on a Seventeenth-Century Anglo-American Faith*, F.J. Bremer, ed. Boston, MA: Massachusetts Historical Society, 1993.
- 'Shepherds, Sheepdogs and Hirelings: The Pastoral Ministry in Post-Reformation England', *The Ministry: Clerical and Lay*, W.J. Sheils and D. Wood, eds. Oxford: Blackwell, 1989.
- 'The vertical and the horizontal in religious history: internal and external integration of the subject', *As by Law Established: The Church of Ireland since the Reformation*, A. Ford, J. McGuire and K. Milne, eds. Dublin: Lilliput Press, 1995.
Cooke, T.R., 'Richard Baxter and the Dictates of the Praying Classes', *Westminster Theological Journal*, 58 (1996), 223-235.
- 'Richard Baxter, Puritan Churchman', Ph.D., University of Western Ontario, 1991.
- '"Uncommon Earnestness and Earthly Toils": Moderate Puritan Richard Baxter's Devotional Writings', *Anglican and Episcopal History*, 63 (1994), 51-72.
Cooper, Tim, *Fear and Polemic in Seventeenth-century England: Richard Baxter and Antinomianism*. Aldershot: Ashgate, 2001.
Cornick, David, 'Pastoral Care in England: Perkins, Baxter and Burnet', *A History of Pastoral Care*, G.R. Evans, ed. London: Cassell, 2000.
- 'The Reformation crisis in pastoral care', *A History of Pastoral Care*, G.R. Evans, ed. London: Cassell, 2000.
Costello, William Thomas, *The Scholastic Curriculum at Early Seventeenth-Century Cambridge*. Cambridge, MA: Harvard University Press, 1958.
Coulton, Barbara, 'The Establishment of Protestantism in a Provincial Town: A Study of Shrewsbury in the Sixteenth Century', *The Sixteenth Century Journal*, 27:2 (1996), 307-335.
Crockett, Bryan, 'The Act of Preaching and the Art of Prophesying', *Sewanee Review*, 105 (1997), 39-52.
Cross, Claire, 'The Church in England 1646-1660', *The Interregnum: The Quest for Settlement 1646-1660*, G.E. Aylmer, ed. London: MacMillan, 1972.
- 'A Metamorphosis of Ministry: Former Yorkshire Monks and Friars in the Sixteenth-Century Protestant Church', *Journal of the United Reformed Church History Society*, 4:5 (1989), 289-304.
- 'Priests into Ministers: The Establishment of Protestant Practice in the City of York 1530-1630', *Reformation Principal and Practice: essays in honour of Arthur Geoffrey Dickens*, P.N. Brooks, ed. London: Scholar Press, 1980.
Curtis, Mark, 'The Alienated Intellectuals of Early Stuart England', *Past and Present*,

23 (1962), 25-43.

- *Oxford and Cambridge in Transition 1558-1642*. Oxford: Clarendon Press, 1959.

Davies, C.M.F., ' "Poor Persecuted Little Flock" or "Commonwealth Christians": Edwardian Protestant Concepts of the Church', *Protestantism and the National Church in Sixteenth Century England*, P. Lake and M. Dowling, eds. London: Croom Helm, 1987.

Davies, C.M.F., and J.M. Facey, 'A reformation dilemma: John Foxe and the problem of discipline', *Journal of Ecclesiastical History*, 39 (1988), 37-65.

Davies, Horton, *Worship and Theology in England: From Andrews to Baxter and Fox, 1603-1690*. Princeton: Princeton University Press, 1975.

- Worship and Theology in England: From Cranmer to Hooker, 1534-1603. Princeton: Princeton University Press, 1970.

- *The Worship of the English Puritans*. London: Dacre Press, 1948.

Davies, J.H., *The Life of Richard Baxter, of Kidderminster, Preacher and Prisoner*. London, 1887.

Davis, Kenneth R., 'No Discipline, No Church: An Anabaptist Contribution to the Reformed Tradition', *Sixteenth Century Journal*, XIII:4 (1982), 43-58.

Derham, A.M., 'Richard Baxter and the Oecumenical Movement', *Evangelical Quarterly*, 23 (1951), 96-115.

Dever, M.E., 'Richard Sibbes and the "Truly Evangelical Church of England"', Ph.D., University of Cambridge, 1991.

- *Richard Sibbes: Puritanism and Calvinism in Late Elizabethan and Early Stuart England*. Macon, GA: Mercer University Press 2000.

Di Bernardino, Angelo, ed., *Encyclopaedia of the Early Church*, 2 vols. Cambridge: Cambridge University Press, 1992.

Dickens, A.G., 'The Early Expansion of Protestantism in England 1520-1558', *Reformation to Revolution: Politics and Religion in Early Modern England*, M. Todd, ed. London: Routledge, 1995.

- *The English Reformation*, 2nd ed. London: Batsford, 1989.

Doerksen, Daniel, *Conforming to the Word: Herbert, Donne, and the English Church before Laud*. Lewisburg, PA: Bucknell University Press, 1997.

Dohar, William J., *The Black Death and Pastoral Leadership: The Diocese of Hereford in the Fourteenth Century*. Philadelphia: University of Pennsylvania Press, 1995.

- ' "Since the pestilence time": pastoral care in the later Middle Ages', *A History of Pastoral Care*, G.R. Evans, ed. London: Cassell, 2000.

Donagan, Barbara, 'Did Ministers Matter? War and Religion in England, 1642-1649', *Journal of British Studies*, 33 (1994), 119-156.

Doran, Susan and Christopher Durston, *Princes, Pastors and People: The Church and Religion in England 1529-1689*. London: Routledge, 1991.

Duffy, Eamon, 'The Godly and the Multitude in Stuart England', *Seventeenth Century*, 1 (1986), 31-55.

- 'The Long Reformation: Catholicism, Protestantism and the Multitude', *England's Long Reformation, 1500-1800*, N. Tyack, ed. London: UCL Press, 1998.

- *The Stripping of the Altars: Traditional Religion in England 1400-1580*. New Haven and London: Yale University Press, 1992.

- *The Voices of Morebath: reformation and rebellion in an English village.* New Haven and London: Yale University Press, 2001.
- 'Wesley and the Counter-Reformation', *Revival and Religion Since 1700: Essays for John Walsh*, J. Garnett and C. Matthew, eds. London: Hambledon, 1993.
Durston, Christopher, 'Puritan Rule and the Failure of Cultural Revolution, 1645-1660', *The Culture of English Puritanism, 1560-1700*, C. Durston and J. Eales, eds. Basingstoke: MacMillan, 1996.
Eales, Jacqueline, 'A Road to Revolution: The Continuity of Puritanism, 1559-1642', *The Culture of English Puritanism, 1560-1700*, C. Durston and J. Eales, eds. Basingstoke: MacMillan, 1996.
- 'Samuel Clarke and the "Lives" of Godly Women in Seventeenth Century England', *Women in the Church, Studies in Church History*, 27, W.J. Sheils and D. Wood, eds. Oxford: Basil Blackwell, 1990.
Eayrs, George, *Richard Baxter and the Revival of Preaching and Pastoral Service.* London: n.p., 1912.
Enssle, Neal, 'Patterns of Godly Life: The Ideal Parish Minister in Sixteenth- and Seventeenth-Century English Thought', *The Sixteenth Century Journal*, 28:1 (1997), 3-28.
Evans, R.J., *In Defence of History.* London: Granta, 1997.
Ferguson, Everett, ed., *Encyclopaedia of Early Christianity.* New York and London, 1997.
Fielding, John, 'Arminians in the Localities: Peterborough Diocese, 1603-1642', *The Early Stuart Church, 1603-1642,* K. Fincham, ed. Basingstoke: MacMillan, 1993.
Fincham, Kenneth, 'Episcopal Government, 1603-1640', *The Early Stuart Church, 1603-1642*, K. Fincham, ed. Basingstoke: MacMillan, 1993.
- *Prelate as Pastor: The Episcopate of James I.* Oxford: Clarendon Press, 1990.
Fincham, Kenneth and Peter Lake, 'The Ecclesiastical Policies of James I and Charles I', *The Early Stuart Church, 1603-1642*, K. Fincham, ed. Basingstoke: MacMillan, 1993.
Firth, C.H. and R.S. Rait, eds, *Acts and Ordinances of the Interregnum 1642-1660.* 3 vols. London: Stationery Office, 1911.
- *Cromwell's Army: a history of the English Soldier during the Civil Wars, the Commonwealth and the Protectorate,* 3rd ed. London: Greenhill, 1992; London: Methuen, 1921.
- *Last Years of the Protectorate 1656-1658.* 2 vols. London: Longmans, Green, 1909.
- *Oliver Cromwell and the Rule of the Puritans in England.* London: Oxford University Press, 1953; London, 1900.
Fish, Stanley, *George Herbert and the Living Temple.* Berkeley: University of California Press, 1978.
Fletcher, Anthony, *A County Community in Peace and War: Sussex 1600-1660.* London: Longman, 1975.
- 'Oliver Cromwell and the godly nation', *Oliver Cromwell and the English Revolution*, J. Morrill, ed. London: Longman, 1990.
Foss, D.B., 'John Mirk's Instructions for Parish Priests', *The Ministry: Clerical and Lay*, W.J. Sheils and D. Wood, eds. Oxford: Basil Blackwell, 1989.

Foster, Joseph, *Alumni Oxoniensis: The Members of the University of Oxford, 1500-1714*. Oxford: Parker, 1891-1892.

Freeman, J., 'The Parish Ministry in the Diocese of Durham, c. 1570-1640', Ph.D., University of Durham, 1979.

Frykenberg, Robert, *History and Belief: The Foundations of Historical Understanding*. Grand Rapids, MI, Cambridge: William B. Eerdmans, 1996.

Gardiner, S.R., *History of the Great Civil War, 1642-1649*. 4 vols. London, 1886.

George, E.A., *Seventeenth Century Men of Latitude: Forerunners of the New Theology*. London: T. Fisher Unwin, 1909.

Gilbert, C.D., 'Baxter and the Work of Catechizing', *Baxter Notes and Studies*, 6:2 (1998), 3-8.

- *A History of King Charles I Grammar School Kidderminster*. Kidderminster: Tomkinson, 1979.

- '"Repent O England": Richard Baxter as Gildas Salvianus', *Baxter Notes and Studies*, 5:1 (1996), 3-10.

- 'Richard Baxter and James Berry', *Baxter Notes & Studies*, 6:1 (1998), 2-10.

- 'Richard Baxter and Nathaniel Brokesby', *Baxter Notes and Studies*, 5:2 (1997), 3-7.

- 'Richard Baxter in Coventry-Again', *Baxter Notes and Studies*, 3:3 (1995).

- 'Richard Baxter's Ministry in Kidderminster, 1641-1661', M.Phil., University of Birmingham, 1996.

- 'Richard Baxter's Visit to Gloucester, 1642', *Baxter Notes and Studies*, 1:3 (1993), 14-16.

- 'Two Irish Ministerial Associations of the 1650s', *Baxter Notes and Studies,* 4:2 (1996), 16-19.

- 'When Richard Baxter Came to Kidderminster', *Journal of the United Reformed Church History Society*, 5:1 (1992), 3-14.

- 'The Worcestershire Association of Ministers', *Baxter Notes and Studies*, 4:2 (1996), 3-15.

Gilbert, C.D., and Richard Warner, *Caldwall Hall Kidderminster*. Kidderminster: Tomkinson, 1999.

Gordon, Alexander, *Heads of English Unitarian History*. London, 1895.

Greaves, Richard L., *John Bunyan and English Nonconformity*. London: Hambledon, 1992.

- *Saints and Rebels: Seven Nonconformists in Stuart England*. Macon, GA: Mercer University Press, 1985.

Graham, J.K., 'Searches for the New Jerusalem: The History and Mystery of Reformation in Mid-Seventeenth Century England', *Religion, Resistance, and Civil War*, G.J. Schochet, ed. Washington, DC: The Folger Institute, 1990.

Graham, Michael F., 'Knox on Discipline: Conversionary Zeal or Rose-tinted Nostalgia?', *John Knox and the British Reformations*, R.A. Mason, ed. Aldershot: Ashgate, 1998.

Green, Ian, *The Christian's The Christian's ABC: Catechisms and Catechizing in England c. 1530-1740*. Oxford: Clarendon Press, 1996.

- ' "Reformed Pastors" and *Bons Cures*: The Changing Role of the Parish in Early Modern Europe', *The Ministry: Clerical and Lay*, W.J. Sheils and D. Wood, eds.

Oxford: Blackwell, 1989.

Gregory, Jeremy, 'The making of a Protestant nation: "success" and "failure" in England's Long Reformation', *England's Long Reformation 1500-1800*, N. Tyacke, ed. London: UCL Press, 1998.

Grimes, Mary Cochran, 'Saving Grace among Puritans and Quakers: a study of 17th and 18th century conversion experiences', *Quaker History*, 72 (1983), 3-26.

Grosart, A.B. 'Richard Baxter: Seraphic Fervour', *Representative Nonconformists*. London, 1879.

Haddon, W.H., 'Baxter's Work', *Baptist Quarterly*, 3 (1926-27), 205-210.

- 'Richard Baxter—the Man', *Baptist Quarterly*, 3 (1926-27), 150-155.

Haigh, Christopher, 'The Church of England, the Catholics and the people', *The Impact of the English Reformation 1500-1640*, P. Marshall, ed. London: Arnold, 1997.

- *English Reformations: Religion, Politics, and Society under the Tudors.* Oxford: Clarendon Press, 1993.

- 'Puritan evangelism in the reign of Elizabeth I', *English Historical Review*, 72 (1977), 30-58.

- 'The Recent Historiography of the English Reformation', *Reformation to Revolution: Politics and Religion in Early Modern England*, M. Todd, ed. London: Routledge, 1995.

Hall, Basil, 'Cranmer, the Eucharist and the Foreign Divines in the Reign of Edward VI', *Thomas Cranmer: Churchman and Scholar*, P. Ayris and D. Selwyn, eds. Woodbridge, Suffolk: The Boydell Press, 1993.

- 'Martin Bucer in England', *Martin Bucer: Reforming Church and Community*, D.F. Wright, ed. Cambridge: Cambridge University Press, 1994.

Hall, David D., *The Faithful Shepherd: A History of the New England Ministry in the Seventeenth Century.* Chapel Hill, NC: University of North Carolina Press, 1972.

Haller, William, *The Rise of Puritanism; or The Way to the New Jerusalem as set forth in pulpit and press from Thomas Cartwright to John Lilburne and John Milton, 1570-1643.* New York: Columbia University Press, 1938.

Hambrick-Stowe, C.E., *The Practice of Piety: Puritan Devotional Disciplines iin Seventeenth-Century New England.* Chapel Hill, NC: University of North Carolina Press, 1982.

- 'The Spirit of the Old Writers: The Great Awakening and the Persistance of Puritan Piety', *Puritanism: A Transatlantic Perspective on a Seventeenth-Century Anglo-American Faith,* F. Bremer, ed. Boston, MA: Massachusetts Historical Society, 1993.

Harris, William, *Richard Baxter: The Making of a Non-conformist.* London: Congregational Union of England and Wales, 1912.

Harrison, Richard L., 'Martin Bucer on the Nature and Purpose of Ministry: The View from Exile', *Lexington Theological Quarterly*, 16:2 (1981), 53-67.

Heal, Felicity, '[Review of] *The Christian's ABC: Catechisms and Catechizing in England c. 1530-1740.* By Ian Green', *Journal of Modern History*, 71 (1999), 185-187.

Heath, Peter, *The English Parish Clergy Prior to the Reformation.* London: Routledge,

1969.

Hill, Christopher, *The Century of Revolution, 1603-1714*. London: Thomas Nelson 1961, repr. London: Nelson, 1980.

- *Society and Puritanism in Pre-Revolutionary England*. London: Secker and Warburg, 1964.

Hirst, Derek, *Authority and Conflict: England 1603-1658*. London: Edward Arnold, 1986.

- 'The Failure of National Reformation in the 1650s' *Religion, Resistance, and Civil War*, G.J. Schochet, ed. Washington, DC: The Folger Institute, 1990.

Hodgkins, Christopher, *Authority, Church, and Society in George Herbert: Return to the Middle Way*. Columbia, MO: University of Missouri Press, 1993.

Hopf, Constantin, *Martin Bucer and the English Reformation*. Oxford: Basil Blackwell, 1946.

Hopkirk, D.S., 'The Reduction: Archbishop Ussher's Historic Effort in Accommodation', *Reformed Theological Review*, 11 (1952), 61-71.

Houlbrooke, Ralph, 'The family and pastoral care', *A History of Pastoral Care*, G.R. Evans, ed. London: Cassell, 2000.

House, R. P., 'Old Testament Historians', *Historians of the Christian Tradition: Their Methodology and Influence on Western Thought*, M. Bauman and M.I. Klauber, eds. Nashville, TN: Broadman and Holman, 1995.

Hudson, W.S., 'The Ministry in the Puritan Age', *The Ministry in Historical Perspective*, H.R. Neibuhr and D.D. Williams, eds. New York: Harper, 1956.

Hughes, Ann, *Godly Reformation and its Opponents in Warwickshire, 1640-1662*. Stratford-upon-Avon: The Dugdale Society, 1993.

- 'The Meaning of Religious Polemic', *Puritanism: A Transatlantic Perspective on a Seventeenth-Century Anglo-American Faith*, F. Bremer, ed. Boston, MA: Massachusetts Historical Society, 1993.

Hunt, Arnold, 'The Lord's Supper in Early Modern England', *Past & Present*, 161 (1998), 39-83.

Hunt, William, *The Puritan Moment: The Coming of Revolution in an English County*. Cambridge, MA: Harvard University Press, 1983.

Ingram, Martin, 'Puritans and the Church Courts, 1560-1640', *The Culture of English Puritanism, 1560-1700*, C. Durston & J. Eales, eds. Basingstoke: MacMillan, 1996.

- 'Religion, Communities and Moral Discipline in Late Sixteenth- and Early Seventeenth-Century England: Case Studies', *Religion and Society in Early Modern Europe 1500-1800*, K. von Greyerz, ed. London: German Historical Institute, 1984.

Jukes, A.L., 'Gunning and the Worcester Agreement', *Modern Churchman*, 7 (1964), 184-186.

Kamperidis, Lambros, 'Catechesis in East and West', *A History of Pastoral Care*, G.R. Evans, ed. London: Cassell, 2000.

Keeble, N.H., 'The Autobiographer as Apologist: *Reliquiae Baxterianae* (1696)', *Prose Studies*, 9:2 (1986).

- *The Literary Culture of Nonconformity in Later Seventeenth-Century England*.

Leicester: Leicester University Press, 1987.

- *'Loving and Free Converse': Richard Baxter in His Letters*, Friends of Dr Williams's Library Forty-Fifth Lecture. London: Dr Williams's Trust, 1991.

- *Richard Baxter: Puritan Man of Letters*. Oxford: Clarendon Press, 1982.

- 'Richard Baxter's Preaching Ministry: its History and Texts' *Journal of Ecclesiastical History*, 35 (1984), 539-559.

Keeble, N.H., and G.F. Nuttall, *Calendar of the Correspondence of Richard Baxter*. Oxford: Clarendon Press, 1991.

Kemp, C.F., *A Pastoral Triumph: The Story of Richard Baxter and his Ministry at Kidderminster*. New York: MacMillan, 1948.

Kendall, R.T., *Calvin and English Calvinism to 1649*. Oxford: Oxford University Press, 1979.

Kilroy, Phil, *Protestant Dissent and Controversy in Ireland 1660-1714*. Cork: Cork University Press, 1994.

Knappen, M.M., *Tudor Puritanism: a chapter in the history of idealism*. Chicago: University of Chicago Press, 1939.

Knott, Jr., J.R., *The Sword of the Spirit: Puritan Responses to the Bible*. Chicago: University of Chicago Press, 1980.

Knox, R.B., *James Ussher: Archbishop of Armaugh*. Cardiff: University of Wales Press, 1967.

Krahn, Henry G., 'Martin Bucer's Strategy Against Sectarian Dissent in Strasbourg', *Mennonite Quarterly Review*, 50:3 (1976), 163-180.

Ladell, A.R., *Richard Baxter: Puritan and Mystic*. London: SPCK, 1925.

Lake, Peter, *Anglicans and Puritans? Presbyterians and English Conformist Thought from Whitgift to Hooker*. London: Unwin and Allen, 1988.

- 'Defining Puritanism—Again?', *Puritanism: Transatlantic Perspectives on a Seventeenth-Century Anglo-American Faith*, F. Bremer, ed. Boston, MA: Massachusetts Historical Society, 1993.

- 'The Laudian Style', *The Early Stuart Church, 1603-1642*, K. Fincham, ed. Basingstoke: MacMillan, 1993.

- *Moderate Puritans and the Elizabethan Church*. Cambridge: Cambridge University Press, 1982.

Lamont, W.M., 'Episcopacy and a "Godly Discipline", 1641-6', *Journal of Ecclesiastical History,* 10 (1959), 74-89.

- *Puritanism and Historical Controversy*. London: UCL Press, 1996.

- 'The Religious Origins of the English Civil War', *Religion, Resistance, and Civil War,* G. Schochet, ed. Washington, DC: The Folger Institute, 1990.

- '[Review of] *Calendar of the Correspondence of Richard Baxter*', *Journal of the United Reformed Church History Society*, 5:1 (1992), 56-58.

- *Richard Baxter and the Millennium: Protestant Imperialism and the English Revolution*. London: Croom Helm, 1979.

Langley, A.S., 'Richard Baxter—The Director of Souls: The Man and His Pastoral Method', *Baptist Quarterly*, 3 (1926-27), 71-80.

Lapidge, Michael, and David Dumville, *Gildas: New Approaches*. Woodbridge, Suffolk: The Boydell Press, 1984.

Lim, Paul Chang-Ha, 'In Pursuit of Unity, Purity and Liberty: Richard Baxter's Puritan Ecclesiology in Context', Ph.D., University of Cambridge, 2001.

Liu, Tai, 'Bibliography [of G.F. Nuttall's published works until 1977)', *Reformation, Conformity and Dissent: Essays in Honour of Geoffrey Nuttall*, R.B. Knox, ed. London: Epworth Press, 1977.

- 'Geoffrey Nuttall: A Bibliography 1977-1996', *The Journal of the United Reformed Church History Society*, 5 (1996), 534-43.

MacCulloch, Diarmaid, 'The change of religion', *The Sixteenth Century*, Patrick Collinson, ed. Oxford: Oxford University Press, 2002.

- *The Later Reformation in England, 1547-1603*. London: MacMillan, 1990.

- *Thomas Cranmer: A Life*. New Haven and London: Yale University Press, 1996.

- *Tudor Church Militant: Edward VI and the Protestant Reformation*. London: Allen Lane The Penguin Press, 1999.

MacFarlane, Alan, *The Family Life of Ralph Josselin: A Seventeenth Century Clergyman*. Cambridge: Cambridge University Press, 1970.

Magee, W.C., 'Richard Baxter, his Life and Times', Lectures delivered Before the Dublin Young Men's Christian Association. Dublin, 1862.

McGinn, D.J., *The Admonition Controversy*. New Brunswick, NJ: Rutgers University Press, 1949.

McGrath, Alister, *Reformation Thought: An Introduction*, 3rd edition. Oxford: Blackwell, 1999.

- *To Know and Serve God: A Biography of James I. Packer*. London: Hodder and Stoughton, 1997.

McGrath, Gavin, 'Puritans and the Human Will: Voluntarism within Mid-Seventeenth Century English Puritanism As Seen in the Works of Richard Baxter and John Owen', Ph.D., University of Durham, 1989.

McIntosh, Marjorie K., 'Local Change and Community Control in England, 1465-1500', *Huntington Library Quarterly*, 49 (1986), 219-242.

McKim, Donald, '[Review of] *Straightening the Altars*', *Church History*, 71:3 (2002), 658-660.

McLachlan. H., English Education Under the Test Acts: Being the History of the Nonconformist Academies 1662-1820. Manchester: Manchester University Press, 1931.

McNeill, J.T., *A History of the Cure of Souls*. New York: Harper, 1951.

Mair, N.H., 'Christian Sanctification and Individual Pastoral Care in Richard Baxter', Th.D., Union Theological Seminary, New York (1966).

Marchant, R.A., *The Puritans and the Church Courts in the Diocese of York 1560-1642*. London: Longmans, 1960.

Marshall, Peter, *The Catholic Priesthood and the English Reformation*. Oxford: Clarendon Press, 1994.

- *The Face of Pastoral Ministry in the East Riding, 1525-1595*. York: Borthwick Institute of Historical Research, 1995.

Martin, Hugh, *Puritanism and Richard Baxter*. London: SCM Press, 1954.

Martin, R.P., *A Guide to the Puritans*. Edinburgh: The Banner of Truth Trust, 1997.

Martin, T.H., 'Richard Baxter and "The Reformed Pastor"', *Baptist Quarterly*, 9 (1938-39), 350-361.

Matthews, A.G., *Calamy Revised: Being a Revision of Edmund Calamy's Account of the Ministers and Others Ejected and Silenced, 1660-2*. Oxford: Clarendon Press,

1988; Oxford: Clarendon Press, 1934.

- *Walker Revised: Being a Revision of John Walker's Sufferings of the Clergy during the Grand Rebellion, 1642-60*. Oxford: Clarendon Press, 1988; Oxford: Clarendon Press, 1948.

- *The Works of Richard Baxter: An Annotated List*. No place: Oxted, 1932

Matthews, H.C.G., and Brian Harrison, eds., *Oxford Dictionary of National Biography, in association with the British Academy,* Oxford, Oxford University Press, forthcoming 2004.

Mayor, Stephen, *The Lord's Supper in Early English Dissent*. London, Epworth Press, 1972.

Mendle, Michael, 'Untimely Compromises: Moderate Proposals for Church Government in 1641', *Conference on Puritanism*, S. Bercovitch, ed. London: n.p., 1975.

Miller, Paul, 'Spirituality, Integrity and Competence: Essentials of Ministry in Richard Baxter's *Reformed Pastor', Evangelical Quarterly*, 69 (1997), 333-342.

Moore, Susan Hardman, 'Arguing for Peace: Giles Firmin on New England and Godly Unity', *Unity and Diversity in the Church*, R.N. Swanson, ed. Oxford: Basil Blackwell, 1996.

Morgan, Irvonwy, *The Godly Preachers of the Elizabethan Church*. London: Epworth Press, 1965.

- *The Nonconformity of Richard Baxter*. London: Epworth Press, 1946.

Morgan, John, *Godly Learning: Puritan Attitudes toward Reason, Learning and Education, 1560-1640*. Cambridge: Cambridge University Press, 1986.

Morrill, John, 'The Coming of War', *Reformation to Revolution: Politics and Religion in Early Modern England*, M. Todd, ed. London: Routledge, 1995.

- [untitled contribution], *The History Debate*, Juliet Gardiner, ed. London: Collins and Brown, 1990.

- 'Cromwell and his contemporaries' *Oliver Cromwell and the English Revolution*, J. Morrill, ed. London: Longman, 1990.

- 'The Historian and the "Historical Filter"', *The Past and the Present: Problems of Understanding*, P. Geach, *et al.*, eds. Oxford: Grandpont House, 1993.

- 'The Impact of Puritanism', *The Impact of the English Civil War*, J. Morrill, ed. London: Collins and Brown, 1991.

- 'Introduction', *Eternity in Time: Christopher Dawson and the Catholic Idea of History*, S. Caldecott and J. Morrill, eds. Edinburgh: T&T Clark. 1997.

- *The Nature of the English Revolution*. London: Longman, 1993.

- 'Politics in an Age of Revolution 1630-1690', *The Oxford Illustrated History of Tudor & Stuart Britain*, J. Morrill, ed. Oxford: Oxford University Press, 1996.

- *The Revolt of the Provinces: Conservatives and Radicals in the English Civil War 1630-1650*, 2nd ed. London: Longman, 1999. London: Longman, 1980.

Murphy, J.M., 'Oliver Cromwell's Church: State and Clergy During the Protectorate', Ph.D., University of Wisconsin, 1997.

Napier, Joseph, *Richard Baxter and His Times. A Lecture*. Dublin, 1855.

Neale, J.E., *Elizabeth I & her Parliaments, 1559-1581*. London: Cape, 1953.

- *Elizabeth I & her Parliaments, 1584-1601*. London: Cape, 1957.

North, R.N., 'Minutes', Reports and Transactions of the Devonshire Association for the Advancement of Science (1887), 279-281.

Nuttall, G.F., 'Advice to a Young Minister', *The Congregational Quarterly*, 30 (1952), 231-235.

- 'Assembly and Association in Dissent, 1689-1831', G.J. Cuming and D Baker, eds., *Councils and Assemblies, Studies in Church History* 7. Cambridge: Cambridge University Press, 1971.

- 'Association Records of the Particular Baptists', *Baptist Quarterly*, 26 (1975), 14-25.

- 'The Baptist Western Association 1653-1658', *Journal of Ecclesiastical History*, 11 (1960), 213-218.

- 'Congregational Commonwealth Incumbents', *Transactions of the Congregational Historical Society*, 14 (1944), 155-167.

- 'The Correspondence of John Lewis, Glasgrug, with Richard Baxter and with Dr. John Ellis, Dolgelley', *Journal of the Merioneth Historical and Record Society*, 2 (1954), 120-134.

- 'The Death of Lady Rous, 1656-Richard Baxter's Account', *Transactions of the Worcestershire Archaeological Society*, 28 (1952), 4-13.

- 'The Essex Classis (1648)', *Journal of the United Reformed Church History Society*, 3:6 (1985), 194-202.

- 'The First Nonconformists', G.F. Nuttall and O. Chadwick, eds., *From Uniformity to Unity 1662-1962*. London: SPCK, 1962.

- *The Holy Spirit in Puritan Faith and Experience*, 2nd edition. Oxford: Basil Blackwell, 1947.

- 'The Last of James Nayler: Robert Rich and the Church of the First-Born', *Friends Quarterly*, 23:11 (1985), 527-534.

- *The Manuscript of the Reliquiae Baxterianae*. London: Dr Williams's Trust, 1954.

- 'The MS of *Reliquiae Baxterianae* (1696)', *Journal of Ecclesiastical History*, 6 (1955), 73-79.

- 'Philip Henry and London', *Journal of the United Reformed Church History Society*, 5:5 (1994), 259-265.

- 'Presbyterians and Independents: Some Movements for Unity 300 years ago', *The Journal of the Presbyterian Historical Society of England*, 10 (1952), 4-15.

- *The Puritan Spirit: Essays and Addresses*. London: Epworth Press, 1967.

- '[Review of] H. Martin, *Puritanism and Richard Baxter'*, *Journal of Ecclesiastical History*, 6 (1955), 240-241.

- *Richard Baxter*. London: Nelson, 1965.

- *Richard Baxter and Philip Doddridge: A Study in a Tradition*. London: Oxford University Press, 1951.

- 'Richard Baxter and *The Grotian Religion'*, D. Baker, ed., *Reform and Reformation: England and the Continent, c. 1500-1750*. Oxford: Basil Blackwell, 1979.

- 'Richard Baxter and the Puritan Movement', F.H. Ballard, ed., *Heroes of the Faith*. London: Livingstone Press, 1949.

- 'Richard Baxter's *Apology* (1654): its Occasion and Composition', *Journal of Ecclesiastical History*, 4 (1953), 69-76.

- 'Richard Baxter's Correspondence: a preliminary survey', *Journal of Ecclesiastical History*, 1 (1950), 89-95.
- 'Stepney Meeting: The pioneers', *Congregational Historical Society Transactions*, 18 (1956), 17-22.
- 'A Transcript of Richard Baxter's Library Catalogue: A Bibliographical Note', *Journal of Ecclesiastical History*, 2 (1951), 207-221.
- *Visible Saints: The Congregational Way 1640-1660*. Oxford: Basil Blackwell, 1957.
- 'The Worcestershire Association: Its Membership', *Journal of Ecclesiastical History*, 1 (1950), 197-206.

Nuttall, G.F., *et al.*, *The Beginnings of Nonconformity*. London: James Clark and Company, 1964.

O'Day, Rosemary, *Education and Society 1500-1800*. London: Longman, 1982.
- *The English Clergy: the emergence and consolidation of a profession 1558-1642*. Leicester: Leicester University Press, 1979.
- 'The reformation of the ministry, 1558-1642', R. O'Day and F. Heal, eds., *Continuity and Change: Personnel and administration of the Church of England 1500-1642*. Leicester: Leicester University Press, 1976.

O'Loughlin, Thomas, 'Penitentials and pastoral care', G.R. Evans, ed., *A History of Pastoral Care*. London: Cassell, 2000.

O'Sullivan, T.D., *The De Excidio of Gildas: Its Authenticity and Date*. Leiden: Brill, 1978.

Oden, Thomas, *Pastoral Care in the Classic Tradition*. Philadelphia: Fortress Press, 1984.

Olsen, G.W., 'Reform after the Pattern of the Primitive Church in the Thought of Salvian of Marseilles', *Catholic Historical Review*, 68 (1982), 1-12.

Packer, J.I., *An Anglican to Remember, William Perkins: Puritan Popularizer*. London: St Antholin's Lectureship Charity, 1996.
- *A Grief Sanctified: Love, loss and hope in the Life of Richard Baxter*. Leicester: Crossway, 1997.
- 'Introducing "A Christian Directory" ', Richard Baxter, *A Christian Directory*. Morgan, PA: Soli Deo Gloria, 1990.
- *A Man for All Ministries*. London: Packer, 1991.
- *A Quest for Godliness: The Puritan Vision of the Christian Life*. Wheaton, IL: Crossway, 1990. Published in the United Kingdom as *Among God's Giants: Aspects of Puritan Christianity*. Eastbourne: Kingsway, 1991.
- 'The Redemption and Restoration of Man in the Though of Richard Baxter', D.Phil., Oxford University (1954).
- 'Richard Baxter', *Theology*, 55 (1953), 174-178.
- 'Richard Baxter on Heaven, Hope and Holiness', J.I. Packer and L. Wilkinson, eds., *Alive to God: Studies in Spirituality presented to James M. Houston*. Downers Grove, IL: InterVarsity Press, 1992.

Packer, J.I., and Timothy Beougher, 'Go Fetch Baxter' *Christianity Today*, 35 (16/12/1991), 26-28.

Palfrey, H.E., 'The Foleys of Stourbridge', *Transactions of the Worcestershire Archeological Society*, new series, xxi (1945), 1-15.

Parker, K.L. and E.J. Carlson, *'Practical Divinity': The Works and Life of Revd. Richard Greenham.* Aldershot: Ashgate, 1998.

Parry, G.J.R., *A Protestant Vision: William Harrison and the Reformation of Elizabethan England.* Cambridge: Cambridge University Press, 1987.

Pauck, Wilhelm, 'Editor's Introduction', *Melanchthon and Bucer*, Library of Christian Classics, XIX. Philadelphia: Westminster Press, 1969.

Paul, R.S., *The Assembly of the Lord: Politics and Religion in the Westminster Assembly.* Edinburgh: T. & T. Clark, 1985.

- 'Ecclesiology in Richard Baxter's Autobiography', D.Y. Hadidian, ed., *From Faith to Faith: Essays in Honor of Donald G. Miller on his Seventieth Birthday.* Pittsburgh, PA: Pickwick Press, 1979.

Pearse, Meic, *The Great Restoration: The Religious Radicals of the 16th and 17th Centuries.* Carlisle: Paternoster, 1998.

Peet, D.J., 'The Mid-Sixteenth century Parish Clergy, with particular consideration of the dioceses of Norwich and York', Ph.D., University of Cambridge, 1980.

Pettegree, Andrew, 'The Clergy and the Reformation: from "devilish priesthood" to new professional elite', Andrew Pettegree, ed., *The Reformation of the parishes: the ministry and the Reformation in town and country.* Manchester: Manchester University Press, 1993.

Pettit, Norman, *The Heart Prepared: Grace and Conversion in Puritan Spiritual Life.* New Haven and London: Yale University Press 1966.

Porter, H.C., *Reformation and Reaction in Tudor Cambridge.* Cambridge: Cambridge University Press, 1958.

Pounds, N.J.G., *A History of the English Parish: The Culture of Religion from Augustine to Victoria.* Cambridge: Cambridge University Press, 2000.

Powicke, F.J., 'Another Lauderdale Letter', *Bulletin of the John Rylands Library*, 10 (1926), 524-531.

- 'Dr. Du Moulin's *Vindication*', *Congregational Historical Society Transactions*, 9 (1924-6), 219-237.

- 'Eleven letters of John Second Earl of Lauderdale (and First Duke), 1616-1682, to the Rev. Richard Baxter (1615-1691)', *Bulletin of the John Rylands Library*, 7 (1922-3), 73-105.

- 'An Episode in the Ministry of the Rev. Henry Newcome, and his Connection with the Rev. Richard Baxter', *Bulletin of the John Rylands Library*, 13 (1929), 63-88.

- *A Life of the Reverend Richard Baxter 1615-1691.* London: Jonathan Cape, 1924.

- *A Puritan Idyll or the Rev. Richard Baxter's Love Story.* Manchester: Manchester University Press, 1918.

- 'The Reverend Richard Baxter and his Lancashire Friend Mr. Henry Ashurst', *Bulletin of the John Rylands Library*, 13 (1929), 309-325.

- *The Reverend Richard Baxter under the Cross, 1662-1691.* London: Jonathan Cape, 1927.

- 'Richard Baxter and The Countess of Balcarres (1621?-1706?)', *Bulletin of the John Rylands Library*, 9 (1925), 585-599.

- 'Richard Baxter and *The Saints Everlasting Rest*', *Congregational Quarterly*, 3

(1925), 280-290.
- 'Richard Baxter and William Penn', *Friends' Quarterly Examiner*, 59 (1925), 151-160.
- 'Richard Baxter's Relation to the Baptists', *Baptist Historical Society Transactions*. 6 (1918-19), 193-215.
- 'Some Unpublished Correspondence of the Reverend Richard Baxter and the Reverend John Eliot...1656-1682', *Bulletin of the John Rylands Library*, 15 (1931), 138-176, 442-466.
- Some Unpublished Correspondence of the Reverend Richard Baxter and the Reverend John Eliot...1656-1682. Manchester: Manchester University Press, 1931.
- 'Story and Significance of the Rev. Richard Baxter's *Saints' Everlasting Rest*', *Bulletin of the John Rylands Library*, 5 (1919-20), 445-479.
Primus, J.H., *Richard Greenham: Portrait of an Elizabethan Pastor*. Macon, GA: Mercer University Press, 1998.
Pruett, John H., *The Parish Clergy under the Later Stuarts: The Leicestershire Experience*. Urbana, IL, and London: University of Illinois Press, 1978.
Reay, Barry, *The Quakers and the English Revolution*. London: Temple Smith, 1985.
Richards, Thomas, *Religious Developments in Wales (1654-1662)*. London: n.p., 1923.
Robson, Michael, 'A ministry of preachers and confessors: the pastoral impact of the friars', G.R. Evans, ed., *A History of Pastoral Care*. London: Cassell, 2000.
Ryle, J.C., *Baxter and His Times*. London, 1853.
- *The Priest, the Puritan and the Preacher*. New York, 1857.
Ryrie, Alec, 'Counting sheep and counting shepherds: the problem of allegiance in the English Reformation', Peter Marshall and Alec Ryrie, eds., *The Beginnings of English Protestantism*. Cambridge: Cambridge University Press, 2002.
Samuel, Raphael, 'The Discovery of Puritanism, 1820-1914: A Preliminary Sketch', J. Garnett and C. Matthew, eds., *Revival and Religion Since 1700, Essays for John Walsh*. London: Hambledon, 1993.
Sceats, David, 'Gildas Salvianas [sic] Redevivus-The Reformed Pastor, Richard Baxter', *Anvil*, 10 (1993), 135-145.
Schilling, Heinz, ' "History of Crime" or "History of Sin"?—Some Reflections on the Social History of Early Modern Church Discipline', E.I. Kouri and T. Scott, eds., *Politics and Society in Reformation Europe: Essays for Sir Geoffrey Elton on his Sixty-fifth Birthday*. London: MacMillan, 1986.
Seaver, Paul, *The Puritan Lectureships: The Politics of Religious Dissent 1560-1662*. Stanford: Stanford University Press, 1970.
Scarisbrick, J.J., *The Reformation and the English People*. Oxford: Basil Blackwell, 1984.
Sharpe, Kevin, 'Archbishop Laud', M. Todd, ed., *Reformation to Revolution: Politics and Religion in Early Modern England*. London: Routledge, 1995.
Shaw, W.A., *A History of the English Church During the Civil War and Under the Commonwealth 1640-1660,* 2 vols. London: Longmans and Company, 1900.
Shealy W.R., 'The Power of the Present: The Pastoral Perspective of Richard Baxter, Puritan Divine, 1615-1691', Ph.D., Drew University, 1966.
Sheldrake, Philip, 'George Herbert and *The Country Parson*', G.R. Evans, ed., *A History*

of Pastoral Care. London: Cassell, 2000.

Shinners, John and William J. Dohar, *Pastors and the Cure of Souls in Medieval England*. Notre Dame, IN: University of Notre Dame Press, 1998.

Spufford, Margaret, 'The Importance of the Lord's Supper to Seventeeth-Century Dissenters', *Journal of the United Reformed Church History Society*, 5, 2 (1993), 62-79.

- 'Puritanism and Social Control?', Anthony Fletcher and John Stevenson, eds., *Order and Disorder in Early Modern England*. Cambridge: Cambridge University Press, 1985.

Spurr, John, *English Puritanism 1603-1689*. Basingstoke: MacMillan, 1998.

- *The Restoration Church of England 1646-1689*. New Haven and London: Yale University Press, 1991.

- '[Review of] *The Christian's The Christian's ABC. Catechisms and Catechizing in England c. 1530-1740*. By Ian Green', *Journal of Theological Studies*, 48 (1997), 330-334.

Stalker, J., 'Richard Baxter', *The Evangelical Succession*. Edinburgh, 1883.

Stauffer, Donald, *English Biography Before 1700*. Cambridge, MA: Harvard University Press, 1930.

Stephen, Sir L., and Sir S. Lee, eds, *Dictionary of National Biography*. London: Oxford University Press, 1908-09.

Stoughton, J., 'Richard Baxter; or Earnest Decision', *Lights of the World*. London, 1853.

Tawney, R.H., *Religion and the Rise of Capitalism*. London: John Murray, 1926.

Thomas, Roger, *The Baxter Treatises: A Catalogue of the Richard Baxter Papers...in Dr. Williams's Library*. London: Dr Williams's Trust, 1959.

- 'The Rise of the Reconcilers', *The English Presbyterians, from Eliazbethan Puritanism to modern Unitarianism*, C.G. Bolam, J. Goring, H.L. Short and R. Thomas, contributors. London: Allen and Unwin, 1968.

Todd, Margo, *Christian Humanism and the Puritan Social Order*. Cambridge: Cambridge University Press, 1987.

Towler, Robert, and A.P.M. Coxon, *The Fate of the Anglican Clergy: A Sociological Study*. London: MacMillan, 1979.

Tulloch, J., 'Baxter', *English Puritanism and its Leaders*. Edinburgh, 1861.

Twigg, John, *The University of Cambridge and the English Revolution*. Cambridge: Cambridge University Press, 1990.

Tyacke, Nicolas, *Anti-Calvinists: The Rise of English Arminianism c. 1590-1640*. Oxford: Clarendon Press, 1987.

- *The Fortunes of English Puritanism 1603-1640*, Friends of Dr Williams's Library, 44th Annual Lecture. London: Dr Williams's Trust, 1990.

- 'Introduction: Re-thinking the "English Reformation"', N. Tyacke, ed., *England's Long Reformation 1500-1800*. London: UCL Press, 1998.

- 'Puritanism, Arminianism and Counter-Revolution', M. Todd, ed., *Reformation to Revolution: Politics and Religion in Early Modern England*. London: Routledge, 1995.

- 'The "Rise of Puritanism" and the Legalizing of Dissent, 1571-1719', O.P. Grell, J.I.

Israel and N. Tyacke, eds., *From Persecution to Toleration: the Glorious Revolution and Religion in England*. Oxford: Clarendon Press, 1991.

Underdown, David, *Fire from Heaven: The Life of an English Town in the Seventeenth Century*. London: Harper-Collins, 1992.

van Dam, Harm-Jan, 'De Imperio Summarum Potestatum Circa Sacra', H.J.M Nellen and E. Rabbie, eds. *Hugo Grotius Theologian*. Leiden: Brill, 1994.

Vander Schaaf, Mark E., 'Archbishop Parker's Efforts Toward a Bucerian Discipline in the Church of England', *Sixteenth Century Journal*, VIII:1 (1977), 85-103.

Venn, John and J.A. Venn, *Alumni Cantabrigienses*. Cambridge: Cambridge University Press, 1924.

Vernon, E.C., 'The Sion College Conclave and London Presbyterianism during the English Revolution', Ph.D., University of Cambridge, 1999.

Wall, John N., 'Introduction', J.N. Wall, ed., *George Herbert: The Country Parson, The Temple*. New York City: Paulist Press, 1981.

Ward, Benedicta, 'Pastoral Care and the monks: "Whose feet do you wash?", G.R. Evans, ed., *A History of Pastoral Care*. London: Cassell, 2000.

Webber, Joan, *The Eloquent 'I': Style and Self in Seventeenth-Century Prose*. Madison WI: University of Wisconsin Press, 1968.

Weber, Max, *The Protestant Ethic and the Spirit of Captialism*. London: Routledge, 2001; c. 1930.

Webster, Tom, *Godly Clergy in Early Stuart England: The Caroline Puritan Movement 1620-1643*. Cambridge: Cambridge University Press, 1997.

Weintraub, K.J., *The Value of the Individual: Self and Circumstance in Autobiography*. Chicago: University of Chicago Press, 1978.

Wenig, Scott A., *Straightening the Altars: The Ecclesiastical Vision and Pastoral Achievement of the Progressive Bishops under Elizabeth I, 1559-1579*. New York: Peter Lang, 2000.

Whiting, C.E., *Studies in English Puritanism from the Restoration to the Revolution*. London: SPCK, 1931.

Whiting, Robert, *Local Responses to the English Reformation*. London: MacMillan, 1998.

Wilkinson, John T., 'Richard Baxter's "The Reformed Pastor" ', *The Expository Times*, 69 (1957), 16-19.

Wilson, Walter, *The History and Antiquities of Dissenting Churches and Meeting Houses in London, Westminster and Southwark: including the Lives of their Ministers*. London, 1810.

Wing, D.G., *Short Title Catalogue of books printed in England, Scotland, Ireland, Wales and British America, and of English books printed in other countries, 1641-1700*, 2nd edition. New York: Modern Language Association of America, 1982-1998.

Wood, A.H., *Church Unity Without Uniformity: A Study of Seventeenth-century English Church Movements and of Richard Baxter's Proposals for a Comprehensive Church*. London: Epworth Press, 1963.

Woolf, D.R., *The Idea of History in Early Stuart England*. Toronto: University of

Toronto Press, 1990.

Woolrych, Austin, *Commonwealth to Protectorate*. Oxford: Clarendon Press, 1982.

Wright, D.F., 'Martin Bucer and England-and Scotland', C. Krieger and M. Lienhard, eds, *Martin Bucer and Sixteenth Century Europe*, ii. Leiden: Brill, 1993.

Wrightson, Keith, *Earthly Necessities: Economic Lives in Early Modern Britain, 1470-1750*. London: Penguin, 2002.

- *English Society 1580-1680*. London: Hutchinson, 1982.

- 'Postscript: Terling Revisited', K. Wrightson and D. Levine, *Poverty and Piety in an English Village: Terling, 1525-1700*. Oxford: Clarendon Press, 1995.

Wrightson, Keith and David Levine, *Poverty and Piety in an English Village: Terling, 1525-1700*. Oxford: Clarendon Press, 1995.

Wykes, David L., *'To reivive the memory of some excellent men.' Edmund Calamy and the Early Historians of Nonconformity*. London: Dr Williams's Trust, 1997.

Index

Studies in Christian History and Thought
(All titles uniform with this volume)
Dates in bold are of projected publication

David Bebbington
Holiness in Nineteenth-Century England
David Bebbington stresses the relationship of movements of spirituality to changes in their cultural setting, especially the legacies of the Enlightenment and Romanticism. He shows that these broad shifts in ideological mood had a profound effect on the ways in which piety was conceptualized and practised. Holiness was intimately bound up with the spirit of the age.

2000 / 0-85364-981-2 / viii + 98pp

J. William Black
Reformation Pastors
Richard Baxter and the Ideal of the Reformed Pastor
This work examines Richard Baxter's *Gildas Salvianus, The Reformed Pastor* (1656) and explores each aspect of his pastoral strategy in light of his own concern for 'reformation' and in the broader context of Edwardian, Elizabethan and early Stuart pastoral ideals and practice.

2003 / 1-84227-190-3 / xxii + 308pp

James Bruce
Prophecy, Miracles, Angels, *and* Heavenly Light?
The Eschatology, Pneumatology and Missiology of Adomnán's Life of Columba
This book surveys approaches to the marvellous in hagiography, providing the first critique of Plummer's hypothesis of Irish saga origin. It then analyses the uniquely systematized phenomena in the *Life of Columba* from Adomnán's seventh-century theological perspective, identifying the coming of the eschatological Kingdom as the key to understanding.

2004 / 1-84227-227-6 / xviii + 286pp

Colin J. Bulley
The Priesthood of Some Believers
Developments from the General to the Special Priesthood in the Christian Literature of the First Three Centuries
The first in-depth treatment of early Christian texts on the priesthood of all believers shows that the developing priesthood of the ordained related closely to the division between laity and clergy and had deleterious effects on the practice of the general priesthood.

2000 / 1-84227-034-6 / xii + 336pp

July 2005

Anthony R. Cross (ed.)
Ecumenism and History
Studies in Honour of John H.Y. Briggs
This collection of essays examines the inter-relationships between the two fields in which Professor Briggs has contributed so much: history—particularly Baptist and Nonconformist—and the ecumenical movement. With contributions from colleagues and former research students from Britain, Europe and North America, *Ecumenism and History* provides wide-ranging studies in important aspects of Christian history, theology and ecumenical studies.
2002 / 1-84227-135-0 / xx + 362pp

Maggi Dawn
Confessions of an Inquiring Spirit
Form as Constitutive of Meaning in S.T. Coleridge's Theological Writing
This study of Coleridge's *Confessions* focuses on its confessional, epistolary and fragmentary form, suggesting that attention to these features significantly affects its interpretation. Bringing a close study of these three literary forms, the author suggests ways in which they nuance the text with particular understandings of the Trinity, and of a kenotic christology. Some parallels are drawn between Romantic and postmodern dilemmas concerning the authority of the biblical text.
2006 / 1-84227-255-1 / approx. 224 pp

Ruth Gouldbourne
The Flesh and the Feminine
Gender and Theology in the Writings of Caspar Schwenckfeld
Caspar Schwenckfeld and his movement exemplify one of the radical communities of the sixteenth century. Challenging theological and liturgical norms, they also found themselves challenging social and particularly gender assumptions. In this book, the issues of the relationship between radical theology and the understanding of gender are considered.
2005 / 1-84227-048-6 / approx. 304pp

Crawford Gribben
Puritan Millennialism
Literature and Theology, 1550–1682
Puritan Millennialism surveys the growth, impact and eventual decline of puritan millennialism throughout England, Scotland and Ireland, arguing that it was much more diverse than has frequently been suggested. This Paternoster edition is revised and extended from the original 2000 text.
2007 / 1-84227-372-8 / approx. 320pp

Galen K. Johnson
Prisoner of Conscience
John Bunyan on Self, Community and Christian Faith
This is an interdisciplinary study of John Bunyan's understanding of conscience across his autobiographical, theological and fictional writings, investigating whether conscience always deserves fidelity, and how Bunyan's view of conscience affects his relationship both to modern Western individualism and historic Christianity.

2003 / 1-84227-223-3 / xvi + 236pp

R.T. Kendall
Calvin and English Calvinism to 1649
The author's thesis is that those who formed the Westminster Confession of Faith, which is regarded as Calvinism, in fact departed from John Calvin on two points: (1) the extent of the atonement and (2) the ground of assurance of salvation.

1997 / 0-85364-827-1 / xii + 264pp

Timothy Larsen
Friends of Religious Equality
Nonconformist Politics in Mid-Victorian England
During the middle decades of the nineteenth century the English Nonconformist community developed a coherent political philosophy of its own, of which a central tenet was the principle of religious equality (in contrast to the stereotype of Evangelical Dissenters). The Dissenting community fought for the civil rights of Roman Catholics, non-Christians and even atheists on an issue of principle which had its flowering in the enthusiastic and undivided support which Nonconformity gave to the campaign for Jewish emancipation. This reissued study examines the political efforts and ideas of English Nonconformists during the period, covering the whole range of national issues raised, from state education to the Crimean War. It offers a case study of a theologically conservative group defending religious pluralism in the civic sphere, showing that the concept of religious equality was a grand vision at the centre of the political philosophy of the Dissenters.

2007 / 1-84227-402-3 / x + 300pp

Byung-Ho Moon
Christ the Mediator of the Law
*Calvin's Christological Understanding of the Law as the Rule of Living
and Life-Giving*
This book explores the coherence between Christology and soteriology in
Calvin's theology of the law, examining its intellectual origins and his position
on the concept and extent of Christ's mediation of the law. A comparative study
between Calvin and contemporary Reformers—Luther, Bucer, Melancthon and
Bullinger—and his opponent Michael Servetus is made for the purpose of
pointing out the unique feature of Calvin's Christological understanding of the
law.

2005 / 1-84227-318-3 / approx. 370pp

John Eifion Morgan-Wynne
Holy Spirit and Religious Experience in Christian Writings, c.AD 90–200
This study examines how far Christians in the third to fifth generations (c.AD
90–200) attributed their sense of encounter with the divine presence, their sense
of illumination in the truth or guidance in decision-making, and their sense of
ethical empowerment to the activity of the Holy Spirit in their lives.

2005 / 1-84227-319-1 / approx. 350pp

James I. Packer
The Redemption and Restoration of Man in the Thought of Richard Baxter
James I. Packer provides a full and sympathetic exposition of Richard Baxter's
doctrine of humanity, created and fallen; its redemption by Christ Jesus; and its
restoration in the image of God through the obedience of faith by the power of
the Holy Spirit.

2002 / 1-84227-147-4 / 432pp

Andrew Partington,
Church and State
*The Contribution of the Church of England Bishops to the House of Lords
during the Thatcher Years*

In *Church and State*, Andrew Partington argues that the contribution of the Church of England bishops to the House of Lords during the Thatcher years was overwhelmingly critical of the government; failed to have a significant influence in the public realm; was inefficient, being undertaken by a minority of those eligible to sit on the Bench of Bishops; and was insufficiently moral and spiritual in its content to be distinctive. On the basis of this, and the likely reduction of the number of places available for Church of England bishops in a fully reformed Second Chamber, the author argues for an evolution in the Church of England's approach to the service of its bishops in the House of Lords. He proposes the Church of England works to overcome the genuine obstacles which hinder busy diocesan bishops from contributing to the debates of the House of Lords and to its life more informally.

2005 / 1-84227-334-5 / approx. 324pp

Michael Pasquarello III
God's Ploughman
Hugh Latimer: A 'Preaching Life' (1490–1555)

This construction of a 'preaching life' situates Hugh Latimer within the larger religious, political and intellectual world of late medieval England. Neither biography, intellectual history, nor analysis of discrete sermon texts, this book is a work of homiletic history which draws from the details of Latimer's milieu to construct an interpretive framework for the preaching performances that formed the core of his identity as a religious reformer. Its goal is to illumine the practical wisdom embodied in the content, form and style of Latimer's preaching, and to recapture a sense of its overarching purpose, movement, and transforming force during the reform of sixteenth-century England.

2006 / 1-84227-336-1 / approx. 250pp

Alan P.F. Sell
Enlightenment, Ecumenism, Evangel
Theological Themes and Thinkers 1550–2000

This book consists of papers in which such interlocking topics as the Enlightenment, the problem of authority, the development of doctrine, spirituality, ecumenism, theological method and the heart of the gospel are discussed. Issues of significance to the church at large are explored with special reference to writers from the Reformed and Dissenting traditions.

2005 / 1-84227-330-2 / xviii + 422pp

Alan P.F. Sell
Hinterland Theology
Some Reformed and Dissenting Adjustments
Many books have been written on theology's 'giants' and significant trends, but what of those lesser-known writers who adjusted to them? In this book some hinterland theologians of the British Reformed and Dissenting traditions, who followed in the wake of toleration, the Evangelical Revival, the rise of modern biblical criticism and Karl Barth, are allowed to have their say. They include Thomas Ridgley, Ralph Wardlaw, T.V. Tymms and N.H.G. Robinson.

2006 / 1-84227-331-0 / approx. 350pp

Alan P.F. Sell and Anthony R. Cross (eds)
Protestant Nonconformity in the Twentieth Century
In this collection of essays scholars representative of a number of Nonconformist traditions reflect thematically on Nonconformists' life and witness during the twentieth century. Among the subjects reviewed are biblical studies, theology, worship, evangelism and spirituality, and ecumenism. Over and above its immediate interest, this collection provides a marker to future scholars and others wishing to know how some of their forebears assessed Nonconformity's contribution to a variety of fields during the century leading up to Christianity's third millennium.

2003 / 1-84227-221-7 / x + 398pp

Mark Smith
Religion in Industrial Society
Oldham and Saddleworth 1740–1865
This book analyses the way British churches sought to meet the challenge of industrialization and urbanization during the period 1740–1865. Working from a case-study of Oldham and Saddleworth, Mark Smith challenges the received view that the Anglican Church in the eighteenth century was characterized by complacency and inertia, and reveals Anglicanism's vigorous and creative response to the new conditions. He reassesses the significance of the centrally directed church reforms of the mid-nineteenth century, and emphasizes the importance of local energy and enthusiasm. Charting the growth of denominational pluralism in Oldham and Saddleworth, Dr Smith compares the strengths and weaknesses of the various Anglican and Nonconformist approaches to promoting church growth. He also demonstrates the extent to which all the churches participated in a common culture shaped by the influence of evangelicalism, and shows that active co-operation between the churches rather than denominational conflict dominated. This revised and updated edition of Dr Smith's challenging and original study makes an important contribution both to the social history of religion and to urban studies.

2006 / 1-84227-335-3 / approx. 300pp

Martin Sutherland
Peace, Toleration and Decay
The Ecclesiology of Later Stuart Dissent
This fresh analysis brings to light the complexity and fragility of the later Stuart Nonconformist consensus. Recent findings on wider seventeenth-century thought are incorporated into a new picture of the dynamics of Dissent and the roots of evangelicalism.
2003 / 1-84227-152-0 / xxii + 216pp

G. Michael Thomas
The Extent of the Atonement
A Dilemma for Reformed Theology from Calvin to the Consensus
A study of the way Reformed theology addressed the question, 'Did Christ die for all, or for the elect only?', commencing with John Calvin, and including debates with Lutheranism, the Synod of Dort and the teaching of Moïse Amyraut.
1997 / 0-85364-828-X / x + 278pp

David M. Thompson
Baptism, Church and Society in Britain from the Evangelical Revival to
Baptism, Eucharist and Ministry
The theology and practice of baptism have not received the attention they deserve. How important is faith? What does baptismal regeneration mean? Is baptism a bond of unity between Christians? This book discusses the theology of baptism and popular belief and practice in England and Wales from the Evangelical Revival to the publication of the World Council of Churches' consensus statement on *Baptism, Eucharist and Ministry* (1982).
2005 / 1-84227-393-0 / approx. 224pp

Mark D. Thompson
A Sure Ground on Which to Stand
The Relation of Authority and Interpretive Method of Luther's Approach to Scripture
The best interpreter of Luther is Luther himself. Unfortunately many modern studies have superimposed contemporary agendas upon this sixteenth-century Reformer's writings. This fresh study examines Luther's own words to find an explanation for his robust confidence in the Scriptures, a confidence that generated the famous 'stand' at Worms in 1521.
2004 / 1-84227-145-8 / xvi + 322pp

Carl R. Trueman and R.S. Clark (eds)
Protestant Scholasticism
Essays in Reassessment
Traditionally Protestant theology, between Luther's early reforming career and the dawn of the Enlightenment, has been seen in terms of decline and fall into the wastelands of rationalism and scholastic speculation. In this volume a number of scholars question such an interpretation. The editors argue that the development of post-Reformation Protestantism can only be understood when a proper historical model of doctrinal change is adopted. This historical concern underlies the subsequent studies of theologians such as Calvin, Beza, Olevian, Baxter, and the two Turrentini. The result is a significantly different reading of the development of Protestant Orthodoxy, one which both challenges the older scholarly interpretations and clichés about the relationship of Protestantism to, among other things, scholasticism and rationalism, and which demonstrates the fruitfulness of the new, historical approach.
1999 / 0-85364-853-0 / xx + 344pp

Shawn D. Wright
Our Sovereign Refuge
The Pastoral Theology of Theodore Beza
Our Sovereign Refuge is a study of the pastoral theology of the Protestant reformer who inherited the mantle of leadership in the Reformed church from John Calvin. Countering a common view of Beza as supremely a 'scholastic' theologian who deviated from Calvin's biblical focus, Wright uncovers a new portrait. He was not a cold and rigid academic theologian obsessed with probing the eternal decrees of God. Rather, by placing him in his pastoral context and by noting his concerns in his pastoral and biblical treatises, Wright shows that Beza was fundamentally a committed Christian who was troubled by the vicissitudes of life in the second half of the sixteenth century. He believed that the biblical truth of the supreme sovereignty of God alone could support Christians on their earthly pilgrimage to heaven. This pastoral and personal portrait forms the heart of Wright's argument.
2004 / 1-84227-252-7 / xviii + 308pp

Paternoster
9 Holdom Avenue,
Bletchley,
Milton Keynes MK1 1QR,
United Kingdom
Web: www.authenticmedia.co.uk/paternoster

July 2005